The
Architecture
of Landscape,
1940–1960

Penn Studies in Landscape Architecture
John Dixon Hunt, Series Editor

This series is dedicated to the study and promotion of
a wide variety of approaches to landscape architecture,
with special emphasis on connections between theory
and practice. It includes monographs on key topics in
history and theory, descriptions of projects by both
established and rising designers, translations of major
foreign-language texts, anthologies of theoretical and historical writings on classic issues, and critical writing by
members of the profession of landscape architecture.

The Architecture of Landscape, 1940–1960

Edited by Marc Treib

PENN

University of Pennsylvania Press
Philadelphia

Support for this book was provided
by the Hubbard Educational Trust,
and the College of Environmental Design
and Department of Architecture
at the University of California, Berkeley.

Designed by Marc Treib

Printed in the United States of America on acid-free paper

10 9 8 7 6 5 4 3 2 1

Published by
University of Pennsylvania Press
Philadelphia, Pennsylvania 19104-4011

Library of Congress Cataloging-in-Publication Data
The architecture of landscape, 1940–1960 / edited by Marc Treib.
    p. cm. — (Penn studies in landscape architecture)
    Includes bibliographical references (p.) and index.
    ISBN 0–8122–3623–8 (cloth: alk. paper)
    1. Landscape architecture — History. 2. Landscape design —
History. I. Treib, Marc. II. Series.
SB470.5 .A725 2002
712'.09'044—dc21   2001057387

In memory of Garrett Eckbo, landscape architect

Contents

MARC TREIB

Introduction

The two decades bracketing the year 1950 were pivotal in defining landscape architecture worldwide and for setting a course still followed today. They were also among the twentieth century's most critical years, during which the world endured military buildup at the expense of the quality and infrastructure of civilian life, suffered the agonies of war, addressed the challenges of reconstruction, and redefined basic questions of human existence. Among these were issues pitting the local and national against the international, capitalism versus socialism and communism, the individual versus society, and the human against the machine. In war, we might safely venture, there are no winners. Only, perhaps, in spurring technological development could any benefit be found to offset, at least in part, the privation and suffering that accompanied bombing, fire, and ruin. By 1945, as hostilities ended, many hoped that life had already sunk to its lowest ebb and that the future could only promise something better. Happily, by 1960, when our study ends, that promise had largely been fulfilled in many quarters of the world.

Perhaps at no other time in history did landscape architecture play such a central role in contemporary life. But defining landscape architecture in those years — as a term and as a practice — remains problematic. No common values, no central definition guided the design of landscapes or the education of those making them. In some countries, landscape design served preparations for war; in others, it offered an escape from that grisly prospect looming on the horizon. In the immediate postwar years, the primary tasks in many countries were land clearance, reformation, and reconstruction; in others, efforts toward bettering living conditions prevailed, in particular the restitution of a functioning infrastructure.

Certainly, the problem of definition that plagued landscape design during the years 1940–1960 also informed the conception of this book. Yet it is this very ambiguity that contributes to the significance of the texts assembled here by generating a variety of material and views. As there was no common definition of landscape architecture among the dozen nations during our period of inquiry, no single approach seemed appropriate to all the authors represented in this book. We need think of this study more as a mosaic of issues, methods, observations, and projects than as contributions to any singular academic position.

If a single definition remains elusive, we can still note certain issues that underlay the design of landscapes during these two decades spanning 1940 to 1960. Many of the findings are surprising; for example, when we witness affinities among postwar garden design in California, Australia, and Denmark. That trends in Sweden, in turn, differed so markedly from the ideas flowering in neighboring Denmark, or that in certain countries it was the railroad rather than the motor road that attracted the attention of landscape designers, despite the growing impact of the automobile in almost all industrialized countries, appears at first curious.

An observation linking almost all of the essays reveals the ranking of social over environmental concerns; in most instances, this was accompanied by an increased democratization of the designed landscape. Given the limited state of ecological awareness, coupled with the daunting task of housing an ever-growing population in drastically reduced housing stock, this privileging is completely understandable. We also see, for example in the United States, the movement toward the suburbs from the central city, with home ownership and privacy as key issues. In Sweden, the park rather than the individual house lay at the core of the landscape architect's interest, and communal rather than privately owned land attracted the attention of the leading policymakers and landscape designers. In Germany, the social problems and political division were even more exaggerated by the ruinous state of the nation. Partition into two states, and the further complications of multinational occupation, led to a schism in both political ideology and the design of landscapes. In West Germany, landscape architects assumed an active role in realizing housing and parks, while in East Germany the profession as a whole languished and plant nurseries disappeared. These examples only suggest the broad range of social ideas and issues that occupied center stage in the postwar years.

If social needs constitute the core programs for these landscapes, we need also examine their styles and manner of their making. In almost all the countries represented in this book, landscape architects directed their primary efforts toward creating spaces rather than designing aesthetic compositions for visual interest alone. In some ways, this seems to have grown from the rootedness of these designs in social practice; in others, it might have been the severity of the task at hand, which demanded addressing the social group rather than the individual avant-garde program or client. Without question, the scale of many of the projects was enormous, embracing designs for rebuilding cities or, in England and Sweden, completely new towns. And in other cases, where the scale of the individual unit remained small, the immense number of those units as an agglomeration demanded a far broader view, for example, in the American suburbs.

This is not to say that innovative form making was neglected. In Belgium, for example, investigations into integrating landscape and architecture, or landscape with the plastic arts of painting and sculpture, continued — sometimes, quite remarkably, during the war years themselves. The desire for self-expression, for a spatial and formal idiom equating with contemporary conditions, had been a hallmark of the modernist landscape project. Christopher Tunnard in England, Jean Canneel-Claes in Belgium, Garrett Eckbo and James Rose in the United States — all had called for a design stance more in accord with life and artistic practices in the twentieth century. In so doing, they consciously rejected both the formal manner characteristic of the estate and the naturalistic manner of the park, arguing for dismissing the axis, and against the emphasis on visual delight alone, and on a landscape that only tangentially engaged human activity. While modernism found expression in countries across the world, acceptance was not complete. In the American South, the endurance of a sensibility aimed toward gracious living emphasized the persistence of tradition rather than any embrace of the new. In other countries, Japan for example, the divergence of old and new values was manifest in two distinct design strains: new plants and foreign influences barely touched traditional garden design; the modern, on the other hand, followed a path to highly sculptural compositions more akin to Western fine arts and garden design than to the historic gardens of Kyoto.

In their search for contemporary expression, almost universally, architects and landscape architects looked to parallel developments in painting and sculpture. In the fine arts, the constraints were reduced, allowing considerable freedom to investigate imagery and form. Designers, in contrast, were bound to address a far greater number of variables, not the least of these being the social relevance cited above. If they could not enter into the free world of plastic investigation, however, landscape designers could at least learn from the aesthetic research produced in the arts, and they could test the relevance of those ideas within the arena of the garden or the plaza.

If we see in the work of many designers the urge toward overtly contemporary plastic expression, we also see a corresponding urge toward a return to nature as model. In the war years and the postwar period, the political dimension of landscape reigned, and naturalism was almost always linked to national identity, tradition, and at times nationalism in its most extreme form — for example, in the plantings of the Reichsautobahn in Germany, or in its occupied territories. The celebrated Stockholm park system, in contrast, practiced a more benign quest for naturalism; but the granite outcropping and the birch as elements of a truly Swedish landscape also spoke to issues of social definition.

The question of national identity held sway in the lands of both the victors and the defeated. In Japan, traditional garden forms, in some ways, helped stabilize a social body adrift in the aftermath of defeat. Brazilian artists and a handful of landscape architects looked to the native jungle as a source of cultural symbols, continuing a project that was inherently linked with the modernization project of the 1920s. In Australia, the bush as a national symbol occupied the consciousness of architects and garden makers and provoked an interest in native species — as it did many places in the world during the late 1940s and 1950s. Although these returns to the native environment smacked of a certain conservatism, or even provincialism, these efforts rarely viewed "nature" in quite the same way as before the war. Tinged by a greater collective social consciousness, an interest in artistic development, and an augmented interest in space rather than forms per se — all of these forced an amalgam of modern societal and professional norms with the traditional view of nature. The gardens and parks became new in the process.

In the first postwar decades, the garden and the park often served as the antidote to architectural severity. In Australia and Brazil, in the Netherlands, and in England one finds planting used to mitigate the perceived impersonality of international modernism. If the modernist project advanced ideas of universality, landscape architects countered that argument with propositions for rooting those buildings in a particular locale. In Denmark, schools, factories, and museums expanded that interest, integrating landscape and building, internal and external spaces, in a manner one would think applicable only to Mediterranean climes.

Only in rare instances did the landscape adopt extreme aesthetic positions — in postwar California, for example; but even here we need to question the extent of the modernity. Vegetation, one might say, is inherently conservative. Rarely is it clipped into some extreme sculptural form or used in modernistically shaped beds to such an extent that plants and trees become in themselves elements of a truly contemporary expression. The landscapes of Roberto Burle Marx in Brazil, of course, like those of his contemporary Garrett Eckbo in California, are notable expressions. But in most instances, people seek the garden for its calm and its balm, not as advanced artistic expression. Besides, there were more important issues on the table following half a decade of horrific belligerence. Only towards the end of our period, inching toward 1960, had recovery advanced to the state that landscape architecture could begin to exhibit sufficient autonomy and display a certain degree of independence.

The reader will note one obvious omission in the content of this book: there is little mention of pioneer American modernists such as Garrett Eckbo, Thomas Church, and James Rose. To date, the history of modern landscape architecture has been only broadly sketched, with barely a handful of significant publications in the English language. But the modernist group has received the weight of that limited scholarship and publication, for example in Peter Walker and Melanie Simo's *Invisible Gardens*, in my own *Modern Landscape Architecture: A Critical Review*, and Dorothée Imbert and my *Garrett Eckbo: Modern Landscape for Living*. Thus, *The Architecture of Landscape, 1940–1960* explores other aspects of midcentury landscape design that have received less attention, from the garden to urban planning.

The Architecture of Landscape, 1940–1960 suggests the scope of efforts to design, on an internationally linked field, viable and vital landscapes around the middle of the twentieth century. The authors included here demonstrate that the issues were complex, involving questions of home ownership, materials, artistic movements, political programs, educational curricula, relations to architecture and urban form, spiritual quests, mobility, and a nearly continual questioning and re-evaluation of landscape architecture in the lives of its users, makers, and owners. There are, of course, gaps in the information, and no single collection can ever hope to address every aspect of the production of landscape architecture internationally. This we admit. We do hope, however, that despite these lacunae, our labors will contribute significantly to understanding the landscape architecture of the mid–twentieth century, in particular those years between 1940 and 1960 when promise itself was the most alluring product.

The
Architecture
of Landscape,
1940–1960

In 1952, Stockholm for the first time hosted the International Federation of Landscape Architects World Congress. On that occasion, Holger Blom, the director of the Stockholm Parks Department could, not without pride, present the results of his work: the city with the world's most progressive park policy. Blom was foremost among the design professionals who had led Swedish landscape architecture into a new era and changed the form as well as the function of the parks. In their form, the parks now constituted a network that infiltrated the city; green space had become an integral part of the urban fabric. In function, the parks served as outdoor living rooms for everyday life, as a critical complement to apartment living. In the 1950s, these new roles for the parks had matured and reached their fulfillment, now harvesting efforts that had begun in the early 1930s. One reason for the parks' success was the part they played in a comprehensive program propelling ideological change for the entire society. It is thus necessary to outline this general ambition for society in order to understand the specific achievements in the field of landscape architecture [Figure 1–1].

1. THORBJÖRN ANDERSSON

To Erase the Garden: Modernity in the Swedish Garden and Landscape

During the decades bracketing the middle of the twentieth century, Sweden demonstrated how political ideas can be successfully implemented within a society using landscape architecture, architecture, and urban planning as their vehicles. Over a period of forty years, from the early 1930s to the 1970s, a shared vision of a new, modern society of the future joined politicians and civil servants, ideologues, and experts in close collegial cooperation. Their efforts resulted in something that can be called a new national identity. This ambitious experiment in social and political reform was eventually to be named the Swedish model, a model that showed a middle way between a market and a planned economy. During these same years, Sweden took the definitive step from a rural agrarian country to an industrial society, and it was the building construction industry—and thus architecture, landscape architecture, and city planning—that generated and became instruments in this process of political change.

The giant project included the transfer of almost half the population from the countryside to the cities. Architects, politicians, and sociologists together defined those requisites they believed necessary for a typical family to live a happy life in a new sort of urban milieu. The ideal apartment was designed, and then stacked one on top of the other to form blocks and towers that in turn defined the new suburbs. Planners estimated the number of square meters of green space sufficient for each inhabitant, as well as determining the size of the sandboxes and the equipment for the playgrounds. The new environment was almost scientifically determined and was thus considered an unquestionably correct environment. In Sweden, this architectural movement to produce a healthy and precise living environment was called functionalism [Figure 1–2].

The functionalist movement was successful as long as the projects were small enough to allow variation and complexity. However, in the late 1960s, as the building industry became more industrialized and oriented toward prefabrication, the architects of Swedish functionalism had a harder time reaching their goals. An informal standard employed by the parks department in Stockholm always let treetops determine the height of roofs. That standard was eventually permitted to lapse; when buildings grew to ten and even fifteen stories, they introduced the environmentally doubtful qualities of monotony and oversized environmental scale.

Possibly the best known of the social scientists who worked with this social engineering (as the total planning of the society has been called) was the married couple Gunnar Myrdal (1898–1987) and Alva Myrdal (1902–86). Each was acclaimed internationally for ideas concerning the construction of a viable and equitable society. Together they authored *Kris i befolkningsfrågan* (Crisis in the Population Issue), published in 1934, a work greatly appreciated in Europe as well as in the United States. The book addressed a question that troubled many of the countries of the Western world at the time, namely the decline in population and the ever-dwindling size of the family. The Myrdals were both members of the Social Democratic Party, and the fact that a labor party invested in family issues in itself marked a political change. Home and family matters, by tradition, had been the domain of the conservatives rather than the progressive element of the political sphere.

With the Myrdals, the Social Democratic Party assumed a more intellectual stance. Both Gunnar and Alva would eventually receive Nobel Prizes; Gunnar received his award in 1974 for his work in economics. His thesis was, in short, that the government should neutralize recessions in the national economy by using strong public financial interventions. Using the building industry as such an economic

Figure 1–1.
Norr Mälarstrand, Stockholm, 1941–43.
Holger Blom and Erik Glemme.
Everyday life in an everyday park. In the political ambition that was to be called the Swedish Model, the parks played an active role.
[C. G. Rosenberg]

Figure 1–2.
Grindtorp, Täby, 1970s. Erik Anjou,
landscape architect; VBB, architects.
The idea of the home environment was
altered by modernism's rational eye. The
garden is transformed into elementary
functions inscribed into geometric figures.
[Oscar Bladh, Arkitekturmuseet]

instrument, Swedish society had, by the time Gunnar Myrdal received his award, utilized his ideas for about forty years. Alva received the Nobel Peace Prize in 1972 for her activities and writings on social matters, where she always saw the family as the fundamental unit.

The Myrdal family lived in Bromma, a suburb some six kilometers west of central Stockholm, in a house designed by Sven Markelius (1889–1972), a noted modernist architect. Markelius also served as Director of Urban Planning for Stockholm from 1944 to 1954. Markelius and the Myrdals actually collaborated on the scheme for the house, using their knowledge of architecture and social science respectively to shape the living space for a modern family living a modern life. Alva and Gunnar Myrdal's close collaboration with Markelius was typical of a society that did not acknowledge confining borders between professionals and politicians. Typical also was the fact that Gunnar Myrdal later was appointed Minister of Trade in the Swedish government (1945–47). At that time the scientist and the politician occupied places on the same side of the table, the very same side where the architect also sat. Alva and Gunnar Myrdal have been termed two of the most important "architects" behind the Swedish welfare model, suggesting that the title architect applies to those who create social or economic schemes as well as to those who design buildings.

During the late 1940s, few countries in the world equaled Sweden's engagement with modern social ideas and their architectural equivalents. Because the past, it was held, meant nothing, there was little to learn from it. Swedish modernity operated with the conviction that every new day was a little bit better than the one that had just passed. The Stockholm Urban Planning Department formulated its vision of a new city in a planning manifesto titled *Stockholm of the Future*, a small but important booklet that was published in 1945. It established the principles for a radical renovation of the city center—with communication and traffic as guiding principles—and for the development of extensive suburban developments around nodes instigated by the projected subway system. For a city of Stockholm's size, the construction of a subway was a bold undertaking. In most foreign countries, a population of one million was regarded as the minimum for such a transportation system. Stockholm in the immediate postwar era comprised only half that number. The city's mayor, Yngve Larsson, who also headed the city council, said from the speaker's chair: "If we are to solve the question about intolerable housing conditions, we must be able to transport Stockholmers from their dwellings to their places of work in no more than thirty minutes."[1]

The decision to build the subway system was made in 1941, in the middle of World War II, when the future was hardly predictable. Göran Sidenbladh, an architect in the city's Urban Planning Department and the main author of *Stockholm of the Future*, caught the atmosphere in the council that night: "To us who were participating it was a feeling of great freedom: after the issue upon which we had worked for nine years was finally decided, we left the city hall and walked out into that fresh June night. The light of day was rising over Lake Mälaren."[2]

The restructuring of the capital was not only the result of a vision; it was also the answer to a strong social need. The general health situation in the urban areas of Sweden was very poor. High-density housing with low sanitary standards left people in diminished physical condition. Tuberculosis epidemics had struck Stockholm in the late 1890s, and the need for improved living conditions had become only too apparent. In fact, the functionalist movement developed in response to just those general health problems. Even during the nineteenth century, well-known Swedish authors such as August Blanche and August Strindberg had engaged this major problem in their writings to stimulate discussion. When the Social Democrats came to power in 1932, they decided to challenge the existing situation. The new prime minister, Per Albin Hansson, argued for the concept of *Folkhemmet*, the People's Home, where the working man could live in a high-quality, modern house, which he himself owned. Thus suburban development began to grow at an increased rate. As a political demonstration, the same year that he was elected, Per Albin Hansson himself moved to a suburb. He left his residence in central Stockholm to live in one of several identical rowhouses in Ålsten, about five kilometers west of the city—out among his electorate.

In the 1950s the time was right to rid Swedish society once and for all of the health nuisance that plagued it. In Stockholm the solution was twofold: a more airy downtown opened to the light and sun, and the implementation of an extensive suburban development program. The times and ideology were now in perfect accord. The 1950s offered the necessary conditions for Sweden to attempt this giant undertaking. Sweden had been spared from the destruction of the two world wars and had been able to establish political stability and a high economic standard. There was a

Figure 1–3.
The aim of the Swedish Model was to create a society that ensured the citizens the necessary ingredients for living a good life. This was eventually termed social engineering.
[Pressens bild]

Figure 1–4.
Sergels torg, Stockholm, 1960–67.
Stockholm Urban Planning Department /
David Helldén et al.
The House of Culture to the right was
designed by Peter Celsing after a competi-
tion in 1965.
[Thorbjörn Andersson]

prevalent belief in the prospects of a bright future with an open mind toward innovation [Figure 1–3].

During the World War II Europe had stood as a closed continent. Its Scandinavian neighbors had fallen to the enemy one after the other, leaving Sweden as an isolated, neutral island in the middle of a sea of belligerence. When the war ended and the frontiers reopened, an eager curiosity about the surrounding world engaged the Swedish public. Private ownership of cars increased significantly, and television came to many households. Through television Sweden explored the world beyond its borders, coming into contact with exotic lifestyles. Young boys adopted the American crew-cut hairstyle and chewed bubblegum; girls wore Bardot-striped dresses and rode on Vespas. Both culture and life-style changed under these foreign influences and so did the city with its buildings, streets, and parks.

Under the supervision of architects and planners—Sven Markelius among them—practically the entire downtown area of Stockholm, with its old houses and narrow lanes, was demolished. In its place came new public open spaces, parks, and high-rise towers. Out of the old bricks grew a new, modern city center. And in the middle of this new vision a public arena was sited, a plaza called Sergels torg. Its realization resulted from an extended design process, culminating in 1957 when the Urban Planning Department presented its definitive scheme. The plaza and its surrounding buildings lay on an axis connecting the royal castle in the Old Town with the Haga Park to the north, where construction at the royal summer residence was left incomplete in the late eighteenth century. This royal axis had been maintained for two hundred years: a boulevard named Sveavägen—Svea being the symbolic mother of Sweden, rooted in the Swedish name for the country, Sverige.

The plan to interrupt this axis, and Sweden's history, was not left unchallenged. Still, it was a symbolic gesture, in the spirit of modernism, to reject the historical Sveavägen and present a modern urban alternative. A new concept of architectural space informed the remaking of central Stockholm. New voids balanced the masses of vertical buildings. The wide skies reflected themselves in the glass facade of the new House of Culture, the result of an architectural competition held in 1965 and won by Peter Celsing [Figure 1–4].

Below the Sergels torg was a sunken pedestrian zone, separated from vehicular traffic, with direct access to the new

Figure 1–5.
Sergels torg, Stockholm, 1960.
Perspective sketch by David Helldén.
The plaza was thought of as a public arena where everybody could take part in cultural events.
[Arkitekturmuseet]

Figure 1–6.
Sergels torg, Stockholm.
"The five trumpet blasts saluting the new era." The perspective sketch was made by the Urban Planning department in 1952.
[Arkitekturmuseet]

subway system, which efficiently transported the citizens to their homes in the suburbs. The floor of the plaza was paved with a striking black-and-white triangular pattern that Markelius had used as a textile design some years before. On one side of the black-and-white plaza, as a symbol of the new aesthetic, the artist Edwin Öhrström erected a one-hundred-foot-high obelisk of glass crystal, the world's highest. It was positioned in a reflecting pool of a shape that no one ever had seen before: the superellipse, conceived especially for the site by the Danish mathematician Piet Hein.[3] Five high-rise buildings, one of them designed by Sven Markelius himself, lined the north side of the plaza. Stockholm's mayor Yngve Larsson, in his inauguration speech, described the towers as five trumpet blasts saluting the new era. Very few, if any, of the world's city centers so strongly reflect the design values of these times as does downtown Stockholm [Figure 1–5].

The old city with its square grid, its horizontal low-rise buildings in brick and stucco, and its rectangular enclosed parks, was rejected and jettisoned. Instead, a modern city, with vertical forms, floating spaces, bright colors, and new materials and patterns, took its place. Clarity, brilliance, and freedom from the burden of outdated history: these were the messages that could be read in every paving stone, in every lamppost, in every form in the new downtown center. A new era in social as well as in architectural dimensions had arrived, and it was conceptualized and realized by talents like Alva and Gunnar Myrdal and Sven Markelius [Figure 1–6].

Simplification, purification, and openness toward new methods were key matters in design issues of all kinds, including the fine arts. Early in the century Pablo Picasso had depicted a bull by using only the handlebars of a bicycle and its metal saddle. Similar modernist inventions now began to appear in landscape architecture in several European countries. Sweden was alone, however, in delivering a modern solution for the society as a whole when most of Europe could cite only solitary examples. Sweden became the pilgrimage site for the young and ambitious architects of postwar Europe, a group in search of a new society to replace the old — now partly, but literally, in ruins. Some of these architects, like Fred Forbat, came from the Bauhaus tradition in Germany. Ralph Erskine arrived from Great Britain in search of a society that showed interest in bold architectural ideas as well as social reinvention.

This modern movement reevaluated landscape design as well as urban form and buildings. As the city underwent renovation, Swedish modernity also turned its back on the traditional garden. As an idea and as an artifact, the garden belonged to the stale, dusty bourgeoisie, relics of an outdated culture. New materials, demands for low maintenance, and the striving to find new values proved to be difficult to integrate with the horticultural world [Figure 1–7].

The traditional garden represented either the manifestation of individualism (if it was a grand garden) or a conservative attitude toward development (since horticulture developed from agrarian society). The garden in its conventional form had no place in modern Sweden. Small, distinct cultivation units—if one chose to see the garden in its utilitarian aspect—or an escapist, decorated dream world—if one chose to see the garden from the aspect of pleasure—did not suit the image of a rational society on its way into the industrial age. Parks, too, until now had served as arenas for the social life of the bourgeoisie. Their design had followed a standard pattern, with flat, well-manicured lawns, extensive arrangements of colorful and often exotic plants, and winding gravel paths where one could undertake see-and-be-seen promenades. Now that society was in need of change, there was also a need for an open, democratic, and informal park that also bore the capacity to improve the health of the citizen.

The search for a new form for a garden reflecting altered values did not occupy only Swedish landscape architects. As early as 1925 — at L'Exposition Internationelle des Arts Décoratifs et Industriels Modernes in Paris — Robert Mallet-Stevens had designed gardens on the Esplanade des Invalides with concrete trees, made by the sculptors Jan and Joel Martel.[4] In this way the undisciplined forms of biological life could be controlled and given a predictable shape. In California, Thomas Church was designing his gardens using easily maintained raised planting beds, zigzag shapes, and asymmetries seldom seen in the old Beaux Arts tradition. Within a decade following the Paris exposition, in Great Britain, Christopher Tunnard had designed his famous garden near Halland, Sussex. Here, the view did not remain confined within a bordering hedge but instead continued outward to the distant landscape. That landscape, in turn, was locked in place by an espalier in the shape of a regular grid. In all of these projects, geometry played a significant role, suggesting that the form of the garden, and the artifice necessary for its creation, should be readily apparent.

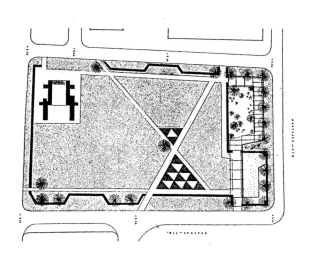

Figure 1–7.
Karl Johans Park, Norrköping, 1870s.
Knut Forssberg, landscape design.
The late nineteenth-century park was primarily meant for the social life of the bourgeoisie, a salon more than an everyday living room.
[Thorbjörn Andersson]

Figure 1–8.
Wilharditurm, Bremen, Germany, 1955.
Competition entry by
Gunnar Martinsson.
Martinsson was relatively alone in Sweden in being inspired more by geometric purification than by the natural world.
[Garten & Landschaft, January 1956]

Similar endeavors with strong geometries appeared in Sweden, where they were used to modernize the traditional garden. Landscape architect Gunnar Martinsson (1924–) addressed the international vogue for two-dimensional patterning with his entry to a competition for new garden concepts. Martinsson here clearly revealed his fascination with his foreign colleagues' interest in simple geometric forms as a basis for garden design. Martinsson's ideas were also influenced by the fine arts of the time and their interest in purifying color and shape. His proposal for the garden at Wilharditurm in Bremen dates from 1955, and it appeared in the German *Garten und Landschaft* in January of the following year. The design, which received second prize, sharply contrasted with the other prize-winning entries.[5] Unlike the other Swedish designs, Martinsson tended to use more curvilinear forms and showed enclosed volumes rather than straight and open spaces [Figure 1–8]. He would continue to explore the formal problems of the garden throughout his entire career, cleansing, distilling, and purifying his designs down to this very core based on simple geometry

The previously mentioned Sergels torg was another example of this tendency to focus on a geometric structure, but among Swedish landscape architects Gunnar Martinsson was relatively alone in following this direction within international modernism. Nils Orento (1922–) also expressed an interest in pattern making and two-dimensional effects in his landscape designs. For the entrance plaza at the Sabbatsberg hospital (completed in 1969) in Stockholm, Orento laid out a strict triangular pattern with considerable visual effect [Figure 1–9]. The pavement was structured as an orthogonal grid. Three shades of gray were used, initiating a secondary play of diagonal alignments. Objects such as pools, benches, and trees all fit within the governing system. Nothing disturbed the continuity of the landscape picture. The pavement was made of concrete: a prefabricated, industrially produced material that represented modernity far more definitively than the granite used in former years. At Sabbatsberg, all the paving units fit into a modular system called 3M, where the parts were multiples of a standard thirty-centimeter (one foot) measure—a modular system frequently used in the construction industry. Orento used the system as if he were virtually possessed by it, illustrating once again how geometry attracted the interest of landscape architects in Sweden as well as in other countries.

Figure 1–9.
Sabbatsberg hospital entry plaza, Stockholm, 1970s. Nils Orento landscape design.
The rationality of modernism created its own aesthetic built on simplification and purity.
[Thorbjörn Andersson]

Biological variety was regarded as an obstacle to a land-scape architecture intended to be squeezed into perfectly regular forms. That is one of the reasons why almost no vegetation interrupted the purity of the plaza at Vällingby, a new town eight miles west of Stockholm, inaugurated in 1954. The architect for the plaza, Erik Glemme (1905–59), worked for several decades at the Stockholm Parks Department. For Vällingby, Glemme laid out a pattern of circular shapes that dominated the reading of the town center [Figure 1–10]. All other design elements, such as benches, fountains, and lampposts, subordinated themselves to this pervasive circular pattern. Vällingby was the first of the so-called ABC towns in Sweden; A for *arbete* (work); B for *bo* (housing), and C for *centrum*, with public and commercial service [Figures 1–11, 1–12]. Inspired by the post-war English new towns, Vällingby was intended to supply each citizen with the possibility for a complete life without having to rely on nearby Stockholm. The new municipality was conceived as the reaction to the crises of the old city that had harbored poverty and disease. And for the second time a Swedish prime minister would move out to the sub-urbs; this time it was the late Olof Palme, who held office during the 1960s and 1970s.

The Stockholm novelist Per Anders Fogelström depicts the bright spirit of the 1950s in the third part of his trilogy about Stockholm, *Stad i världen* (The City in the World). In the novel, the young Social Democrat and municipal politician Erik Karge decides to move out to Vällingby. Spellbound, he sees a brand-new town and a new society take shape simultaneously:

> Erik Karge was fascinated by the game, by the construction itself. Man's victory over nature, the possibility to construct a completely new society, to build with social ambitions, to create a scientifically correct, designed environment. The city was nothing more than a consumer article after all, he thought. A machine that hundreds of thousands of people worked with every day and which like all machines would wear down and had to be eventually exchanged. If all those people who yelled about the preservation of the old would have their way, the whole city would turn into some sort of a museum. Far too long we have stayed content with mending and patching, restoring and repairing in little pieces. Now was the time for radical changes, for complete-ly new cities like Vällingby. Old junk and dirt would have to go away, and with it everything he thought was connected with the old, rotting city of poverty.[6]

Vällingby was a planner's triumph, bringing international review and praise. The stream of visitors was so intense

Figure 1–10.
Vällingby, 1954. Erik Glemme.
The circular pattern on the ground was applied consistently and, in modernism's typical way, was only vaguely spatially connected. It did, however, impose a strong architectural identity.
[Thorbjörn Andersson]

Figure 1–11.
Vällingby town center, 1954.
Erik Glemme, landscape design;
Backström & Reinius, architects.
A new transportation system, the subway,
allowed the planners to expand Stockholm,
with dwellings at increased distances from
the central city.
[Stadsmuseet]

that the municipality employed hostesses, typically dressed in specially designed uniforms. Foreign scholars used Vällingby as a model case study; an American economist wrote a thesis called *Vällingby and Farsta: From Idea to Reality*.[7]

But it was not the controlled and graphic landscape design found in the circular pattern in Vällingby which was to become Sweden's main contribution to modernist landscape architecture. Instead it was the explicit utilization of a natural landscape as a garden or a park that Swedish landscape designers would explore and refine. Again, this distinct change in direction for Swedish landscape architecture derived from the health crisis in the cities. For these problems, fresh air and exercise were the best-known cures. To address these new programs park design abandoned its turn-of-the-century forms for those based on more contemporary ideas. Now the healing powers of nature were considered more important than the pleasures gained by the bourgeoisie from having a pleasant place to stroll. The new parks turned to nature as the source of their form; in their function they emphasized the recreational use of what had in earlier times served only as decorative lawns and plantings. Play, physical exercise, and social use became keywords for the new natural park movement.

In the history of garden design nature is normally used as a counterbalance to the idea of the designed garden. Nature is that untouched territory we colonize and reform as a garden. Nature is to be conquered, modified, and provided with new features that in turn bear witness to the human presence and, perhaps, even human dominance. The Christian and Muslim paradise gardens well illustrate this position, clearly established in earlier centuries. The walled gardens of Eden protected its original inhabitants from the threatening wilderness beyond. In Swedish modernism, this archetypal idea of a garden was put on trial — and ultimately rejected. Sven Hermelin (1900–1984), one of the leading landscape personalities from the 1940s through the 1960s, compared the garden traditions of neighboring Denmark and Sweden while on an excursion in 1934. His comments suggest that the Swedish and Danish gardens were headed in two quite different directions.

> *Gardens in central Sweden face outwards; so much more is offered by our countryside that the task of the landscape architect becomes a matter of carefully integrating the building with the existing site conditions and arranging the transitional zone between the two. The Danes are not lucky enough to possess countryside of this merit and their gardens*

13

Figure 1–12.
Vällingby, Stockholm, 1954.
Erik Glemme used geometry in a playful way, skillfully avoiding rigidity and monotony. Vällingby is among the most internationally recognized works of postwar Swedish planning.
[Sune Sundahl, Arkitekturmuseet]

Figure 1–13.
Swift, 1885. Bruno Liljefors.
Oil on canvas.
Functionalist gardens echoed a Swedish
feeling for the natural world.
[Private collection]

Figure 1–14.
Fox and Crows, 1884. Bruno Liljefors.
Oil on canvas.
Liljefors depicts natural scenes without
romanticism but with the factual tone of
reports.
[Private collection]

*thus have to compensate for this lack of aspect. Instead,
their gardens face inwards, marking their boundaries with the
open agricultural landscape by using substantial plantings.*[8]

Hermelin's observations focus on a Swedish conception of
nature that differs considerably from Danish ideas, which
fell definitely within the continental tradition. In the Swedish
mind wilderness produces no threat. Hermelin interprets
the forest as a safe and desirable place for residence, a
place removed from the complexity — and dangers — of
contemporary urban life.

Etymologically speaking, one can establish that the Swedish
word for forest (*skog*) does not share the same linguistic
origin as its equivalents in English, Italian, or French, a trait
that is otherwise fairly common among Swedish words. The
term forest seems to have evolved from the Latin *foresta*,
which is related to *foris*, meaning "outside." The forest zone
was found outside the jurisdiction of the city and was pop-
ulated by outsiders such as lunatics, robbers, hermits and
lepers.[9] The forest is the shadow that civilization casts
behind itself, a world of twilight. Not only do the terms for
forest have different origins (and thus different meanings)
in Sweden and the above-cited cultures, but the inherent
importance of the word within the culture also differs. *Skog*
is a separate and distinctive Nordic word. Linguistically, it
has a Germanic origin and may be derived from the Old
Norse word *skogr*, meaning something that rises up from
the ground. Unlike the Latin reading of forest as a land
beyond civilization, in the north forests were perceived as
friendly, quiet, and even lush; they provided variety and
were useful because they could be harvested for firewood.
The forest, as a concept, in fact, stood as an equivalent of
the garden, since it satisfied many of the criteria by which a
garden is normally defined.[10]

The forest as a safe place pervades the Swedish perception
of nature. This is evident, for example, in the production of
the turn-of-the-century painter Bruno Liljefors (1860–1939).
Regarded as one of Sweden's national painters, Liljefors's
subjects depicted key aspects of the national psyche. Nature
was his lifelong habitat. In nature, the painter found contexts
of an existential kind, for example in the painting *Swift*, from
1895, in which black swallows cut across the tapestry of
summer flowers and dancing insects [Figure 1–13].[11]

In *Fox with Crows* (1884), he renders a specific landscape in
central Sweden: the hilly topography with its typical vegetation, the elaborate pattern of the rustic fence, the fox, and

the screaming crows [Figure 1–14]. Despite these folk subjects, Liljefors was influenced by modern times and his notations were razor-sharp in detail. He often depicted the dramas in nature that today fall under the rubric of ecology. Modern painters such as Paul Klee, Piet Mondrian, and Pablo Picasso offered to designers of the continental garden a potential vocabulary involving new modes of geometry and constructed form. As abroad, the fine arts also led the way into Swedish modernism, but it was of a different kind. Liljefors focused on nature, but he observed and investigated nature in an analytic manner that had little to do with the romantic landscape movement earlier in the nineteenth century. He recognized that nature is a self-repairing, well-functioning system that has the capacity to bring itself into balance. Similarly, Alva and Gunnar Myrdal hoped to apply these principles to the reformation of Swedish society. Through his artistic skill and through the broad distribution of his work, Liljefors communicated his vision of nature to many Swedes. Others would adopt his vision and use it as a prototype for a new garden.

Such a fragment of nature was Sven Markelius's house in Kevinge, where Alva and Gunnar Myrdal also lived; the architect had moved there from Bromma in 1945 [Figure 1–15]. One particular photograph of the Markelius villa greatly influenced the Swedish landscape architecture of the time. Here the garden in its traditional form has vanished and a new conception has taken its place. The house does not dominate the image, as is often the case. Instead, the house serves as a background for the garden. A few forest trees, birches, imply that the garden is unbounded and continues to the rear of the photographer or, alternately, that there is no garden. Given its central position in the picture, the little pool appears merely as stormwater which has collected in a rock crevice. The young girl is turned away from us. She does not pose but finds her place naturally in this very special garden. She belongs to the first generation who will live a completely modern life. She stands in a landscape that looks more like a clearing in a forest than a designed garden. In this new concept of a garden a historic remnant remains. The picture testifies to an unbroken tradition of Swedish landscape with a certain perception of nature: where humans have a place in the wild, living in a meaningful relation with nature [Figure 1–16].

The landscape architect Sven Hermelin, mentioned earlier, was also a writer, a teacher, and the first landscape architect in Sweden to practice exclusively as a private consultant in

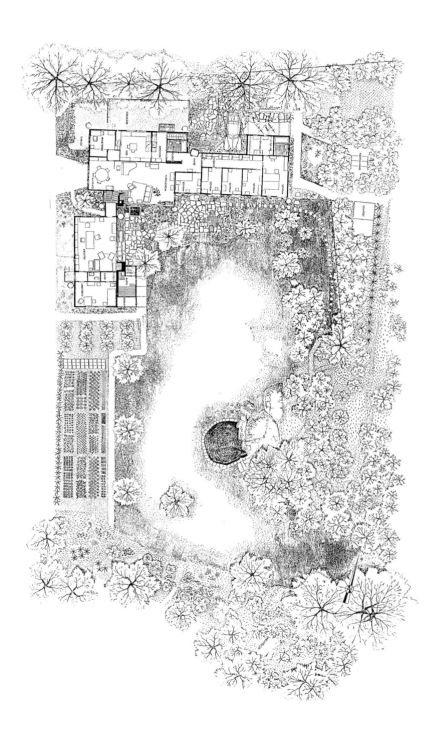

Figure 1–15.
Villa Markelius, Kevinge, Stockholm, 1945.
Sven Markelius.
A new kind of garden was introduced that
took nature as its model.
[Arkitekturmuseet]

Figure 1–16.
Villa Markelius, Kevinge, Stockholm, 1945.
Sven Markelius.
The plan with its careful detailing indicates
a growing interest in the outdoors.
[*Byggmästaren*, 1945]

Figure 1–17.
The Poacher, 1894. Bruno Liljefors.
Oil on canvas.
This painting was one of Sven Hermelin's
personal favorites, showing man listening
to what nature has to tell him.
[Private collection]

Figure 1–18.
Marabou Park, Sundbyberg, 1945.
Sven Hermelin and Inger Wedborn.
This park was brought into existence to
fulfill an ambition to compensate industrial
workers for their monotonous working
surroundings.
[Office of Sven Hermelin]

landscape design. In earlier times, designers had always worked with a contracting firm, what today would be termed design/build. Hermelin's career was a lifelong struggle to define the profession in a new way. He expanded the role of the landscape architect from garden designer to that of a comprehensive design professional, while he established nature as a valid concept for the making of gardens. From the inception of garden design in Sweden during the sixteenth century, Sweden had followed international trends. The bosque, the parterre, and the cascade were all traditional ingredients in Swedish garden design, although they were utilized not without difficulty. Boxwood, for instance, did not thrive in this northern climate. Hermelin, who made restoration designs for several historical noble gardens, modified foreign practice; for example, for the parterres of Hässelby Slott he exchanged the boxwood common to the gardens of southern Europe for pruned spruce, the most typical of all Swedish trees.[12]

Sven Hermelin attended to local conditions, and he had a true love for nature; but he was also aware that he lived in a time when society was undergoing major changes. In response, he left classical ideas of the garden behind, instead introducing elements from the surrounding landscape. In his projects glades, lakes, inlets, meadows, pastures, groves, and forest edges were stylized and used as artistic points of departure. Hermelin deeply admired Bruno Liljefors for his reading of the natural world, and although he had received a traditional training in garden design, he more and more turned to nature as his source of inspiration.

In Liljefors's painting *The Poacher*, of 1894, the subject listens with one hand behind his ear, paying close attention to what nature has to tell him [Figure 1–17]. The landscape architect must also listen to what nature tells him or her. One of Hermelin's many landscape aphorisms is "that looks as if it were planted, it is supposed to look like it grows."[13] Hermelin, although born a baron, talked about the "socialization of garden design" in an effort to describe the new role of parks as open spaces accessible to everyone and as a health-promoting counterweight to the ever-growing density of the city. Since parks served the general public, their facilities were to address everyday demands. Hermelin said in an interview shortly before his death in 1984: "Go easy on the flowers, they can easily become too much of a good thing. To my mind, a lawn that is full of children is far prettier than a lawn with colorful borders."[14]

Hermelin's conviction that parks were important to the well-being and health of the people found a substantial expression in his work for the Marabou chocolate factory in Sundbyberg [Figure 1–18]. In connection with this project, he had visited several industrial companies in Britain and had studied how considerately designed parklike surroundings could mitigate the monotonous and tiring work of the factory. In addition, his contacts in Germany brought him in touch with the Schönheit der Arbeit, an organization that arranged architectural competitions to beautify the surroundings of industrial complexes. These foreign efforts matched Swedish society's goal to provide good everyday environments for all its citizens [Figure 1–19].

In the spring of 1937, the Hermelin office received a commission from the Marabou chocolate factory, a commission that would occupy Hermelin until 1943. The Norwegian owner of the company, Henning Throne-Holst, was philanthropic in mind and intended that two hectares (about five acres) of land adjacent to the factory should be transformed into a park. The park would be used as recreational grounds for the workers during their breaks, and on weekends it would be opened to the public. The site had a considerable level change of about ten meters between an extended rock ridge and a lower plain. Deciduous trees shaded the dramatic ridge. In Hermelin's design, one descends along stepped walkways to the large, sun-drenched lawn that carpets the lower part of the site intended to offer space for recreation and physical exercise. At the end farthest from the factory buildings is a pond with a small pavilion [Figure 1–20]. Depressed into the ground as if by a giant thumb, the pond's paved bottom slips into the soft grass with no distinct edge to define its borders. A few large trees create a changing pattern of shadows on the lawn, an effect quite welcome in a northern country like Sweden with its low winter sun.

Park benches occupy shaded areas beneath the canopies along the edge of the ridge. "The transition between that which is fixed and that which is free has often occupied my imagination," Hermelin wrote in a letter in 1983.[15] It could have been his credo. Unfortunately, the landscape architect's relations with Throne-Holst's successor, his son Johan, were imperfect. Shortly after World War II Johan Throne-Holst returned from a trip to Washington, D.C., where he had seen the pink blooms of the Japanese cherries planted around the edge of the Tidal Basin. He now suggested that the large trees at the foot of the ridge should be cut down

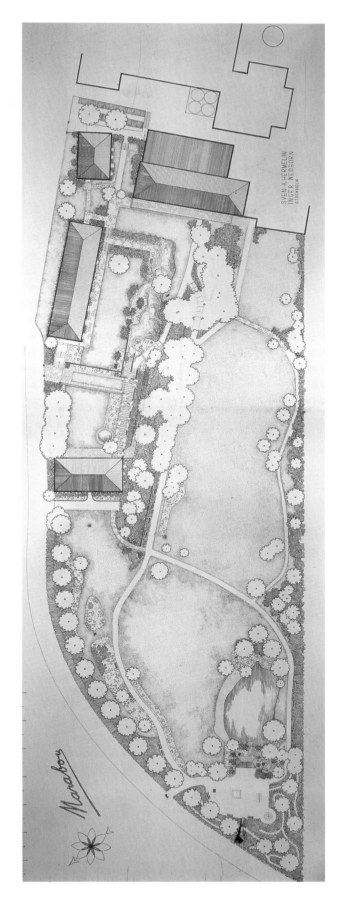

Figure 1–19.
Marabou Park, Sundbyberg, 1945.
Sven Hermelin and Inger Wedborn.
During the weekends, when the factory is closed, the park is kept open for the use of the public.
[Åke E:son Lindman]

Figure 1–20.
Marabou Park, Sundbyberg, 1945.
Sven Hermelin and Inger Wedborn.
The little Japanese-style pavilion at the pond was designed by Arthur von Schmalensee, one of the more prominent architects in Sweden at the time.
[Åke E:son Lindman]

and replaced by flowering cherry trees, standing in a bed of yellow daffodils. Hermelin waved this suggestion away, commenting that it revealed bad taste, and was subsequently released from his commission.

The photo of Sven Markelius's villa in Kevinge in which the young girl stretches her arms toward nature and toward the bright future that belongs to her and to the Swedish modernist garden had a strong propagandistic effect. A second image by the photographer K. W. Gullers, showing the children's pond in Stockholm's Fredhäll Park, was equally influential [Figure 1–21]. Here we see a peaceful environment, with children playing in what could be a natural lake inlet or stream. Old oak and ash trees, growing freely, their branches reaching out over pastureland, frame the picture. If not for the apartment buildings that appear in the rear of the photo the scene could have been somewhere out in the Swedish countryside: the landscape and the atmosphere are about the same in both settings.

But Fredhäll is located in the middle of central Stockholm and the lake inlet is a children's pool cast in concrete. Fredhäll Park was yet another influential representative of the new attitude in Swedish landscape design that intended to erase the garden. The municipal park department designed so many parks in this style, of such consistently high quality, that they were later grouped together and labeled the Stockholm School of Landscape Design. The Stockholm School took the regional landscape around Lake Mälaren as an aesthetic program and point of departure, purifying, distilling, and stylizing the site's natural assets, or at times, creating them in places that lacked natural advantages.

The programs for the new municipal parks also differed from the old ones. Rather than being restricted to green refuges, parks were now regarded as active and essential urban elements. Parks were seen as indivisible parts of the social housing program, on the same list of necessities as the flush toilet, the balcony, and hot and cold running water. For the first time, landscapes were planned for active use by the general public, where it was possible to walk on the grass, to bathe in the sun, to share a picnic lunch. All this despite the fact that for the first time a person had been appointed Director of Parks in Stockholm who knew almost nothing about making gardens.

The man was Holger Blom (1906–96), who served in office over three decades, from 1938 to 1971 [Figure 1–22]. He

was trained as an urban planner and had practiced with Lars Israel Wahlman in Stockholm, with Krüger & Toll in Amsterdam, and with Le Corbusier in Paris. Blom's contribution was twofold. The first was his park program; he displayed a strong, strategic mind devoted to questions of park policy. The second was his success in realizing a system in which parks penetrated almost all areas of the inner city.

Blom's park program was simple, tersely worded, and striking in effect. It comprised several different levels, each developed with a different degree of detail that could be condensed into a single effective picture, repeatedly used in conversation with politicians, colleagues, and the general public. The four main points were as follows:

1. The park relieves the city.
   (The urban planning aspect)
2. The park provides space for outdoor recreation.
   (The sanitary and general health aspect)
3. The park offers space for public gatherings.
   (The social aspect)
4. The park preserves nature and culture.
   (The ecological aspect) [16]

Norr Mälarstrand, built 1941–43, possibly best exemplifies the Stockholm concept of a naturistic urban landscape combined with recreational facilities. The park is a narrow green finger — two miles long and in most parts only seventy-five feet wide — extending along the north shore of Lake Mälaren. The park cuts through the entire inner city, starting at its center fronting the city hall and ending at the very outskirts of town. Today, Stockholmers generally believe that Norr Mälarstrand is an area of preserved nature of particular beauty, when as a matter of fact it is a thoroughly constructed environment. [17] Before development, the land was a desolate strip of marshes dotted with storage sheds; it had no visual or physical amenities. [18] The architect for most of the parks in Stockholm during the period of the Stockholm School was the multitalented Erik Glemme, mentioned earlier in connection with the Vällingby town center. Glemme worked for Holger Blom at the parks department and was the chief designer for Norr Mälarstrand. To him must be credited the delicate texture and continual variety experienced along the linear sweep of the shoreline [Figures 1–23, 1–24, 1–25].

Holger Blom served in public office; Sven Hermelin worked in private practice. This was certainly not the sole way in

Figure 1–21. Children's pond,
Fredhäll Park, Stockholm, 1936–38.
Oswald Almquist and Erik Glemme.
This photograph taken by the legendary
Swedish photographer K. W. Gullers was
published in many international maga-
zines. It witnessed a new attitude in land-
scape design, in form as well as in content.
[Nordiska museet]

Figure 1–22.
Holger Blom (1906–96).
The man who implemented the Stockholm
School of park design.
[Gösta Glase]

24

Figure 1–23. [*above*]
Norr Mälarstrand, Stockholm, 1941–43.
Holger Blom and Erik Glemme.
Despite its width of only about 15 meters
(48 feet), this park is overwhelmingly rich
in functional as well as aesthetic elements.
[Thorbjörn Andersson]

Figure 1–24. [*facing page, top*]
Mobile stage for a small group of
musicians, 1940s. Erik Glemme.
The development of parks amenable to mul-
tiple uses was typical of the Stockholm
School of park design.
[C. G. Rosenberg]

Figure 1–25. [*facing page, bottom*]
Norr Mälarstrand, Stockholm, 1941–43.
Holger Blom and Erik Glemme.
Although Stockholmers of today generally
believe this park to be a natural area that
has survived in the city, older photos show
that it is a thoroughly constructed park.
[C. G. Rosenberg]

which the two men differed, however. Hermelin was a land-scape architect with rigorous horticultural training. Blom, in contrast, was educated as a building architect with extensive experience in urban planning. Before Blom was appointed Director of Parks, the national organization of landscape architects (Landskaparkitekternas Riksförbund, or LAR), through its spokesman, Sven Hermelin, directed sharp criti-cism toward the way that the position had been formulated in the job announcement. Its wording favored an architect with a planning background rather than a landscape archi-tect with horticultural experience. In spite of their differing competencies, however, these two individuals promoted a new attitude toward gardens in Sweden that excluded old notions of the garden.

The Swedish book with the widest international distribution is neither a novel nor a social or political history: it is the children's story of Pippi Långstrump (or Pippi Longstocking in English), by Astrid Lindgren. The book has been translated into more than sixty languages, and perhaps more than any other national cultural expression, Pippi has become the symbol of Swedish spirit abroad. Pippi defies propriety and authority; she liberates us from the burden of narrow-minded moralism. When Lindgren wrote the first book in 1945, she was not unaffected by the change of values in Swedish society. And the garden was an active part of that change. Lindgren writes: "In a country setting we find a garden and a house. In that house lived a father and a mother with their two cute little children, a boy and a girl. The boy was Tommy and the girl Annika. They were both very nice and well-raised and obedient little children. Never did Tommy chew his nails; he always did what his mother asked him to do. Annika would never make trouble when she did not get what she wanted, and she was always very neatly dressed in little well-ironed cotton dresses. They also have an equally neat and tidy garden."[19]

Illustrations from the book show Tommy and Annika playing croquet in their parents' garden. The lawn is neatly cut, and a flower border surrounds the square garden. Tommy's hair is neatly combed and he wears a sailor suit. Annika wears a summer dress and her index finger is coquettishly placed in her mouth. In Villa Villekulla, the neighboring home, a red-haired girl with oversized shoes is just moving in. She even-tually will change the lives of Tommy and Annika. Her lawn is not mowed, and the trees grow old and crooked, offering tantalizing targets for climbing. Frogs croak in her wild gar-den, which looks more like a natural feature than anything that someone had created. Pippi's garden bears similarities with the Markelius garden in Kevinge, as well as with the landscape at the children's pond in Fredhäll. In the course of the story, Tommy and Annika step out of their restrained garden and into Pippi's world: more alive, more rebellious, less predictable. Astrid Lindgren uses the description of the garden to reflect the changing society around her [Figures 1–26, 1–27].

The garden is a part of Swedish culture and thus bonds the story with the forest and sea still so much a part of Swedish life; in essence, the garden reflects a view of society. How landscape architects treat outdoor space tells more than that, however. It also says something about our conception of nature, our conception of society, and our conception of our fellow human beings. Modernism threw the idea of the garden into crisis because the traditional garden had very little in common with the values and the needs of the twentieth-century city. Figures such as Holger Blom, Sven Hermelin, Alva Myrdal, and even Pippi Långstrump — each in his or her own way and through their differing positions in society — made this a mutual cause and launched the garden into a new direction. In his book *Gardens in the Modern Landscape* (first published in 1938), Christopher Tunnard concluded his description of the Swedish message with the following statement: "The full significance lies in the fact that it was a group effort and not the product of any one individual's ideas."[20] As a result of that process, the form of the garden faded into the woods and the sea, leaving in its place a landscape of humanized nature [Figure 1–28].

26

Figure 1–26.
From *Pippi Longstocking* by Astrid Lindgren; illustration by Ingrid Vang Nyman.
Tommy and Annika's garden, an orderly place in which to be proper.
[Courtesy Peder Nyman]

Figure 1–27.
From *Pippi Longstocking* by Astrid Lindgren; illustration by Ingrid Vang Nyman.
Pippi's garden at Villa Villekulla.
[Courtesy Peder Nyman]

NOTES

For their support of this essay as well as other projects, I wish to thank The Visual Arts Fund, Stockholm; the Anders & Ivar Tengbom Fund; and the FFNS Research Fund.

1. Cited in Magnus Andersson, *Stockholms årsringar* (Stockholm's Annual Rings) (Stockholm: Stockholmia förlag, 1997), p. 153.

2. Cited in ibid., p. 195.

3. The superellipse derived from the super-imposition of the rectangle and the circle; it had various applications from table designs to the plaza at Sergels torg.

4. See Dorothée Imbert, *The Modernist Garden in France* (New Haven: Yale University Press, 1993), p. 38.

5. Bengt Isling and Torbjörn Sunesson, *Gunnar Martinsson landskapsarkitekt* (Gunnar Martinsson, Landscape Architect) (Stockholm: Byggforskningsrådet, unpublished research report).

6. Per Anders Fogelström, *Stad i världen* (The City in the World) (Stockholm, 1968).

7. David Pass, *Vällingby and Farsta: From Idea to Reality*, Ph.D. diss. (KTH) Royal Institute of Technology, 1969. Thorbjörn Andersson, *Utanför staden* (Outside the City) (Stockholm: Stockholmia förlag, 2000).

8. Sven Hermelin, "Dansk trädgårdskonst och svensk. Några intryck från föreningen Svenska Trädgårdsarkitekters resa i Danmark" (Danish and Swedish Garden Art: Some Impressions from the Swedish Landscape Architects' Excursion to Denmark), *Havekunst* (1934), p. 25.

9. Thorbjörn Andersson, "Appearances and Beyond: Time and Change in Swedish Landscape Architecture," *Journal of Garden History* (1997), p. 285.

10. Thorbjörn Andersson, "The Functionalism of Gardening Art," in Claes Caldenby, ed., *Sweden* (Munich: Prestel, 1999), p. 233.

11. Allan Ellenius, *Bruno Liljefors: Naturen som livsrum* (Bruno Liljefors: Space for Life) (Stockholm: Bonnier Alba, 1996), p. 45.

12. Thorbjörn Andersson, "Sven Hermelin 1900–1984," in Thorbjörn Andersson, Tove Jonstoij, and Kjell Lundquist, ed., *Svensk Trädgårdskonst under fyra århundraden* (Stockholm: Byggförlaget, 2000), pp. 206–16.

13. Cited in Sven-Ingvar Andersson, "Sven Hermelin 70 år miljövårdsåret," *Landskab* 8 (1970), p. 146.

14. Cited in Lotte Möller, "Det långsamma skådespelets regissör," *Vi* 40 (1982), p. 12.

15. Cited in Sven-Ingvar Andersson, "Breven berättar," *Utblick Landskap* 1 (1985), p. 7.

16. Holger Blom, "Stockholms gröna ytor," *Byggmästaren* 16 (1946), pp. 1–36.

17. In like manner, many New Yorkers believe that the seeming naturalism of Central Park is, in fact, terrain surviving the city's construction. In fact, it is completely constructed, being the work of Frederick Law Olmsted and Calvert Vaux, dating from around the middle of the nineteenth century.

18. Thorbjörn Andersson, "Erik Glemme and the Stockholm Park System," in Marc Treib, ed., *Modern Landscape Architecture: A Critical Review* (Cambridge, Mass.: MIT Press, 1993), p. 122.

19. Astrid Lindgren (illustrations by Ingrid Vang Nyman), *Boken om Pippi Långstrump* (Stockholm: Rabén & Sjögren, 1945), p. 13.

20. Christopher Tunnard, *Gardens in the Modern Landscape* (London: Architectural Press, 1938).

Figure 1–28.
Holger Blom directs his workers to use nature to create a new park.
Illustration by Birger Lundquist.
[Courtesy Tarras Blom]

In the decades between the first and second world wars, a new tolerance toward nature, the original, and the childlike influenced the course of Danish culture. This trend found expression in the radicalism of the reform and democratic movements, in modern theories of education, in dance and music, and in the admiration of the natural, untouched, and original landscape. The ideal of the era embodied a pastoral idyll, romanticizing everyday middle-class life. Freedom was the first priority.

After World War II it became the human goal to conquer nature, sexual instincts, and animalism—to distance oneself from all that was natural. As a result, the cultured, the cultivated, and the constructed were regarded as the correct and the beautiful. The liberation of human instincts in the interwar period had also found its reflection in the liberation of nature outdoors. After the war, the struggle against human nature was paralleled by the struggle against nature outside the body and the house.

By cultivating nature, by uniting the inner and the outer, by making the garden a constructed outdoor room, the language of aesthetics could be used as a tool to understand the new society. Within the limits of Danish society, the garden as a constructed realm enforced calmness, purity and regularity, control, standards of propriety, and even democracy. Everything made by man became beautiful; the garden came under the aegis of the builder and the gardener rather than that of the shepherd. Although the aesthetics of the architect triumphed over the aesthetics of the manager, it was only for a short period. When imagination was recalled and restored in 1968, that era ended. At the beginning of the 1970s, impelled by new cultural, social, and economic situations, the attitude toward the relation between humans and nature changed. But in the years following the end of World War II, a new aesthetic language, which had its beginnings in art, had demonstrated the connections between the language of aesthetics and the values we consider important.

2.

MALENE HAUXNER

With the Sky as Ceiling: Landscape and Garden Art in Denmark

G. N. BRANDT AS THE GRAND MASTER

In the first half of the twentieth century Danish landscape architects actively fought the Beaux Arts style, which they termed the "old ugliness." To this generation the Beaux Arts represented falsehood, romantic superficiality, and a facade with no content. Where the young architects and landscape

Figure 2–1.
Hellerup Strand Park, Hellerup, Denmark,
1912–16. G. N. Brandt.
[Malene Hauxner, *Fantasiens Have*]

Figure 2–2.
Brandt garden, Ørnekulsvej, Ordrup,
Denmark, 1916. G. N. Brandt.
[Hauxner, *Fantasiens Have*]

architects adopted Reginald Blomfield's historicism, G. N. Brandt (1878–1945) picked only Edwin Lutyens's spatial clarity and William Robinson's and Gertrude Jekyll's view of the unique value of plants from the English "renaissance" Arts and Craft garden.[1] Brandt instigated a search for the past, for old familiar ways, but in order to find solutions to contemporary social problems, he also demanded organization, standardization, and innovative views of plant use. These demands were met, for example, in his own garden on Ørnekulsvej in Ordrup (1916), Hellerup Strandpark (1912–16) [Figure 2–1], and Mariebjerg Cemetery (1925–36).

The small garden at Brandt's own house combined the classical organization with equipment and elements of the Arts and Craft garden. But at the same time, it also utilized modern ideas [Figure 2–2]. From the house, which is now gone, one could retreat into a lawn without paths and lie down naked among daisies under apple trees. One of the garden rooms was furnished with an idealized irrigation ditch, in actuality a concrete canal with plants on its banks and a short pipe set in the brick-covered wall. Brandt's aesthetic intention in incorporating these elements was to prevent the wall from appearing too flat. The feeling was that of something unbounded, something endless, to free the imagination.

In 1925 Brandt received the assignment to create a modern cemetery [Figures 2–3, 2–4]. What he saw as his first and most important task was to reestablish the missing connection between the cemetery and its elements: the graves and the monuments. The grave was accepted in all its ugliness, organized as an organic system of regularly shaped rooms linked by avenues. Brandt, always a classicist, rebelled against prewar ideals. Nevertheless, he acquired a central role in another rebellion, which propelled a final shift between paradigms around 1930.[2]

Farmers had created the country's woods, commons, meadows, hedgerows, paths, fences, and ditches; but poets, painters, and architects first saw their wonder. In Denmark, Brandt was the first to show how such images of the countryside could improve garden design [Figure 2–5]. What was at first no more than an artistic vision was made a "glorious reality" in a large number of Brandt's gardens (for example, the Svastika, realized in Rungsted in 1925). All were constructed from one particular concept, which turned its back on rational town life in order to satisfy the

new notion of "infinite" space and nurture the life of individual plants. Throughout a generation, Brandt applied this concept—first outlined in his 1930 article "Der kommende Garten" (The Future Garden) — using plantings whose basic elements were a frame of some sort, smooth grass, and individual stands of trees that were thus set off as "a jewel amidst neutral green" (for example, the garden at Nympha in Vedbæk, 1930) [Figure 2–6].[3]

Brandt's preparations for this free individual growth, perhaps the most important artistic idea in modern garden and landscape architecture, whose beginning can be precisely dated to 1930, were first outlined before and during World War I in two key publications: *Stauder* (Perennials, 1914) and *Vand- og Stenhøjsplanter* (Water and Rock-plants, 1917).[4] Brandt selected nature's own plants, ascribed to each its own value and character, and allowed each its normal rate of growth. In certain ways this attitude provided a way to determine value and to read modern life. Modern man, demanding individuality, wanted the right to think and act freely; in a similar way, plants should also be treated individually, following their natural properties and habits. Whereas in Germany the removal of man and the creative spirit was a culture-critical act that turned dictatorial, to Brandt the

idea was to work like the jeweler, to leave a precious stone unworked within a finely worked frame, allowing man to live in a natural balance, in fellowship with animals and plants. The more systematic modern life became, the more the world was organized, standardized, mechanized, and rationalized, the greater the desire for irrationality and thrill and the greater the longing for a variety of sensual experiences. The garden became a haven of romanticism and lyricism which counterbalanced the monotony of life. To achieve this aim, Brandt used the deliberate veiling of view, a veiling that was intended to lead to conjecture and dreams. With his remark "not what has been drawn, and hardly even shaped," Brandt eschewed clarity and avant-garde posturing. Using growth, free association, and a deliberate murmur, as it were, he left interpretation to the observer and, with it, the interest in the architect's intentions. That stance did not represent any conservative or unrealistic romanticism but, instead, was meant to provoke the viewer's creativity or action. Imagination, dreams, and thought may lead us out of the natural world, but they may also lead us to democracy, to a way of managing one's life—a view Brandt shared with Poul Henningsen (1894–1967), the chief proponent of Danish intellectual radicalism.

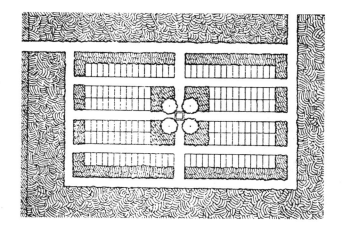

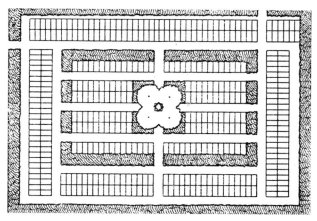

Figure 2–4. [*above left*]
Mariebjerg Cemetery, Gentofte, Denmark,
1925–36. G. N. Brandt.
[Hauxner, *Fantasiens Have*]

Figure 2–5.
Ordrup Cemetery, Ordrup, Denmark.
G. N. Brandt.
[Hauxner, *Fantasiens Have*]

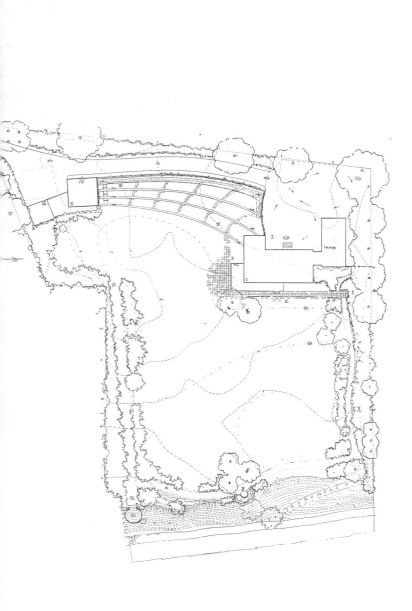

At the close of World War II, Danish garden art had accepted as tradition the modern pastoral garden based on ideas that Brandt had propagated. Among gardens designed using his concepts were Carl Theodor Sørensen's proposal for the grounds of Århus University (1931) [Figures 2–7, 2–8], his Bellevue Strandpark (1930), and park director Jacob Bergmann's plans for Utterslev Mose, the Damhusengen, Bispebjerg, Valby and Sundbyvester parks in Copenhagen. The last great masterpiece in this style was Mindelunden at Ryvangen (a memorial landscape commemorating the Danish Resistance), designed by Kaj Gottlob and Aksel Andersen (1945) [Figure 2–9].

Brandt's practices differed from those common today. He employed young architects and landscape architects as designers and draftsmen in such a manner that their office years served as a formative educational apprenticeship. In this way he managed to influence a generation of landscape architects. This distinguished group of Brandt "graduates" included Georg Georgsen (1893–1976), who later became professor at the Royal Veterinary and Agricultural University; Aksel Andersen (1902–52), who followed him as park director in Gentofte; C. Th. Sørensen (1893–1979), who acted as both park manager in Gentofte and professor at the Royal Academy of Fine Arts; and Troels Erstad (1911– 49), who became Brandt's partner in his last years, marked by the senior man's illness. Erstad's own life ended tragically, but during his short career he proposed a series of gardens that were both personal and harmonious with their times. At their best they represented a modern poetic tradition that reached above and beyond their era. In his own Ordrup garden (1940) he employed an artistic language learned from late Roman culture, from William Robinson, Gertrude Jekyll, Willy Lange, Brandt, Sørensen, and Mogens Lassen. Here he sublimely coupled light with color, new with old, house with garden, simple with complex, and exotic with native [Figure 2–10]. G. N. Brandt died in 1945. His last great works were the Garden of Parterres at Tivoli Gardens, also known as "the 32 Fountains" (1943) [Figure 2–11], and the gardens and roof terraces for Denmark's Radio House (1943). Both were created in a new aesthetic language, far away from the 1930s, which proposed the garden as a courtyard where beauty lay in the human construct.

Entering the Tivoli Gardens through the gate opposite Copenhagen's City Hall and following the undulating wall, one receives a marvelous view of Brandt's fountain garden. The wall of bricks is the permanent element, a technical

Figure 2–6. [*facing page*]
Nympha Garden, Vedbæk, Denmark, 1930.
G. N. Brandt.
[Hauxner, *Fantasiens Have*]

Figure 2–7. [*above*]
Århus University, Århus, Denmark.
Competition, 1931; 1933–47.
C. Th. Sørensen, landscape architect;
C. F. Møller, Kay Fisker, Poul Stegmann,
architects.
[Marc Treib]

Figure 2–8. [*left*]
Århus University, Århus, Denmark.
Competition, 1931; 1933–47. Plan.
C. Th. Sørensen, landscape architect;
C. F. Møller, Kay Fisker, Poul Stegmann,
architects.
[Hauxner, *Fantasiens Have*]

Figure 2–9.
Mindelunden, Ryvangen, Denmark, 1945.
Kaj Gottlieb and Aksel Andersen.
[Marc Treib]

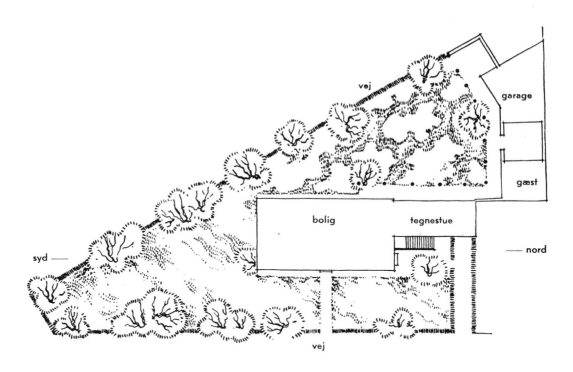

Figure 2–10.
Erstad garden, Ordrup, Denmark, 1947.
Troels Erstad.
View.
[Walter Bauer, courtesy Vibe Erstad]
Plan.
[*Havekunst*, 1944]

solution for supporting terrain that occupies two different
levels. The war had also contributed to the look of the garden. The yellow bricks — the only paving materials available
at the time — created a fine floor; the water vessels beneath
the fountains were made of wood because construction in
concrete was prohibited during the Occupation. To Brandt
the garden was like a memory, an old voyage realized. The
special character of the garden derived from its equal mixture of water and flowers distributed over the ground in a
steady rhythm without accentuation, centers, or stated axes.
The garden's plan resembled a fragment of a wallpaper pattern, with the geometrical figures melting together while
appearing as squares and circles. A regular modular system
of parallel lines emerges in one direction, a rhythmic partition in the other. A landscape like Tivoli's fountain garden
had not been seen in Denmark before 1943. It was fundamentally contemporary, with a functional content and an
expression that corresponded to technique and economy.
The garden was neither nostalgic nor sentimental but to a
considerable extent, poetic. And lastly it was a garden that
pointed to the garden of the future.

Figure 2–11.
The thirty-two fountains, Tivoli Gardens,
Copenhagen, Denmark, 1943. G. N. Brandt.
[Gentofte Kommune]

SVEN HANSEN

During the 1930s Sven Hansen had worked for G. N. Brandt as a draftsman for the design of the celebrated Mariebjerg Cemetery, where he later became its landscape manager. In the office he had witnessed and aided Brandt's breakthrough into a more modern idiom. Among other things, Hansen designed a prototype cubic gravestone in granite, which, together with the neatly trimmed paths of grass in the spirit of the "grand master," made the "wilderness" section of the cemetery recognizably reformed by man. At Hillerød Cemetery (1956), Hansen used Brandt's characteristic contrast between trimmed and untrimmed grass and between looking at a plant as an individual element and as a building stone [Figure 2–12]. Hedges, rows of trees, and drystone walls surrounded defined spatial zones. One also recognizes scenes that recall the dramatically situated trees on the hilltop of the Woodland Cemetery in Enskede, Sweden, outside Stockholm (1915–40). As a totality though, the Hillerød Cemetery differed significantly from Gunnar Asplund's and Sigurd Lewerentz's Woodland Cemetery and Brandt's Mariebjerg design. The Hillerød landscape can be laid within an implied elliptically

Figure 2–12.
Hillerød Cemetery, Hillerød, Denmark, 1956. Sven Hansen and Max Büel.
[Malene Hauxner]

shaped space, with walls made from fieldstone, planted with hawthorn (*Crataegus* sp.) and a single inner row of trees. The elliptical lines of a paved road emphasized the identity of the space, like the line between the trimmed green grass and the untrimmed yellow grasses during the summer. Square rooms bounded and overlapped by one another followed the shape of the outer oval, while meandering angled hedges contoured the inner figure. As the ground rose, the hedge-enclosed spaces also rose toward a simple cubic chapel, and beyond toward the dramatic earthworks crowned by lindens (*Tilia* sp.).

At the Copenhagen County Hospital in Glostrup (1952), Hansen had imagined the large hospital building to be a huge rock brought to the site by a glacier that had cut deep traces in the soft Danish topsoil and had pushed it forward as a rampart around a large plain. He helped re-duce the apparent size of the large building by planting black locusts (*Robinia* sp.) in front of the building and oaks (*Quercus* sp.) on the ramparts; the patients gained some-thing beautiful to look at in the process. A collaboration with the architects to fully join building and landscape did not quite succeed, even though an attempt was made to reflect one of the hospital's facades in a rectangular pool, like that of a Renaissance garden [Figure 2–13]. The gardens at Glostrup Hospital, like those at Hillerød Cemetery, are grand earthworks that helped inspire Hansen's approach to later projects of the 1960s such as the high-rise apartment blocks at Høje Gladsaxe (1963), the Entreprenørskolen (Builders' School) at Ebeltoft (1961), Aswan Dam in Egypt (1962), and the TV and Radio House in Århus (1971).

Although Hansen was fully capable of creating powerful grounds on his own, a close collaboration with architects — common at the time — characterized his work. The extreme example of a joint project was the architect Jørgen Bo's residence in Hjortekær, where it is difficult to see just who did what [Figures 2–14, 2–15]. The house, almost square in outline, was not very large. But the walls extended along the full length of the long rectangular site, causing the build-ing to appear much larger than it actually measured. The house was situated to the rear of the land, making room for a large lawn in the front. Tall, white walls sheltered the internal spaces and reflected the sun upon exotic plants. Cut from the square terrace pavement were beds for yucca, the sculptural Mexican species known in Denmark from Gordon Cullen's drawings and from photographs of Frank

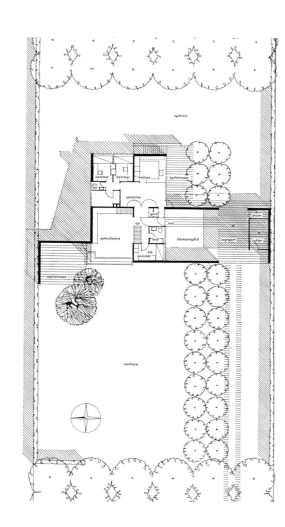

Figure 2–13. [*facing page*]
Copenhagen County Hospital, Glostrup,
Denmark, 1952. Sven Hansen.
[C. Th. Sørensen Archives]

Figure 2–14.
Bo house and garden, Hjortekær, Denmark,
1954. Jørgen Bo and Sven Hansen. View.
[Else Tholstrup; Jørgen Bo/Malene Hauxner
Archives]

Figure 2–15.
Bo house and garden, Hjortekær, Denmark,
1954. Jørgen Bo and Sven Hansen. Site plan.
[*Arkitektur DK*, 3/1957]

Lloyd Wright's Taliesin West, and Roberto Burle Marx's Brazilian garden designs. Two rows of flagstones set in the grass were flanked by an allée of flowering plums (*Prunus* "Mount Fuji") — which grew almost horizontally and bloomed in white — and led toward the garage, which in 1954 was a modern addition to the domestic landscape. Jørgen Bo's building and Sven Hansen's allée intersected to form an asymmetrical cross that constituted an inviolable whole. But despite the strength of this plan, it was the vertical dimension, and the walls of the house, that most conclusively defined the garden. They stretched outward, making spaces and rooms, dividing front and back, and separating children from adults.

ARNE JACOBSEN

To look at plants as a building element is not an unknown practice in the history of garden art. But in the modern Danish garden, as it took form during the period between the wars, that was not their main role. If we exclude some sporadic experiments in the 1920s, plants tended to appear during this period in their natural forms—as a poetic touch in pastoral landscapes, which did not relate to the architecture through a sure use of geometry. In this way the architect Arne Jacobsen (1902–71) had directed planting in his

designs for the House of the Future at Forum (1929) and at the town halls for Søllerød and Århus (1937). In other projects from the 1930s, Jacobsen shaped an arcade of lindens around a car park or filled in the interstices with trimmed shrubs, almost as a background for the individual trees left to grow in their habitual forms. A deliberate, artistic use of plants as space-creating components belongs, however, to the postwar period.

Almost on the seashore at Øresund, north of Copenhagen, rising like a bastion on a windy point, lay Arne Jacobsen's own garden, completed in 1950 [Figures 2–16, 2–17]. Bamboo cut into square forms enclosed the garden on three sides; on the fourth, a humble but elegant house created the last wall. This south facade read as a perfectly proportioned composition of rectangular forms of varying sizes and materials. Glass, wood painted white, yellow bricks, and fabric window shades joined with the garden's spatial components to create a unified entity. With the facade as its backdrop, the paving and planting elements suggested a painting in three dimensions, a concrete materialization of a garden view. The floor was carpeted with Norwegian marble divided into rectangular modules. In the gaps between the planters *Sagina* pushed upward in stripes and amorphous

Figure 2–16. [*facing page*]
Jacobsen house and garden, Klampenborg, Denmark,
1950. Arne Jacobsen.
[*Marc Treib*, 1999]

Figure 2–17.
Jacobsen house and garden, Klampenborg, Denmark,
1950. Arne Jacobsen. Plan.
[*Bo Bedre*, 9/1965]

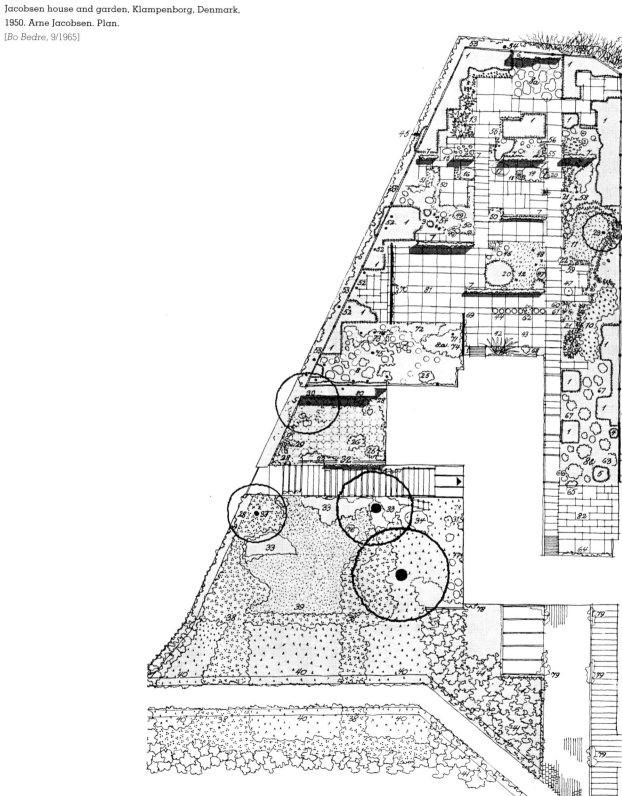

cushions, making it possible to experience the poetical variations of these small-scale plants. The freestanding hedges of larch (*Larix* sp.)—only 4–6 inches in width—were cut at different heights, although their consistent alignment organized the garden space and created visual clarity. G. N. Brandt's modern garden, as he described it in 1930, was a pastoral garden with grass upon which to play and stroll. The internal scenery of its spaces, bounded by untrimmed shrubs, was blurred, even hidden, thereby stimulating the human imagination. In Arne Jacobsen's garden, to the contrary, a different spatial division served a clarifying purpose. Here, we are closer to Brandt's own garden in Ordrup (1916), which was divided into imagined boxes bounded by hedges arranged according to the Golden Section.

Jacobsen's Munkegårds school buildings of 1950 were set horizontally, inserted into a slope, like a bastion rising above a grass-covered playing field [Figures 2–18, 2–19]. Five parallel corridors combined to give admission to crossing bands of classrooms in three single-story buildings; a fourth building contained studios and classrooms in a two-story wing. This organization yielded an inner landscape of seventeen courtyards experienced from the corridors through glass walls, and from the classrooms through low child-friendly windows. The courtyards were paved with flagstones identical in material yet differing in shape and configuration: rectangular, square, triangular, circular, and hexagonal. They were laid principally in a manner encouraging gaps in which grew the low *sagina,* like a natural caulking that will swell into biomorphic cushions. The shapes of the bed could be either irregular or regular; their placement at angles or parallel; but the modular net always lay beneath the vegetation, providing its support structure. In planting beds cut within the flagstone field grew exotic and sculptural plants such as hydrangea, magnolia, pyracanthus, bamboo, juniper, and lilies. And perhaps as a very special gift for the children, boxwood was cut into animal shapes such as chickens and dogs. Casts of Greek, Egyptian, and classical Danish art—for example, a portrait bust set on a freestanding pedestal or a relief mounted on a wall—completed a succinct evocation of an atmosphere of 1950s progressive, enlightened childrearing. At the same time, its historical and aesthetic references added a feeling of admiration for humankind's cultural achievements.

A room in which plane trees created the ceiling, and grass the floor, divided into two paved yards an extensive asphalt schoolyard that surrounded the gymnasiums, bicycle shelters,

Figure 2–18. [*facing page*]
Munkegård School, Gentofte, Denmark,
1950. Arne Jacobsen.
[C. Th. Sørensen Archives]

Figure 2–19.
Munkegård School, Gentofte, Denmark,
1950. Arne Jacobsen.
[C. Th. Sørensen Archives]

and restrooms. Along the street front, the direction of the pavement was reinforced by a line of pollarded plane trees. Green walls of beech adjacent to the administration buildings continued these spatial divisions between private and public domains and inside and out. This Gesamtkunstverk, whose buildings have been recognized as a milestone in Jacobsen's career, and more broadly in modern architecture as a whole, also pointed out the most prominent directions in Danish postwar landscape and garden art: the enlargement of indoor space outward in the landscape.

In 1924, when Arne Jacobsen began to study at the Kunstakademiet in Copenhagen, G. N. Brandt became its associate professor of garden art. By that time Brandt had already compiled a significant list of publications and was held in considerable professional regard. Since 1918, he had discussed in his lectures the relationship between the clear and the unclear, between a unit and a unified whole, and between the mass and the individual. In an article titled "Træer" (Trees), Brandt discussed plants' ability to create aesthetic order and clarity, as well as to strengthen the deliberately unclear, the obscure, the poetic, which stimulate imagination.[5] It is very likely that Jacobsen was familiar with this essay and other aspects of Brandt's theories, as Jacob-

sen's manner of working with plants reflects a similar consciousness. He knows the quality of the plant. It can perform as a building block used to define rooms as well as a poetic troublemaker. Jacobsen created simplicity in his gardens by basic means: using green vertical planes of hedges, rows of trees, and horizontal planes of flagstones, configured as modular units. His deliberately imprecise planning reveals a poetic dimension derived from plantings in beds carved into the flagstone floor. As interpreted from his work in the garden, it appears evident that Arne Jacobsen entered a new era resenting neither the past nor his predecessors. Although he died in 1945, Brandt remained the great master. Unlike in the United States, there had been little urge to overcome the pastoral, poetical garden tradition in order to create room for new growth and works. In Denmark, the new garden was welcomed as part of contemporary life.

C. TH. SØRENSEN

In his book *Parkpolitik i Sogn og Købstad* (Park Policy in Parish and Market Town), C. Th. Sørensen (1893–1979) suggested replacing the mixed planting characteristic of municipal parks with hedges and groves of the Danish cultural landscape: oak groves, beech woodlands, hedges of hawthorn, and fences covered with wild roses.[6] Although his program was adopted to some degree, as time passed the aesthetic language changed radically. Now, as buildings spread into the pastoral landscape they were ordered in blocks, and the order of the trees increased over time. Plants once allowed to grow naturally now formed part of the architectural works. While the native oaks surrounding the buildings at Århus University, for example, were allowed to grow naturally from seed, the exotic honey locusts that created the spaces between the prefabricated houses in Hjortekær (1948) were planted in rows. At the Åbenrå Stadium (1950) the allée of horse chestnut trees took form from its function as a circulation way; the remainder of the plantings stood upright in the landscape like baroque allées, independent and powerful. At the Risø nuclear plant (1956) the buildings were tied together by a gridded road system, whose main street was marked by an allée of erect poplars. And the principal allée accompanying the gigantic red brick building for the F. L. Smidt corporation (1957) was planted with Canadian poplars (*Populus canadensis*) [Figure 2–20].

To transform and refine plant cultures from the agricultural landscape into an architectonic work of art became one of C. Th. Sørensen's most profound contributions to modern garden art. If you consider the principal materials of garden art to be soil, water, and plants, and if you use the aesthetic language of the agricultural landscape, you might end with a composition of essentially three components: the embankment, the canal, and the row of trees. In Åbenrå, for example, a canal surrounded by levees planted with rows of poplars (1950) issued from this way of thinking [Figure 2–21]. From its form, one could believe this to be a functional landscape, but this is not the case. It is a spiritual piece of work, an artistic landscape design, a place of beauty utilizing a deliberately aesthetic language.

Throughout his lengthy career, Sørensen applied the formal studies he started in the 1920s, for example in designing the sculpture garden at the Angli IV factory in Herning (1956) [Figure 2–22]. In the Nærum allotment gardens (1948), the elliptical hedged enclosures are the principal elements, creating an image part horticultural, part pastoral. By coordinating the layout of these elements with the hilly, grass-covered terrain, important secondary spaces were created between the hedges.

In the interwar period Sørensen had experimented with circles, squares, ovals, spirals, and free shapes. After the war,

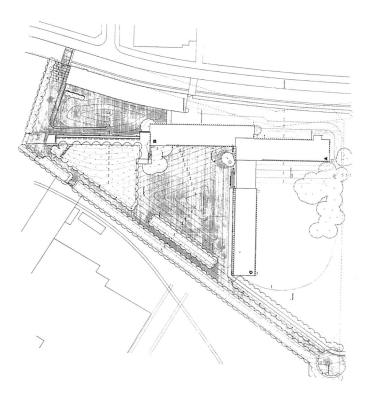

Figure 2–20.
F. L. Smidt Corporation, Copenhagen, 1957.
Plan. C. Th. Sørensen.
[Arkitekten Palle Suenson]

Figure 2–21.
The Poplar Allée, Åbenrå, Denmark, 1950.
C. Th. Sørensen.
[Malene Hauxner]

Figure 2–22.
Sculpture Garden, Angli IV, Herning,
Denmark, 1956. C. Th. Sørensen.
[C. Th. Sørensen Archives]

Figure 2–23. [*facing page, left*]
Eidsvold Værk, Oslo, Norway, 1959.
C. Th. Sørensen. Axonometric.
[C. Th. Sørensen, *Haver, Tanker, & Arbejder*]

Figure 2–24. [*facing page, right*]
City Hall Square, Tårnby, Denmark, 1956.
Ole Nørgaard.
[Malene Hauxner]

46

the forms became more tightly connected to their function and construction, embodying functionalism or constructivism in a purer form. In these later projects, the circle and the curve still survived in Sørensen's landscapes, but the straight line and the right angle proposed the formal vehicles of his future designs. In the unrealized proposal for Eidsvold Værk in Norway (1959), a green tunnel of vegetation, in a strange fashion, unified the vegetation of the baroque garden and the hedges that defined the limits of the fields [Figure 2–23]. Seen from eye level it read as a piece of theatrical scenery. Seen from above, the park landscape read as a component of a constructivist painting. Sørensen's ongoing mission was fulfilled: to create a certain sense of enclosure while at the same time maintaining distant vistas of the landscape, creating coherence between inside and outside, near and far. Sørensen's Eidsvold scheme embodied a syntax that by the end of the 1960s appeared in the designs of his successor, Sven-Ingvar Andersson. But he did not move to Denmark until the 1960s.[7]

THE NEXT GENERATION

The almost archetypal landscape typologies endemic to earth and vegetation that C. Th. Sørensen used as unifying and space-creating forms—the canal, the dike, and the row of trees—became important components in the work of other Danish landscape architects who followed him. Among these was his disciple Ole Nørgaard (1925–78). In the fall of 1953, the architects Halldor Gunnløgsson and Jørn Nielsen won an open competition for a new city hall for the municipality of Tårnby; Nørgaard served as landscape architect. In the competition entry, two parallel rows of trees created a linear space and roofed a field of parking spaces set obliquely to the trees. Twenty rectangular beds with flowering bushes complemented this arboreal cover. Six years later, in 1959, the city hall was finally inaugurated. By that time, several significant aspects of the landscape plan had evolved from the original plan. In the final design, for example, the front yard had changed. The oblique lines of the parking spaces now ran parallel, and rows of trees enclosed a driveway pointing to the entrance of an office providing social services. In total, they created an architecture of vegetal elements as powerful as a baroque allée. But it was not baroque: set against the main entrance of the city hall, the alignments of poplars and a grove of shaped plane trees became the walls of a rectangular space and, at the same time, a component of an asymmetrical composition of rectangular volumes. Two stone stripes in the field of granite pavers directed the eye toward the main entrance

of the city hall. In the building's great hall, with light beige brick and dark steel gray walls, rhododendrons in pots surrounded groups of furniture designed by Poul Kjærholm. With C. Th. Sørensen as a consultant, Ole Nørgaard designed this monumental but supple composition of spaces, which relied on the implication of spaces rather than their physical enclosure. The deep shade between the branches of the plane trees contrasted markedly with the sunny and open square, giving the city hall a set of spaces almost southern European in atmosphere [Figure 2–24].

As a result of the great educational explosion and reformation in the postwar years, the Polytechnic Institute at Nørrevold moved to the suburbs in 1958. The existing landscape there was sloped and warped, falling fifty feet from the highest point in the south to the lowest point in the northwest. Ole Nørgaard had this slope regraded into terraces with a level difference of about ten feet, to correspond in dimension to the height of the buildings. By this intelligent manipulation of land form, and to maximize access to light and ventilation, the academic buildings would expose two stories on the uphill side and three stories below. Where no building occupied the terrace, a retaining wall of concrete covered with Opdal shells held the soil in

place. A two-hundred-fifty-foot wide, one-and-a-half-mile long, ceiling of beech foliage created an inner esplanade with the character of a ballroom, a sort of spatial corridor within the more grandly scaled landscape. Because this "hall" would function as a car park, it was screened by beech hedges and reinforced with concrete pavers set in regular patterns derived from parking's functional requirements. Ceilings of plane trees, linden, horse chestnut, hawthorn, and pine contrived a spatial composition that is in no way inferior to the dynamic spatial composition of Theo van Doesburg's drawing Design for a House (1922).[8] Seen from the exterior, Danmarks Tekniske Universitet (the Danish Technical University, as the school was later renamed) appears to be a woodland. From the inside, however, it appears as an open meadow with a free distribution of buildings and planting elements like a glade in an oak wood [Figure 2–25].

Other members of the next generation also made formal experiments, but using geometries differing from those of Nørgaard and Sørensen. The following landscapes are examples: Næstved Central Cemetery (1948) by Georg Boye (1906–72) and Knud Preisler (1918–); the proposal for a central cemetery in Lyngby (1951) by Jørgen Arevad-Jacobsen (1917–); the courtyard of the Baltica Life Insurance

Figure 2–25.
Danish Technical University, Lundtofte,
Denmark, 1958. Ole Nørgaard.
[Malene Hauxner]

Figure 2–26. [*facing page, left*]
The Small Garden, 17 Haver i Én
(Seventeen Gardens in One) exhibition,
Haveselskabets Have, Frederiksberg,
Denmark, 1955. J. Palle Schmidt.
[Hauxner, *Fantasiens Have*]

Figure 2–27. [*facing page, right*]
The Grass Garden, 17 Haver i Én
(Seventeen Gardens in One) exhibition,
Haveselskabets Have, Frederiksberg,
Denmark, 1955. Morten Klint.
[Hauxner, *Fantasiens Have*]

Company (1958) by Eywin Langkilde (1919–97); and the
gardens at the exhibition "17 Haver i Én" (17 Gardens in
One) in Haveselskabets Have (1955) [Figures 2–26, 2–27]
by J. Palle Schmidt (1923–) and Morten Klint (1918–78).

EDUCATION AND DISSEMINATION

Georg Georgsen and C. Th. Sørensen ended their careers
in the 1950s and the 1960s, respectively. Both had come to
professional maturity in the age of neoclassicism and the
avant-garde experimentation of the 1920s; innovation in the
design language had presumably seemed natural to them.
Georgsen became the first spokesman for a theory of spatial
construction and syntax. His proposal for a central cemetery in Næstved (1948) told of a new tectonic aesthetic;
however, it was Sørensen who became this language's most
profound spokesman and widespread disseminator for a
new generation. For a number of years, this pair of landscape
architects had offered classes for students at the Royal
Academy of Fine Arts. Intense discussions about founding
a common educational program failed, and in 1963 both
the Landbohøjskolen (the Royal Veterinary and Agricultural
University) and the architecture school at the Royal Academy
of Fine Arts established special departments for landscape
studies. Typically, the leading figures of the period had not

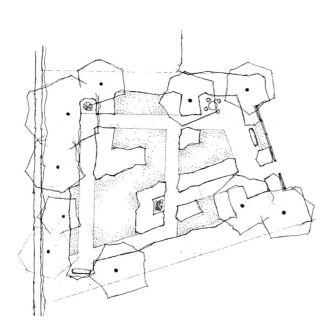

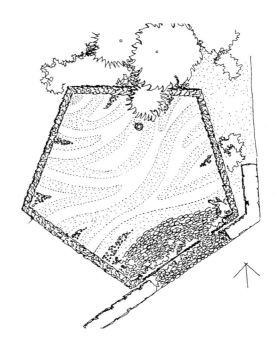

received academic degrees within the landscape profession. Arne Jacobsen and Ole Nørgaard, for example, were architects by profession. G. N. Brandt and C. Th. Sørensen had apprenticed as gardeners. Morten Klint received a degree in garden art as a special student at the Royal Academy of Fine Arts. The remainder of the leading practitioners held degrees in horticulture.

Brandt was an excellent author whose writings no landscape architect has ever exceeded. His last written work introduced the development plan for Tivoli Gardens in Copenhagen, produced in collaboration with Poul Henningsen (and, later, with Hans Hansen).[9] Georgsen was an active and analytical debater who strongly influenced the decisions of the competition juries upon which he served. Sørensen, in addition to studies of Copenhagen's park space, wrote *Europas Havekunst: Fra Alhambra til Liselund* (European Garden Art: From the Alhambra to Liselund), in which his theory of garden design as a stylization of the landscape was presented for the first time.[10] His unpretentious *39 Haveplaner: Typiske haver til et typehus:* (39 Garden Plans: Typical Gardens for a Typical House) demonstrated to the lay public how history and contemporary observation could be reformed and applied to the contemporary small garden.[11] Troels Erstad actively participated in newspaper debates; in 1956, Eywin Langkilde collected examples of gardens for detached houses in *Nye Danske Haver: Modern Danish Gardens*.[12] Georg Boye wrote *Anlægsgartneri: Håndbog i fagets teknik* (Landscape Construction: A Handbook of Professional Techniques).[13] Perhaps most important for the design professions in the English-speaking countries was Steen Eiler Rasmussen's *Om at opleve Arkitektur* (Experiencing Architecture), which remained in print for several decades.[14] The journal *Havekunst* (Garden Art) was published in collaboration with Swedish garden architects, since they published no professional journal of their own. The Danish editors were Troels Erstad, Sven Hansen, Georg Boye, Ursula Hansen, and Agnete Mygind, suggesting the comprehensive vision held by active practitioners at that time: *Arkitekten Ugehæfte/Arkitekten* (The Architect) , and *Arkitekten Maanedshæfte/Arkitektur* (Architecture) were excellent and informative periodicals, edited by the outstanding architecture writers Hans Erling Langkilde and Poul Erik Skriver.

Figure 2–28.
Louisiana Art Museum, Humlebæk,
Denmark, 1958. Jørgen Bo, Vilhelm Wohlert,
and Agnete Petersen.
[Jesper Høm; Jørgen Bo/Malene Hauxner
Archive]

BUILDINGS AND LANDSCAPE

A characteristic design attitude for this era was to regard gardens and landscapes as architecture, as outdoor rooms that formed a part of the architectural ensemble. The interaction between building and landscape — where the modeling of the landscape forms and structures the buildings, and the buildings actively enter into modeling the landscape — is regarded as the essence of a particularly Scandinavian architectural idea, which has been called both empirical and organic. Nonetheless, the method presumably derived from the United States, in particular the work of Frank Lloyd Wright at the turn of the century. One of the best examples is the art museum Louisiana, designed by Jørgen Bo and Vilhelm Wohlert in the years 1955–58. Excavations for a derelict military harbor dating back to the Napoleonic Wars had left in their wake an unobtrusive cliff and a ravine that extended almost as far inland as a lake set on a rise in the land thirty-five feet above the sea. Here the merchant Knud W. Jensen had thought of building a museum that would bring together modern painting, sculpture, graphic arts, crafts, architecture, and garden art [Figures 2–28, 2–29]. Set back from the shoreline was an elegant nineteenth-century neo-classical house situated in a landscape garden with grass lawns, winding paths, native and exotic trees, and an orchard — slightly hidden from view as was customary in these middle-class pastoral gardens. To make a modern building and a fragile manmade landscape — almost as a surviving shard of prior occupancy — harmonize with their natural setting was quite an achievement. The determining element of the architectural solution was a glazed corridor connecting the entrance in the renovated villa with the garden, various galleries, a library, and a café with an open fireplace and a glass wall open to the land and sea.

Here, with a stabile by Alexander Calder seen in silhouette, visitors were offered a view of the sea. During this promenade, they could detour to a larger hall with Alberto Giacometti's figural sculptures set against the reflective surface of a pond beyond a two-story-high glass wall. When a gallery was not glazed on two sides, paintings were hung on the closed side. The ceiling and floor planes continued past the glass walls, which formed the actual boundaries of the corridor. As a result, the link between outside and inside was fluid and perceptually inexact. The galleries were situated in such a way that the old trees were preserved and deliberately used as a significant force in planning the site. A branch of one beech tree, for example, determined the overall sequence of the built elements.

The landscape garden was not popular in the mid-1950s. But by continually utilizing the themes of movement with carefully considered pauses in the exhibit rooms, which take their identity from the landscape, the architects fashioned something new. In addition to the possibilities for making gardens and outdoor spaces with particular characters structured by the architecture, this string of buildings in the landscape lent a certain identity to each exhibition space. The first garden on the tour toward the sea was a rose garden by Agnete Petersen, designed so unpretentiously that one is led to believe it has always been there. Beyond, a female figure by Astrid Noack stood beneath some black locusts as if it were walking toward the house on a path of stone that continued as steppingstones across a reflecting pool. The brick relief of one of the many white walls, inside as well as outside, merited particular attention. In rows of rectangular planting beds grew rose-colored spirea in a ground of gray and gray-green perennials. In general, color remained muted throughout the landscape. Paintings and flowers are seen at different times, and only calm green courtyards can be enjoyed from the interiors of the buildings. In the white brick containers, placed on the rough point, grow compact mountain pines (*Pinus mugo*). Thus, at Louisiana there is demonstrated a balance between conceiving the landscape as nature needing to be preserved and nature as a medium for artistic adaptation.

During the postwar years this balance may be seen in the joint efforts of the architect and garden designer: it is often the architect who looks at the picturesque landscape with the eyes of the shepherd, and the garden designer who focuses on the cultivation of plants. One of Louisiana's architects, Jørgen Bo, wrote:

> The preservation of natural areas [in Denmark] has been based primarily on the principle that landscape is something given, something which cannot be improved, but alone needs to be protected as it is. However, the landscape has its own life. Left alone it will change, and thereby take many different orders. This suggests that saying that the landscape must be left in its present form is illusionary. It is no longer sufficient to make a decision about what is not allowed to happen; in many instances this is necessary but not enough. The growth of the landscape must be planned to develop in harmony with the use desired of it.

He continued by outlining a new direction for the landscape profession:

> With this new recognition, a new profession is developing. It is difficult to find a suitable name for it, but perhaps "Land-

Figure 2–29.
Louisiana Art Museum, Humlebæk,
Denmark, 1958. Jørgen Bo, Vilhelm Wohlert,
and Agnete Petersen.
[Jesper Høm; Jørgen Bo / Malene Hauxner
Archive]

Figure 2–30. [*facing page, top*]
Kingo housing estate, Helsingør, Denmark,
1958. Jørn Utzon.
[Model by Peter Raaschou]

Figure 2–31. [*facing page, bottom*]
Kingo housing estate, Helsingør, Denmark,
1958. Jørn Utzon.
[Malene Hauxner]

scape Treatment" might be suitable. It concerns something *practical and something artistic; it implies training in a new technique, especially one of analyzing and developing land-scape values, securing for natural areas their correct utiliza-tion and management. It is a profession which concerns regional planning at one level and garden and landscape art at the other.*[15]

This organic idea of addition seems at first quite humble. On second look, however, it suggests a very deliberate effort, as it was at Louisiana. The museum's buildings, without question, remain conspicuous, sited along the ridge at a point equally of sea and land, of architecture and landscape. And yet there is a humility and quietness about the relation of structure to landscape that has found few equals any-where in the world, and which profoundly characterizes a prominent strain of Danish landscape design in the 1950s.

At the very north of Denmark, outside Helsingør, Jørn Utzon constructed the Kingo housing estate in 1958. Also known locally as the Roman houses, from their resemblance to the southern European atrium houses [Figures 2–30, 2–31], they were based on a typical L-shaped dwelling unit that, paired with two low walls, created a square yard paved with the same yellow brick as the building facades. Tiled roofs sloped toward the courts and emphasized their cen-tral location and function. The inner facades were glazed; the exterior walls were almost solid with few apertures. Each house was an element of a greater plan, as a cell might join with its mates to create an organism. Together, the conglomerate blocks appeared as a fortress on the ter-rain that cast the pond and its sloping valley into noticeable relief. Five larger spaces, varying in profile from concave to convex, shared grass underfoot and walls of yellow brick but differed in their orientation and ability to catch sunlight. As a group, the buildings not only emphasized but in some respects reinvented the terrain. The tools and elements used were few and simple; yet they were effectively employed to create a richness of landscape details, even more noticeable in places where the grass was left unmowed. Vertical and horizontal planes cultivated the ground form: vertically with building groupings, horizontally by creating mounds and ravines. The entire site, a former gravel pit, enjoyed extensive tree plantings that complemented and punctuated the mod-eling of the earth. Regulated variation governed the selec-tion of the tree species, including a mixture of birches, wil-lows, beech, and pine planted along the streets. Points and plateaus as components, and addition as syntax, recur in Jørn

Utzon's aesthetic language, as much in the Roman houses as in his better-known Sydney Opera House.

CONCLUSION

For Denmark, the years 1940–60 cannot really be described as an era. In the period between the first and second world wars, and through a good deal of the 1940s, Denmark was oriented toward the European continent, and Germany in particular. But in 1949 the nation did choose a side, joining the North Atlantic Pact countries, and the world began to look quite different. The postwar period was first marked by privation, unemployment, shame, guilt, and fear. The structures of the farming community, the village, and the family were beginning to erode. Danish society needed to be reestablished and strengthened socially, mentally, and physically. After the defeat of Nazism and the end of World War II, Denmark stood shattered with the painful knowledge that human nature was unreliable and dangerous if uncontrolled. After the decision to build a new democratic welfare community—with man as its center—mechanisms had to be put in place to create, lead, govern, control, and cultivate this nature, in such a way that man would never again make the wrong choices. Denmark reemerged with the help of American capital. Industrialization, urbanization, growth, and a belief in the future developed with little fear of moving in the wrong direction or of disappearing. The atomic bomb, the Cold War, and the fear of Communism made the feeling of community even more important.

Parallel to these political, economic, and cultural changes came a change in the aesthetic language of landscape and garden art. Gardens assumed a form more obviously man-made. They became architectural spaces equal in definition and strength to those of buildings. They became bounded boxes with floors of stones and walls that did not meet at the corners, or free spaces constructed of soil and plants —with the sky as their ceilings. The spaces were pure and simply created by vertical and horizontal planes. The syntax relied on the geometry of the right angle and on a serial, rhythmical, or deliberately syncopated composition. The construction of form gradually replaced formal experiments as the primary motivation for the designer's work. To cultivate nature, to combine culture and nature, to interweave inside and outside, to make gardens constructed spaces of both architecture and garden art—these intentions and efforts marked the postwar Danish landscape. It was made according to a new aesthetic language controlled and

ascetic in its idea and architectonic in its forms. This restrained language continued through a good deal of the 1960s, prompted by social accord, technical possibilities, and increased material prosperity. It stopped only in 1968, when students demanded that imagination should return to power; as a result, the inner as well as the outer nature was released once again.

Translated by Marianne Borup and Marc Treib.

NOTES

1. Reginald Blomfield, *The Formal Garden in England* (1892; reprint, London: Waterstone, 1985).

2. Malene Hauxner, *Fantasiens Have: Det moderne gennembrud i havekunsten og sporene i byens landskab* (The Modern Breakthrough in Garden Art and Its Traces in the Landscape of the City) (Copenhagen: Arkitektens Forlag, 1993).

3. G. N. Brandt, "Der kommende Garten," *Wasmuth's Monatshefte für Baukunst und Städtebau*, no. 4, 1930, pp. 161–76.

4. G. N. Brandt, *Stauder* (Perennials) (Copenhagen, 1914); G. N. Brandt, *Vand- og Stenhøjsplanter* (Water and Rock-Plants) (Copenhagen, 1917).

5. G. N. Brandt, "Træer" (Trees), *Architekten*, 1919, pp. 361–69.

6. C. Th. Sørensen, *Parkpolitik i Sogn og Købstad* (Park Policy in Parish and Market Town) (Copenhagen: Christian Ellings Forlag, 1931).

7. For further reading on Sørensen, see Sven-Ingvar Andersson and Steen Høyer, *C. Th. Sørensen—en havekunstner* (Copenhagen: Arkitektens Forlag, 1993). An English edition of this book, translated by Anne Whiston Spirn, will be published by the Arkitektens Forlag; see also Hauxner, *Fantasiens Have*. For information about Sven-Ingvar Andersson, see Steen Høyer, ed., *Sven-Ingvar Andersson* (Copenhagen: Arkitektens Forlag, 1994).

8. Part of van Doesburg's painting is illustrated in Siegfried Giedion, *Space, Time, and Architecture: The Growth of a New Tradition* (Cambridge, Mass.: Harvard University Press, 1941).

9. G. N. Brandt and Poul Henningsen, *Tivoli: Udviklingsplan*, March 1945.

10. C. Th. Sørensen, *Europas Havekunst: Fra Alhambra til Liselund* (European Garden Art from the Alhambra to Liselund) (Copenhagen: G. E. C. Gads Forlag, 1959).

11. C. Th. Sørensen, *39 Haveplaner: Typiske haver til et typehus:* (39 Garden Plans: Typical Gardens for a Typical House) (Copenhagen: Arkitektens Forlag, 1966).

12. Eywin Langkilde, *Nye Danske Haver: Modern Danish Gardens* (Copenhagen: Høst og Søn, 1956).

13. Georg Boye, *Anlægsgartneri: Håndbog i fagets teknik* (Landscape Construction: A Handbook of Professional Techniques) (Copenhagen: Almindelig Dansk Gartnerforenings Forlag, 1959).

14. Steen Eiler Rasmussen, *Om at opleve Arkitektur* (Copenhagen: G. E. C. Gads Forlag, 1957); English edition: *Experiencing Architecture* (Cambridge, Mass.: MIT Press, 1962).

15. Jørgen Bo, "Landskabsbehandling," (Landscape Treatment), *Byplan*, no. 84, 1963.

The period 1940–1960 saw the emergence of the profession of landscape architecture in Britain, building on tentative beginnings in the 1930s to achieve an important role in postwar reconstruction. During that period, modernism in architecture and the arts developed from its specialized, marginal position of the 1930s to achieve considerable official sanction and a limited popularity. There was a mutual interaction between these two events that had long-term consequences for British culture in general, in ways that have not yet been fully recognized.[1]

BACKGROUND IN THE 1920S AND 1930S

The 1920s was a period in which the actual landscape, particularly in southern England, was seriously threatened by modernity in the form of building development, the break-up of large landed estates, increased travel and tourism, and the impact of the motor car. The Campaign for the Preservation of Rural England (CPRE) was founded in 1926, and Clough Williams-Ellis's book *England and the Octopus* (1928) emphasized the sense of betrayal suffered by the generation who thought they had fought World War I to save the physical country of England, only to see a surrender to short-term economic gain, unchecked by protective legislation. The transference of ideas and emotions between the landscape and the abstract idea of nationhood and its values, familiar as part of English culture since at least the romantic movement, helped to stir popular interest in defending the second by means of the first. *England and the Octopus* was part of a counterattack that grew in pressure through the 1930s, by a mixture of legislation and opinion-forming, until at the end of World War II there was a political climate ready for radical steps to be taken in controlling the ownership and use of land [Figure 3–1].

Clough Williams-Ellis (1883–1978) was an architect with a diversity of cultural and political agendas who enjoyed extending his purview to planning and landscape design, playing the role of the "improving" squire on his own and other people's estates. In later life, he referred to the "Amenity Brigade," a loose association of architects, planners, journalists, civic leaders, industrialists, and other activists who successfully used modern media to articulate alternative visions of the future, as well as developing techniques of planning survey and recommending specific strategies for controlling growth and development.[2]

3. ALAN POWERS

Landscape in Britain

Figure 3–2.
Bentley Wood, Halland, East Sussex, 1938.
Serge Chermayeff, architect, Terrace with
Henry Moore's *Recumbent Figure*.
[Dell & Wainwright. Courtesy
Architectural Press]

Figure 3–3.
Bentley Wood, Halland, East Sussex, 1938.
Serge Chermayeff, architect. Interior with
painting by John Piper.
[Dell & Wainwright. Courtesy
Architectural Press]

The result was similar in effect to a park-like setting such as might have been designed by Capability Brown, with the difference that the two terraces provide a structure through which to observe the distant views, one in front of the house and one extending at right angles, backed by a brick wall and terminated by a wood-and-glass screen of rectangles. This served practically as a transparent windbreak and, despite its simple form, had a strong if subliminal imaginative appeal like some of Paul Nash's imaginary geometric structures in nature. The Moore figure stood on a special plinth beside steps rising from the grass to the terrace, looking away from the house and into the landscape. Bentley Wood was immediately popular, and it seems important in retrospect in the way it made modernism entirely at home in England as an extension of the existing culture. Its broad, spatial approach to the relationship between building and landscape went beyond any previous conceptions of what a modern garden might be, to reach something beyond time and style.

In 1938, the year that Bentley Wood was completed, Christopher Tunnard published *Gardens in the Modern Landscape*, using as frontispiece a photograph of Chermayeff's wife Barbara reclining on the terrace with the Moore sculpture and the screen beyond. This book was the first important attempt at a theoretical statement in England about the possible equivalents in landscape and garden design for modernism in architecture. In his practice as a garden designer, limited to a handful of projects, Tunnard was able to provide examples of a form of garden that he considered appropriate to modern architecture, consisting of a hybrid between a park landscape, as at Bentley Wood and at Tunnard's own shared modern movement residence, St. Ann's Hill, Chertsey, and a formal geometrical structure, demonstrated in the areas close to the house at St. Ann's Hill. By emigrating to the United States in 1939, however, Tunnard separated himself from the current of ideas in England and increasingly from landscape practice.

Tunnard's book came at the end of a decade of increasing interest in the practice of landscape design as an independent discipline, for which the foundation of the Institute of Landscape Architects in 1929 provides a convenient starting date. The term landscape architect had been used before in Britain but was still not a recognized professional designation. The institute grew largely from the impulse of a group of young designers engaged in private garden work, including Richard Sudell (1900–68) and Brenda Colvin (1897–1981), soon joined by the architects Geoffrey Jellicoe (1900–1996),

Gilbert Jenkins (c. 1876–1957), Oliver Hill (1887–1968), and the landscape designer Sylvia Crowe (1901–97). Percy Cane (1881–1976), one of the more established garden designers, was, in Colvin's words, "seen prowling about the small circle listening to our proceedings but taking no part."[9] The garden designer and contractor Thomas Mawson (1861–1933), who had diversified into urban and regional planning, was persuaded to become the first president. As Brenda Colvin wrote in 1979, "In those early years, we had only the faintest notion of how the Institute might develop or how the work and influence of the profession could expand through joint efforts. We were concerned with the need for communication and the sharing of information among members. We felt the need for better means of education and more public recognition than was available, but our sights were still set low."[10]

Among the most important activities of the young institute was the foundation, in 1934, of a journal, *Landscape and Garden*, edited by Richard Sudell. Much of its content was concerned with private gardens, new and old, although the wider social scope of landscape was also an important preoccupation. The editorial of winter 1934 caught the spirit of national renewal and the need for some separation from the nostalgia for the past. Marjory Allen (Lady Allen of Hurtwood, 1897–1976), a practitioner of garden design with a strong interest in the social questions of the time, such as slum clearance and progressive education, contributed an article entitled "New Slums for Old?" in the same issue.[11] The editorial in the winter number of 1935 on "Civic and Social Centres" sought to give aesthetic content to recreational and sports facilities in order to improve their social efficiency, emphasizing that "our landscape designs must meet the need for social intercourse."[12] At the time, such schemes would normally have been designed by the Borough Engineer, a local government employee with no aesthetic training, probably in a debased Beaux Arts style. Even the London County Council's lidos (open-air swimming pools) and park buildings, designed by H. W. Rowbotham in a style derived from W. M. Dudok, were axial compositions. The open-air bathing place at Lausanne by Marc Picard was one of several European examples of social landscapes for leisure much admired in England at this time as an alternative.

The magazine published articles by Christopher Tunnard (writing initially as Arthur C. Tunnard) on "The Influence of Japan on the English Garden," on "Interplanting," "Garden

Making on the Riviera," and "Garden Design at the Chelsea Show," which indicate the small-scale focus on gardens. These preceded his awakening to the wider issues of landscape as witnessed in a series of articles in the *Architectural Review* between 1936 and 1938 which had a more specifically modernist direction, particularly in a Corbusian scheme for developing the park at Claremont, Surrey, then threatened with division into standard suburban house plots. *Landscape and Garden* published some anonymous and highly critical comments on F. R. S. Yorke and Marcel Breuer's proposals for twelve-story slab blocks in "Concrete City," exhibited in 1937 and 1938, asking its readers to remember that "the background and foreground of Nature are 'given'; we cannot dispute with them. What we add must be adapted or assimilated to what we already have."[13] Among committed modern architects, criticism was often seen as a form of betrayal or heresy, but the culture of landscape seems to have been more open at this point. This may have owed something to Geoffrey Jellicoe, who in his practice as an architect in the 1930s alternated between flat-roofed and pitch-roofed schemes in a way that would have embarrassed the purist members of the MARS (Modern Architectural Research) Group. By 1939, however, many modern architects had already indicated a change of direction toward a richer palette of materials that was combined with an increased awareness of landscape to create more consciously regional designs, such as the Girls' High School at Richmond, North Yorkshire, by Denis Clarke-Hall (1939–41).

WARTIME DEVELOPMENTS

The outbreak of war in 1939 opened the way for radical changes in national life that had remained only projects during the 1930s; the development of landscape architecture was one of them. The movement for postwar reconstruction was initiated by Churchill's wartime government after the fall of France in 1940, partly as a way of improving morale. The former Director General of the BBC, Sir John Reith (late Lord Reith), began the administrative process as Minister for Works and Buildings in 1941, recruiting the architect-planner William Holford as one of his chief advisers, under whom Thomas Sharp, already well known as an author and practitioner, and Gordon Stephenson, trained in Paris and at MIT, were also recruited. Reith was sympathetic to the cause of landscape architecture and later became an honorary council member of the Institute of Landscape Architects. He lost his job in 1942, but Holford continued

to work with the planners Sharp, Stephenson, George Pepler, and John Dower on a variety of policies relating to land use and national parks. A new Ministry of Town and Country Planning was created in 1943, and for a time high hopes were held concerning the opportunities for a coordinated and radical reconstruction. Political reality modified these hopes, but the extent of planning and development controls embodied in the Town and Country Planning Act of 1947 still radically altered the balance between freedom and control. In the controlled economy of the postwar years, government departments played a significant role in the distribution of resources, and it was relatively easy for them to act in a coordinated way.

As Geoffrey Jellicoe, the wartime president of the Institute of Landscape Architects, wrote in 1984, the reports of Lord Uthwatt (Compensation and Betterment, 1941), together with others by Sir Thomas Barlow (Location of Industry, 1940), Sir William Beveridge (Health and Social Security, 1942–43), and Lord Justice Scott (Land Utilization in Rural Areas, 1942), suggested that "a great new landscape profession was in the offing," and the institute decided to increase its influence at high levels, expand its membership, and set up an educational system.[14] These reports were of such general public interest that they were summarized and published by Penguin Books.[15] Jellicoe also acknowledged Holford's importance in introducing the concept of landscape architecture into official circles and explaining the value of the specialized skills it offered. This period, although it did not produce tangible results in the form of projects, was pivotal in preparing the way for an altered perception among a wider public.

The war brought an end to the private garden work that most landscape designers had relied on for a living in the 1930s, but it opened up wider possibilities. Sylvia Crowe, while serving in the ATS (Auxiliary Territorial Service, the women's organization attached to the army) in the Medway area, began to see the potential (still largely unrealized at the turn of the twenty-first century) for its development as a leisure area for Londoners.[16] One project undertaken by Jellicoe in 1942, for the landscaping of Hope's Cement Works, in Derbyshire, was indicative of a new feeling of long-term concern for assimilating modern industry into the English landscape. Although initially conceived as a finite and conventional scheme, owing to Jellicoe's involvement over a period of fifty years, it came instead to exemplify, in his mind, the theory of John Dewey according to which he conceived that "art … was not merely the finished object, but the whole experience of creation."[17] The scheme developed partly because the quarry and its plant continued to encroach on the landscape; Jellicoe used its waste to make a platform on the hillside, overlooking a fertile valley.

One of the most significant boosts for landscape architecture was the appointment of Lord Reith as Chairman of the New Towns Committee in 1945–46. From this position he was able to ensure that each of the postwar new towns had a landscape architect on the design team from the outset. This resulted in the employment of Sylvia Crowe at Harlow, H. F. (Frank) Clark (1902–71) at Stevenage, and Brenda Colvin at East Kilbride, among many others. At Harlow, the planner was the architect Frederick Gibberd (1908–84), who had a considerable sympathy for landscape and who was able to work harmoniously with Crowe to make the most of the understated features of the landscape he found there, keeping existing trees and streams in the bottoms of the shallow valleys, putting the buildings on the higher ground, and linking housing areas with old lanes turned into cycle tracks [Figure 3–4]. Gibberd traveled abroad every summer with Geoffrey Jellicoe, looking at rebuilding schemes in Holland, Scandinavia, and elsewhere; he relished sharp-edged contrasts between built form and nature. His "point block," The Lawns, 1951, resembles the tall blocks of flats at Vällingby in its brick solidity and encircling trees. Sven Markelius, the City Planning Director of Stockholm responsible for Vällingby, on the other hand, denied having learned anything from England, saying, "I have no feeling that Vällingby is copied from the New Towns, even though they were planned at about the same time and there are some general ideas they have in common."[18] The town center, placed on top of the highest hill in the site, worked by contrast to achieve formality in its streets and buildings and in an area of terraced water garden, embellished with modern sculpture and calculated to get the best views of the landscape beyond.

The New Towns were a third way between pressures for growth, usually taking the form of suburban expansion, and the high-minded if dogmatic campaigning for low-density habitation on the part of the Town and Country Planning Association. The designers of the New Towns hoped that the skill of designers would provide a quality of place more akin to English market towns than the widely spread Welwyn Garden City, planned in the 1920s. Once built, the New Towns were a disappointment, with fields of mud and

Figure 3–4.
Harlow New Town, 1947. Frederick Gibberd, Model of landscape.
The original caption reads, "The shapes of the areas are determined by the existing topography; the field patterns, trees, valleys and existing buildings being worked into the design so that each has its own character." [*Architectural Review*, March 1948]

Figure 3–5.
Hemel Hempstead New Town, 1947.
Geoffrey Jellicoe. Aerial perspective of
proposed town center,
Ronald Rutherford, artist.
Jellicoe's scheme was abandoned, but he was
retained as designer for the water gardens.
[© The Landscape Institute Library]

too many houses of uniform size and quality. They gained a bad reputation architecturally, being castigated as early as 1953 in J. M. Richards's article "The Failure of the New Towns" in the *Architectural Review* (July) and sociologically in Michael Young and Peter Willmott's book *Family and Kinship in East London*, 1957, which emphasized the closeness of the old dense urban communities and their effectiveness in human terms. The landscape design of new towns inevitably needed time to mature, and visually they now justify the faith of their founders, even though some social and economic problems persist [Figures 3–5, 3–6, 3–7].

The increase in education for landscape architects was achieved partly by establishing professional qualification standards within the institute itself in 1946, and partly by the setting up of courses. Visitors to America were impressed by the number of schools and their contribution to the status of the profession. The only prewar course in Britain, in contrast, was a three-year diploma at Reading University under A. J. Cobb, run by H. F. Clark from 1946 to 1957. Thomas Sharp became head of a new course at Durham University in 1948 and the University of London set up a course under Brian Hackett in the same year, both within departments of town planning. Further courses took longer to develop but emerged in the 1960s from schools of art and design. By the mid-1960s, it was realized that demand for places had overtaken supply.

Despite these advances, landscape architecture remained a small profession, still very closely linked to architecture and town planning. A decisive moment came early in 1946 when the Institute of Landscape Architecture was on the point of entering negotiations with the Royal Institute of British Architects with a view to amalgamation. At a meeting, Brenda Colvin and Sylvia Crowe argued strongly against this and carried the rest of the members with them. Unlike some of their male colleagues, Colvin and Crowe were not trained initially as architects and were therefore more able to see the separation between the two disciplines. Two years later, Lady Allen proposed the establishment of an International Federation of Landscape Architects (IFLA), which resulted in a conference held in London in 1948, organized by a committee chaired by Sylvia Crowe, who remained closely involved with international activities thereafter, giving British landscape architecture a source of identity and symbolic strength separate from the architectural profession.

Figure 3–6.
Water Gardens, Hemel Hempstead New Town, 1957-59. Geoffrey Jellicoe.
[© The Landscape Institute Library]

Figure 3–7.
Water Gardens, Hemel Hempstead New
Town, 1957-59. Geoffrey Jellicoe.
[© The Landscape Institute Library]

Another important source of influence in the wartime years was the *Architectural Review*. During the immediate postwar period, four editors were listed jointly: J. M. Richards, who worked full time; Nikolaus Pevsner, then beginning to achieve his standing as an academic in England; Osbert Lancaster, who also produced a regular cartoon for the *Daily Express*; and H. de C. Hastings, who although apparently a background figure retained a strong control of policy and content. There was little new architecture to publish, and he took the opportunity to continue his 1930s task of placing architecture in a wider social and artistic context. The publication of Tunnard's articles and other pieces on the history of landscape had already set this process in motion, and it went on to include an important series of articles by John Piper in which his drawings and photographs explored a new range of visual phenomena in England, such as the black-and-white character of seaside buildings, the quality of "pleasing decay," and the decoration of Victorian pubs. These were seen by Hastings as part of a shock campaign to open up architects' visual sensibility.[19]

The general public was exposed to the special flavor of the *Review*, with its brilliant combination of text and pictures, in small handbooks that accompanied the exhibitions *Your Inheritance* (1942) and *Rebuilding Britain* (1943). The former, subtitled *The Land: An Uncomic Strip*, was based on material about landscape history mostly taken from an important issue of the *Review* in July 1935, which exposed the perils of suburbanization and offered alternative methods for planned development. The latter offered visions of modern buildings in landscape settings, mixing British, European, and American images without differentiation to construct a model of the future [Figures 3–8, 3–9].

Hastings encouraged Pevsner to investigate the history of the picturesque movement, which had been broached by Christopher Hussey's book *The Picturesque*, published in 1927.[20] Hastings went farther than Pevsner in drawing out of picturesque theory a new and startling set of conclusions in relation to contemporary design, which have largely been forgotten. In the article at the beginning of 1944, "Exterior Furnishing or Sharawaggi: The Art of Making Urban Landscape," he wrote of the need to liberate architecture and urban design from the tedium of both modernism and the Beaux Arts style by proposing a system of pluralism and deliberate contrast. This he saw principally as a further stage of modernism, which was anticipated in the more decorative or even surreal work of Le Corbusier in the 1930s and his

 *but still*

ASLEEP

look again. The eyes are open
but see nothing because the
child is a doll. Millions of
people are like this doll—they
look but they don't see. That's
why the street opposite is
possible. But can human
beings really spread themselves

5 in this kind of neighbourhood?

6 Or would they be better off
here? who is going to decide?
We are asking you to decide.

Figure 3–8.
Spread from *Your Inheritance: The Land:
An Uncomic Strip.* Cheam: Architectural
Press, 1942.

Figure 3–9.
Spread from *Your Inheritance: The Land:
An Uncomic Strip.* Cheam: Architectural
Press, 1942.

English followers like Berthold Lubetkin. Hastings recognized in this loosening and broadening process an English kind of common sense, tolerance, and fantasy mixed together, in which both the principles of landscape and the actual deployment of growing forms would play a part [Figure 3–10].[21] In the same issue, the *Review* proposed keeping the ruins of bombed churches in London as open space, with appropriate planting, as ornamental objects with recreational potential. In 1949, Hastings (under his pseudonym I. de Wolfe) wrote a further remarkable article, "Townscape," subtitled "A Plea for an English Visual Philosophy Founded

on the True Rock of Sir Uvedale Price," which extended the political and national dimensions of "Exterior Furnishing." Both articles proposed a radical reworking of the relationship between existing buildings and modern ones, relishing their conjunctions rather than trying to avoid them, and dependent more on the eye and sensibility of the modern artist than on the conventional training of the architect.[22] This was at a time when a number of alternative proposals were under discussion for the rebuilding of London and other bombed cities, most of which proposed the clearance of large areas and their replacement with homogeneous architecture, whether semitraditional or modern.

When *Townscape* finally appeared as a book in 1961, it included the drawings by Gordon Cullen that formed the second part of the original article but not the political

Figure 3–10.
Illustration for "Exterior Furnishing or Sharawaggi: The Art of Making Urban Landscape." Kenneth Rowntree.
[*Architectural Review*, January 1944]

introduction by Hastings, and it was issued entirely under Cullen's name. He was personally sympathetic to this cause, having, among much other graphic work before the war, made the drawings of proposed schemes by Tunnard which illustrated *Gardens in the Modern Landscape*. Cullen was a brilliant exponent of the visual principles, but the theoretical point of the original statement was rather too easily absorbed in diluted form as a style manual. Other writers in *Architectural Review* pursued Hastings's conjunctions between landscape and politics, notably Eric de Maré, with his enthusiasm for making linear parks alongside the many abandoned and neglected canals from the early industrial revolution, and along the River Thames.[23]

Apart from Pevsner's articles, the *Review* encouraged other historians to research and publish on landscape history in a context of contemporary creativity, including H. F. Clark, whose short book *The English Landscape Garden*, covering some of the major sites of the eighteenth century, was published in 1948 (Pleiades Books). The painter and illustrator Barbara Jones was another regular contributor to the *Architectural Review*, and her book, *Follies and Grottoes* of 1953, opened up a poetic aspect of English landscape pleasingly at odds with the utilitarianism of the liberal postwar consensus. The magazine's continuing attention to landscape matters did much to establish the credibility of landscape within the context of architecture, not least with its fine photographs and graphics by a number of artists with an interest in topography. The camp taste for Victoriana and folk art, which the *Review* promoted alongside its landscape enthusiasm, was probably the point at which it diverged from the more sober tastes of the Institute of Landscape Architecture.

LANDSCAPE AS A VALUE SYSTEM AND AS A CRITIQUE OF CIVILIZATION

With the development of landscape architecture as a separate profession in the wartime years there emerged a distinctive set of values that provided a theoretical basis for practice. Brenda Colvin's book *Land and Landscape*, published in 1948, was one of the first comprehensive statements of the new synthesis in Britain. It begins in terms reminiscent of Lewis Mumford's *Culture of Cities* with a broad statement about modern civilization and the necessity for a deeper relationship to landscape in terms of individual and social well-being. The succeeding chapters look at the historical formation of landscape in England and at the developing awareness of its cultural and artistic poten-

tial. This area of study was supported by texts newly published in the 1930s on ecology and the history of British landscape, such as J. W. Bews, *Human Ecology* (1935), Dudley Stamp, *The Structure and Scenery of Britain*, and A. C. Tansley, *The British Islands and Their Vegetation*. While elements of the past are valued and understood, Colvin is clear that there was no golden age or canonic style and that the potential for landscape lies in the future, if it can be realized through appropriate skills.

The text reads in many ways as an explanation of the landscape architect's skills for those new to the idea, encompassing the whole land area and all different forms of use. The ideal of a functional landscape is celebrated, although in terms far removed from the mechanistic analogies of functional architecture. In fact, Tunnard's quest for a "new style" in garden design is specifically rejected, since this would be too restrictive and insufficiently sensitive to context. "Environment and purpose must be brought into relationship," Colvin wrote, "in the same way that the sails and shape of a sailing vessel bear relationship to the water and the wind. Design approached in this spirit will never remain static nor greatly moulded by tradition, but will be dynamic, constantly changing to meet new conditions. It will be essentially of its own time—contemporary, individual and true to the needs of humanity."[24]

In enlarging the practical and theoretical scope of landscape architecture so far beyond visual composition, Colvin was undoubtedly influenced by American examples, such as the Tennessee Valley Authority, much admired in England during the war years as an exemplar of functional uses, ecology, and aesthetics working in harmony to ameliorate a social situation. She wrote of the necessity for a balance of uses and an ecological understanding of the interaction of soil, plants, animals, and man as the foundation for beauty. This was an opportunity and a necessity for modern man, since "the time is long past when it could be left to nature or to blind chance."[25] Thus the prejudice that a designed landscape is second-best because "unnatural" was dismissed as a luxury no longer affordable in an industrial age.

On a more practical level, Brenda Colvin collaborated with the planner Jaqueline Tyrwhitt and the artist S. R. Badmin to publish *Trees for Town and Country* in 1947, a finely produced picture book with concise information, which well conveyed the feeling of optimism well-rooted in the past that characterized the 1940s in the landscape world [Figure

3–11]. Trees were almost a symbol of the spirit of reconstruction, since it was noted that much felling had taken place during the two world wars and stocks needed replenishment. Urban trees were seen as equally important, and the Ministry of Housing and Local Government issued its own lucid and well-presented guidelines in *Trees in Town and City* in 1958. Brenda Colvin noted in *Land and Landscape* the extent to which individual trees were featured in the design of gardens, while hilltop plantations, seen from a passing car, were a gift from the past that needed special care.

Land and Landscape also reflects a moment of optimism about British farming, looking back to the time between the wars when some argued that farming could be abandoned in favor of recreational uses of land, a situation that the physical isolation of World War II and the need to grow the majority of food for the population at home altered, as it then seemed, forever. Even before the war there was a contest between advocates of industrialized monoculture and others with a more organic concern for mixed farming and soil quality. On economic grounds, the traditional small farm gave way in the 1960s to more mechanized larger units.

The cultural status of landscape was enhanced by the publication in 1949 of *Landscape into Art* by Kenneth Clark, the Director of the National Gallery and a leading collector and promoter of artists such as Graham Sutherland and John Piper, who called cautiously in his conclusion for revaluation of the relationship of man and nature as expressed through the depiction of landscape. He described some of the symbolic meaning of landscape in the past, as well as discussing the link between a civilization's psyche and its attitude toward landscape. These terms were similar to those in which Geoffrey Jellicoe began to talk about landscape in later years. During the 1940s and 1950s, Jellicoe's theoretical writings consisted of lectures and articles. He expressed the opposition between science and humanity in terms of deep-rooted divisions between Eastern and Western systems of belief. In an article of 1947, he quoted Tolstoy, writing in *Anna Karenina*, about the creative process as a form of uncovering something seen in the mind's eye as already present.[26] This already hints at his later adoption of C. G. Jung's theory of archetypes — ideas and images that are latent in the shared consciousness of man and that the artist has a special duty to bring out into the open, through his sensitivity to the subconscious.

Especially suitable for Common, Clipped Hedge, Meadow, Village Green, Windscreen, Woodlan

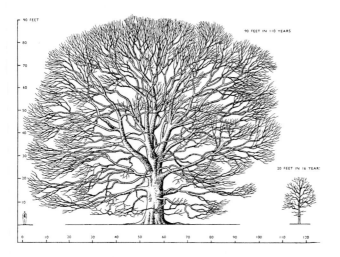

70

Figure 3–11.
"Beech," from Brenda Colvin, Jaqueline Tyrwhitt, and S. R. Badmin, *Trees for Town and Country*, 1947. Drawings by S. R. Badmin. [Frederick Watson. Courtesy Colvin & Moggridge].

Sylvia Crowe's book *Tomorrow's Landscape*, published by Architectural Press in 1956, covered some of the same ground as Colvin's book but made a special feature of forestry planning. After World War I, the Forestry Commission had planted large areas of conifers with little thought about visual impact or ecology. By the 1950s, it was possible to propose a greater variety of species for an improved visual effect and to encourage biodiversity. When she became landscape consultant to the Forestry Commission in 1963, Crowe worked effectively toward these ends on a great number of sites, as well as emphasizing the recreational use of forests by providing picnic and parking areas.

Colvin and Crowe's books presented a comprehensive and unified vision of landscape as a subject and achieved balance without loss of vigor. They hinted at greater depths of meaning but retained a surface appearance of pragmatism, which was necessary in an English context. In their examination of geology they avoided the more romantic approach of Jacquetta Hawkes's *A Land*, a popular book of 1951, although there is a strand of sympathy between these texts. There were more radical writers in the field of planning, such as E. A. Gutkind, whose book *The Expanding Environment: The End of Cities, the Rise of Communities* was published by the anarchist Freedom Press in 1953; it advocated dispersal of the population into small communities. The mood of the time was generally antiurban, but the ideal of the small town with abundant planting and irregular plan form, as illustrated in many of Colvin and Crowe's photographs, was reproduced in the planning theory of "neighborhoods."

THE FESTIVAL OF BRITAIN AND THE SMALL GARDEN

The Festival of Britain in 1951 represented a coming together of many of the cultural concerns of the previous twenty years. The chief manifestations of the festival were the South Bank Exhibition in London and the Festival Gardens in Battersea Park, both in the tradition of international exhibitions offering education and entertainment. The South Bank was planned by the Director of Architecture, Hugh Casson (1910–99), to have a circuitous route through various pavilions, exploiting the picturesque quality of the site and using water, plant tubs, and small–scale planting to enhance a domestic feeling rather than following an axial layout. The landscape design also had a practical intention of absorbing large crowds and allowing "backwaters" in which the public could sit and watch others go past. Borrowing

Figure 3–12.
Water Garden, Unicorn Café, Festival of Britain, 1951. Peter Shepheard.
[Courtesy Architectural Press]

the new terminology of the *Architectural Review*, the aim was described as "consciously designed townscape in the informal English tradition."[27] H. F. Clark was landscape consultant to the Festival Office, assisted by the Italian émigré designer Maria Parpagliolo Shephard (d. 1974). Peter Shepheard (1913–), a young architect with wartime planning experience, designed the landscape for the downstream site, around the Royal Festival Hall, and the remainder was in the hands of Clark, Shephard, and Peter Youngman (1911–) [Figure 3–12].

The effect was more dynamic than formal, largely dependent on hard landscaping, while the site was also a lexicon of new techniques of planting, edging, plant containers, and uses of rough stone and pebbles. Many of these devices derived from Scandinavian and American examples, and the commemorative book on the Royal Festival Hall noted the inspiration of the landscaping of Stockholm's lake frontage. The planting, which originally extended inside the building and onto its roof terraces in a much more prominent way than at present, was praised by the book's author, Clough Williams-Ellis, for the way that it softened the modernism of the architecture and enlarged the sense of space.[28]

The festival was the first time a large public had seen an alternative to the standard practices of municipal gardening based on Victorian principles of bedding out. The principle of selecting plants for their interesting leaf shapes was demonstrated for the first time, but there was an eclectic mixture of a new informality with plenty of bright color and regular geometry, since much of the planting had to be protected within small curbed beds in the public areas. To architects and planners, it showed the range of possible techniques of hard landscaping as ways of controlling the flow of crowds without signs or barriers, a point emphasized by *Architectural Review*, which described it as "a town-builder's pattern book" and took credit for its own promotion of the picturesque revival [Figure 3–13].[29]

Organic shapes in the Regatta Restaurant gardens by Clark and Shephard, which could be viewed directly from above, showed the influence of Burle Marx. The effect at night was studied, with various forms of lighting dispersed among the plantings. Water, lit from below, was also an important element. The exhibition site was notable for its use of open air sculpture, continuing the informal but deliberate manner of placing sculpture that originated with the Henry Moore piece at Bentley Wood.

Figure 3–13.
Water Garden, Harvey's Department Store, Guildford, Surrey, 1956-57.
Geoffrey Jellicoe.
[© The Landscape Institute Library]

The domestic scale of the landscape design at the festival was intended, through its many small and intimate spaces, to inspire people making small gardens at home. Apart from examples of a new Mediterranean-style informality offered in the magazine *House and Garden*, launched in 1947, aspiring garden makers could consult Peter Shepheard's book *Modern Gardens* in 1953, with a well-illustrated selection of international examples, and *The New Small Garden* by Susan Jellicoe and Lady Allen of Hurtwood (1956), both titles published by Architectural Press [Figure 3–14]. These books showed the influence of Thomas Church and Garrett Eckbo in California in widening the range of compositional devices for gardens, such as the wooden decking and overlapping geometries of the Donnell Garden by Church, whom Shepheard, although he had not been able to visit America at all, described as "outstanding, even among the notable work of the whole modern school of landscape architects in the USA."[30] The 1950s also saw a revival in indoor planting, demonstrated at the Festival and given book form by H. F. Clark and Margaret Jones in *Indoor Plants and Gardens* in 1952.

The value of small gardens in housing projects was not universally appreciated but was given convincing demonstration through the personal interests of particular architects. Eric Lyons designed housing developments in conjunction with the developer Span, the first of which took over the site of a nursery garden at Ham in Surrey and had a ready-made stock of plants. Later developments at Blackheath worked around existing nineteenth-century trees (one of which stands in the middle of a narrow access road) and made model use of the public spaces around houses and flats. The architects Tayler & Green, whose private work was represented in Peter Shepheard's book, designed a great deal of state-funded housing in Norfolk villages. They gave the houses traditional front gardens with hedges and white-painted wooden gates when the normal tendency was to make continuous open spaces. Herbert Tayler, who was a student of Jellicoe's at the Architectural Association in the early 1930s, explained, "I have come, slowly and unfashionably, to believe in the hedged front garden, because the English will often garden like gods in the front. Have we forgotten what inspired William Robinson and Gertrude Jekyll?"[31] An early photograph of Whiteways, a small development in the hamlet of Wheatacre, shows the gates in position, even though the hedges are hardly grown. The rural road is allowed to merge into the grass verges, while the houses are composed against the background of an

Figure 3–14.
Garden at 19 Grove Terrace, Highgate, circa 1960. Geoffrey and Susan Jellicoe.
This was Jellicoe's own house. He and his wife, Susan, often published their typical narrow London terrace garden as an exemplar of a modern treatment.
[© The Landscape Institute Library]

existing dense group of trees and bushes. This scheme was given one of the Festival of Britain awards for architecture in 1951.

The English gardens illustrated in these books tended to be designed by architects or artists for themselves. Sylvia Crowe's book *Garden Design* (1958) took a broad view of the subject, linking it to landscape design. She noted the current influences from Japan and northern Europe in forming the contemporary style in America, which, in the work of Lawrence Halprin and Burle Marx had, she felt, come "into concord with the contemporary spirit of the other arts and have reaffirmed the close sisterhood of painting and landscape."[32] She noted the influence of recent if more traditional gardens in England open to the public, naming Sissinghurst, Hidcote (presented to the National Trust in 1947), and Tintinhull, all of which were characterized by their use of strong forms of architectural enclosure, offering inspiration for small-scale gardening. The photographs in Crowe's book were disappointing, however. *Architectural Review* led the way in showing buildings in their settings of garden and landscape, and the painters John Piper and Paul Nash were influential in producing a poetic vision of English landscape with a touch of alienation and strangeness. Edwin Smith (1912–71) developed their vision in his varied and prolific work. His photographs for *The English Garden*, by Edward Hyams, produced in large quarto by Thames and Hudson in 1964, mark a breakthrough in the presentation of gardens [Figure 3–15].

CHANGES IN THE 1950S

Crowe's later books, *The Landscape of Power* (1958) and *The Landscape of Roads* (1960), reflect a turn from the pastoral vision of the 1940s toward anxiety about the proliferation of technology. This emphasizes how, during the 1940s and early 1950s, much of what now seems like the inevitable movement of the time toward mechanization and urban growth was held in check and alternative projections of the future were realistically considered.

Electric power was a means for dispersing industry and population and breaking the ties between the land and economic activities. Its postwar development came faster than expected. Lord Holford was a member of the Central Electricity Generating Board from its establishment as a postwar nationalized industry. When the 1957 Electricity Act opened the way for the first nuclear power stations set

Figure 3–15.
The Topiary Lawn, Great Dixter,
East Sussex. Nathaniel Lloyd.
[Edwin Smith. Courtesy Olive Cook]

Figure 3–16.
Dame Sylvia Crowe on site at
Trawsfynydd Power Station (Sir Basil
Spence, architect), with engineers from
the Central Electricity Generating Board,
circa 1962.
[© The Landscape Institute Library]

Figure 3–17. [facing page]
Trawsfynydd Power Station.
The mature landscape.
[© The Landscape Institute Library]

in remote coastal locations, Holford ensured that engineers and landscape architects worked together from the outset. As Crowe wrote in the introduction to *The Landscape of Power*, "Our generation blames the industrialists of the nineteenth century bitterly for having destroyed so much of the landscape and left us a legacy of a few thousand acres of ugly and derelict land, but this is nothing compared with the havoc we shall leave to our descendants unless we take avoiding action now and find a means of reconciling our need for power with our need for a landscape fit to live in."[33] Her work at Trawsfynydd Nuclear Power Station, in North Wales, and at Wylfa, in Anglesey, in the early 1960s helped to reduce the impact of these buildings in the landscape and prevent the suburbanization of the surroundings [Figures 3–16, 3–17]. When challenged on her proposed access roads at Trawsfynydd, without curbs or lighting, edged only with the heather of the surrounding moor land, she replied, "Don't vehicles have headlights?" and won the argument. At Wylfa, she created two artificial hills to diminish the impact of the substation on a flat and open coastal site.

Crowe's commentary on road planning, a response to the unpromising beginnings of motorway (highway) building in Britain, focused on the choice available between skillful and positive planning and inappropriate dressing up of roads and their surroundings. Her philosophical attitude is apparent although never overstated, as in her assurance that "good landscape will ensure that there is pleasure both in traveling and in being."[34] In dealing with both power stations and roads, Crowe acknowledged the new kind of design problem they represented, in terms of scale and speed. In both cases, contemporary art offered parallels and paradigms, such as the grid structures found in works by Paul Klee, Paul Nash, and Ben Nicholson, and in the concept of kinetic design developed in the Bauhaus. As Crowe wrote in *The Landscape of Roads*, "Another enjoyment of fast travel is the sense of penetrating swiftly into the heart of the landscape. Many of the most delightful roads owe their attraction to this strong feeling of direction and penetration. It echoes a trend in modern painting and sculpture which exploits the strong directional line exploring the depths of a composition, where the older traditions of both painting and landscape achieved their sense of penetration in a more leisurely way."[35] As a result of her comments, highways in Britain have benefited from a sensitive and intelligent approach to landscaping, although Crowe's only personal work in this area was on an interchange with pedestrian routes through it, the Cumberland Piazza at Clifton of 1964.

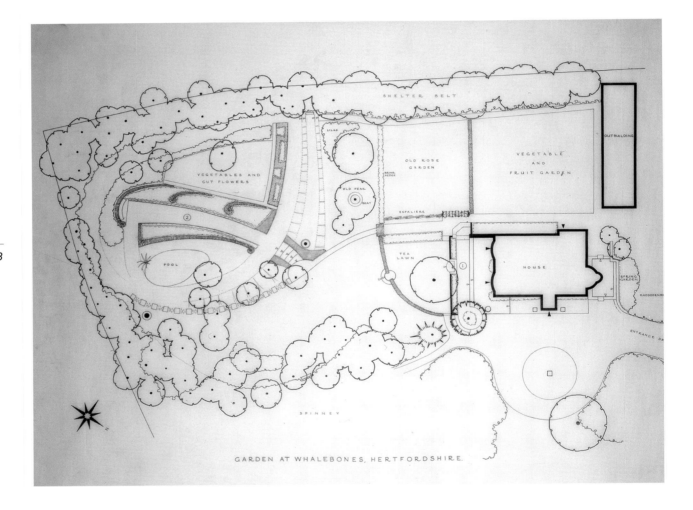

GARDEN AT WHALEBONES, HERTFORDSHIRE.

Figure 3–18.
Design for garden, Whalebones, Barnet,
Hertfordshire, 1956. Sylvia Crowe.
Dynamic, asymmetrical planting in a small
private garden.
[© The Landscape Institute Library]

Geoffrey Jellicoe is more closely associated with the influence of modern art on landscape than Sylvia Crowe or any other designer, partly because he revealed some of his sources of inspiration in lectures and essays. His design for the power station at Oldbury-on-Severn, commissioned in 1963, for example, was generated by Ben Nicholson's reliefs of over-lapping rectangles [Figure 3–17]. He admitted that, although aware of modern art, he did not begin to understand and enjoy it until he was inspired by Frederick Gibberd's personal collection in the 1940s.[36] In *The Landscape of Power*, Crowe refers to the book *The New Landscape in Art and Science*, edited by László Moholy-Nagy's former associate Gyorgy Kepes in 1956 and based on an exhibition at MIT. The book is not literally about landscape but uses the word as an inclusive metaphor for the connection of visual and functional appearances on a wide variety of scales, moving from a single viewpoint in space to seeing through the microscope and the telescope at once. Something of this kind of viewing of landscape had begun in the 1930s, however, when John Piper wrote "Prehistory from the Air" for *Axis* magazine and put a painting by Joan Miró beside aerial photographs of prehistoric English earthworks.[37]

Writing a foreword to the second edition of *Land and Landscape* in 1970, Brenda Colvin saw the unity of art and science, as explored in Kepes's book, as the wider task for landscape as a profession and as a way of understanding the world. "Landscape design is the youngest art, since the refinement of our natural joy in landscape comes late in history. The understanding and perception of the visual scene goes deeper than what the eye sees and owes much to scientific knowledge that the study of landscape design must now bridge the chasm between art and science. It is becoming ever more necessary for art and science to come to terms—their isolation and separate development is a danger to society."[38] The concept of ecology, which was only just beginning to emerge into its present importance in the early 1960s, was recognizable in the texts of these pioneer writers on landscape, although by 1970 Colvin saw it as the means by which limits on growth could be imposed. In their book *The Landscape of Man*, published in 1975, Geoffrey Jellicoe and his wife, Susan, presented an overview of landscape as a history of civilization in a manner appropriate to the age of the "green revolution," a phrase included in quotation marks on the first page of text. Thus one can trace, through one man's developing awareness of the significance of landscape, its transformation from a private

and professional concern to a matter of worldwide political significance.

The optimism about landscape practice generated in the wartime years was temporarily thwarted but never suppressed by the pace of expansion in the 1960s. On a professional level, British landscape architects were internationally well known, as indicated by the book *Space for Living*, the proceedings of the 1960 conference of the IFLA chaired and edited by Sylvia Crowe with contributions from Jellicoe and Shepheard. The backwardness of Britain in landscape and the values connected with it, relative to America and Scandinavia, had been remedied to some extent by the official adoption of landscape architects to work on new towns, highways, industrial sites, reservoirs, university campuses, and power stations, even though these left many other problems of existing ugliness unattended.

Subsequent years have shown more strongly the relationship between politics and landscape, which H. de C. Hastings raised in "Exterior Furnishing" in 1944. A new generation of landscape scholars has found more interest in the political meaning of historic landscape than in its functional, spiritual, and aesthetic qualities, or even in the Jungian symbolism and meaning expounded by Jellicoe in later years. Recent studies of landscape ideology of this period have nonetheless unaccountably neglected the quietly revolutionary practice of landscape architecture at that time, so much of which has become second nature that its presence is all too easily taken for granted.[39]

NOTES

1. The general cultural histories of the period give little attention to landscape; for example, volumes 8 and 9 of *The Cambridge Guide to the Arts in Britain*, ed. Boris Ford (Cambridge: Cambridge University Press, 1988 and 1989); and Arthur Marwick, *Culture in Britain Since 1945* (Oxford: Blackwell Publishers, 1991). The interaction between issues of landscape preservation and the general culture has been explored in David Matless, *Landscape and Englishness* (London: Reaktion Books, 1999). For a partially revisionist view of modernism in England in the 1930s, see the exhibition catalogue *Modern Britain, 1929–1939*, ed. James Peto and Donna Loveday, commissioning ed. Alan Powers (London: Design Museum, 1999).

2. Members of the "Amenity Brigade" in the 1930s would have included Patrick Abercrombie (planner), Harry Peach (industrialist), Charles Reilly (architect and educator), and Thomas Sharp (writer and planner).

3. W. H. Auden, *Look, Stranger!* (London: Faber & Faber, 1936), p. 15. Printed by kind permission of Faber and Faber Ltd.

4. See Samuel Hynes, *The Auden Generation: Literature and Politics in England in the 1930s* (London: Faber and Faber, 1976) chap. 6; and J. A. Morris, *Writers and Politics in Modern Britain* (London: Hodder and Stoughton, 1977) chap. 3, "The Despair of Systems."

5. The term neoromantic, which later became a standard label for the artistic movement of the 1940s, was apparently first used by the critic Raymond Mortimer when writing about Paul Nash's photographs in the article "Nature Imitates Art," *Architectural Review*, 77, 1935, p. 28, where he describes French surrealism as "the neo-romantic revolt against reason."

6. See Herbert Read, ed., *Unit One* (London: Cassell, 1934); *Unit 1*, exhibition catalogue, Portsmouth City Museum and Art Gallery, 1978.

7. See Alan Powers, "Une maison moderne de Serge Chermayeff," *Le moniteur architecture AMC*, March 1996, pp. 44–51, and *Serge Chermayeff: Designer, architect, teacher* (London: RIBA Publications, 2001).

8. Christopher Tunnard, *Gardens in the Modern Landscape* (London: Architectural Press, 1938), p. 76. The relative involvement of Tunnard and Chermayeff in designing the landscape at Bentley Wood has been a controversial issue for which conclusive evidence will probably never be found. Tunnard published his own account, "Planning a Modern Garden: An Experience in Collaboration," in *Landscape and Garden*, spring 1939, pp. 23–27. Ian Kitson offers a well-documented account in "Christopher Tunnard at Bentley Wood," in *Landscape Design*, December–January 1990–91, pp. 10–15, not challenging Tunnard's claim as designer. In a letter to Geoffrey Jellicoe of 17 March 1957, not quoted by Kitson, Chermayeff wrote, "The site plan, the architectural design, in its entirety had been completed by myself; and Christopher Tunnard, whose services at the time cannot be underestimated, contributed plant material and advice on plant arrangement exclusively to form my own specific landscape plans" (Chermayeff Archive, Avery Collection of Manuscripts and Drawings, Avery Library, Columbia University). In a note to his essay on Tunnard in *Modern Landscape: A Critical Review*, Marc Treib, ed. (Cambridge, Mass.: MIT Press, 1993), p. 147, Lance M. Necker records that in an interview in 1989, Chermayeff "claimed that Tunnard only made suggestions about the thinning of the trees that occurred as part of the site preparation." In later life, Chermayeff was inclined to emphasize his own part in collaborative ventures, so that this evidence may not be conclusive.

9. Brenda Colvin, "Beginnings," *Landscape Design*, February 1979, p. 8.

10. Ibid.

11. Lady Allen of Hurtwood, "New Slums for Old?" *Landscape and Garden*, winter 1934, p. 33. Born Marjory Gill, and a cousin of the artist Eric Gill, Lady Allen married the Labour politician and pacifist Clifford Allen (1889–1939), who was given a peerage in 1932. They ran a progressive coeducational school in Surrey with flat-roofed buildings designed by Clough Williams-Ellis. See Marjory Allen, *Memoirs of an Uneducated Lady* (London: Thames and Hudson, 1975).

12. "Civic and Social Centres," editorial, *Landscape and Garden*, Winter 1935, p. 131.

13. "MARS and Jupiter," unsigned review, *Landscape and Garden*, spring 1938, pp. 52–53.

14. Geoffrey Jellicoe, "The Wartime Journal of the Institute of Landscape Architects," in S. Harvey and S. Rettig, eds., *Fifty Years of Landscape Design* (London: Landscape Press, 1985), p. 16.

15. *Country and Town: A Summary of the Scott and Uthwatt Reports*, intro. G. M. Young (Harmondsworth: Penguin Books, 1943).

16. Sylvia Crowe, letter of 4 October 1941, quoted in Geoffrey Jellicoe, "The Wartime Journal of the Institute of Landscape Architects," p. 14.

17. Geoffrey Jellicoe, *The Guelph Lectures on Landscape Design* (Ontario: University of Guelph, 1983), p. 130.

18. Sven Markelius, "The Structure of the Town of Stockholm," *Byggmästaren*, 1956, p. 74, quoted in David Pass, *Vällingby and Farsta: From Idea to Reality* (Cambridge, Mass.: MIT Press, 1973). See also Frederick Gibberd, Ben Hyde Harvey, Len White, et al., *Harlow: The Story of a New Town* (Stevenage: Publications for Companies, 1980); and "Landscape Architecture in the New Towns: A Symposium," with papers by Brenda Colvin, Sylvia Crowe, and H. F. Clark, given at a General Meeting of the Institute of Landscape Architects on 11 May 1950 and published in *Journal of the Institute of Landscape Architects*, July 1950, pp. 3–10.

19. Several of Piper's articles were collected in his book *Buildings and Prospects* (London: Architectural Press, 1947).

20. Pevsner's key articles were "Price on Picturesque Planning," *Architectural Review*, 95, February 1944, pp. 47–50; and "The Genesis of the Picturesque," *Architectural Review*, 96, November 1944, pp. 139–46. He also contributed to the *Architectural Review* under the pseudonym Peter R. F. Donner.

21. Editor [H. de C. Hastings], "Exterior Furnishing or Sharawaggi: The Art of Making Urban Landscape," *Architectural Review*, 95, January 1944, pp. 1–8.

22. I. De Wolfe [H. de C. Hastings], "Townscape: A Plea for an English Visual Philosophy Founded on the True Rock of Sir Uvedale Price," *Architectural Review*, 106, December 1949, pp. 355–74.

23. See *Architectural Review*, 106, special number on canals, July 1949.

24. Brenda Colvin, *Land and Landscape* (London: John Murray, 1948), p. 62.

25. Ibid., p. 83.

26. Geoffrey Jellicoe, "A Philosophy of Landscape II," in *Architects' Yearbook*, ed. Jane B. Drew (London: Paul Elek, 1947), p. 40.

27. Peter Shepheard, *Modern Gardens* (London: Architectural Press, 1953), p. 72.

28. Clough Williams-Ellis, *Royal Festival Hall* (London: Max Parrish, 1951), pp. 58–65.

29. *Architectural Review*, 110, August 1951, special issue on the South Bank. Technical information on hard landscaping in postfestival style was given in Elizabeth Beazley's *Design and Detail of the Space Between Buildings* (London: Architectural Press, 1960).

30. Shepheard, *Modern Gardens*, p. 63. Eckbo's work was published, with his own text, in *Architectural Review*, 105, January 1949, pp. 25–32.

31. Herbert Tayler, "Houses 1953," *Architect and Building News*, 205, January 1954, p. 45. See Alan Powers and Elain Harwood, *Tayler and Green, Architects, 1938–1973: The Spirit of Place in Modern Housing* (London: Prince of Wales's Institute of Architecture, 1998).

32. Sylvia Crowe, *Garden Design* (London: Country Life, 1958), p. 77.

33. Sylvia Crowe, *The Landscape of Power* (London: Architectural Press, 1958), p. 10. See also Geoffrey Collens and Wendy Powell, eds., *Sylvia Crowe*, LDT Monographs no. 2 (Reigate: Landscape Design Trust, 1999).

34. Sylvia Crowe, *The Landscape of Roads* (London: Architectural Press, 1960), p. 27.

35. Ibid., p. 33.

36. See the now copious literature on Jellicoe, but particularly Sheila Harvey, ed., *Geoffrey Jellicoe*, LDT Monographs no. 1 (Reigate: Landscape Design Trust, 1998).

37. John Piper, "Prehistory from the Air," *Axis*, 8, 1937, pp. 3–6.

38. Brenda Colvin, *Land and Landscape*, rev. ed. (London: John Murray, 1970), p. xxii.

39. For example, David Matless, *Landscape and Englishness* (London: Reaktion Books, 1999).

A common trajectory shaped the landscapes of Belgium and France in the first half of the twentieth century, from the formal garden designs of the interwar years to the generic *espaces verts* of the 1950s and 1960s.[1] Similar forces shaped the development of landscape architecture in both countries, a discipline that in turn was determined by the impetus of planning. Modernist landscape architecture, particularly in France, suffered from the uncertainties of a developing profession. The certified landscape architect replaced the pluralistic garden architect-landscape planner. The field of landscape architecture still addressed a variety of scales—from garden and park design to planning—but drifted into the domain of horticulturists. Having become specialists, the late 1940s French landscape architects often acted as consultants to the architects and planners who governed the country's reconstruction. Similarly, Belgian landscape architects faced the simple dialectic of garden versus espace vert, unable to draw from the prewar collaborative spirit of architects and landscape designers. In both countries, the landscape products that came with, and in the wake of, post–World War II reconstruction expressed a rift between a sort of green engineering, in which trees and stretches of turf were quantified, and a very publicized decorative branch of garden design that resorted to dazzling displays of flowers.

4. DOROTHÉE IMBERT

Counting Trees and Flowers: The Reconstructed Landscapes of Belgium and France

Although European reconstruction after World War I still acknowledged regional variations with new and past models, the post-1945 recovery of cities was far more homogeneous. Reborn harbor cities evoked similar atmospheres, independent of geographic or cultural climates.[2] The tabula rasa operation, which is equated with the housing projects of the 1960s and 1970s, proved a convenient antidote to the trauma of war and/or occupation in several countries. With this removal of historical context from the design process came the degrounding of architecture. Site plans displayed housing slabs set against the irregularity of an abstracted green tone. Paradoxically, the perceptual severance of the building from its soil, and the landscape from its heritage, went hand in hand with the protection of an idealized countryside. As planning strategies cited the Athens Charter to modernize housing and cities, the tree and the forest were either memorialized against urban growth and industry or used as a foil to the "good" progress of modern road engineering.

Indeed the parallels and ties between France and Belgium are numerous, with geographic and (partial) linguistic prox-

Figure 4–1.
Cité Le Logis-Floréal, Watermael-Boitsfort,
Belgium, 1922. Louis van der Swaelmen.
Site plan with "Funnel," "Horseshoe,"
"Trapeze," "Triangle," and "Square"
formal nodes.
[La Cité]

Figure 4–2.
Cité Le Logis-Floréal, Watermael-Boitsfort,
Belgium, 1922. Louis van der Swaelmen.
A residential street. Jean-Jules Eggericx,
architect.
[Dorothée Imbert]

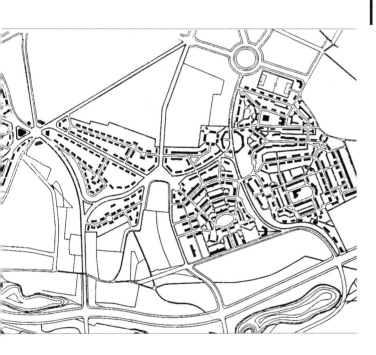

imity, intermittent common history, and occasional cultural affinities. The two world wars as well as colonialism marked the development of architecture, urbanism, and, ultimately, landscape architecture in these countries. Both Belgium and France suffered important material and psychological damage in the 1914–18 conflict with Germany. The reconstruction of the devastated provinces, mostly situated between France and Belgium, became part and parcel of the propaganda for the newly popularized discipline of urbanism. Both Belgium and France signed an armistice with Germany early in World War II, lived under German occupation, and suffered a second wave of destruction under Allied fire. Finally, their colonial empires presented planners and landscape architects with testing grounds for their theories.[3]

BELGIUM BETWEEN THE WARS

Reconstruction after World War I was intended to provide modern housing and to plan the territory at regional and national levels. By 1941, however, these ambitions were deemed unfulfilled. Because of expedience and nostalgia, as well as the prevalence of individualism over cooperation, both Belgium and France had seen their towns and houses re-created to match their pre–World War I images.[4] The commemorative garden cities, conceived in the spirit of a cooperative Belgian society between 1922 and 1930, were exceptions to this trend.[5] Although these architectural and urbanistic experiments varied in their degree of innovation — both formally and technically — they expressed the contribution of landscape architecture to town planning.

Louis van der Swaelmen, who participated in the design of several garden cities, left a strong mark on the field of Belgian planning and landscape architecture, under the self-ascribed title of "architecte-urbaniste." He published *Préliminaires d'art civique* in 1916, the treatise that would provide the theoretical basis for the country's postwar reconstruction.[6] In 1927, van der Swaelmen became the first Professor of Urbanism and the Art of Gardens at the Decorative Arts School of La Cambre.[7] The duality of scales expressed in the title of his chair, planning and gardens, revealed the breadth of van der Swaelmen's approach, as well as demonstrating the necessity of making landscape architecture an integral part of urban design. Among the concrete manifestations of his planning concepts are the garden cities of Logis-Floréal, Kapelleveld, and Berchem-Ste Agathe. Formally, these developments expressed modernistic élans as well as solid revisions of traditional and pseudovernacular architec-

83

Figure 4–3.
Canneel Garden, Auderghem, Belgium,
1931. Jean Canneel-Claes. Axonometric
view of the garden as an extension of the
house. Louis-Herman de Koninck, architect.
[Archives d'Architecture Moderne, Brussels]

ture.[8] In 1922, he planned the fifteen-hundred-unit Logis-Floréal twin garden city, outside of Brussels, mitigating the irregular shape of the site with a sequence of formal civic clusters: "Triangle," "Square," "Horseshoe," "Trapeze," and "Funnel" [Figures 4–1, 4–2]. The master plan reflected a sophisticated hierarchy of private and public spaces. Seeking the effect of a continuous park, he proscribed fences on front lawns and carefully orchestrated masses, densities, and colors of vegetation. At the Kapelleveld garden city, built in 1923–26 in Woluwé, van der Swaelmen used vegetation and gardens to create a coherent urbanistic ensemble that would mitigate the divergent stylistic tendencies of its architects. He located the houses on streets perpendicular to the existing thoroughfares, so as to limit the impact of traffic noise. A local network of pathways and plazas connected the private gardens.[9]

The Belgian garden cities of the 1920s expressed the confluence of landscape architecture and town planning. Van der Swaelmen used garden units and vegetation as spatial structure rather than decoration. During the 1930s, the garden would become the fundamental counterpart to a modernist architecture concerned with outdoor living and a comprehensive attitude toward house and site. Several landscape designers proposed a simplified and reduced formalism to answer the more modest means of their clients. Rarely was there an attempt to truly establish the precepts of the modern garden. In this respect, Jean Canneel-Claes remains an emblematic figure of the 1930s Belgian landscape.[10]

The first significant connection between Canneel and modernist architecture involved his own house. On 29 April 1929, Canneel contacted Le Corbusier to design a house for a "young couple in Brussels."[11] The project never materialized because of cost, a change of sites, and Le Corbusier's disregard for his client's requests. Canneel had expressed his desire to the architect that the garden be "designed in perfect accordance with the interior arrangement."[12] Ignoring this concern, Le Corbusier conceived the house in accord with his Five Points for a New Architecture: he raised the living spaces from the ground, devoting this level to services and the automobile, and shifted the garden to the roof terrace.[13]

As negotiations with Le Corbusier stalled, Canneel found a local, cheaper, and more attentive modernist architect, Louis-Herman de Koninck [Figure 4–3]. This decision proved a judicious one for Canneel, since the design of his garden

Figure 4–4.
Heeremans Garden, Liedekerke, Belgium,
1938. Jean Canneel-Claes.
Huib Hoste, architect.
View from the upper floor toward the valley
of the Dendre River.
[Courtesy Dr. Karl Heeremans]

would launch his career as a landscape architect. Completed in 1931, the Canneel house and garden expressed a tranquil equilibrium between indoors and out. The garden did not compete with, nor did it recede from, the house; it simply took its cues from the geometries of the architecture. The simple, yet formal, arrangement of the garden and its addressing contemporary functions brought Canneel international recognition.

De Koninck and Canneel opened the house to sun and air and furnished the upper solarium with exercise equipment. As if to balance this penetration of architecture by the elements, Canneel formed the garden with a clearly defined structure. The typical components—sandbox, flowers, trees—were graphically and functionally arranged. The intermittent stripes of flowers punched out of paving or emerging from lawn allowed easy access for tending; the rectangle of sand took full advantage of the southwest exposure; the discontinuous line of poplars and the dissolving corner of the plan suggested the continuation of the landscape beyond; and the metal trellis structure echoed the terrace's railing.

To Canneel, the garden was a geometric and spatial arrangement of voids and solids that he termed "furnished" spaces, expressing a precise architectural rhythm. He stressed the necessity to avoid the sentimentality of the wild garden, the artificiality of the landscape style, or the intellectualism of the jardin à la française. Canneel thus became the proponent and exclusive representative of what he termed the "functionalist garden." His was a landscape that fulfilled social and hygienic functions, that would be both hospitable and practical.[14]

Unlike the formal exercises constructed in France during the 1920s and 1930s, Canneel's gardens expressed proportional harmony and a respect for vegetation and the site. He became the advocate of a new sort of composite style that combined architectural elements with a "harmoniously simple" green framework. With its architectonic structure interspersed with floral or sculptural accents, commented Canneel, such a garden satisfied physical as well as "emotional" needs while remaining within organic limits [Figure 4–4].[15]

Canneel refused the role of landscape architect as a mere selector of plants, a steward, or an improver of nature. To him, garden architecture posed a multifaceted problem whose solution needed to be formal, psychological, and

practical. By 1933, Canneel was questioning the validity of Le Corbusier's severance of architecture from ground. He saw the architectural prism of the Villa Savoye, raised on pilotis and floating above its site, as lacking warmth.[16] He then proceeded to suggest a few improvements that would reconcile Le Corbusier's architecture with nature: regular plantings, a courtyard with flowers, and perhaps a sculptural element. To complement a restful roof garden, sheltered and yet offering panoramic views, Canneel furnished the ground level with "organs" for corporeal living: a children's sandbox, exercise porticoes, pools, planes for the practice of games and sports, and squares for sunbathing, as well as a vegetable garden and an orchard. This concern for health and sports would resurface in the wartime projects of "Nature Baths" and his public town squares.

Publications such as Tekhné, La Cité, Bâtir, and La Revue documentaire featured the houses of Louis-Herman de Koninck, Huib Hoste, Jean-Jules Eggericx, and Victor Bourgeois, as well as the complementary new "functionalist" gardens of Canneel. Master of the reduced geometric and graphically composed landscape and promoter of an international movement of modernist designers, Canneel would rapidly dominate the field of Belgian garden design during the 1930s. He also proved to be a superior self-publicist, expressing his modernist convictions through axonometric representation, whose language he borrowed from modernist architecture. Axonometry implicitly suggested modernity. Furthermore, it placed the garden on an equal footing with architecture. The axonometric view described the way the space was structured rather than the way it was perceived. Since it removed the viewer from the composition, it presented the garden as an analytical and synthetic object that responded to the geometries and proportions of the house, its asymmetrical dynamism fully revealed. Canneel represented his landscapes as a series of spaces seen from above, not as a sequence of pictures that would be experienced. The modular and structural nature of the "functionalist" garden was reinforced, and the abstraction of its colored planes clarified.

Indeed Canneel's designs departed strikingly from the typical garden fare found in contemporary periodicals, both for their elegant architectural graphics and for their photogenic qualities. Photography provided the details and textures of life. In the modest scale of the modern garden, architectonic elements such as paving, pools of water, and geometrically arranged plantings served the design focus of the photographic composition. Canneel's gardens benefited from the modernist allies of large expanses of glass and accessible rooftops. The exterior space was photographed as a continuation of the interior through the large windows or from the upper terrace.

Canneel was a unique player in the field of modernist landscape architecture in Belgium. He also attempted to open his profession to architectural, artistic, and international currents, following the example of the first International Congress of Garden Architects, held in Paris in 1937. Its chairman, theorist and garden architect Achille Duchêne, bemoaned the death of the art of gardens. Discussions at the Paris congress revolved around parks and playgrounds, schools and sports fields. True luxury had dwindled. Landscape architecture was no longer a private or public display of artful garden design. It needed to consider the "education of the masses" with factory gardens and school playgrounds. According to Duchêne's report, the sports park of an industrial city needed to include zones for recreation, education, rest, spectator sports, physical education, swimming, camping, and tourism. Landscape architect and future sports field expert Albert Audias dismissed stadiums as wasteful. There, "thousands of people stood still to watch a dozen players frantically run professionally." He saw the small private garden complete with vegetable plot and playground as doing far more "for the improvement of the race" than a forty-thousand-seat stadium.[17] The dwindling of economic means and the disappearance of large estates marked the death of Duchêne's garden tradition, that of grand formal gardens and Gallic ambitions. Landscape design answered social and functional needs, both quantifiable and abstract. Sports parks and roadways responded to the concern for exercise and speed. Utilitarian and botanical gardens and suburban parks fulfilled the needs for education and leisure. Gardens were also part and parcel of urbanism. Duchêne's report recommended that the department of Promenades et Plantations should include a garden architect to complement the work of engineers and gardeners. This was a concern Robert Joffet would reiterate during the next decade and implement during his tenure as the head of the Paris Parks Service. The garden section of the 1937 Paris Exposition seemed to warrant Duchêne's pessimism regarding the state of his discipline. The International Congress of Garden Architects signaled a changing of the guards.

Unlike Duchêne, Canneel answered the challenge of designing a garden reduced in scale and means by addressing the demands of contemporary garden owners in function and form. He extended his publicity and didactic interests to the profession of landscape architecture in Europe. One year after the 1937 Paris meeting, Canneel joined English landscape architect Christopher Tunnard to form the International Association of Modernist Garden Architects, itself modeled on the Congrès Internationaux d'Architecture Moderne (CIAM).[18] The Belgian landscape architect acted as the Secretary General. This group was to include not only garden designers of all nationalities but also urbanists, architects, sculptors, painters, writers, and all individuals concerned with the problems of present times. The association's manifesto was printed in French, English, and German. Although the text remained general, one could detect Canneel's influence in several of its points. The association was to defend the cause of "rationalist" gardens, a main concern of Canneel. It echoed the 1937 Paris meeting by stressing the need to study and develop the relationship among garden design, urbanism, and architecture. Thus if the scope of design of landscape architects was reduced from estates to the urban garden, it would benefit from being integrated into the process of city reform. In fact, garden design was to be considered not a decorative art but a branch of architecture, intimately connected with the questions of dwelling and city. It was a discipline with social responsibilities. It bore a direct influence on the physical and moral development of human beings, both as individuals and as communities. But garden art was also an aesthetic discipline. Canneel saw the dictum "form follows function" as applicable to the modern garden, as long as one also sought beauty in harmony and rhythm. Nature was to be respected, but not imitated. He concluded that although geometry was the foundation of garden design, it must remain flexible to allow for functional and site constraints. The Belgian designer affirmed that the relationship among landscape and other arts be studied with a particular emphasis on the impact of science on these arts. This point mirrored the argument raised by American landscape architect James Rose in his article "Why Not Try Science?"[19]

Canneel called for a greater landscape that crossed geographical frontiers, an effort that his contemporary fellow garden designer René Pechère would repeat in the 1950s. In 1938, internationalization was seen as essential if only to offer a passive defense of humanism in its pursuit of intellectual diversity and universality.[20]

A year after creating the International Association of Modernist Garden Architects, Canneel expanded the formal and functional principles that shaped his residential designs into the public scale of the Exposition de l'Eau. [21] The exposition was held in Liège in 1939 to celebrate the completion of the Canal Albert, a new waterway that linked Liège to Antwerp, thus freeing its constricted metallurgic industry. Pavilions were dedicated to the glory of Belgium and to the theme of water, like the Palace of the Sea, the Palace of Naval Construction, and the Palace of Civil Engineering and Metallurgy. Typical of exposition landscapes, Canneel's design for Liège needed to fulfill immediate goals—those of show and shade. But his scheme also involved the design of permanent structures, including a fifty-acre park and playing fields. It was reported that this project required importing 100,000 cubic meters of topsoil, 100,000 tulips, 20,000 rose bushes, and 3,000 "young trees with rustling foliage." His plan featured a dahlia garden, a rose garden, a zoological garden, a water garden, and a checkerboard of hydrangea and pools, completed by fifty-five rows of twenty-five jets of water [Figure 4–5]. [22]

The Exposition de l'Eau represented a milestone in Canneel's career. There he applied his spatial theories on an expansive and public scale and mastered the multiplicity of time frames, responding to both the temporary needs of visitors and to those of future permanent users. He also reconciled his love for functionalism with his love of plants, and in particular flowers [Figure 4–6]. But the exposition gardens also represented one of Canneel's last exercises in formalism and geometry.

In addition to honoring grand public works such as the Canal Albert, the exposition announced the future ambitions of Liège's city planners. In the name of urbanism, hygiene, and commercial expansion, the organizers justified the removal of old neighborhoods, reform, and reconstruction, all to bring the region to the level of "power," "order," and "beauty" it deserved. To the architects of the exposition and the planners of the Grand Liège, who would later extend their new order under the German occupation, urbanism meant discipline and regulation, homogeneity and unity, as if to announce the future. [23]

The Liège exposition opened in May 1939. On 23 August Leopold III, king of the Belgians, broadcast a call for peace. On 1 September Germany invaded Poland, and two days later, France and England declared war on Germany.

Figure 4–5. [top]
Exposition de l'Eau, Liège, Belgium, 1939.
Jean Canneel-Claes. Flower and water
parterre.
[Willy Kessels; Archives d'Architecture
Moderne, Brussels]

Figure 4–6. [*facing page, bottom*]
Exposition de l'Eau, Liège, Belgium, 1939.
Jean Canneel-Claes. Axonometric view of
the Rose Garden.
The roses were displayed in tiers according
to species and color, and interspersed with
water jets. Trees screened an outdoor
amphitheater.
[Archives d'Architecture Moderne, Brussels]

Figure 4–7. [*below*]
Front cover. *Reconstruction*, February 1941.

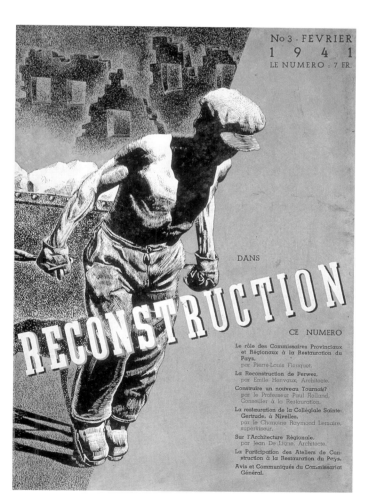

Belgium took a neutral position. On 10 May 1940, Germany
attacked Belgium. Early in the morning of 28 May 1940,
Belgium capitulated.

THE OCCUPIED LANDSCAPE OF BELGIUM

Belgium began its reconstruction, from industry to infrastructure, under the control of Germany. A fair amount of
independence was given to the local collaborating authorities,
and the Commissariat Général à la Restauration du Pays
(Agency for the Restoration of the Nation) was nominally
placed in the hands of Belgian professionals. Personalities
such as the architect Henry van de Velde and the planner
Raphaël Verwilghen would direct the reconstruction of
Belgium [Figure 4–7]. Canneel headed the agency's landscape bureau, which was placed under the aegis of the
urbanism section. Canneel's team would design or restore
village squares, athletic fields, monuments, cemeteries, parks
and public gardens, and roadside plantings. The pursuit of
modernization and reconstruction advertised the respect of
regional characteristics, just as in Vichy France. The order
and discipline that issued from the designs of the landscape
bureau were to serve the national community. As in France,
the whole country was a family and the land its house.

Canneel designed housing developments, established planning rules and guidelines for setbacks, laid out garden necro-
polises, and inserted baths in naturalistic settings [Figures
4–8, 4–9, 4–10]. If axonometry had resurfaced in the pages
of the magazine *Reconstruction*, it lacked the modern flair
that had marked Canneel's earlier drawings. Although he
maintained a private practice throughout the Occupation,
his designs for the grande bourgeoisie retained little of the
graphic tension expressed in the geometries of the 1930s
gardens. The rural estate in Borsbeke that Canneel created
for the de Vuyst family in 1945 featured many of his typical
prewar design components [Figures 4–11, 4–12].[24] A terrace of wide square concrete pavers framed a very traditional house; it was lined with roses and a herbaceous border. Nearby, the children's garden set a sandbox and exercise equipment within a bosk of fruit trees. Swimming pool,
tennis court, and vegetable garden would have formed the
productive core and a direct extension of the pleasure garden. A vast apple and pear orchard and allées framed the
garden proper, directed views, and formed an ordered foil
to the surrounding agricultural fields. In plan and in reality,
however, the sum of these design parts failed to conjure
the taut juxtaposition of spaces and geometries that had
characterized Canneel's earlier gardens.

89

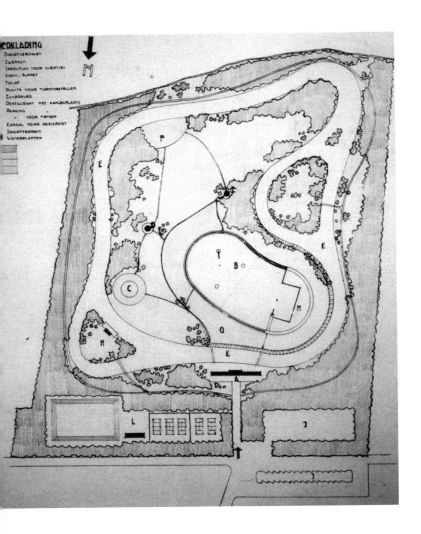

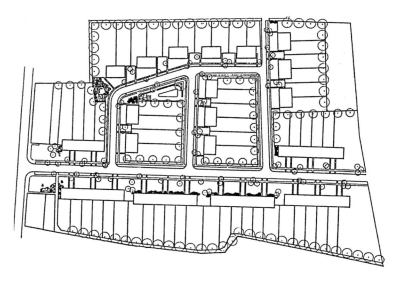

Figure 4–8.
Natuurbad de Rietbeemden, Brasschaat, Belgium, 1942. Jean Canneel-Claes, Commissariat Général à la Restauration du Pays. Site plan.
The Nature Bath was sited within a frame of heather and pine groves; it featured various swimming, wading and canoeing areas, a large expanse of turf for exercising, bicycle and car parks, and sports fields.
[Archives d'Architecture Moderne, Brussels]

Figure 4–9.
Cité de l'État, Tessenderloo, Limbourg, Belgium, circa 1943. Jean Canneel-Claes, Commissariat Général à la Restauration du Pays. Jos. Ritzen, architect.
Canneel's landscape bureau formulated the site plan for sixty dwellings. The setback allowed individual front yards to be used as a collective landscape planted with clumps of white birch.
[Reconstruction]

Figure 4–10.
Cité de l'État, Tessenderloo, Limbourg,
Belgium, circa 1943. Jean Canneel-Claes,
Commissariat Général à la Restauration
du Pays. Private garden with study of
shadows. Plan and section.
Canneel proposed two types of gardens for
the Cité de l'État. The first, illustrated below,
devoted a significant portion of its surface to
vegetable beds and orchard, and the other
to turf.
[Archives d'Architecture Moderne, Brussels]

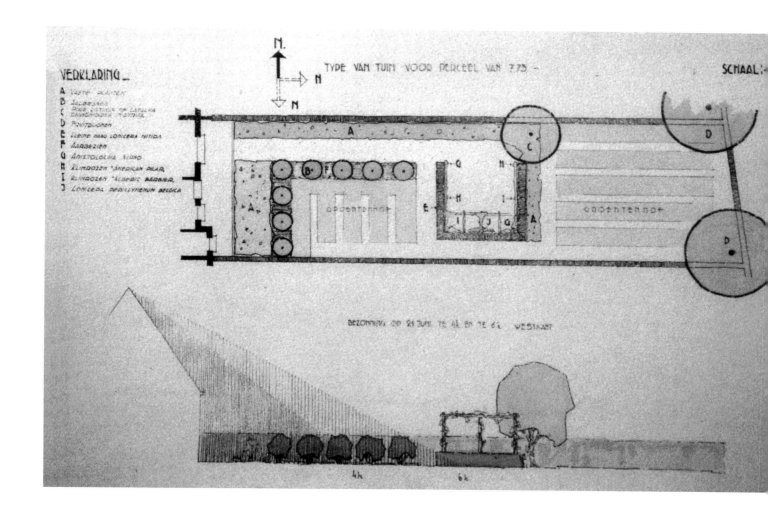

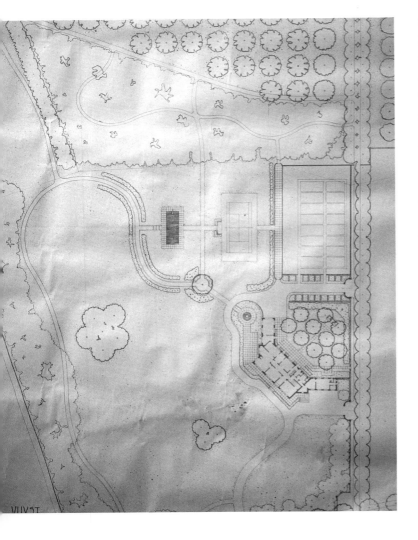

Occasionally, Canneel's gardens complemented modern houses. In 1946, he collaborated with Huib Hoste on a design in West Flanders [Figure 4–13].[25] The large expanse of glass in the living room allowed the living room to extend visually onto a broad terrace, complete with pool and pergola. A series of architectonic elements framed distant views of the countryside and supposedly added perspectival depth to the garden. Trees served as both armature and focal points; tall plantings screened the mandatory tennis court and swimming pool. The formality of spaces dissolved toward the south, where an intimate pond and a willow offered a destination to the undulating path. To further tie the garden to its site, Canneel relied essentially on plants found locally, like maple, linden, willow, and poplar.[26] During the 1940s he continued to publish articles that reiterated his tenets for a simple and functional garden in accordance with the house. Perhaps the difficulty he experienced in furthering his formal design research was that clients who could afford to drive automobiles and to build gardens with pools and tennis courts during the 1940s were usually not interested in modern architecture or landscape. More often than not, the gardens that Canneel designed during that period answered traditionally styled houses with tiled roofs and conventional plans, and his gardens remained more traditional. He addressed contemporary requirements with productive gardens, essential during times of rationing.

In addition to designing projects and establishing guidelines, the section Canneel headed within the Commissariat worked on the preservation and enhancement of the countryside for its touristic and regional attributes. His team acted as "curators of the landscape." The focus of the section rested on the creation of "natural parks" and on the rehabilitation of areas touched by industry and traversed by freeways.[27] The practice of controller and protector within the profession was most likely modeled after the German *Landschaftanwalt*, which in turn was echoed by the contemporary French *Avocat du paysage*.

Although one may think — especially in light of today's profession — that a landscape architect would hardly influence the future of a country, Canneel attempted to efface his collaboration with the Agency for the Restoration of the Nation. He removed the title blocks identifying the projects executed during these years but kept the drawings nevertheless, as if his investment in design were worth preserving.

Canneel had attempted to reinforce the design affinities of landscape architects in various countries with his International Association of Modernist Garden Architects. Similarities in form and intent were shared among France, Belgium, and England, and between the United States and Japan. These similarities expressed a regionalism of the mind, as landscape design sought to answer the contemporary needs of its inhabitants. Parallels between the landscape and architecture promoted by the French and Belgian regimes during the 1940s continued, but instead of fulfilling real needs and functions, they served as moralistic propaganda. Sadly, the flexible and poetic regionalism of the mind had given way to a standardized regionalism of deed.

THE RECONSTRUCTIONS OF FRANCE

The French interwar period witnessed both the radical formalism of garden design and the development of landscape planning. The lack of definition of the profession allowed all interventions to take place under the vague denomination of "garden architecture." Jean-Claude Nicolas Forestier, for instance, acted as a landscape engineer/gardener creating plans for the cities of Havana and Buenos Aires, exposition grounds for Barcelona and Seville, and small gardens around Paris.[28] Architects conceived parks and gardens, and artists linked indoors and outdoors with architectonic compositions that came closer to scenography than to landscape design.[29]

Designers saw the destruction of France during World War I as a splendid opportunity for testing their urban theories. Hundreds of thousands of buildings were destroyed and entire cities razed in the northern *départements*. Achille Duchêne, a garden artist-planner like Forestier, devoted his attention to the reconstruction of the town of Albert, in the Somme.[30] The implementation of modern industrial, commercial, hygienic, and social facilities would presumably entice the populations of towns like Albert to return. Duchêne's plan for the new Albert included institutions controlling the lives of inhabitants from birth to death. It also featured a park, whose style was left unspecified. He advised, however, avoiding both "classical solemnity" and pastiches of nature.[31] While walking, listening to music, or practicing sports in the park, the masses would "widen their intellectual and moral horizon"—and, not incidentally, find their desire to work for progress stimulated.[32] Unlike his renovations of formal estates, Duchêne's landscape of reconstruction was not to embody French stylistic supremacy but rather to function as a vehicle for economic recovery.

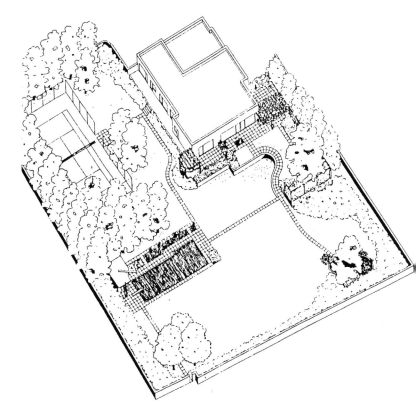

Figure 4–11. [facing page, top]
De Vuyst Estate, Borsbeke, Belgium, 1945.
Jean Canneel-Claes. Site plan.
[Courtesy Notaire de Vuyst]

Figure 4–12. [facing page, bottom]
De Vuyst Estate, Borsbeke, Belgium, 1945.
Jean Canneel-Claes.
Allée leading to the main orchard, with agricultural fields beyond.
[Dorothée Imbert]

Figure 4–13.
Estate, Haecht, Belgium, 1946.
Jean Canneel-Claes. Axonometric view of garden with house. Huib Hoste, architect.
The functional elements, such as swimming pool and tennis court, no longer complete the graphic composition but are screened by vegetation.
[La Maison]

As Duchêne had pointed out in his 1918 essay on Albert, reconstruction was not merely a matter of architecture, landscape design, or even urbanism, but essentially a question of planning. With World War II another opportunity for planning on a territorial scale arose. On 22 June 1940, less than a month after the Belgian army had capitulated, France signed its armistice with Germany. Marshal Philippe Pétain became head of the French State on 10 July 1940. Urbanists developed strategies for the reconstruction of France. It was hoped that this reconstruction would avoid the piecemeal solutions that had prevailed over a coherent regional effort in 1919.

The material destruction incurred during the six weeks of the so-called Funny War affected a far greater number of départements than did the Great War.[33] The scale of reconstruction varied widely. Cities like Amiens or Dunkirk and villages in Champagne or Ardennes had to be rebuilt almost entirely; industrial cities and regions like the Loiret needed to be restructured; and historic neighborhoods like those of Rouen needed to be restored and reconfigured.[34]

Under the leadership of Pétain, France advertised a "return to the real" with the idealized "Man of the Soil" as antidote to intellectualism and individualism.[35] Although the years of German occupation are often simplistically equated with regionalism in opposition to modernism, the interruption of the early 1940s was far from drastic, expressing instead a continuity between the 1930s and the postwar years. André Vera, for instance, would reiterate the necessity of cultivating regionalist modernity and of redeveloping crafts from the 1910s well into the 1950s. Under the Vichy regime, the French farmer and craftsman had become the "moral repository" of the nation.

Landscape planning was to be studied at the regional and national level. Henri Pasquier, who called himself *paysagiste-urbaniste* (landscape architect-urbanist), saw the future of his profession directed toward managing, protecting, and, if necessary, reconstituting the French landscape, not toward the making of gardens or parks.[36] Such paysagistes-urbanistes would act as "landscape advocates" who could read the land in geographic, ethnic, economic, and sociological terms and devise aesthetic plans. To Pasquier, a road expressed "the human trace necessary for the rational possession of nature" and formed the essential link between the various regions; it functioned as a window onto the regional character, through layout, decoration, and planting.[37] Ideally,

Figure 4–14.
Roadway planting diagrams, 1939. Henri Pasquier.
In the upper scheme, the pedestrian path is situated between two thoroughfares. Meandering amidst irregular plantings, the path affords varied views of the landscape beyond. The lower diagram shows a two-way road with the path on one shoulder. Planting is described as "soft."
[*Urbanisme*]

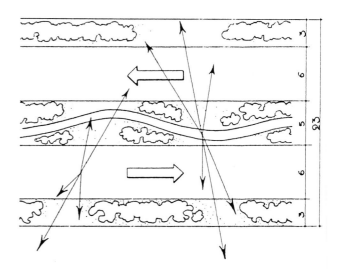

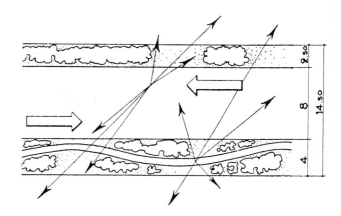

he hoped the French landscape advocate would emulate its counterpart in a "great neighboring country," most likely Germany.[38] There, the model Landschaftsanwalt collaborated with the engineer to devise freeway layouts, plantings, and views.[39]

Pasquier's attention to the landscape of roads perhaps best expressed the period's tug of war between progress and tradition, planning and nostalgia.[40] He considered that if the automobile had killed the private garden, it should dictate the creation of a collective garden. The road was to the landscape what the allée was to a park.[41] Previously, the route nationale had derived its alignments from the surrounding fields and their drainage and windbreak patterns. The shoulders of the modern-day road were no longer to be lined with plane trees. Instead, the faster and straighter road was beautified with irregular clumps of trees, so as to create a multiplicity of viewpoints and a transition to nature beyond [Figure 4–14]. In the spirit of contemporary trends and of the German Autobahn model, the engineered landscape was connected to its surrounding through plantings of indigenous specimens.[42] Thus the so-called noble species of oak, beech, and chestnut were to link the manmade path to nature. By overlaying science and aesthetics with economy, Pasquier concluded, one could line the road with fruit trees and transform France into an orchard.

André Vera also gave a vote of confidence to Pétain. He saw in the Vichy government the much-needed opportunity to banish the "negative style" of the 1930s and lead the country into an era of renewed morals and arts and crafts.[43] To Vera, urbanists needed to stop thinking about circulation and focus instead on houses and towns. He requested that designers consider squares, streets, trees, sculpture, and architecture, not only in plan but also in elevation. Bypassing Camillo Sitte, he cited the scenographic perspectives of Serlio as inspiration. Vera belittled specialization — comparing the dispute between "engineer-urbanist" and "architect-urbanist" to one between a hornet and a bee — preferring instead the notion of a Renaissance architect, master of gardens as well as of cities.[44]

The projects conceived during the Occupation were either halted until the Liberation, like the reconstruction of Orléans, or often remained unbuilt.[45] A few examples that straddled the fields of urbanism and landscape design were executed, however. The conversion of the zone non aedificandi outside the Thiers fortifications of Paris was voted as

part of the Grands Travaux (Great Works) at the end of 1940.[46] To fight unemployment, 120 designers worked on this project under Édouard Crevel and Robert Joffet.[47] Although the cleansing of slums to create an annular system of hygienic, recreational, and exercise spaces was not novel, it fit perfectly the Vichy government's propagandistic dialectic of city versus nature. The parks were not only to improve living conditions, both physically and morally, but also to circumscribe in a green cinch Paris and its uncontrolled expansion.[48] In the late nineteenth-century park, the contact with both nature and the bourgeoisie was seen as a potential improvement of the working class. Joffet's ring of parks offered recreation and health facilities for the varied socioeconomic Parisian neighborhoods it adjoined. High(er) and low(er) cultures would meet in the promenades, restaurants, guinguettes, racetracks, and sports fields; the aim of improving physical conditions was explicit and that of reforming morality implicit. Joffet rationalized the grouping of leisure and sports activities in the multiuse park as limiting high building and maintenance costs. Such a generic landscape — framing the different sports, educational, and recreational facilities — announced the astylistic quantification of the post-Occupation years. The technical research that accompanied the Parisian health ring also anticipated the programmatic and scientific aspects of the future landscape architecture profession.[49]

The Services Techniques des Parcs et Jardins de la Préfecture de la Seine of Joffet and his team presented their work at the 1943 Salon des Urbanistes. The exhibition featured the new projects in a historical context that underlined the disappearance of private city gardens and the scarcity of parks created since the Second Empire. Against these quantitative and qualitative inadequacies, the park service promoted a landscape for physical education, health, and leisure at the urban, periurban, and departmental levels. By 1943, it had become apparent that the means necessary for the realization of these "beautiful projects" were unavailable. Joffet's ring park was only partially realized; the "departmental" projects like the Parc Pétain in La Courneuve would be executed later.[50]

On the eve of war, Pasquier had asserted that codifying the espaces verts was not enough; the gardener was essential to counter the engineer's supremacy in landscape planning that had begun with Haussmann. Landscape architects needed to act. His concern for the increased density of the housing ring that had replaced the fortifications ring was

Figure 4–15.
Parc Kellerman, Paris, 1937, 1941–1950.
Jacques Gréber.
View from the upper terrace looking south
toward the lower pools.
[Marc Treib]

answered by Jacques Gréber's Parc Kellerman [Figure 4–15].[51]
Gréber was the chief architect for the 1937 Paris Exposition
and the author of *Jardins modernes*, which presented the
fair's garden section. The project for the Parc Kellerman was
conceived as part of the exposition. Work continued during
the Occupation and was completed in 1950. Anchored on
the edge of Paris, it stepped along remnants of ramparts
down to the southern suburbs. It featured the usual contemporary Paris park structures in concrete and brick, like
guard pavilions and a solarium/shelter. The Parc Kellerman
balanced the urbane formal typology of pruned allées and

a ceremonial viewpoint with the roughness of stone and
the irregularity of plantings. The upper circles of water cas-
caded in lessening degrees of formality down to the large,
kidney-shaped pool at the lower level, next to a broad
expanse of turf for informal games.

Although the profession of landscape architect may have
emerged officially with the creation of an educational system, it evolved fluidly from the interwar years to the post-
1945 reconstruction era. The issues that modeled the field
of postwar landscape architecture were current in the 1930s
and remained so during the Occupation. The quantification
of green spaces and the specialization of the profession
dominated discussions at the International Congress of
Garden Architects held in Paris in 1937 [Figure 4–16].[52] The
Floralies Joffet organized in 1959 at the ultramodern La
Défense were in fact reminiscent of the horticulturally
heavy garden section of the 1937 exposition. Indeed the
Occupation did not interrupt the practice of French landscape planners, engineers, and designers. Pasquier, Joffet, and
their contemporaries practiced or wrote during the Vichy
regime and played a central role in the rebuilding of the
territory. Albert Audias brought his horticultural and design
experience to Joffet's department in 1941 and later to the
planning of cities like Saint-Nazaire. He was a founding

Figure 4–16.
Urban density diagram, 1939.
Henri Pasquier.
The upper row illustrates the number of
inhabitants per "green hectare" and the
lower per "built hectare."
[*Urbanisme*]

member of the landscape department within the Versailles horticulture school in 1946.

Although urban housing and the imperilment of France's cultural landscape and forest by peripheral development dominated the postwar reconstruction debate, these issues had surfaced earlier.[53] In 1937 André Vera had argued for "ruralism"—the creation and protection of national parks and forests—a concept he judged as essential as its pendant, urbanism.[54] He would also publish an article entitled "Nature et urbanisme" just before the war, which called for the urgent need to integrate vegetation in planning.[55] Choosing the familiar case study of Greater Paris, he first recommended preserving sites such as Le Nôtre's terrace at Saint-Germain-en-Laye and its adjoining orchards.[56] Next, he proposed reconstituting "incomplete landscapes" such as those "mutilated by industry," in order to establish a continuous green flow across several suburban communes. Finally, Vera insisted on the necessity for urbanists to design with trees. Vegetation treated as an architectonic volume or as isolated specimens would inculcate moral values in the urban dweller, whose mental as well as physical state he saw as threatened.[57] Forests needed to be evaluated not only commercially (bois d'exploitation) but also as destinations for leisure (bois de promenade) and thus requiring protection against roads and suburbs (bois sacrés). Contemporaneously, Pasquier focused on the shrinking of forests and of the "pristine" countryside. He warned that with the proliferation of satellite towns and industry, suburban areas would see their fields, vineyards, and woods dwindle.[58] Also in 1939, Pasquier had catalogued urban and suburban espaces verts according to function and percentage, established the need for rural preserves, and considered the rapidly developing field of tourism and the issue of landscape design for roads.[59]

The landscape was quantified following the ratio of open space to inhabitant; likewise, the forest was a resource to be exploited not only for its wood but also as a destination for tourism. With the rise of leisure and automobile travel, planners saw the green reservations of the distant suburbs as easily accessible to city dwellers. Thus landscape and recreation became intimately linked with roadways and circulation management. A peripheral boulevard to relieve traffic congestion in and around Paris and to facilitate egress toward the rest of France was proposed in 1943. It would become the boulevard périphérique (ring road) of the 1960s. Joffet's greenbelt of sports fields, playgrounds, and parks was

slowly eroded by additional housing and finally girdled by the Périphérique.[60]

Forests fell under the technical aegis of the Eaux et Forêts corps, but their aesthetic and human component was assessed by tourist entities.[61] The preservation of forest and countryside went hand in hand with the development of mass leisure and tourism. In 1919, Duchêne had predicted the potential of battlefields as an economic draw for out-of-town visitors.[62] The landscape served the double purpose of health reservoir and monument to the glory of the country. As memorials to the dead were erected across towns, trees symbolized the enduring and untainted past of France and its future. Both architectural and green patrimony were to be protected. The forest became a historical, moral, and didactic ground for recreation.[63]

On weekends, Fontainebleau functioned as a playground for the young Parisian—the naturalist, artist, student, or flâneur. To those interested in botany, mycology, geology, entomology, painting, or archaeology, the forest and its cliffs appeared as a large laboratory. The park of Parilly, executed in the early 1950s next to Lyons, served a similar scientific function. As a cross between an exposition landscape and an outdoor classroom, the park featured various zones of activity: an education zone with daycare, classrooms, and other "social services"; an alpine zone and an aquatic zone; a zone of silence; a pleasure zone; and a sports zone complete with stadiums, swimming pools, and tracks.

The articles on landscape preservation, planning, and design, which appeared on a fairly regular basis in French periodicals from the late 1930s through the 1950s—particularly in Urbanisme—reflected the evolution of the landscape architecture profession and its perception. Authors like Henri Pasquier, Robert Joffet, and Daniel Collin anticipated the future with a quantifiable landscape made of trees and typified open spaces. André Vera, knighted "counselor of urbanism," still exemplified the old guard concerned with style, poetry, and morals. Perhaps it was writing that carried Vera from his antebellum idealistic and Catholic landscape stance through the German occupation and well into the 1950s.[64]

Although Pasquier used scientific and quantitative arguments to demonstrate the necessity for open spaces and greenery, he professed a distrust of landscape engineering. Reaffirming Duchêne's wish expressed at the 1937 International Congress of Garden Architects, Pasquier demanded that a landscape specialist design the urban espaces verts.[65] He valued the input of the much-underestimated gardener, who he thought should join the team of architects and engineers in regional studies.[66] Henri Pasquier's measuring of the landscape went hand in hand with a romantic idealism of nature and region — a recurring theme of the Vichy regime. His 1939 article on espaces verts in cities outlined the agenda for both the Occupation and the postwar landscape. Following the focus of the late 1930s on specialized spaces, Pasquier's landscape comprised sports fields, playgrounds, public parks, cemeteries, nature preserves, roads, and planning. Like Canneel, Pasquier frequently associated the word "rational" with "landscape." But unlike Canneel, Pasquier avoided formal issues altogether. Prescient of the moribund landscapes of 1960s planning, the so-called espaces verts were sized and sited primarily according to the ratio of open space to building and to the density of population. Aesthetics appeared secondary.

With the aerial bombings of 1944, France would experience a second and ravaging wave of destruction. General De Gaulle, then provisional chief of government, placed Raoul Dautry at the head of the newly created Ministry of Reconstruction and Urbanism. Architects and urbanists were assigned projects for reconstructing recently bombed cities such as Le Havre, Royan, Boulogne-sur-mer, and Maubeuge. Long-awaited commissions materialized for rebuilding towns like Orléans which were heavily damaged in 1940.[67] Dautry did not reject the initiatives of Vichy's previous reconstruction efforts, a policy that allowed Henri Pasquier, among others, to play an active role in the new ministry, in spite of his Occupation activities.

The last reconstruction of France still needed to answer practical and urgent demands like housing and infrastructure, which were in turn linked to structural issues such as *remembrement* and the protection of forested domains. Remembrement, which refers to both land reform and urban reallotment, would significantly alter the physiognomy of France. If landscape engineers like Pasquier studied the visual relationship between roadway and countryside, other specialists assessed the regional and national landscape in quantifiable terms. Agronomists, engineers from Ponts et chaussées and Eaux et forêts, planners, and legislators debated how to restructure France economically and functionally. Little was said of the effect their reforms would have on the visual character of various regions.

In 1946, France remained extremely regionalized agriculturally. Farmland in the north and east was divided into long rectangular plots arranged in bundles; buildings were clustered. The irregular fields of Normandy were lined with hedges, and their constructions scattered. In the south, the parcels varied in size and form.[68] In the spirit of modernization, productivity, and economy of infrastructure, the entire landscape of France was reformed. Although articles and reports advocated the preservation of the countryside for its touristic and symbolic values — free of visual pollutants like sports fields, air strips, and roads — the agricultural landscape was assessed strictly scientifically by agronomists, geologists, and hydrologists. A planner saw the technocratic approach as the only alternative for redeeming the rural slums of the old order.[69]

A decade later, landscape architect Jacques Sgard sought a national vision for the French landscape abroad: in the Netherlands — there, the reconstruction effort centered on the creation and the restoration of polders, and on agrarian reform.[70] To Sgard, the Dutch model was worth studying for its pairing of private initiative and state regulation, but above all for its landscape consciousness. Landscape preservation was a matter for both specialists and the general public. The new twentieth-century agricultural landscape was conceived for the rural population. Although Sgard described the result as functional and eschewing all picturesque tendencies, he revealed the romantic vision of a modernist when he described the efficient and utilitarian countryside as the perfect "natural" antidote to the overcrowded urban centers.[71] Sgard's exposure to the expansive scale of Dutch landscape planning would, however, strongly influence his subsequent reclamation projects.

During the interwar years architects, urbanists, artists, contractors, and engineers concerned with garden and park design and landscape planning had alternatively called themselves landscape architects, landscape engineers, and garden architects. They had specialized in forestry or horticulture. While the École du Breuil in Vincennes directed its students toward the maintenance of the existing domain of parks and gardens, the École Nationale d'Horticulture at Versailles trained landscape contractors and designers.[72] With the establishment of the Society of Architects in 1940, the architectes-paysagistes had to give up their architectural title and part of their identity.[73] For several years the landscape profession would fight for accreditation and statutory recognition.[74]

At De Gaulle's request, a landscape design program was created in 1946 within the National School of Horticulture of Versailles and placed under the tutelage of the Ministry of Agriculture. The degree of "Paysagiste D.P.L.G." complemented the study of horticulture with that of the art of gardens. This ambivalence between a scientific and an artistic education may be both cause and symptom of the dichotomy at the heart of the profession. The first generation of paysagistes answered the need for specialization and a formal understanding of design that went beyond the technical knowledge of horticulturists. The early graduates of Versailles were said to have moved into the field of urbanism, where the opportunity of large-scale projects lay. Other design tendencies were reflected in the teachings of André Riousse and Henri Thébaud.[75]

Although Riousse was trained as an architect, he is best remembered for his gardens and courtyards. For the 1925 Exposition des Arts Décoratifs Industriels et Modernes, he conceived a garden court that was awarded a Grand Prix. His inheriting a landscape contracting firm during the 1930s allowed him to extend his design practice to estates and urban gardens [Figure 4–17]. Although he focused on the residential scale, he also studied the recasting of gardens and parks into espaces verts and their impact on social housing. He had designed the grounds for the garden suburb of La Butte Rouge in Chatenay-Malabry in 1931. At Versailles, planting design was taught by Henri Thébaud, a strong proponent of the *style régulier*. Throughout the 1930s he had promoted a garden that was reformed by modern living and yet was decorative. To him, cubism offered motifs and color combinations that could easily translate into the flower beds of a modern garden.[76] Another contributor to the 1925 Exposition des Arts Décoratifs, Marguerite Charageat, lectured on garden history. Less focused on the decorative were the teachings of Albert Audias, who added a planning and horticultural dimension to the new landscape section of Versailles.[77]

With only one year of design education following the standard horticultural training, the school of Versailles failed to fashion paysagistes who carried the clout of predecessors such as Duchêne and Forestier. As the reconstruction debate converged toward housing and urbanism, the surrounding espaces verts became by-products of architectural and zoning requirements. Surfaces replaced spaces in the shaping of landscapes; paysagistes, unable to bridge the gap between garden design and planning, served as technical consultants

Figure 4–17.
Le Bois Fleuri estate, Bougival, France, circa 1950. André Riousse.
Allée with dwarf weeping rose bushes and Lombardy poplars.
[*Petits jardins d'aujourd'hui*, volume 1]

for grading, drainage, and planting. The newly defined profession already suffered from the schism between art and science.

THE 1950S AND ONWARD: AMNESIC RECOVERY

Robert Joffet transitioned smoothly between the Vichy years and his tenure as head of parks, gardens, and espaces verts for the city of Paris and the Seine département. Representing the French interests of landscape architecture at the 1951 World Urbanism Day, he assessed the state of public open space and the future plans for increasing the ratio of vegetation to inhabitants.[78] His report included the mandatory numbers, planning schemes, and various types of espaces verts duly classified. His mission included the preservation of the existing domain of gardens and parks, the management of street trees, new use requirements, and the reduction of maintenance costs. Modern parks were to address the functions of the past as well as the demands of sports and health with contemporary means. The projects he chose to illustrate his arguments indicated the ambiguous position of landscape architecture among the design professions. He alternated the formality of existing grounds like the Champ-de-Mars with the rusticity of restored forests; matter-of-fact neighborhood playing fields designed by architects with restored parterres and flower beds in traffic rotaries; and collaborative projects between the park service and the corps of the Ponts et chaussées. A few years later Joffet reiterated his call for the preservation of public open spaces, whether fields, forests, or vineyards, and for the respect of French soil and streams.[79] He demanded the education of both public and designer. Believing that the landscape architect should join the architectural team from the onset of projects, he suggested that their collaboration would be more fertile were their training more similar. While landscape studies fell under the Ministry of Agriculture, like the school of Eaux et forêts, architecture followed the directives of the National Ministry of Education and Fine Arts. Joffet also saw in the growing importance of "vegetal decor" the necessity for the "man of art" to master aesthetics in addition to grading, drainage, and planting.[80] In the same issue of *Urbanisme*, he reviewed the Floralies Internationales.

Robert Joffet's Floralies were modeled after the popular Belgian floral displays at Ghent.[81] The show opened on 24 April 1959 as the inaugural event for the Palais du Centre National des Industries et Techniques (CNIT) at La Défense; it lasted ten days. With its one-hundred-sixty-foot-tall vault

spanning over seven hundred feet and resting on three points, the CNIT building offered a futuristic, if incongruous, framework for the flower show. Eighteen acres of display were distributed on five floors around a central open core, which allowed viewing from above. With the Floralies Joffet mastered the recovery of garden design as art and effaced his recent image as the head landscape architect for Parisian public works under the Occupation. The 1959 event became a promotional operation for both horticulturists and landscape designers. Joffet presented his Floralies as a didactic project that equated garden design with art, bound to improve the morals of the masses. He saw the moral calm of flower contemplation as the necessary antidote to a contemporary life dominated by mechanization. Finally, the various displays were to represent international amity and celebrate cultural differences. Although a symbol of France, the Floralies were also an international event with the participation of twenty countries. Landscape architecture was not merely an artistic discipline, it was grounded in technology and science; thus various displays promoted the progress made in the fields of genetics and plant pathology.

Within the triangulated plan of the CNIT Joffet sought the "unity of composition and the vistas that are to be found in a beautiful landscape [while] giving a particular character to each of its diverse parts."[82] The intensity and density of the floral displays formed a hyperlandscape, where permanent monitoring and replacement of nonperforming specimens allowed perfect and continuous blooms. In this Disneyfied landscape, time and temperature stood still; the garden was objectified as a self-contained entity within the greater mosaic of the Floralies.

If the 1959 event carried a didactic mission in educating the masses about beauty and flowers, it also served as a giant billboard for landscape architects and contractors. In these times of renewed affluence, gardens were objects of consumption affordable to most. The second level featured fifty thousand square feet of exhibition space devoted to the "Fine Arts"—books, tapestries, and photographs—with a particular emphasis on the work of contemporary designers, including the renovation and creation of landscapes, parks, and residential gardens. To Joffet, the midcentury art of designing landscapes and gardens had fallen into a sort of obsolescence. Through the CNIT exhibition he hoped to revive this lost art. Ignoring the recent past and the diminutive scale of most contemporary gardens, he cited the seventeenth-century's "superb pleasure of forcing nature."

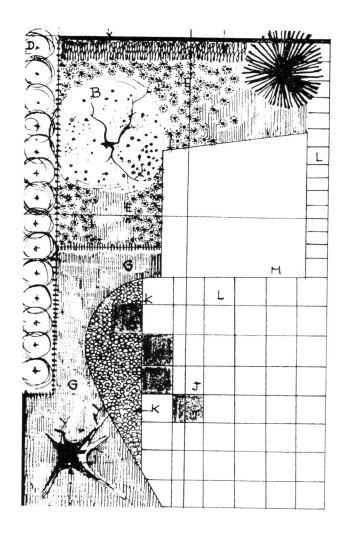

Figure 4–18.
Floralies Internationales, La Défense, 1959.
Daniel Collin. Robert Joffet, head land-
scape architect. Garden for the Glassware
Syndicate.
[Urbanisme]

Figure 4–19.
Floralies Internationales, La Défense, 1959.
Mrs. Couette. Robert Joffet, head land-
scape architect. Garden for the Galeries
Lafayette.
[Urbanisme]

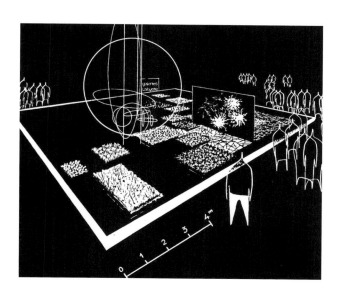

Appealing to the patriotic strain of garden consumers, he described gardens and planted terraces as "dazzling manifestations of culture and taste."[83] Gardens were for sale, and they helped to sell tourist destinations and consumer goods. There were gardens representing Parisian Perfumers and the Glassware Syndicate by Daniel Collin; the booth of the department store Galeries Lafayette was a garden "decorated" by a Mrs. Couette [Figures 4–18, 4–19]. Gardens advertised the tourist attractions of "great French cities" or regions, like the Rose nurseries of the Loire Valley by Henri Brison, another early graduate of Versailles, like Collin.

The additional weight of soil, the difficulty of waterproofing the concrete slabs and allowing for drainage did not deter the committee. The Floralies were a marketing and media success, in spite of the astronomical cost of the event and its limited duration. Joffet boasted that there were 1,700,000 visitors during the nine days the show was open to the public.[84] At La Défense, the combination of the CNIT's engineering feat with the horticultural brilliance of its Floralies fully expressed the postwar economic recovery of *Les Trente Glorieuses*, and for De Gaulle, the "genius of France."[85] Under the "largest vault on earth," Joffet had orchestrated the revival of the garden, a garden that was decorative and photogenic, a garden that appealed to the masses [Figure 4–20]. Landscape architects became celebrities, like decorators and actors.

One popular magazine, *Connaissance des arts*, led an inquiry into finding the appropriate style for the mid-1950s garden.[86] The article featured the garden of actor and singer Maurice Chevalier and sought the opinions of Joffet, Pasquier, and the Englishman Russell Page. Comfort and ease of maintenance, and respite from agitation and speed, were invoked as generators of new designs. The contemporary garden need not represent nature, for that could be reached with the automobile and experienced while camping. The Frenchman was no gardener, and "his" garden, reduced in size, should rely on perennials, turf, and paved paths. The landscape architect, or "man of art," needed to address psychological, functional, and material issues to design a garden.[87] In his answer to what the contemporary garden may be, Joffet deemed the psychological aspect essential to design. To him, French gardens were not based on a love of plants but on the desire for décor. The classical designer had orchestrated the transition between architecture and nature through strict parterres and broad perspectives leading to the forest and surrounding countryside. Similarly,

Figure 4–20.
Floralies Internationales, La Défense, 1964.
Daniel Collin, head landscape architect.
View of the central hall on Level 3; the pools of water form a molecular structure.
[*Floralies*]

Figure 4–23.
Parc André Malraux, Nanterre, France,
1967. Jacques Sgard.
The park becomes a superlative evocation
of nature, with strong concrete modeling
forming the adventure landscape and an
undulating pond answering the waves of
the towers of La Défense in the distance.
[Dorothée Imbert]

Figure 4–24.
Playground. France, circa 1958.
[*Urbanisme*]

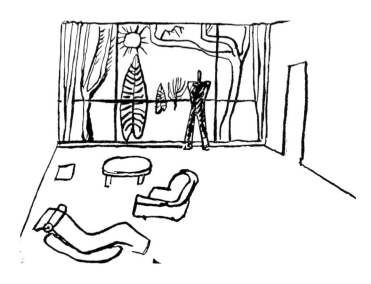

Figure 4–25.
**"The essential pleasures have entered
dwellings," 1948. Le Corbusier.**
Eugène Claudius-Petit would praise the
corbusian "radiant cities" from which man
could admire the cycle of nature from a
window.
[*L'Architecture d'aujourd'hui*]

faintly present landscape planner. In the French reconstruction years, architects and urbanists remained more visible: Jacques Gréber worked on restructuring Rouen, and Théo Leveau, Dunkirk. Michel Béjot, class of 1946 at Versailles, was part of the espaces verts department of Le Havre from 1950 to 1990; he described the city as twice destroyed, first by the war and again by the architecture and urbanism of Auguste Perret.[105] The early graduates of the newly refurbished school of Versailles supposedly joined the ranks of urbanists, but the paysagistes' contributions were hardly represented in the pages of *Urbanisme*, where such projects were published. Articles on the restructuring of Boulogne-sur-mer, Royan, and Florange did not credit landscape architects. Jean-Bernard Perrin, who graduated with Jacques Sgard in 1947, would play an important role in the development of Paris and the preservation of existing espaces verts.[106] Sgard himself would be influenced by the Dutch model and would overlay planning with landscape architecture. Although he attained renown with the sculpture garden of the Parc Floral in Vincennes and the Parc André Malraux in Nanterre, both conceived in 1967, and designed espaces verts for several housing projects, he would aim his landscape practice toward environmental planning and land reclamation [Figure 4–23]. Other graduates like Henri Brison and Daniel Collin remained mostly within the domain of residential design, with a particular attention to plants.[107] The class of 1953 included Martine Canneel, Jean Canneel-Claes's daughter and future collaborator, and Michel Bourne, who would be associated with the *grands ensembles*, large-scale housing projects such as Les Minguettes, near Lyons.

Henri Pasquier's earlier classification of espaces verts — private and semipublic gardens, playgrounds and educational gardens, sports fields, "society" gardens, cemeteries, and edible gardens—had announced the specialization of the landscape [Figure 4–24]. Different users and different functions called for different landscapes.[108] This scientific approach allowed the modernization of a field whose primary material, vegetation, did not structurally evolve. The park was essentially modified by its use: contemporaneity was manifest in the surface of a running track rather than in the alignment of trees. The terms *espace libre* and *espace vert* were assessed comparatively in the 1952 issue of *Urbanisme*. One author qualified the espace vert as an espace libre with "green garnish." Both fell under the responsibility of urbanists. Another article requested that the city be

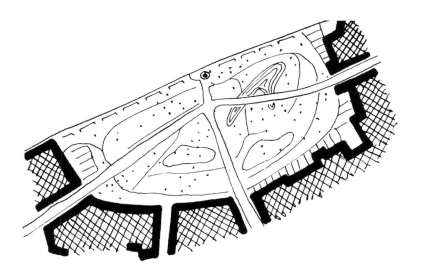

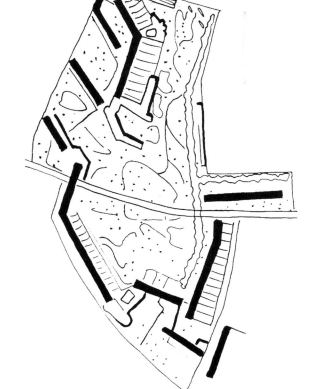

Figure 4–26.
Cité Rotterdam, Strasbourg, France, 1951.
Eugène Beaudouin. Housing slabs with
central garden.
The development of Parc Monceau (above)
was seen as the ideal urban precedent,
where residents lived close to nature and
the semi-public open space served the
entire city. Similarly, Beaudouin's "garden"
was to be at the heart of both housing project and the park system of Strasbourg.
[*Urbanisme*]

Figure 4–27.
Parc Saint-John Perse. Reims, France, 1970.
Jacques Simon.
Large plantings of *Populus alba* "Nivea"
filter the views. Stairs lead to the rim of the
grassy bowl.
[Dorothée Imbert]

shaped by "horticultural urbanism" and, instead of gardens within the city, envisioned the city within a garden.[109]

The arrival of Eugène Claudius-Petit at the Ministry of Reconstruction and Urbanism in 1948 expressed a shift toward the Corbusian attitude of rebuilding cities. Urban blocks became further disengaged from historical structures and from the landscape. A strong proponent of Le Corbusier's urban theories, Claudius-Petit advocated the "reconciliation of houses with nature" through the erasure of the traditional Haussmannian block, which he deemed responsible for transforming cities into "deserts of stone." Paraphrasing the architect from whom he would commission the Unité d'habitation in Marseilles, Claudius-Petit described radiant cities in which man could admire the cycle of nature from his windows [Figure 4–25].[110] The block had exploded, moving away from the dusty and noisy street. Hygiene would result from the combined parameters of greenery, sun, and ventilation. To replace the sparse town square or public gar-den of the overcrowded city, architects evoked idyllic visions of housing blocks "intimately connect-ed to the garden."[111] There was little innovation in their image of the landscape, however. The nineteenth-century development of the eighteenth-century Parc Monceau, a perennial favorite of Le Corbusier, was deemed ideal [Figure 4–26]. It afforded views and physical access to the people living around it. The appeal of the Parc Monceau did not rest on the quality or the arrangement of its plantings or the composition of its vistas and fabrics, but simply on its accessibility and its social amenities. The slabs and towers that replaced the old order of the closed urban block rarely established such a close connection to the landscape around them; however. The new world was distributed according to four distinct uses — housing, work, recreation, and circulation. Within such a scheme, the zoning of the landscape as a quantifiable and use-specific space would ultimately lead to its abstraction.

Théo Leveau, a disciple of Forestier and a professor at Ver-sailles, evaluated the relationship of housing and espaces verts as falling short of the much-advertised insertion of architecture in nature.[112] He conceded that the rejection of street alignment had perhaps improved the orientation of buildings to sun and air but had left only residual spaces surrounded by slabs and towers at ground level. Poor plant-ing, ravaged soil, and paltry budgets prevented these frag-ments from ever becoming the parks trumpeted by planners and architects. To Leveau, the landscape plan conceived after

the fact was only a filler. The previously private estate offered an alternative for a ready-to-use park or garden, as long as the siting and construction of buildings respected the exist-ing terrain and plantings. For the espaces verts to fulfill their mission as new landscapes, however, it was necessary to conceive the site plan well ahead of construction. Leveau considered that the ideal delay between preliminary site design and completion of a project was thirty years. Then the essential principles of landscape design — namely the play of masses and voids, of constructed and planted vol-umes, of colors, and the variations of light and shade — could be fully developed. Unfortunately, rarely did the housing industry allow the necessary budget and time for the completion of the essential garden. Thus, concluded Leveau, it would be wise to abandon the open site plan and return to the more traditional block aligned with the street, so as to keep housing from floating into acres and acres of wastelands.[113]

The housing projects that sprung up on the outskirts of cities such as Paris, Lyons, and Marseilles reflected both the Corbusian heritage of planned urbanism and the housing crisis of the 1950s and 1960s. The residual espace vert, constricted by the geometries of towers and slabs, remained an insufficient palliative to technocratic and monofunctional architecture. In this global programming for dwellings, land-scape was dominated by planning logic. The 1960s crystallized not only the questioning of the architect's role in society but also the ambiguity of a landscape architect's profession riddled with specialization. Leveau's concern for the future of espaces verts revealed once more the lag between archi-tectural forces and the shaping of the landscape. The latter reacted to the former: as the urban block dissolved, vegeta-tion lost its spatial definition. The grands ensembles featured large housing slabs or towers floating within space defined, or divided, by circulation axes rather than by the landscape. Indeed, paysagistes seldom participated in the original stages of site planning. At best, they could draw on existing parks, save mature trees, and minimize the grading impact of streets and pathways on soils. Architects imposed a new order; paysagistes responded with the remnants of a displaced landscape. The profession, split between the quantifiers of trees per hectare and the floral decorators, lacked a formal vision that would not only stand against, but subvert, the new planning practices.

CODA

Perhaps the curriculum of Versailles originally lacked the design focus necessary for its graduates to establish a dialogue with architects and urbanists. Nevertheless, the late 1960s witnessed the renewal, or the true beginning, of the profession of paysagiste. Jacques Simon, who graduated from Versailles in 1959, and Michel Corajoud, who brought his decorative arts education to landscape design, both joined the multidisciplinary team of Atelier d'Architecture et d'Urbanisme (AUA) at the end of the 1960s.[114] Simon expressed the power of site work in projects like Les Châtillons (1967) and Parc Saint-John Perse (1970), in Reims. The density of planting and the undulating terrain physically and perceptually resisted the harsh surrounding housing blocks of Les Châtillons. Parc Saint-John Perse has become a green enclave within the adjacent suburban development. Simon modeled the ten-acre site by bulldozing forty thousand cubic meters of earth left from the construction of the housing units [Figure 4–27]. A series of grassy bowls and berms emerged from, and disappeared in, large expanses of single-species plantings to compose a "hyperlandscape," one that reinforced both nature and the manipulation of machinery.

Thus the 1970s would witness a renewed contribution of paysagistes to French urbanism and housing. If specialization had simultaneously outlined and diminished their professional arena, landscape designers would mark their territory by appropriating anew the artistic and cultural forces that had receded behind technical education. The distinctive formalism with which Simon and Corajoud stamped the suburban no-man's landscape established a mediation between natural and Cartesian worlds. These compositions remembered the sensuousness of the earth and yet coincided with the forces of urbanism. The destruction of World War II had offered a tabula rasa for planning. A rupture occurred not only in the urban fabric but also in the evolution of a landscape tradition rooted in history. Landscape practice initially redesigned its foundations upon horticulture; three decades later it would emerge as a design discipline capable of shaping the land both formally and culturally, not simply in response to, but in conjunction with, architecture and planning.

NOTES

1. I avoided translating the term *espace vert* as open space, to allow for the differentiation between *espace vert* and *espace libre*. The first term attempted to establish a direct equivalence with the prior tradition of parks and gardens; the second appeared as the reality of a sort of space left unbuilt.

2. See Rémi Baudouï, "Imaginaire culturel et représentations des processus de reconstruction en Europe après 1945," in *Les reconstructions en Europe* (1945–1949), Dominique Barjot, Rémi Baudouï, and Danièle Voldman, eds. (Caen: Éditions Complexe, 1997), pp. 309–21.

3. Overseas territories provided fields for experimentation, both in landscape and in urbanism. Henri Pasquier, who began practicing landscape architecture in the late 1920s, praised Henri Prost's and Albert Laprade's plans and designs for Casablanca, Rabat, and Marrakech. He saw that the city centers of Indochina, western French Africa, and Algeria were clearly marked by the rational and "tasteful" designs of French planners. "Les surfaces vertes dans la ville," *Urbanisme*, 8, no. 68, 1939, p. 16. Raphaël Verwilghen began planning cities in the Belgian Congo in the late 1920s. The landscape planner Louis van der Swaelmen lauded Verwilghen for his "survey" approach, which allowed him to site towns and neighborhoods ideally through an analysis of natural and social factors at both a regional and a local scale. Verwilghen played an important role in both reconstructions. After World War I, he headed the Office des Régions Dévastées; in 1940 he directed the urbanism and architecture section of the Commissariat Général à la Restauration du Pays. Louis van der Swaelmen, "Raphaël Verwilghen urbaniste au Congo," *La cité*, 7, no. 8, 1929, pp. 103–4. For Verwilghen's plans, see Xavier Carton de Wiart, "Les lois de l'urbanisme au Congo Belge," *Reconstruction*, 3, nos. 22, 23, 1942, pp. 6–10, 10–13, respectively. Landscape architect Jean Canneel-Claes also participated in Belgium's colonial expansion. See Archives Verwilghen, Katholieke Universiteit Leuven and Archives Africaines, Brussels.

4. Jean Royer, of the Ministry of Building Reconstruction and founder of the periodical *Urbanisme* in 1932, defined the reconstruction of 1919 as an "exceptional opportunity and a missed opportunity" for French urbanism. See "Reconstruction 1941," *Urbanisme*, 10, no. 72, 1941, p. 65. Similarly, Victor Bourgeois regretted that the reconstruction of devastated regions had not been based on "today's reality but on images of yester-day." "Belgique," *Architecture d'aujourd'hui*, 17, nos. 7–8, 1946, p. 103.

5. See *Cités-Jardins, 1920–1940* (Brussels: Archives d'Architecture Moderne, 1994), and *Rassegna* (L'architettura in Belgio, 1920–1940), 34, 1988. Belgian modernist architecture took its cues from the Netherlands, Germany, and France. For instance, Louis-Herman de Koninck paid a tribute to the Viennese Secession, a rite of passage on his path toward modernism, in the 1922 project for the city of Veterans at Dour. Unlike in England and the Netherlands, there were no subsidies for social housing in Belgium until after World War I. Architects, theorists, planners, and landscape architects strove to influence the legislation in order to facilitate the advent of this new environment. As in France, however, the advocates of this "planning order" did not quite succeed: nostalgia and private enterprise took the lead, and towns and cities were essentially rebuilt the way they used to look.

6. Although van der Swaelmen (1883–1929) is essentially remembered as an urbanist, his apprenticeship with his father, the landscape architect Louis-Léopold van der Swaelmen, left a strong imprint on his vision of town and city planning. He fled Belgium for the Netherlands during World War I, where he created the Dutch-Belgian Committee for Civic Art with another Belgian expatriate, Paul Otlet (Le Corbusier's patron for the 1929 Mundaneum project). Van der Swaelmen also planned the housing development Les Pins Noirs in Woluwé St-Pierre (1923–26) and collaborated with Huib Hoste on Klein Rusland in Selzaete (1921–23). Van der Swaelmen founded the periodical *La Cité* with planner Raphaël Verwilghen and architect Huib Hoste in 1919; he also edited the column "Parks and Gardens" in the magazine *Tekné*. Van der Swaelmen designed formal gardens for the estate of Maillard. For a list of his contributions to the fields of urbanism and garden design, see "Bref aperçu de l'œuvre de Louis van der Swaelmen," *La cité*, 7, no. 6, 1929, p. 100, and *Cités-Jardins, 1920–1940*, p. 108.

7. Architect Henry van de Velde created the school following a royal decree of 2 March 1926; it opened its doors in 1927. Van der Swaelmen died in 1929. See *La Cambre, 1928–1978* (Brussels: Archives d'Architecture Moderne, 1979).

8. Victor Bourgeois, a significant player in the development of social housing, acknowledged the formative influence of De Stijl in his Cité Moderne at Berchem-Ste Agathe, a tenants' cooperative built 1922–25. The houses that lined "rue du Cubisme" and the central urban square, designed by Louis van der Swaelmen, would bring him recognition on the international scene. Hannes Meyer selected a view of Bourgeois's Cité Moderne to illustrate his article on the Belgian avant-garde. See "Junge Kunst In Belgien," *Das Werk*, 12, 1925, pp. 257–76. Le Logis-Floréal expressed in its coherence the harmonious collaboration of three young architects: Jean-Jules Eggericx, Lucien François, and Raymond Moenaert. Kapelleveld, in contrast, revealed the formal disagreements that arose between the modernist Huib Hoste and the more traditional Antoine Pompe, Paul Rubbers, and G. F. Hoeben.

9. See "Cité du Kapelleveld à Woluwé-Saint-Lambert," *Cités-Jardins, 1920–1940*, pp. 76–83.

10. Jean Canneel-Claes was born to a family of painters and sculptors on 12 July 1909, in Schaerbeek, near Brussels. He studied at La Cambre under Louis van der Swaelmen before apprenticing with the more traditional garden designer Jules Buyssens. Buyssens held a significant public role, as a frequent contributor to periodicals, as the head of Brussels' parks department, and as gardener-in-chief of the 1935 Belgian centennial exposition. The sculptures of Eugène Canneel, Jean Canneel-Claes's father, were displayed in a garden designed by Jules Buyssens at the 1925 Paris Exposition Internationale des Arts Décoratifs et Industriels Modernes. In 1930, Canneel returned to La Cambre to study under Jean-Jules Eggericx, one of the architects for the garden cities of Logis-Floréal.

11. The project correspondence reveals Canneel's admiration for Le Corbusier, the architect's tenuous commitment to the project, and the lack of patience of the commissioner, Henri Leclercq, banker and Canneel's future father-in-law. See the Canneel Archives at Fondation Le Corbusier, Paris. For a comparative description of Le Corbusier's and de Koninck's projects for Canneel, see Marc Dubois, "La virtuosité individualiste de Le Corbusier: Le fonctionnalisme parfait de Koninck," *Maisons d'hier et d'aujourd'hui*, no. 67, 1985, pp. 50–75. The Canneel/Leclercq house was published in Le Corbusier's *Œuvre complète* as "Maison de Mr. X à Bruxelles 1929." See Le Corbusier et Pierre Jeanneret *Œuvre complète de 1910–1929* (Zurich: Les Éditions d'Architecture, 1929), pp. 204–5.

12. Fondation Le Corbusier, 12–14–52.

13. Le Corbusier's Canneel House featured a swimming pool on the garage's roof, which was dismissed by Leclerq for being inappropriate for the Belgian climate. See "Observations," dated 14 September 1929, Fondation Le Corbusier, 12–14–55.

14. P. L. Flouquet, "Le jardin fonctionnel," interview with Jean Canneel-Claes, *Bâtir*, no. 24, 1934, pp. 926–29.

15. Jean Canneel-Claes, "Le jardin fonctionnel," *Bâtir*, no. 5, 1933, p. 179.

16. Jean Canneel-Claes, "Le rôle du jardin dans l'architecture fonctionnelle," *La Revue documentaire*, no. 4, 1933, pp. 49–50.

17. Albert Audias cited by Achille Duchêne in "Premier Congrès International des Architectes de Jardins," typescript (Paris: Société Française des Architectes de Jardins, 1937), pp. 27–28, 37–38.

18. P. L. Flouquet, "L'Association Internationale des Architectes de Jardins Modernistes," *Bâtir*, no. 64, 1938, pp. 130–33. This association was seen as complementary, rather than detrimental, to other professional groups. The Association Professionnelle des Architectes de Jardins was founded in 1934. Louis van der Swaelmen had created the Société Belge des Urbanistes et Architectes Modernistes (SBUAM) in 1919; it was dissolved in 1968.

19. James Rose, "Why Not Try Science?" *Pencil Points*, 20, no. 12, 1939, pp. 777–79.

20. P. L. Flouquet, "L'Association Internationale," pp. 130–31.

21. Canneel had previously visited the 1925 Exposition des Arts Décoratifs et Industriels Modernes in Paris, which featured several of the radical garden designs of the French interwar years; he worked with Jules Buyssens on the Belgian Centennial fair and participated in the design for the Belgian pavilion at the Paris 1937 international exposition.

22. See "'L'amitié des fleurs et des arbres': Les jardins et parterres de l'exposition," *Bâtir*, no. 78, 1939, pp. 214–15; "Vues sur l'architecture de l'exposition," interview with Ivon Falise, chief architect of the Exposition Internationale de l'Eau, *Bâtir*, no. 78, 1939, pp. 207–9.

23. See the interview of Georges Truffaut, deputy mayor for Liège's public works department, "L'exposition et le Grand-Liège," *Bâtir*, no. 78, 1939, pp. 204–6.

24. For a plan and early photographs of the de Vuyst estate, see "Propriété en Flandres," *La Maison*, 3, no. 9, 1947, pp. 233–36.

25. See ibid., p. 294.

26. The plants were described as autochtones, that is, native of, or long-adapted to, the region.

27. See "Principes et activités de la section d'architecture paysagère au Commissariat Général à la Restauration du Pays," *Reconstruction*, 4, nos. 36–37, 1943, p. 4.

28. The Parque de María Luisa was dedicated in 1914 and the Ibero-American Fair inaugurated in 1929, almost simultaneously with the Barcelona exposition. Théo Leveau, who became a central figure in the hazy postwar landscape architecture scene, collaborated with Forestier on the plan for Havana from 1926 to 1930. A fine example of Forestier's smaller-scale designs remains in the 1906 Iris Garden at Bagatelle, in Paris. See Jean-Claude Nicolas Forestier, *Grandes villes et systèmes de parcs* (Paris: Hachette, 1906, reprint, Paris: Institut Français d'Architecture, Norma, 1997); Jean-Claude Nicolas Forestier, *Jardins: Carnet de plans et de dessins* (Paris: Émile-Paul, 1920); and Dorothée Imbert, "J. C. N. Forestier: Plants and Planning," in *The Modernist Garden in France* (New Haven: Yale University Press, 1993), pp. 11–25.

29. Jean-Charles Moreux designed several gardens. His Square Croulebarbe (1930) in Paris still stands today, like Jacques Gréber's Parc Kellerman on the southern edge of the city. Paul Vera, mostly remembered for his murals and tapestries, collaborated with Moreux on numerous city gardens. See Imbert, *The Modernist Garden in France*; and Susan Day, *Jean-Charles Moreux: Architecte-décorateur-paysagiste* (Paris: Institut Français d'Architecture, Norma, 1999).

30. Henri Duchêne and Achille Duchêne in particular are mostly remembered for their recreation of the gardens of Vaux-le-Vicomte and Champs-sur-Marne. On Albert's social planning, see Achille Duchêne, *Pour la reconstruction des cités industrielles (étude économique et sociale)* (Paris: Bibliothèque de la renaissance des cités, 1919). Paul Otlet, who was Le Corbusier's patron for the Mundaneum and the cofounder of the Comité Néerlando-Belge d'Art Civique with Louis van der Swaelmen, wrote the preface to Duchêne's text.

31. Duchêne, *Pour la reconstruction des cités industrielles*, p. 54.

32. Ibid., pp. 54–55.

33. For maps comparing the extent of destruction in November 1918 and September 1941, see Jean Royer, "Reconstruction 1941." The number of buildings destroyed in 1940 was double that of World War I; France lost 20 percent of its housing.

34. The reconstruction of the Val-de-Loire became a symbolic project for the Vichy Government and expressed a compromise between functionalism and regionalism; however, construction had not yet begun when the Allies landed. See Rémi Baudouï, "Dalla tradizione alla modernità: La ricostruzione in Francia." *Rassegna (La ricostruzione in Europa nel secondo dopoguerra)*, 54, 1993, pp. 68–75.

35. See Romy Golan, "Conclusion: A Moralized Tale," in *Modernity and Nostalgia: Art and Politics in France Between the Wars* (New Haven: Yale University Press, 1995), pp. 155–63.

36. Henri Pasquier, "Les Avocats du paysage," *Urbanisme (Jardins et espaces verts)*, no. 86, 1943, pp. 16–19. Before joining the Ministry of Reconstruction and Urbanism, Pasquier taught horticulture at Versailles and designed numerous gardens. See André Riousse, *Petits jardins d'aujourd'hui*, and René Pechère, *Petits jardins d'aujourd'hui, deuxième série* (Paris: Éditions d'art, Charles Moreau, n.d. [c. 1952]).

37. Pasquier, "Les Avocats du paysage," pp. 18–19.

38. In "Les Avocats du paysage," Pasquier repeated the arguments he had presented earlier in "Les Routes fleuries et la reconstitution du paysage." In the prewar version, however, he openly praised the interaction between the German landscape architect and civil engineer in the design of freeways. See Henri Pasquier, "Les Routes fleuries et la reconstitution du paysage," *Urbanisme*, 8, no. 68, 1939, pp. 40–45. See Gert Gröning, "Teutonic Myth, Rubble, and Recovery: Landscape Architecture in Germany," in this volume.

39. For a description of the case for native vegetation along the Autobahn, see "Roadside Planting on Hitler's Highways: An Inquiry from Germany and an American Answer," reply by Frederick Law Olmsted, Jr., *Landscape Architecture*, 30, no. 4, 1940, pp.179–82.

40. Pasquier had discussed the topic of plantings along roads and freeways as part of the

urbanism of espaces verts in the late 1930s. He refused the Ponts et chaussées vision of the modern road as a treeless and impermeable monolith, like the naked ribbons that unraveled through the Tunisian, Palestinian, and Syrian deserts. Instead Pasquier praised the efforts of the Germans and Italians to integrate their roads with the landscape and to beautify their roadsides. The design and planting of roadways continued to be a topic of interest well into the 1950s.

41. Henri Pasquier, "Les Surfaces vertes dans la ville," pp. 13, 40.

42. André Vera offered the same advice and recommended selecting trees within the regional flora, not for picturesque effect, but to prove one's attachment to the province. Thus, one should prefer French trees and shrubs over the Cedar of Lebanon or the catalpa. André Vera, "Manifeste pour le renouveau de l'art français," *Urbanisme*, 10, no. 72, 1941, p. 56.

43. Vera, "Manifeste pour le renouveau de l'art français." Vera promoted arts and crafts as the true essence of France in several articles throughout the 1930s and 1940s. He saw crafts as being to the region and nation what native plants were to the landscape. As the peasant was linked to the soil, so the region to the nation. France advertised itself as a decentralized state with revived regional identities, in direct contradiction with the technocratic policies of its authoritarian regime.

44. Vera, "Manifeste pour le renouveau de l'art français," p. 55.

45. See Baudouï, "Dalla tradizione alla modernità: La ricostruzione in Francia."

46. See Jean-Louis Cohen and André Lortie, *Des fortifs au périf* (Paris: Picard, 1991), pp. 236–37.

47. Crevel was head of the architecture section for the city of Paris and the Seine Department. Joffet headed the Paris civil engineering section and the planning department for the zone. See Cohen and Lortie, "Un Grand ensemble annulaire sur la zone," in *Des fortifs au périf*, pp. 234–40. In spite of its brevity, the war had a heavy impact. In six weeks 400,000 apartment buildings were damaged, 3,300 bridges destroyed, and industrial production severely diminished. The number of unemployed reached 800,000.

48. For a study of Vichy's impact on Paris, see Rémi Baudouï, *À l'assaut de la région parisienne: Les conditions de naissance d'une politique d'aménagement régional, 1919–1945* (Paris: École d'architecture Paris-Villemin / Bureau de la recherche architecturale, 1990). Cited by Cohen and Lortie, "Un Grand ensemble annulaire," p. 237.

49. Auto workers cleared a 100-hectare (250-acre) site near Porte de Versailles to build a "Centre de recherches techniques et sportives." On this laboratory site methods were tested to assess the grading, drainage, and soil composition best adapted to the various playing fields. Cohen and Lortie, "Un Grand ensemble annulaire," p. 240. The institute was presented at the 1943 Salon des Urbanistes under the title "Centre d'Expériences et d'Information d'Équipement Sportif" in parallel with the project for the Parc Olympique National in Vincennes. See "Les Services Techniques des Parcs et Jardins de la Préfecture de la Seine," *Urbanisme*, 12, nos. 92–93, 1943, pp. 172–74. Several of the projects presented in 1943 were not yet built in 1952. The Parc Pétain was then renamed Parc de La Courneuve. See Robert Joffet, "Le point de vue du Conservateur des Jardins de Paris," *Urbanisme*, 21, nos. 3–4, 1952, pp. 109–24. Unlike the Service de la Conservation des Parcs, Jardins, et Espaces Verts, which maintained the existing landscape body of Paris, Joffet's department concretized new designs. See Bernadette Blanchon, "Les paysagistes en France depuis 1945: L'amorce d'une indiscipline ou la naissance d'une profession," in *Les Espaces publics modernes: Situations et propositions*, Virginie Picon-Lefebvre, ed. (Paris: Le Moniteur, 1997), pp. 191–210.

50. "Les Services Techniques des Parcs et Jardins de la Préfecture de la Seine," pp. 172–74.

51. To Pasquier, the twenty miles of fortifications around Paris could have become a greenbelt of a thousand acres instead of the seventy-four acres of public promenades that were implemented between 1919 and 1936. The glacis of lawn gave way to construction; the wall of low-income housing not only replaced possible linear parks but also made the perimeter of Paris denser and its need for open space more acutely felt. Pasquier, "Les Surfaces vertes dans la ville," pp. 17–18.

52. Recalling the resolutions of the International Congress of Garden Architects, Pasquier advocated that the city's open spaces be designed by "specialists," rather than by architects, since their geometries reduced in scale increased cost. With high maintenance and limited accessibility, architectonic gardens were, to Pasquier, unattractive to both administration and users. The new public garden ought to be specialized and not primarily decorative. At the same time he trusted the urbanist with the siting and sizing of the green space within the city. Pasquier, "Les Surfaces vertes dans la ville," pp. 17–19.

53. Similarly, Louis van der Swaelmen had devoted his attention to protecting Belgian forests as "National Reserves" before World War I. See Louis van der Swaelmen, "Guide du promeneur dans la forêt de Soignes," in collaboration with René Stevens, 2 vols. (Paris: Librairie d'art et d'histoire G. Van Oest et Cie., 1914); and "Étude sur l'aménagement (sylvicole) et le traitement spécial qu'il conviendrait d'appliquer en général aux forêts décrétées 'Réserves Nationales' à titre de patrimoine collectif de beauté naturelle pour la Nation, et en particulier à la forêt de Soignes aux portes de Bruxelles," Proceedings of the Fourth International Congress on Public Art, Brussels 8–12 October 1910. See *Congrès International de l'Art Public: Rapports et comptes rendus* (Brussels: A. Lesigne, 1910).

54. Vera, "Une Phase nouvelle dans l'évolution du jardin," *L'Architecture d'aujourd'hui*, 1937, p. 3.

55. Vera, "Nature et urbanisme," *Urbanisme*, 8, no. 68, 1939.

56. The Commission départementale des Monuments naturels et des Sites de Seine-et-Oise had voted on 12 December 1932 for the protection of the terrace with a buffer zone. See "Pour la protection des Sites et Paysages," *Urbanisme*, no. 19, 1933, pp. 300–304. Unfortunately, the historical landscape would finally lose to the demands of circulation. The A14 motorway was just recently completed, in spite of efforts to limit its impact on the terrace. The superb views are now marred by the constant noise of a freeway deemed in the public interest.

57. Vera saw the rise in crime and insanity and the lack of physical fitness (only 75 percent of young men were deemed fit for military service in 1937) as direct consequences of man's severance from nature. "Nature et urbanisme," p. 2.

58. Pasquier, "Les Surfaces vertes dans la ville," p. 35.

59. Ibid., pp. 10–47.

60. In 1943, Jacques Gréber praised the work of Joffet and of the various reconstruction ministries. To him, the cleansing of *îlots insalubres* and the creation of expansive sites within the city's boundaries by the removal of industries offered a fantastic opportunity for inserting new open spaces within the dense urban fabric. "Les Réseaux d'espaces libres dans les grandes villes," *Urbanisme*, no. 86, 1943, pp. 5–9. The early annular circulation scheme was conceived to relieve traffic within the city proper—to be clearly differentiated from its suburbs—and to facilitate transit toward regional tourist destinations. See Cohen and Lortie, "Un Grand ensemble annulaire."

61. See Henri Gasquet, Président du Touring-Club de France, "La Forêt et la ville," and Henry de Ségogne, "D'un urbanisme de la forêt," *Urbanisme*, 14, nos. 107–8, 1946, pp. 89–90, 91–92, respectively.

62. "N'oublions pas non plus qu'une ville, aussi séduisante que nous la voulons, et qui de plus, se trouvera située sur un champ de bataille historique, ne manquera pas d'attirer les étrangers," Achille Duchêne, "Pour la reconstruction des cités industrielles," p. 29.

63. The 1958 Espaces Verts Plan for Greater Paris reiterated the same issues of protection of historical monuments and sites and tourism management for regional green spaces. See *Espaces verts de la région parisienne* (Paris: Ministère de la Construction, 1958); and Jean-Bernard Perrin, "Protection et aménagement des espaces verts de la région parisienne," *Urbanisme*, 28, no. 64, 1959, pp. 48–61.

64. Landscape designers rarely expressed themselves in print. André Vera, who designed a few gardens with his brother Paul, was an exception; he remained the advocate for the French *jardin régulier* from the beginning of the century to the 1950s. Jean-Claude Nicolas Forestier published several texts on garden design and likely would have continued to publicize his views as well as landscape planning projects had he not died in 1930. Vera was described as "Counselor of Urbanism" in 1947. See Léon Moine, "Urbanisme 115," *Urbanisme*, 16, no. 115, 1947, p. 79.

65. Pasquier, "Les surfaces vertes dans la ville," p. 18.

66. Pasquier saw the elevation of gardeners to the status of esteem granted them in England, Germany, and the United States as necessary to reverse Haussmann's favoring of engineers. Postscript to "Les Surfaces vertes dans la ville," p. 47.

67. Auguste Perret headed the reconstruction of Le Havre; Claude Ferret redesigned Royan; Pierre Vivien reorganized Boulogne-sur-mer; André Lurçat was the urbanist and architect for Maubeuge.

68. See J. Roche, "Le Remembrement," *Techniques et architecture*, 6, nos. 3–4, 1946, pp. 98–100.

69. Guy Pison, "Vers un aménagement rural nouveau," *Techniques et architecture*, 6, nos. 3–4, 1946, pp. 92–94.

70. These interventions included the new polder of Wieringermeer, the rehabilitation of the landscape destroyed by water during the war or in 1953 (Walcheren and Zeeland). The surface of reformed land covered 2.5 million acres. Jacques Sgard, "Le Délassement et l'espace vert aux Pays-Bas: Un Problème national," *Urbanisme*, 28, no. 64, 1959, pp. 28–32.

71. Ibid., p. 32.

72. The École du Breuil issued from the École d'Horticulture de Saint-Mandé, which was created in 1867 by Haussmann in order to train the maintenance personnel for the parks and promenades of Paris.

73. See Blanchon, "Les paysagistes en France depuis 1945," p. 194.

74. The Société Française des Architectes de Jardins, headed by Ferdinand Duprat, began to lobby for the creation of a garden design department within the École Nationale d'Horticulture in 1941. See Blanchon, "Pratiques paysagères en France de 1945 à 1975 dans les grands ensembles d'habitation," research sponsored by the Ministère de l'Équipement, des Transports, et du Logement; Plan Construction et Architecture; Programme Cités Projets, June 1998, pp. 24–25.

75. Jacques Sgard (1929–) graduated from Versailles in 1947 and recalled the teaching of landscape contractor Riousse as being centered on urban squares and gardens, even though the new curriculum answered the desires of the Ministry of Reconstruction and Urbanism. He condemned the spirit of the reconstruction for favoring espaces verts over the landscape. See Annette Vigny, *Jacques Sgard: Paysagiste et urbaniste* (Liège: Pierre Mardaga, 1995), pp. 11, 13.

76. See Henri Thébaud, "La décoration moderne des jardins," in *Jardins d'aujourd'hui* (Paris: Studios "Vie à la Campagne," 1932), pp. 109–14. These instructors were at Versailles from 1945 to 1952. André Riousse taught Composition (Design). I thank Bernadette Blanchon for this information.

77. After graduating as a horticultural engineer in 1925 and working for Ferdinand Duprat, Audias joined Joffet's department in 1941. The Occupation years allowed him to design contextually within the perimeter of the zone and to plan for the future extension of Paris. Audias taught at Versailles from 1946 to 1969; he also lectured at the École d'Ingénieurs des Travaux Publics on the design of sports facilities. See Blanchon, "Pratiques paysagères en France," p. 28.

78. See Joffet, "Le Point de vue du Conservateur des Jardins de Paris," *Urbanisme*, 21, nos. 3–4, 1952, pp. 109–24.

79. Joffet, "L'Espace planté, cadre idéal de la vie," *Urbanisme*, 28, no. 64, 1959, pp. 42–47.

80. Ibid., p. 46.

81. See Joffet, "Les Floralies internationales de Paris 1959," *Urbanisme*, 28, no. 64, 1959, pp. 2–7.

82. Ibid., p. 7.

83. Ibid.

84. The cost was one billion francs, divided between exhibitors and organizers. Joffet assessed that his goal had been met, since the attendance at the Floralies was twice that at the most popular shows at the Grand Palais. Ibid., pp. 4, 7.

85. The development of La Défense as well as grand infrastructure projects like the Boulevard Périphérique and freeways was part of the nation's modernization in the second half of the 1950s. Between 1950 and 1958, France's Gross National Product increased 41 percent. *Les Trente Glorieuses* refers to the thirty years of economic growth that followed the end of World War II. For his Floralies, Joffet received the Legion of Honor. Apparently, De Gaulle described the Floralies and the bridge at Tancarville as equally characteristic of Gallic genius. Cited by Blanchon in "Pratiques paysagères en France de 1945 à 1975 dans les grands ensembles d'habitation," p. 32.

86. "Une grande enquête de 'Connaissance des arts' sur l'art des jardins," *Connaissance des arts*, no. 41, 1955, pp. 20–25.

87. Ibid., p. 20.

88. Ibid., p. 25.

89. See Imbert, *The Modernist Garden in France.*

90. Neither volume of *Petits jardins d'aujourd'hui* bears a date. The first volume was published after 1940, as André Riousse, who died on 3 March 1952, mentioned the "two wars that weakened and ruined [France]." The attribution of various designs to a "Paysagiste D.P.L.G." implies that the book was published after the creation of the landscape department at Versailles (1946). The second volume, which was edited by René Pechère, included a photograph of the Regatta Restaurant Garden, by H. F. Clark and Maria Shephard, for the 1951 Festival of Britain; the book was reviewed in *La maison* in September 1953. See *Petits jardins d'aujourd'hui, première série* (Paris: Éditions d'Art Charles Moreau, n.d. (c. 1947); and *Petits jardins d'aujourd'hui, deuxième série* (Paris: Éditions d'Art Charles Moreau, n.d. (c. 1953).

91. André Riousse, introduction to *Petits jardins d'aujourd'hui, première série,* n.p.

92. The Hungria Machado Garden in Rio de Janeiro, which Roberto Burle Marx designed in 1938, and the "Jardin japonais" situated on the property previously owned by Albert Kahn in Boulogne-sur-Seine, were the only exotic illustrations in volume 1.

93. See René Pechère, "The Garden of the Future May Be an Instrument of Education," in "Progress in Garden Design," *Gardens and Gardening,* 1939, F. A. Mercer, ed. (London: The Studio, 1939), p. 18.

94. René Pechère, "Présentation," in *Petits jardins d'aujourd'hui, deuxième série,* n.p.

95. See René Pechère, "L'Organisation des espaces verts en Belgique," *Urbanisme,* 28, no. 64, 1959, pp. 18–21. Pechère praised the work of van der Swaelmen and Jules Buyssens. To my knowledge Pechère never mentioned Canneel.

96. See René Pechère, *L'Aménagement du territoire et les espaces verts, Cahiers d'urbanisme no. 29* (Bruxelles: Éditions Art et Technique, 1958), pp. 6–7.

97. Pechère, "L'Organisation des espaces verts en Belgique," p. 18.

98. See René Pechère, "La Journée mondiale de l'urbanisme: Les Espaces verts," *La Maison,* 7, no. 12, 1951, pp. 400–401.

99. See René Pechère, "Témoignage d'un jardinier à la recherche d'un style," *Reflets du monde,* c. 1957, pp. 1–15.

100. Ibid., pp. 3–4.

101. Ibid., p. 6.

102. Pechère described the affinities between his own work and that of an American colleague (possibly Thomas Church), which proved he himself had not reinvented the wheel. Ibid., p. 7.

103. See "Projet de parc pour la ville de Renaix—Conception de René Pechère," *La Maison,* 5, no. 9, 1949, p. 275. His design for the Reine Astrid school playground and park was described by P. L. Flouquet in "Plaines de jeux," *Bâtir,* 7, no. 69, 1938, pp. 341–44, and by Pierre Gilles in "Au Plateau du Heysel: Le Parc d'enfants 'Reine Astrid,'" *Bâtir,* no. 81, 1939, pp. 348–52.

104. The conspicuous position of garden designers in the Belgian profession is reinforced by the international stature of Jacques Wirtz. The control of private enterprise is brought a step farther with Wirtz's own nursery. He was placed in the lineage of Pechère and Canneel in the exhibition "L'Architecture du paysage au XX siècle: Jean Canneel-Claes, René Pechère, Jacques Wirtz," which was held at the Archives d'Architecture Moderne in Brussels in 1993.

105. "J'y ai subi l'architecture et l'urbanisme obsolètes d'Auguste Perret, excellent exemple du 'drame français,' dans une ville qui s'est ainsi trouvée deux fois sinistrée," Michel Béjot cited by Blanchon, "Pratiques paysagères en France," p. 29. The few public gardens and plazas published with the accounts of Perret's reconstruction of Le Havre were themselves fairly traditional. See "Le Havre: Auguste Perret urbaniste," *Urbanisme,* 27, no. 59, 1958, pp. 32–38.

106. See *Espaces verts de la région parisienne.* Perrin founded the Agence de l'arbre within the Ministry of Construction and Urbanism in 1962. See Blanchon, "Pratiques paysagères en France," p. 43.

107. See Henri Brison and Daniel Collin, *Jardins d'agrément* (Paris: J. B. Baillère et Fils, 1959).

108. Pasquier, "Les Surfaces vertes dans la ville;" Pasquier, "L'Étude et l'aménagement des villes," *Urbanisme,* 15, no. 109, 1946, pp. 118–21.

109. R. Puget, "Espaces verts, espaces libres," *Urbanisme,* 21, nos. 3–4, 1952, pp. 90–93.

110. Eugène Claudius-Petit, "Pour des maisons réconciliées avec la nature," *Urbanisme,* 20, nos. 11–12, 1951, p. 6.

111. "Habiter autour d'un jardin: Trois projets de E.-E. Beaudouin," *Urbanisme,* 20, nos. 7–8, 1951, p. 5.

112. See Théo Leveau, "Espaces verts de l'habitat," *Urbanisme,* 24, nos. 39–40, 1955, pp. 177–80. Leveau taught design and construction at Versailles between 1952 and 1962.

113. The term *terrain vague* best describes the undefined nature of these sites.

114. Michel Corajoud is a graduate of the École Nationale Supérieure des Arts Décoratifs; he met Jacques Simon at the AUA. There he would form the team CCH with architects Henri Ciriani and Borja Huidobro; among his most noted early projects are the Parc des Coudrays, in Maurepas-Élancourt, and Villeneuve de Grenoble (1966–73). See *Michel Corajoud* (Versailles: Hartmann Editions, 2000).

During the twelve years of National Socialism—from 1933
to 1945—the term landscape described the design of both
gardens at home and the occupied territories in the East.
On 1 September 1939 Germany had invaded Poland. On 7
October 1939 Adolf Hitler appointed Heinrich Himmler
State Commissioner for Strengthening German Identity
(*Volkstum*) by secret decree. Of his new assignments
Himmler seems to have been particularly engaged in the
design of new areas for German settlement in the East, that
is, in Poland.[1] The team that was formed by Himmler for
the implementation of this task included Heinrich Friedrich
Wiepking-Jürgensmann (1891–1973).[2]

Since Wiepking-Jürgensmann was fairly influential in German
landscape architecture until the late 1960s it is important
to know some of his thinking developed during National
Socialism. In 1940 Wiepking declared that "aesthetic thoughts
play no role in today's landscape policy," an ideology he
repeated in his *Landschaftsfibel* (Landscape primer).[3] Wiepking
also wanted to preserve German identity,
and more than that, he felt that he "must
restore Germanity to a considerable seg-
ment of our population, including those
from the rural population, into a landscape
of the soul which corresponds to our being and our spirit."
To do this he asserted, "we must create German landscapes."[4]

5.   GERT GRÖNING

Teutonic Myth, Rubble, and Recovery: Landscape Architecture in Germany

Wiepking deliberately turned away from the project to
provide publicly accessible open space for the populations
of large cities. Although substantial professional activity in
landscape architecture would still address the design of
private gardens and urban open spaces, the professional
engagement with communal urban open space planning—
a stronghold of democratic self-administration during the
Weimar Republic—received considerably less attention. In
1939 Wiepking changed the name of the Institute for
Garden Design at the Friedrich-Wilhelm-University in
Berlin to Institute for Landscape and Garden Design. This
shift followed his belief that "landscape design must primarily care for the rural people and their activities in the landscape."[5] Of the more than seventy documented theses
supervised by Wiepking during National Socialism, only
about one-fifth related to urban open space planning topics;
about four-fifths concerned rural landscape issues. Two of

the leading landscape architects during National Socialism—Wiepking-Jürgensmann and Alwin Seifert (1890–1972)—and their followers made landscapes, especially landscapes in Poland, their primary professional concern.[6] Seifert was made Reichslandschaftsanwalt (State Landscape Director) by Adolf Hitler in 1940 [Figure 5–1]. The group of landscape architects who saw Seifert as their leader called themselves *Landschaftsanwälte* (literally, "attorneys at landscape," or state landscape officers). Although they were at first mostly concerned with planting along the newly constructed motorways, they became more and more involved in camouflaging bunkers for the military and buildings for strategic war industries during the course of the war.

According to Heinrich Himmler the landscape in the East needed to become thoroughly Germanized.[7] In 1942 he wrote: "It is our task not to Germanize the East in the old way, that is to teach the people the German language and German laws, but to assure that only those of truly German Teutonic blood should live in the East."[8] Landscape architects were eager to follow this guideline and developed landscape regulations which clearly specified the elimination of foreign peoples as a precondition for proper landscape

design.[9] "It is not sufficient to settle our people in those areas and to eliminate foreign stock [*Volkstum*]," however. "Instead," the regulations stated, "the area must be given a structure which corresponds to our type of being [*Wesensart*], so that the Teutonic German will feel at home; he settles there and is ready to love and defend his new home."[10]

In the course of National Socialism, the sociology of plants, derived from von Humboldt's geography of plants, had been "Teutonized" and had become accepted dogma for landscape architects.[11] It provided "a useful criterion for artistic taste" and would inform the landscape architect of unacceptable combinations of plant species. In 1936 the first chair for plant sociology in Germany was granted to Erwin Aichinger at Freiburg University; three years later Aichinger received the chair at the College for Soil Culture in Vienna (Austria had already been absorbed into the sphere of National Socialist Germany). In what he called a "biological comparison," Aichinger proved "scientifically" the relation between poorly developed vegetation and "primitive" people: "As in the land of the tundra," he wrote, "where the vegetation can not develop due to the inclemency of the conditions, so man stagnates in a primary stage in this territory, because a further interest in adaptation does not emerge . . . so tundra man is thrown back into those locations with the worst living conditions; . . . which higher differentiated people, forced to operate on their own, cannot bear."[12] This distortion of empirical findings was typical of the "science" that informed many academic programs during National Socialism.

In a similar way, and in striking analogy to Hitler's injunction that "the German people has to be cleansed," Reinhold Tüxen (1899–1980) wanted "to cleanse the German landscape of unharmonious foreign bodies."[13] Tüxen, the leading plant sociologist during National Socialism, became professor in 1939 and in the same year established the Office for Theoretical and Applied Plant Sociology at the College for Veterinary Medicine in Hanover.[14] Tüxen continued to teach until the late 1960s in the landscape architecture program at Hanover University, which Wiepking-Jürgensmann had established in 1947.

Figure 5–1.
Adolf Hitler meets Alwin Seifert on the occasion of the completion of the first thousand kilometers of state motorways in 1936.
[Gert Gröning and Joachim Wolschke-Bulmahn, *1913–1988, 75 Jahre BDLA*]

THE LANDSCAPE ARCHITECTURE OF NATIONAL SOCIALISM

After graduation Wiepking's students entered the employ of the National Socialist state. They would design landscapes in the vast lands east of Germany, in Poland and the Soviet Union. The landscape in these territories, they were told, had been spoiled by the cultural inability—another term in the vocabulary of Teutonic mythology—of the people who inhabited them [Figure 5–2]. Specific studies justified the activity of landscape architects in such areas. It may come as no surprise that in 1943 Wiepking supervised a thesis addressing the greening of the new town of Auschwitz.

One image, published in 1940, carried the caption "Worst confirmation that the people design the landscape." The example related to Old Pomerania, an area along the south shore of the Baltic Sea where Polish and German people had lived for centuries. Without theoretical reasoning, which might have indicated the strangeness of the issue, Wiepking-Jürgensmann and his students tried to prove the connection between blood and soil. They found that both the net yields from land tax per hectare and the percentage of German blood in the population decreased rapidly as one moved eastward. Far from recognizing other variables that might have been operating, Wiepking claimed that the state of culture and landscape diminished in exactly the same way as did human achievement. After the military had conquered such territory, and after it had been cleansed of the members of the inferior races, landscape architects would develop spatial plans to improve the situation. Landscape architects would turn the territory into terrain where Germanic man would feel at home[15] and where his "Nordic longing for landscape" would be met.[16] In Wiepking's mystical language, "No people on earth was more plantlike and rooted to a beautiful life-affirming environment than ours, which is sensibly incorporated into the circling of the stars and of organic life."[17]

Wiepking-Jürgensmann conceived of the new German landscape in the East as a *Wehrlandschaft*, a defensive military landscape resembling the mythic *Midgard* [Figure 5–3].[18] "Today," Wiepking wrote in 1942, "the forest is our last Utgard, the last piece of soil, which, with no regard to its real owner, belongs to all, where we still can walk on soil and grasp it without getting punished, where we feel free as free beings and members of the great creation and the entire world."[19] In his writing Wiepking claimed that he "completely confirmed the myth of Midgard and Utgard, of this world and the other world of our species-linked world of imagination."[20]

Figure 5–2.
Landscape spoiled by the "cultural inability" of the people (above), and the same landscape turned into territory where Germanic man would feel at home (below). 1943. Heinrich Friedrich Wiepking-Jürgensmann. [Gert Gröning and Joachim Wolschke-Bulmahn, *Die Liebe zur Landschaft, Der Drang nach Osten*]

The use of plants in garden design also had to follow

National Socialist ideology.[21] The blood-and-soil garden became the standard model, an acceptable design executed in a softened landscape style. The design was curvilinear with irregularly planted shrubbery. No paths would interrupt the mood of natural landscape.[22]

Since the commissions for landscape architects were immense — landscapes for new motorways, the design of new cities and settlements in the East, and greening of villages — new institutions for garden design were to be established by 1941. Graduating after two years as state-certified garden designers allowed them to further study at the university level. After another three years of practical experience the graduates could then take an exam as Baumeister der Gartengestaltung (architect for garden design).[23] In a meeting on 14 January 1942, representatives from the National Socialist ministries of the interior, nutrition and agriculture, forestry, and finances, the Saxon ministry of people's education, and the Reichsnährstand, the all-embracing National Socialist corporation for everything related to agriculture and horticulture, could not agree on establishing such schools for garden designers. Since the matter was not considered important to the war effort, further consultation was postponed until after the end of the war.[24]

If not the experience of war, then certainly the liberation from National Socialism in 1945 ended these prospects for landscape architecture in Germany. Peace also blew away the idea of a network of state-employed landscape architects extending from Poznan in Poland to Novosibirsk or even Vladivostok in the Soviet Union. The careers of those landscape architects who had been actively involved in its advocacy continued, however. Although Teutonic myth as a root for professional activity had been severely shaken, aspects of this myth survived in professional landscape architecture during the decades to come.

FROM RUBBLE TO RECONSTRUCTION: IN THE WESTERN ZONE, IN BERLIN, AND IN THE EASTERN ZONE, 1945–1949

At the end of World War II the Allies divided Germany into four zones of occupation; Berlin was surrounded by the Soviet occupation zone.[25] In the following years the mounting tension between the Western Allies and the Soviet Union led to a division of the country into Western and Eastern spheres; Berlin was also divided.[26]

Figure 5–3.
Wehrlandschaft, around 1940. Heinrich Friedrich Wiepking-Jürgensmann.

Rows of hardwood trees 18 inches in diameter, planted in a north-south direction, with deep ditches on either side to form an obstacle to expected attack from the east. Wiepking-Jürgensmann credited such planting with eternal value if maintained properly. [Heinrich Friedrich Wiepking-Jürgensmann, *Die Landschaftsfibel*]

Some ten million refugees had to be accommodated within a German territory that had shrunk by roughly one-third.[27] To provide housing for the local population and for the refugees from the East was the major concern after the close of the war in 1945.[28] The city park in Hamburg housed countless homeless in Quonset huts, half-tube-shaped shelters of prefabricated sheets of corrugated iron. The central meadow in this park became a refugee camp and was no longer used as a place for recreation.[29]

Statements by Germans who recognized that their own misery was a direct consequence of National Socialist depredations at home and elsewhere in the world were rare in those days. One of the notable exceptions was a report by Carl Alwin Schenck, a German forester and founder of the Biltmore Forest School in North Carolina. In 1948 he wrote: "No sane man in Germany fails to see that the resurrection of the cities destroyed in England, in France, in the Netherlands, in Belgium, in Poland, in Russia will have precedence over the reconstruction of the cities destroyed in Germany."[30] After World War II, landscape architecture in Germany was shattered. Much of Germany lay in ruins, and any prospects for a future in landscape architecture looked bleak. Johannes Reinhold claimed that a disproportionately high number of university graduates in landscape architecture and horticulture had died in the war.[31] Hans Karl Möhring noted that "Entire generations of younger, but also elderly and experienced gardeners were missing. Education stagnated for years; professional schools offered no programs." There was no capital for investments. "Cheap, cheap, cheap will be the slogans for a long time," prophesied Möhring.[32]

Instead of preparing plans and designs for Teutonic landscapes in the vast evacuated lands in the East — most of which had never been conquered — the rubble of war required clearing. Much of it was recycled by associations for the productive use of rubble.[33] The need to deal with huge amounts of debris considerably changed the design of public open space but also created new sites for recreation. In Berlin the remains of the as yet unfinished military-technical faculty which Hitler wanted to establish in the Grunewald vanished under a mountain of rubble that had grown to more than ten million cubic meters by the end of 1960.[34] The mountain was later covered with topsoil and shaped for recreational purposes.[35] The Berlin architect Max Taut (1884–1967) suggested spreading debris in the open space between building blocks, thus creating foundations for

flowering terraces. In East Berlin the rubble had to be cleared before soil could be added to grow plants again.[36]

In the final stages of World War II the Allied air forces had extensively bombed throughout Germany. In Berlin close to four-fifths of the features of the city's open spaces had been completely destroyed. Some five thousand acres of forest land had been entirely cleared for firewood; another three thousand acres were cleared to such an extent that they hardly resembled forests any longer. In West Berlin alone some 110,000 trees along the streets were cut for firewood; the remainder were badly damaged — often by bullets. Wooden benches had disappeared from public parks for similar reasons.[37] Schoolyards were likewise denuded.[38] Some 5,500 acres of public green space were devastated and only fragments remained.[39] In many cities the remnants of public parks had been subdivided, serving as garden plots for the growth of vegetables and fruit as late as 1951. In Dresden, for example, the "gradual restitution and redesign of the remaining open spaces began in 1948. Since early 1950 it may be said, there have been extraordinary achievements in redesign and restitution."[40]

After the war, municipal parks departments had planted vegetables to secure food for the population.[41] Ammunition and debris filled the lakes in parks and elsewhere. Tunnels for military activities criss-crossed many public parks, a number of which housed aboveground bomb shelters making reconstruction difficult. In Berlin, for example, in Humboldt Park and Friedrichshain, and elsewhere, those bomb shelters proved so difficult to demolish that they were left in place.[42] They were filled with fragments of demolished buildings, covered with topsoil, planted with shrubs and trees, and gradually turned into green mountains that changed the contour of the city [Figures 5–4, 5–5].

Topographical changes of a different kind took place in the parks of Treptow and Schönholz in the Russian sector of Berlin between 1947 and 1949. A huge memorial for some five thousand Russian soldiers who had died in the fight for Berlin during the last days of World War II displaced the hippodrome-shaped children's playground.[43] Another Berlin memorial in Schönholzer Heide commemorates the death of some thirteen thousand Russian soldiers.[44] Open spaces that once had been planned for recreation thus became places of commemoration.

Figure 5–4.
Demolished bomb shelter left in place,
Berlin, 1945.
[Garten und Landschaft]

Figure 5–5.
The same bomb shelter as in Figure 5–4,
filled with rubble, Berlin, 1952.

The professional credo behind the principles of reconstruction in those days was to rebuild in a simple but nevertheless design-oriented way.[45] Also there were many sites where ruins were turned into green spaces.[46] Landscape architect Camillo Schneider (1876–1951) offered suggestions for tending Berlin's green spaces now in ruins: "one will proceed in the simplest way, for no other reason than there are no materials available from nurseries and because the maintenance costs must be kept as low as possible."[47] Schneider then referred to the example of the Sachsenplatz and suggested that designers "simplify quite a bit and . . . select those plants which have proven viable in spite of all the years of nonmaintenance and uncultivation."[48]

RECONSTRUCTING THE DISCIPLINE OF LANDSCAPE ARCHITECTURE

The only university-level landscape architecture institute had ceased to exist with the Russian takeover of Berlin in April 1945. Its chair, Heinrich Friedrich Wiepking-Jürgensmann, fled from Berlin and became active again in 1946 in the British Zone under his dehyphenated name, Wiepking. A year later Wiepking, who had difficulty saying farewell to National Socialism after the end of World War II, and others managed to establish a new school of horticulture and landscape studies in Hanover with an overall floor plan just short of a swastika [Figure 5–6].[49] Wiepking learned to exclude National Socialist terminology from his lectures but basically continued his earlier program with a strong emphasis on what he considered landscape.

At Friedrich Wilhelm University in Berlin, Georg Bela Pniower (1896–1960) succeeded Wiepking as professor of garden art and landscape design, changing its name to the Institute for Garden and Landscape Studies [Figure 5–7].[50] For the first time in German history there were now two chairs in landscape architecture, one in Berlin and the new one in Hanover. In a society accustomed to believing almost everything spoken or written by a professor, for the first time different approaches to landscape architecture were feasible at the university level; a new quality of scholarly debate could have emerged.

Georg Pniower was an outspoken former member of the Social Democratic Party in the Weimar Republic. His appointment as chair revealed several anomalies, not the least of them being geographic. For racial and political reasons Pniower had been forbidden to practice as a land-

scape architect by the National Socialist Party's Fine Arts Board. He now lived and taught in the American sector of Berlin, although his chair was administered by the faculty for agriculture and horticulture, which belonged to Friedrich Wilhelm University, located on Unter den Linden in the Russian sector. In the past, lecture and seminar rooms in landscape architecture were located in the Berlin-Dahlem district, which now belonged to the American sector.[51] Pniower indirectly criticized Seifert's and Wiepking's National Socialist landscape architecture, thus showing his interest in landscape architecture as a scholarly activity.[52] Wiepking and Seifert, for their part, preferred not to mention Pniower at all. They were not interested in stimulating professional debate. Pniower believed that the so-called landscape officers had died; Seifert, of course, had served as State Landscape Director.[53] Pniower also thought that the National Socialist idea of a Nordic, that is, a Scandinavian landscape (which Wiepking-Jürgensmann had favored) and "the re-creation of the catastrophe-generated poverty of species of our flora" (which Seifert had envisioned during National Socialism) "has vanished."[54] Instead of improving the landscape through "nordification," Pniower suggested eliminating the "life-destructive traces of the Ice Age." To do so he called for the "southernization" of the landscape, returning "to our landscape a wealth of life which it had possessed several times before under the same macroclimatic conditions, but with essentially less favorable technical preconditions."[55] Here Pniower renewed a creative line of thinking he had already developed during the late years of the Weimar Republic, for example, with his design for the Gourmenia House in Berlin.[56]

In 1945 Pniower designed the Kleistpark in Berlin [Figure 5–8].[57] There was hardly a park area in Berlin which could have had more personal meaning for Pniower as a landscape architect than this park.[58] Pniower's strong interest in the history of horticulture and dendrology is reflected in the history of this garden. In the seventeenth century the site had been used as a royal garden where hops were grown for beer production. It then became a kitchen garden; some North American trees were planted there as specimens, and during the eighteenth century the area was planted as a botanical garden.[59] Pniower's interest in a university curriculum for landscape architecture is reflected in its history.

This park symbolized another aspect of Pniower's life, the suppression of his work as a landscape architect. The earlier

126

Figure 5–6.
Hochschule für Gartenbau und Landeskultur, Hanover, c. 1957, aerial view.
[*Fakultät für Gartenbau und Landeskultur Hannover*]

Figure 5–7.
Georg Bela Pniower (1896–1960), professor, Institut für Garten- und Landschaftskultur from 1946 to 1960, Berlin, c. 1955.
[*Berliner Forschung und Lehre in den Landwirtschaftswissenschaften*]

botanical garden was turned into an open space named Kleistpark for the centennial of the death of the poet Heinrich von Kleist (1777–1811), who had committed suicide because he felt suppressed by the then-state chancellor of Prussia, Count Hardenberg. Pniower had been forbidden to work as a landscape architect under National Socialism because he was considered half Jewish and because he had been a member of the Social Democratic Party. Since 1913 the Prussian Supreme Court building occupied the western section of the park. In this very building most of the notorious trials of the National Socialist Volksgerichtshof (People's Court) took place,[60] including the trial of the conspirators who unsuccessfully tried to kill Adolf Hitler on 20 July 1944. In 1945 the building became the seat of the Allied Council for Berlin and thus became a symbol of the liberation, which allowed Pniower to practice again.

A few years later Pniower proposed a design for Berlin's Tiergarten, which had been completely destroyed during the war. Pniower believed that the Tiergarten should become a people's park that would respond to the needs for mass recreation: "Its design needs to be unconventional and must clearly reveal that it belongs to the built organism and the rhythm of a world-class city."[61] Although there was some support for Pniower's outstanding design the opposition proved stronger [Figure 5–9]. For example, Hubert Hoffmann (1904–1999), who from 1948 to 1952 headed West Berlin's city planning office, strongly rejected the design as a late example of the Jugendstil movement.[62] Instead, it provided a different approach to park design, one associated with the Weimar Republic. During this short period, which lasted from 1919 to 1933, the range of designs for parks and gardens had been wider than ever before. Pniower's asymmetric and dynamic design for the Tiergarten clearly opposed the nineteenth-century school of landscape design, which by the early twentieth century was considered outdated. Obviously preferring a pastoral central park for Berlin, Hoffmann also opposed Pniower's idea for introducing a number of public attractions such as a vaudeville theater, a circus, and tobogganing as part of the overall plan for the Tiergarten.[63]

The magistrate of Berlin had commissioned Pniower for the park's design. However, Reinhold Lingner (1902–68), a landscape architect then director of the Municipal Parks Department, also preferred an early nineteenth-century park design. Behaving as if he wished to return to pedestrian and equestrian times, Lingner proposed a design for the

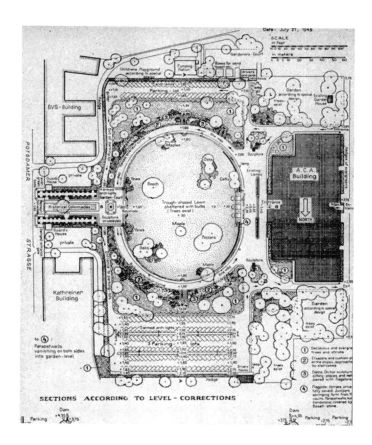

Figure 5–8.
Kleistpark, Berlin-Schöneberg, Allied Control Authority, 1945. Georg Bela Pniower, landscape architect. Site plan.
[*Garten und Landschaft*, 5, 1950]

Figure 5–9. Tiergarten, Berlin, 1948, model.
Georg Bela Pniower.
[*Die Neue Stadt*]

Tiergarten that approached the late nineteenth-century school of Lenné and Meyer; he even suggested converting its heavily trafficked thoroughfare, which ran through the park from east to west, into a meadow.[64] This plan remained unexecuted [Figure 5–10]. With the split of Berlin into Eastern and Western administrations, another conservative design in the late landscape style by Willy Alverdes (1896–1980) from the gradually emerging West Berlin parks administration served as the guideline for the reconstruction in the decades to come.[65]

In 1948 Pniower published *Bodenreform und Gartenbau* (Agrarian Reform and Horticulture), which addressed the contemporary needs of many people in Germany [Figure 5–11].[66] One of the most urgent needs was to produce food. For that Pniower suggested the creation of "fruit landscapes," that is, garden-citylike settlements where gardens attached to single-family homes would provide fruits and vegetables and thus reduce the widespread need for these foods. Pniower also demonstrated how landscape architects could find a professional role (if they found one at all) during those troubled years. This book seems to have been the only publication to make explicit references to the achievements of landscape architecture in the Weimar Republic.[67] To cite one example, Pniower found that "even the social green policy of the Weimar Republic would no longer be adequate today."[68] A rational design was required which rested on the life needs of the people and replaced the models of a few "blood-and-soil fanatics" with a "rational socialism," a "synthesis between nature and technology" in contemporary designs for gardens and landscapes.[69]

Another of Pniower's research interests focused upon the creation of a model landscape, in an area of about 110 square kilometers in the northeastern promontory of the Harz Mountains, which had been devastated to a large extent by inappropriate cultivation. This landscape ideally would provide a lasting increase in agricultural yields. Work seems to have started in 1953.[70] Pniower and his collaborators felt that in these exemplary landscapes, "science has the chance for basic research. . . . Continued observation of the scientific experiments and continuing studies will deepen the knowledge needed to continually improve the method. Similarly the permanent exchange of experience between authorities and people-owned institutions serves this task and favors close and ongoing cooperation between science and practice."[71]

Here Pniower's design ideas extended far beyond the traditional design of parks and gardens as singular entities.

Although he did not explicitly refer to it, the late eighteenth- and early nineteenth-century idea of land embellishment comes to mind. This concept resembled that of the ornamented farm in England and the *ferme ornée* in France. Land embellishment combined in large estates if not in an entire state the useful (agriculture) with the beautiful (landscape architecture). The most progressive modes of agriculture joined with the aesthetic idea of a rural landscape.[72] Some 150 years later, "progressive economy was [for Pniower] to change nature according to a plan which followed a line of continuing enrichment of nature with all creative means at hand and thus to an ever larger extent by means of technology."[73]

The gradually developing Cold War between the former Allies led to the establishment of different administrations in East and West Berlin. After the American and British military occupation authorities had refused to help reconstruct Friedrich Wilhelm University, the Soviet Military Administration in Germany (SMAD) reopened it in 1946.[74] The institutes and laboratories of the university were scattered all over the city, in the East as well as the West, with its main building in East Berlin. The municipal administration of West Berlin threatened to evict Friedrich Wilhelm University (which had been renamed Humboldt University in 1949) from its premises in West Berlin. Consequently the school of agriculture and horticulture, which had been located primarily in what became East Berlin, lost eleven of its twenty-seven institutes, which had been located in what was now West Berlin.[75] This also affected Pniower's institute, which was located in Dahlem, since ultimately the U.S. military confiscated the building and land on behalf of the West Berlin administration. On 12 August 1951 Pniower was restrained from entering the old building; he consequently started a new Institute for Garden and Land Studies (Institut für Garten- und Landes-kultur) in another university building on Invalidenstrasse in East Berlin.[76] Still commuting between West and East Berlin, Pniower moved from his home in Dahlem to a new home in Grünau in East Berlin in 1953. He reasoned that the "separation of the institute from its natural hinterland" would sterilize its research and practice.[77] Obviously this applied to the research in agriculture and forestry he had initiated near the Harz Mountains in the Huy-Hakel area and in expanses devastated by coal mining south of Berlin in the Niederlausitz.[78] When Pniower died, however, his research interests died with him and nothing came of his far-reaching visions.[79]

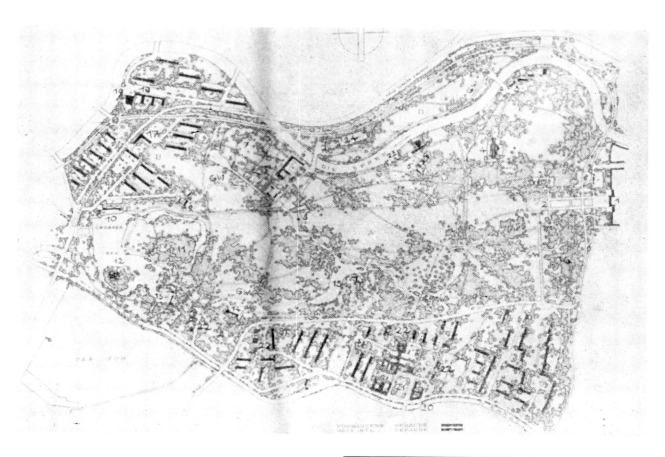

Figure 5–10.
Tiergarten, Berlin, 1948, Reinhold Lingner.
Brandenburg Gate to the far right.
[*Die Neue Stadt*]

Figure 5–11.
Bodenreform und Gartenbau (Agrarian
Reform and Horticulture). Cover,
Georg Pniower.

In 1953 the curriculum for landscape architects at Humboldt University had been extended from three to five years. It included elementary courses in Marxism-Leninism, in political economy, and in the Russian language.[80] Three years later the curriculum was again expanded to six years.[81] In East Germany, the need for such a curriculum was explained thus:

> The vague desire to make "little gardens" and "nice green open spaces" is not enough. One must know that the mental equipment for a garden architect consists not only of some simple plant knowledge but includes also down-to-earth knowledge with respect to technical, organizational, scientific—and last but not least—artistic matters. The abilities for creative design must already exist; these can only be developed and carefully promoted here.[82]

In the West the position was similar, although there the curriculum was only four years.[83] A university curriculum in open space planning and landscape maintenance urged:

> Science and art—as opposite poles—both encompass what we call culture in the widest sense. If the one or the other becomes neglected, a perfect culture in garden and landscape design would be impossible. The profession of garden and landscape architects takes its legitimation from the task to create culture through good garden and landscape design. . . . If we are not ready to position science first, the [role of the] garden and landscape architect will be degraded to a landscape decorator one . . . to practice art is not the job of such a university institute. It [art] is to be taken into account only . . . in a discipline; science must not be suppressed in favor of art. Only together both produce garden and landscape culture.[84]

THE POLITICAL DIVISION OF GERMANY AND ITS LANDSCAPE REPERCUSSIONS

Pniower's decision to stay with Humboldt University in East Berlin created a need for a new chair in landscape architecture in the West. In 1952 Gustav Allinger (1891–1974), once a member of the National Socialist German Workers' Party (NSDAP) and actively involved in the National Socialist political redirection of landscape architects, was appointed to the newly established chair at the Technical University in West Berlin. As a consequence of the political division of the city, a new school for agriculture was established, joining the eleven institutes from the prior school of agriculture and horticulture of Humboldt University. Since Allinger's past as a National Socialist was well known, he had some

difficulty in receiving the appointment. Landscape architect Wilhelm Hübotter (1895–1976) recalled Allinger's role during National Socialism: "We freelance landscape architects vividly remember this meeting here in Hanover in '33 when Gustav Allinger in storm trooper uniform and with a gun on his belt tried to coerce all of us."[85] In a lengthy process the state board of education investigated Allinger's activities before and during the war.[86] He was asked to be fairly precise in his curriculum vitae about the years between 1933 and 1945; he rewrote the information several times before it was finally accepted.

Landscape architect Hübotter, later one of the founders of the Bund deutscher Gartenarchitekten (Federation of German Landscape Architects), was himself not a peace dove. In 1934 he had purchased land for the National Socialist SS, or security echelon. Founded in 1929 as Hitler's bodyguard, this organization evolved into what was, in effect, a police army with a membership by the end of the war of about one million.[87] On the land he had purchased, Hübotter designed the Saxons' Grove, a reference to Teutonic mythology, near Verden/Aller.[88] Despite this damning record, a decade later, after World War II, Hübotter was commissioned to design a memorial for an earlier National Socialist concentration camp near Bergen-Belsen in Lower Saxony.[89]

The scale of destruction in the large cities forced landscape architects and city planners to consider decentralization as part of the reconstruction process. "Berlin in Reconstruction" was the title of the first renewal plan for the city, proposed in 1946. The architect Max Taut saw the landscape as the most important factor in city planning and thus "fully shared the soul of the green-planners."[90] The architect and city planner Fritz Schumacher (1869–1947), who had served as Hamburg's city architect and planner until the National Socialists came to power, gave the open spaces top ranking:

> I place open spaces first because they are the most difficult and most important task for city planning. Buildings arise even if one does not care; open spaces disappear if one does not speak for them. They can only be guaranteed as a permanent asset of a living organism which becomes more dense by systematic care in city planning. While it may appear quite often to the outsider as if city planning were invented to create sites for building, the expert knows it exists primarily for the preservation of open spaces.[91]

Suggestions for the spatial dispersion of large cities were also debated by the members of the Academy for Spatial Research and Land Planning at their second meeting in

1947 in Wiesbaden.[92] Plans for the preservation and reconstruction of parks were prepared;[93] other planners suggested new standards for the provision of open spaces in 1947. Under the headline "Light–Air–Cleanliness" they demanded one square meter (about ten square feet) of public park, garden, and sports areas for each person and two hundred square meters of garden for each apartment.[94] It was believed that not only minor cities but also large cities could meet such standards. "For Berlin," Georg Heyer claimed, "it has been proven that by ordering the existing urban space it is possible to provide a home in a single-family rowhouse with a small garden; additionally, within the residential community open spaces and sports areas of the desired size can be provided within a distance of from 100 to 500 meters distance. . . . The garden, an open-air room of 150 square meters, is connected to the 12-square-meter living room by an arbor."[95] Standards such as these mushroomed all over Germany. In 1960 the Deutsche Olympische Gesellschaft published its Golden Plan, introducing standards and guidelines for the establishment of recreation, play, and sports facilities, which became widely accepted in the years that followed.[96]

The Kollektivplan developed in 1946 by the architect Hans Scharoun (1893–1972) and his team (which included landscape architect Reinhold Lingner) envisioned "landscape in the city."[97] The plan took the Urstromtal, the broad valley shaped by large rivers in prehistoric times in which Berlin is located, as a guideline for a cellular structure. Following a rather biological but nevertheless common line of thinking, this structure was to consist of large and middle-sized cells [Figure 5–12].[98] The plan was based on ideas from a wartime study, "The Subdivided and Decentralized City," by architect Hubert Hoffmann; architect and city councillor of Braunschweig, Johannes Göderitz (1888–1978); and architect Roland Rainer.[99] The plan was left unimplemented, however.[100] A major reason seems to have been that much of the subsurface infrastructure — lines for electricity, gas pipes, canals for water and sewage, subways, and many cellars buildings — could still serve as the basis for urban reconstruction. The study had been conducted during World War II and had been printed in January 1945 under the auspices of architect and Reichsminister for armament and war production Albert Speer (1905–81). An inaccessible book at the time of its writing, the report was published for the first time in an expanded version in 1957.[101]

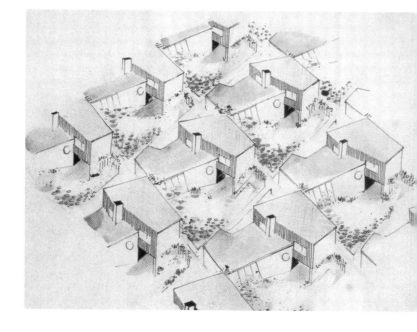

Figure 5–12.
Gardens and houses as part of a cellular structure, c. 1950. Hans Scharoun et al.
[1945, Krieg—Zerstörung—Aufbau, Architektur und Stadtplanung 1940–1960]

Instead, "The Plan Berlin 1948," proposed by architect Karl Bonatz (1882–1951), who succeeded Scharoun in 1947, was implemented.[102] The plan carefully considered the importance of the Tiergarten and referred to a design by Reinhold Lingner of the same time. Lingner suggested turning Berlin's traditional central axis, which ran from East to West, into a lawn with a large lake at its western end; only one road through the southern part of the park was to be maintained. Bonatz objected to the axis-as-lawn idea, however, and called attention to the traditional meaning of this road and its function of leading from the West into the heart of the city. Positive readings of the plan were not universal. Another landscape architect, for example, argued that the plan had "dropped the landscape as basis," and was thus unacceptable.[103]

Whereas architects thought that reconstructed cities must include a fair amount of open space, landscape architects resurrected the concept of a productive landscape full of gardens surrounding cities and villages.[104] Their goal was

> a wreath of flowering gardens around our cities, a zone of extremely intensive use, which provides the necessary fresh vegetables and fruit, framed by protective plantings of wild-fruit shrubs and precious wood for use, which also improve the climate and provide food and places for small animals to hide. Ultimately, we thus achieve a beautiful landscape which at the same time also fully corresponds in every respect to the demand for living space, space for nutrition and home.[105]

Given the devastated country, horticulture may have appeared as the one and only way to survive. Nevertheless it is surprising that neither industry nor commerce was conceived in terms of future development. This may have been a reflection of the Morgenthau Plan, developed by Henry Morgenthau, Jr., U.S. Secretary of the Treasury from 1934 to 1945. Morgenthau proposed controlling Germany by converting it from an industrial to an agricultural economy. It was not put into operation and soon became replaced by the plan developed by George Catlett Marshall, the Chief of Staff of the American Army from 1939 to 1945. The Marshall Plan supported postwar economic recovery in Europe and ultimately in Germany as well.

TRACES OF PROFESSIONAL RENEWAL

Although much of the war debris gradually vanished under grass and shrubbery, it took some time before the organizational structures for landscape architects operated effectively once again. It seemed easier to achieve in West than in East Germany. Organization was critical to voicing more than an individual interest and participating in the gradual process of establishing a democracy. Rather than being appointed — the National Socialists' method — now presidents of professional organizations were chosen through open elections.

Many Germans found it difficult to accept American and Russian leadership in politics because they believed Germany still possessed a "culture" superior to that of either the United States or the Soviet Union: they felt no real defeat. With respect to the United States, such attitudes had been nourished as part of National Socialist landscape architecture. One example, which relates to the need to grow hedges as part of a truly German landscape, may suffice. The "psychic and cultural impact" of hedges was considered more important than their economic impact:

> The German people will only exist and remain creative if allowed to grow according to her species. A bond with nature belongs to her species, however. This is most apparent in the neverending longing for nature by the inhabitants of large cities, who still yearn for villagelike circumstances. This longing will die away, only when nothing more is offered to fulfill it. At that time, however, we would have a human who is better suited for America than for Germany. And this is why the hedge is a symbol of the nature-connected German human.[106]

In the West, such attitudes accounted for considerable resentment against America; in the East, resentment against Russia would continue for years to come.

Owing to the new political organization in Germany, there were national, state, and city interests whose policies had to mesh. In all three instances, professional positions as well as funding for landscape projects were a concern. At the city level, the parks department sought to equal the building department in stature. At the state level, the interests of cities with respect to legislative action needed representation, and at the national level the focus was on laws concerning garden and landscape issues. Independent landscape architects and state- and city-employed landscape architects shared an interest in these issues.[107]

From 1951 to 1958 Reinhold Lingner headed the department for open-space planning within the Institute for City Planning of the German Academy for Building in East Berlin [Figure 5–13]. With these words he began a 1954 article about the embellishment of cities as part of a national task for reconstruction: "For the National Reconstruction Work the transition from the clearance of rubble to the creation of green open spaces represents work on a new, higher level of quality."[108] This new level, however, proved difficult to achieve, in part because landscape architects in the Russian occupation zone found it difficult to organize effective professional organizations. The organizations and institutions tended to lose autonomy and suffered from Communist Party political involvement.[109]

Given the complete political failure and military defeat of National Socialism, it is remarkable that explicit references to democracy during the Weimar Republic or the horrors of National Socialism were extremely scant in both West and East Germany in the postwar years. Rather than talking about National Socialism directly, various strategies were developed to avoid any explicit reference to the regime. A characteristic book, by landscape architect Gustav Allinger, examined horticultural exhibitions in Germany in the 150 years prior to its writing. In this 1963 text Allinger avoided the words National Socialism or any derivative and instead referred to the time of National Socialism as the "episode of the Reichsnährstand," a National Socialist organization that claimed to encompass all the professions that contributed to food and nutrition.[110]

After 1945 the interest in physically reconstructing what had been turned to ruins and rubble was paramount. Among survivors of the war, rebuilding was such a central concern that many considered any reflection on what had been destroyed mentally and socially during National Socialism in Germany counterproductive. In a similar way, with particular respect to the city of Frankfurt am Main, the graphic artist Hans Leistikow found that "the silk-blue sky above Frankfurt has not been injured, and all the old towers remain to again hinder the traffic as they did before, and the gardens try to cover the wounds to their houses."[111] One sentence in the introduction to the five "principles of reconstruction," published as a manifesto in March 1947 by a number of people who felt obligated to the "old idea of the Werkbund," voiced it thus: "With a feeling of liberation we once believed we could go to work again. Today after two years we realize how much the visible collapse is only an expression of the mental derangement, and [we] could persist in desperation."[112]

Figure 5–13.
Reinhold Lingner, landscape architect.
[Deutsche Gartenarchitektur]

Compared to the entirely new approaches to the parks and gardens design, which had structured landscape architecture during the first years of democracy in the Weimar Republic, the new efforts were quite meager. Georg Pniower was, at first, an exception. After five years of East-West quarrels, however, he had chosen to live in a state that gradually dismissed almost all the design aspects of landscape architecture.

RECOVERY, 1950–1960: THE RETURN OF GARDEN EXHIBITIONS

National Socialism and World War II caused a ten-year hiatus for garden exhibitions small and large, which had been held annually between 1880 and 1914 and from 1921 to 1939. The last National Socialist garden exhibition had been opened after twenty-six months of labor to convert a former quarry of some seventy-five acres into an exhibition ground in Stuttgart on 22 April 1939 [Figures 5–14, 5–15]. Due to the beginning of World War II on September first of that year, it was closed prematurely later that month. It had been designed by landscape architect Hermann Mattern (1902–1971) and architect Gerhard Graubner in 1936 and implemented by landscape architect Eugen Bauer (1897–1970) [Figure 5–16].[113] Among the striking design elements were the terraces and retaining walls as well as many stairs of red sandstone, which shaped the entire site with a maximum height differential of almost two hundred feet. The first big garden show after the liberation took place in 1948 in Leipzig-Markkleeberg, in the Russian zone [Figure 5–17]. It was followed by the Südwestdeutsche Gartenbau-Ausstellung in Landau, Pfalz, in the French zone, which opened its doors on 15 July 1949 [Figure 5–18].[114]

The year 1950 saw a garden show in Stuttgart,[115] and one in Erfurt, Thuringia, in East Germany. The Stuttgart exhibition of 1950 again was designed by landscape architect Hermann Mattern, the Erfurt exhibition by landscape architect Walter Funcke (1907–1987). Between 1929 and 1945 Funcke and Mattern as well as landscape architect Herta Hammerbacher (1900–1985) and perennial plant breeder Karl Foerster (1874–1970) had collaborated in Potsdam and Berlin. After the war Funcke no longer worked for Mattern; nevertheless, he still admired Mattern's design.[116] For Erfurt he explicitly tried to design a garden exhibition reflecting values for a future socialist society in East Germany.[117] There was a need for both exhibitions, since both offered landscape models for their respective societies. Wilhelm Hübotter

Figure 5–15.
The hilltop café and its overlook. National Garden Show, 1939.
[*Das Erlebnis einer Landschaft*]

Figure 5–14.
Water feature in the Valley of the Roses. National Garden Show, 1939.
[*Das Erlebnis einer Landschaft*]

commented: "Since we just came from Stuttgart we could easily compare [the two exhibitions] and my opinion is that there is only one possible conclusion: it can never be Stuttgart or Erfurt but only Stuttgart and Erfurt."[118]

The first national garden show in West Germany took place in Hanover in 1951; Hübotter had won the competition for the design of this show in 1949, but it was not realized.[119] Instead, the head of the parks department in Hanover executed the design with the help of an artistic advisory board, namely the landscape architects Oskar Langerhans, Karl Heydenreich, Josef Breloer, and Heinrich Friedrich Wiepking.[120] The fifty acres of this show were divided by a thoroughfare crossed by a pedestrian bridge. Both parts centered on a fairly large meadow surrounded by such exhibits as a rose garden, water gardens, and a perennials meadow. Many related associations held their annual meetings on the occasion of such shows. In Hanover some 650 exhibitors presented their work to approximately 1,600,000 visitors.

In 1955, landscape architect Gerda Gollwitzer (1907–96) found that the "German miracle," the rapid economic rise in West Germany, "has been only partly effective in the for-

Figure 5–16.
Hermann Mattern, landscape architect.
[Das Gartenamt]

mer capital of Berlin."[121] Nevertheless, by then the recovery was well on its way in most cities in West Germany.[122] As the garden shows were visible signs of recovery, so were other related improvements to urban open space. In 1953 a landscape architect from the city of Chemnitz, then named Karl-Marx-Stadt, East Germany, felt that "the essential improvement of our economic situation" justified that "we no longer use the front yards for growing vegetables"; a new garden design should create "a street space without objectionable features."[123] There is no way to ascertain how successful the suggested new street design was, however.

The implementation of the plans for the first green socialist city, the new residential quarters near Fürstenberg, East Germany, proved disappointing. From 1952 to 1954 landscape architect Walter Funcke and his team had prepared the plans for Stalinstadt, as the place was named in 1953; in 1961, its name was again changed, to Steelworks City [Figure 5–19]. In 1954 Funcke was dismissed; a more formal design was proposed but was not executed. Although it had always been the goal to reduce the costs for maintaining green space, the amount of available funding was "often radically reduced," which again resulted "in low quality in both design and technical aspects."[124] Perhaps the authors of a manual for socialist residential complexes, issued by the East German ministry for building, had in mind the Stalinstadt example when they ruled several years later that "the composition of the open spaces must follow a clear artistic statement."[125] They felt that the design of the open spaces should form a unit with the built spaces.

Professional relations in landscape architecture in those years reflected the competitiveness of life in East and West Germany; professional contacts seemed to stimulate it.[126] In 1957, for example, the German-Canadian landscape architect Gunter A. Schoch reported favorably in a West German professional journal about the achievements in garden design in Moscow. Schoch based his article on a piece published by the head of the Moscow parks department, K. F. Kashirsky, in the Ohio-based Tree magazine in 1956. Schoch's article began as follows: "It is still fairly seldom that we in the Western world receive professional articles from countries behind the Iron Curtain. We do not know if authors are afraid of repercussions from their own regime if they publish neutral articles in the Western press — or if they feel inferior to the West professionally."[127]

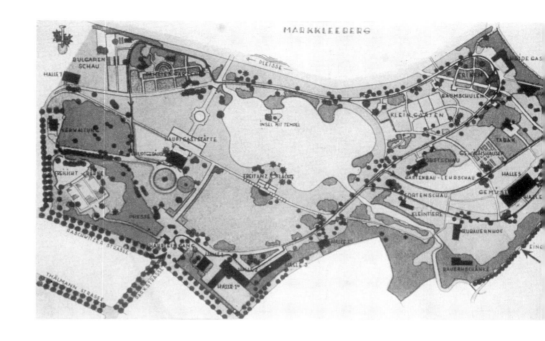

Figure 5–17.
Horticultural Exhibition, Leipzig-
Markkleeberg, 1948. Helmut Lichey,
landscape architect.
[Das Hohelied von Gartenbau und
Gartenkunst]

Figure 5–18.
Horticultural Exhibition, SÜWEGA,
Landau, Pfalz, 1949. Walter Rieger,
landscape architect.
[Das Hohelied von Gartenbau und
Gartenkunst]

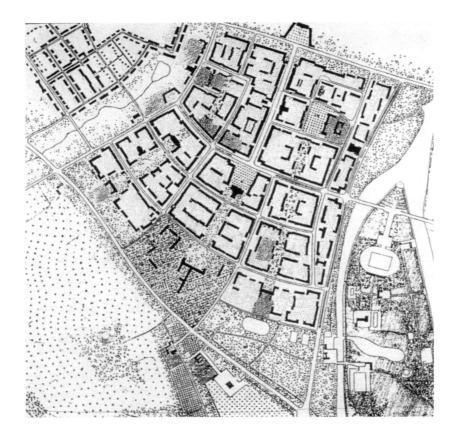

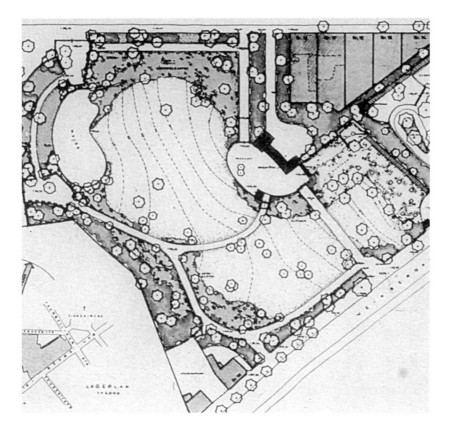

Figure 5–19.
Stalinstadt, the first socialist city in the
green. Open space plan for residential
complexes I–IV, 1953. Walter Meissner and
Walter Funcke, landscape architects.
[*Deutsche Gärtnerpost*]

Figure 5–20.
People's Park Weinbergsweg, central East
Berlin, 1955.
[*Der Deutsche Gartenbau*]

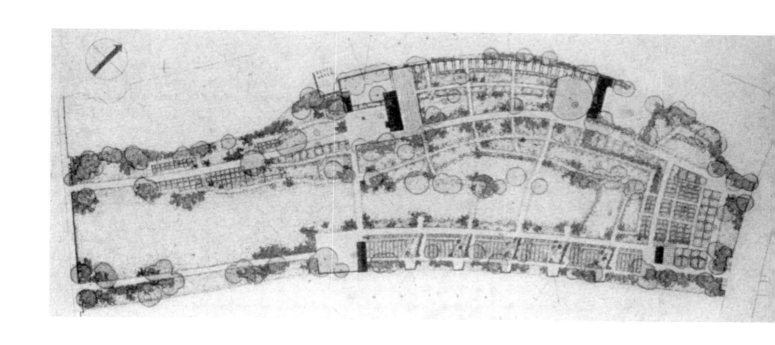

Figure 5–21.
Freundschaftsinsel, Potsdam, 1955.
Hermann Mattern and Walter Funcke,
landscape architects.
[*Der Deutsche Gartenbau*]

Another example documenting this intra-German professional competitiveness of landscape architects was the Weinbergsweg Park in central East Berlin. The design, which was in the late landscape style, was published first in an East German journal in July 1955 and again a month later in a West German professional journal [Figure 5–20].[128] The park included a children's playground, a lake, a rose garden, a restaurant, and a meadow for recreation which was bordered by irregularly planted shrubs and trees; a circumferential path ran through most of the site.

In the mid-1950s some people believed the chances for reunification had increased and that a thaw in the Cold War lay ahead. On several occasions, wishes for unification were expressed by East German landscape architects. In 1954, Johannes Reinhold envisioned "that a great development in the education of trained personnel in horticulture is just beginning. We also trust that such development will not be restricted to the eastern part of our fatherland but that we will find much greater possibilities for truly scholarly work which will serve the reconstruction of a modern, scientifically operated horticulture in a unified, peace-loving Germany."[129] As a consequence, in the mid-1950s there were more students than ever at the College of Agriculture and Horticulture of Humboldt University.[130] In 1955 the newly established section for garden architects in East Germany hoped for correspondence, conferences, and workshops in cooperation with West German landscape architects.[131]

The journal *Der Deutsche Gartenbau* voiced the 1955 New Year's desire that "with our common effort the wish for a German fatherland reunited in peace and affluence may be actualized."[132] A few months earlier, Friedrich Bergann had considered the reanimation of German dendrology after World War II and hoped for "a German collective arboretum . . . with which no other institution in the world could compare."[133] From 1930 to 1933 the head of the parks department in Dortmund, Richard Nose (1881–1965), had designed and built an arboretum of about ten acres in Romberg Park. During World War II bombs badly damaged many plants in the arboretum. Between 1951 and 1953 another twenty acres were added in three stages to the already existing arboretum as a comparative garden.[134] Since a Central Office for the Management of Hardy Trees and Shrubs had been established by Gerd Krüssmann, a dendrologist who succeeded Nose with the parks department in Dortmund in 1951, a similar office was also requested in East Germany.[135]

As early as 1950 landscape architect Walter Funcke had designed a perennial garden at Erfurt. He designed another one with nurseryman Karl Foerster on Freundschaftsinsel in Potsdam, between 1952 and 1955 [Figure 5–21]. The gardens were meant as an East German contribution to an all-German plant selection, in which species from nurseries were tested against a number of criteria, such as length of flowering, influence of rain on flowers and their colors, and resistance to frost and to fungal infection. In technical terms these gardens function as outdoor laboratories that tested plant material for nurseries and landscape architects.[136] Funcke referred to similar gardens in West Germany, such as in Hamburg, Nymphenburg, Weihenstephan, and Hanover-Herrenhausen, and demanded: "In order to get a most comprehensive impression of the behavior and the value of various species it is necessary to establish these gardens for plant selection under the most varying environmental conditions throughout Germany and to further develop those which exist already."[137]

In a response to Bergann's 1954 article published in the same year, it was made clear that the political split between East and West Germany had cut off the East from the specialized plant production in the West—especially in Holstein, one of the largest tree nursery areas in the world—and that no common institution would be established. The propagation of rare species and varieties in the East was said to have "failed" and was attributed "to the nonexistence of propagation material rather than to the question of economy and distribution."[138] Nevertheless, before the unification of Germany in 1990, the Foerster firm sold about three-quarters of its production in perennial plants to private nurseries in West Berlin and West Germany.[139]

In the 1950s, some felt that the political division of Germany had become irreversible. As the debate concerning plant propagation indicated, there was an economic side to the division, which affected landscape architecture: it caused the loss of propagation possibilities for East Germany and thus reduced the number of species available for garden designers. In addition, special plants needed for restoring or maintaining historical gardens were no longer cultivated. It is not surprising, then, that the horticultural department of the East German academy for agricultural sciences suggested that it begin by "providing lists of shrubs and perennials, biannuals, and annuals, as the basis for mass propagation. A dendrological inventory of economically valuable shrubs and trees in the area of the German Democratic Republic should be implemented. First of all, exotics need to be listed, in order that they may serve as the basis for propagation and breeding."[140]

The East-West separation even led to a name change for a number of plants. For example the *Salvia × superba* "Ostfriesland," a very popular herbaceous perennial bred in West Germany, was named after Ostfriesland, a region bordering the Netherlands. Since East Germany did not want their garden enthusiasts to be continually reminded of that rural region in West Germany when they looked at that plant, the plant was renamed *Salvia × superba* "Rügen." Rügen was the name of a very popular island in the Baltic Sea which belonged to East Germany.[141]

NEW PRINCIPLES INSTEAD OF ECONOMIC RECOVERY

The gradual end of landscape architecture in East Germany was hastened by a special event that took place in 1950. From 12 April to 25 May, a delegation of East German architects and city planners visited the Soviet Union. They spent thirty-two days in Moscow, two in Stalingrad, three in Kiev, and three in Leningrad (now St. Petersburg again). The journey deeply influenced architecture, landscape architecture, and city planning in East Germany thereafter. From an East German perspective the journey was meant to demonstrate to everyone, meaning the West Germans as well, that "the better Germany, the European alternative, is located in the East."[142] Consequently, according to architectural historian Simone Hain, "the entire organizational, administrative, planning-theoretical, and urbanistic-conceptional system for building in the GDR was turned upside down."[143]

The credo for this change, the "principles of planning," had been proposed in the ministry for city planning in Moscow on 29 April 1950[144] and they were adopted by the Ministerrat in East Berlin in July 1950 as the result of the Soviet excursion. Surprisingly, the principles first appeared in a professional West German journal that August.[145] They were also published in an official journal in East Germany the following month.[146] In words that clearly indicated the Communist belief that all of Germany would become Communist one day, the article stated that these principles were meant not only to guide city planning in the GDR but also to "express the great goals which challenge reconstruction in all of Germany."[147]

Principle 12 explicitly referred to landscape architecture and clearly opposed the earlier visions of "landscape in the city": "It is impossible to change a city into a garden. Of course, sufficient greenery must be provided. That principle cannot be overruled, however: in the city one lives in a more urban manner; at the periphery or beyond the city one lives in a more rural way."[148] In a presentation in July 1950 in Erfurt, Reinhold Lingner, then head of the East Berlin parks department, attempted to modify this principle. Because "the large city cannot be developed as a garden city, a far-reaching greening of the city must be sought."[149] However, Lothar Bolz, then the East German minister for reconstruction, contradicted Lingner's assertion in his explanation of the new doctrine: "One cannot build a garden city without politically demoralizing the population. Not without reason is the garden city the ideal of American and English heads of the police force: since their goal is to turn the worker into a breeder of rabbits and grower of cauliflower and prevent his participation in political demonstrations."[150] Ironically, only three years later the participation of many of these workers in political demonstrations throughout East Germany was quite contrary to what Bolz had imagined.

The "principles of city planning" marked the end of the municipal parks departments in East Berlin and other East German cities for the decades to come.[151] As late as 1950 the name of this branch of local administration—established in Berlin in 1870—was the Agency for Green Spaces and Horticulture. Whereas this name continued in West Berlin, and thus clearly signaled the importance of open spaces within municipalities, it almost ceased to exist in East Berlin in 1951. The municipal parks department was hidden behind a wall of higher-ranking authorities. If a citizen wanted to address a request to this branch of government, she or he would have to know that matters of open space provision and maintenance had been subsumed under an office for reconstruction, which again was a division of a department for economy. Thus were green issues administratively removed from the citizens' purview.[152]

When a new administrative structure was introduced in East Germany in 1952, the parks departments, which had been part of a longstanding tradition of local administration, were "forcibly terminated."[153] A characteristic new label for the groups who were assigned to the tasks of the earlier municipal parks departments was State Design Office for City and Village Planning, Dresden, Brigade Green Planning.[154] "This meant that a qualified, municipal administrative body no longer existed for maintaining parks and gardens" and that "the VEBs [*Volkseigener Betrieb*, or state-owned business] were fully integrated into the planned economy" of the state.[155] The disorder seems to have been considerable. With respect to the new administrative structures and their meaning for park design and maintenance a critical East German voice noted in 1954: "In the GDR one can hardly speak of a unified organizational reconstruction."[156] A few years later an article about the future of planning in landscape design in East Germany made it clear that "planning for landscape always means planning of a 'territory' which again is always the object of economic development as part of the totality of political economy."[157]

The professional field of freelance landscape architecture did not recover in East Germany and almost dried out completely in the late 1950s. In what may be the only contemporary statement from a West German landscape architect about the decline of professional activities in East Germany, Wilhelm Hübotter remarked in 1956: "It is correct, that our friends in the Eastern Zone have now lived for a decade under a law which is totally alien to us and which they daily have to deal with anew. The notion of the freelance landscape architect has changed into the land-consultant and –planner."[158]

The meagerness of his "efforts for a socialist building and garden art," which East German landscape architect Frank Erich Carl (1904–94) presented as the brief final chapter of his book *Small Architecture in German Garden Art*, in 1956, seems to have been felt by the author himself, who promised to publish a second book with more examples. It never appeared.[159] Out of 140 pages in Carl's book, 100 dealt with baroque gardens, landscape parks, and some parks and gardens of the early twentieth century. The last chapter, on socialist garden art — barely two of the nine pages are text — shows designs for Lomonossow University and a public square in Moscow, a site plan and a few details for Stalin-allée in East Berlin designed by the Kollektiv R. Lingner.

As a consequence of collectivization campaigns in 1960 and 1971, almost all freelance landscape architects had to abandon their practices. For example, in Leipzig and its surroundings, with a population of roughly 750,000 inhabitants, not a single private park, garden, or landscaping business existed prior to reunification.[160] In 1958 the garden design and construction branch which Karl Foerster had established in 1928 in Potsdam was liquidated.[161] The Foerster firm itself became half state-owned in 1960 and fully state-owned in

1970 after the death of its founder. After the unification of Germany in 1989 and 1990, Hermann Goeritz (1902–98) was apparently the only surviving independent landscape architect from East Germany. Only in the late 1990s, one and a half generations later, did a partial recovery of the profession begin in what were then the new states of the Federal Republic of Germany.[162]

NEW DEVELOPMENTS IN THE WEST

In West Germany landscape architects had reorganized in 1948.[163] It already seemed that "the possibilities [for the creation of new open spaces] which the great chaos [after World War II] left have in many cases been ruined; ahead is the urgent task to make use of what may be the last chance."[164] Contradictory as it may seem, the fear of losing gardens, parks, and other open spaces — which had been saved from development and reconstruction—was a sign of prosperity. The rising number of private cars was one of its more visible signs in West Germany. New and broader roads were needed, roads that often encroached upon open spaces and thus reduced their size and quality.[165] Paradoxically, landscape architects assumed the professional task of integrating these new roads into the urban and rural areas.[166]

An outstanding example of West German open-space planning from the 1950s is associated with landscape architect Günther Grzimek (1915–96), who was head of the parks department in Ulm, Baden-Württemberg, from 1947 to 1960. Grzimek took a decisive step on the road to democratic planning procedures, developing a concept of urban planning considered unusual by his contemporaries.[167] Grzimek had realized that "it is good to have the public participate" and worked along with citizens from the early 1950s on—almost two decades before comparable participatory activities in landscape architecture.

From the early twentieth century on, many a landscape architect in Germany could survive economically only when also engaged in commercial activities as a landscape contractor. In the postwar years, however, the professional climate changed. In 1953 the Essen Resolutions of the German Association of Garden Architects excluded commercially active landscape architects from membership, a clear sign of economic recovery in the profession. Compared to the interest in new design ideas during the years of the Weimar Republic, this may not have suggested any form of recovery — and indeed, in terms of design it was more like stagnation.

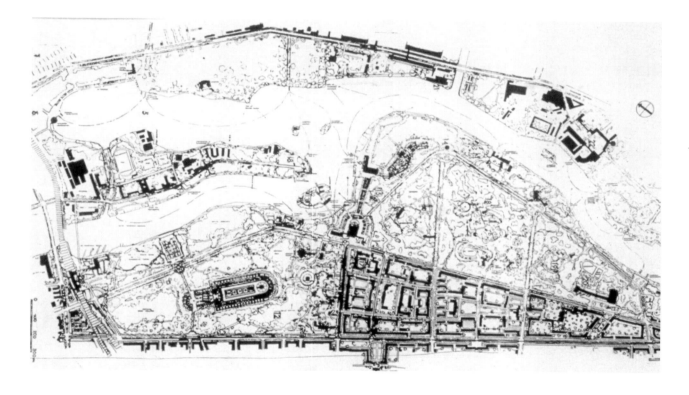

Figure 5–22.
Kulturpark Treptow, Berlin, 1957.
Walter Hinkefuss, landscape architect.
[Deutsche Architektur]

In 1954 the landscape architects in West Germany established an office in Bonn, then the capital of the Federal Republic of Germany, and began to develop a program of increased professional and strategic activities.[168] Committees for public relations, economic policy, science, and education were formed. Lobbying for the parliamentary acceptance of landscape architects as freelance professionals began and aimed at achieving equal legal status with architects.[169]

NEW DEVELOPMENTS IN THE EAST

Similar signs of recovery appeared in East Germany, although not at the same level as in the West. With respect to public open space, the word *Kulturpark* first appeared in East Germany in the 1950s [Figure 5–22]. In a comparable way the Plan for the National Work of Reconstruction had decreed for the city of Erfurt, Thuringia, in 1953, that "the area of the horticultural exhibition has to be changed into a generously designed culture park for the Erfurt working people."[170] It is difficult to see how the newly advocated Kulturpark differed from earlier parks. Following a decision of the Erfurt assembly of city deputies in 1923, some thirty years earlier, the land surrounding the former castle on Mount Cyriak was converted to an urban park.[171]

In 1954 East German landscape architect Helmut Lichey (1910–1991) reported on his visit to the Soviet agricultural exposition in Moscow and found that the "central culture park, named after Maxim Gorki, is nowadays an older design which no longer can compete with new creations."[172] For Lichey such a Kulturpark was outdated. His view seems to have changed somewhat, however, after he had been to Moscow again in 1956 and had visited a flower show at Moscow's Maxim Gorki Kulturpark.[173] In the same year Lichey called a fairly large open space in the south part of Leipzig a Kulturpark. Here the first Agricultural Exhibition in Markkleeberg had taken place in 1953. The center of this area was a traditional public park, Goethe Park. Adjacent to the north were track and field areas; a forest bordered to the west, adjacent to the south were allotment gardens and the site for the largest agricultural exhibition in East Germany. In 1957 Lichey again organized a flower show in the Gorki Kultur Park in Moscow.[174]

The Arbeitskreis Gartenarchitektur und Landschaftsgestaltung, the professional organization for landscape architects in East Germany, chose as the topic for its first meeting Central Parks and Their Meaning for City Planning in the German Democratic Republic. The meeting took place in Dresden in late 1956.[175] The exhibition of projects at this meeting included nine Kulturparks. Each of the plans seems to have presented a different version of the idea and thus caused some confusion about what a cultural park might be. As one participant later noted, "A precise wording of this category is urgently needed because the labeling on the exhibition plans only created a very imprecise image of the culture park for the spectator."[176] Obviously, it was quite difficult to clearly explain the difference between a Kulturpark and the earlier version of a park for people.[177] Although communication between landscape architects in East and West Germany had become more and more difficult after 1953, a few landscape architects from West Germany did attend the conference. One of them, the senior Wilhelm Hübotter, reported that at first the program had caused him some anxiety, but later it proved to be less problematic. Nevertheless he felt a "red thread" running through the presentations. Since Hübotter had put the words "red thread" in quotation marks, those familiar with the situation in Germany in those days understood that he was alluding to the Communist undertone he sensed in the presentations.[178]

Another milestone involved the renewed interest in school gardens, which differed considerably in East and West Germany.[179] In school gardens, it was believed, children should learn how to cultivate and maintain plants as practical applications of lessons taught in botany and biology. Although school gardens were often neglected in West Germany after World War II, they prospered in East Germany. In West Germany those who strongly advocated school gardens gradually vanished after the war.[180] In a 1956 publication, West German landscape architect Gerda Gollwitzer, also editor of *Garten und Landschaft* from 1954 to 1974, reacted to what had become reality in many schools in West Germany and condemned "schoolwork gardens" as a "theory," and thus implied that school gardens were no longer practical.[181] Quite to the contrary, school gardens in East Germany received an official boost, supported by a number of publications translated from Russian, which promoted the Michurin school garden, based on the ideas of the Russian botanist and pomologist Ivan Vladimirovich Michurin (1855–1935). Michurin bred fruit and vegetable varieties that could grow in the harsh climate of the northern Soviet Union; he wanted to bring a knowledge of plants to every child.[182]

The interest in allotment gardens, a century-old tradition, remained strong in both parts of the country, and landscape architects were involved in their design in many instances.[183] Last but not least there was in both East and West Germany a nearly obsessive occupation of landscape architects with cemeteries—a longstanding tradition.[184]

This essay is hardly more than an overview of some of the ideas, events, and designs that shaped landscape architecture in Germany in the years between 1940 and 1960. My choices have been fairly selective. The first five years in this period were dominated by the belief in a Teutonic myth that was especially strong during National Socialism and that directed landscape architecture between 1940 and 1945. The following fifteen years, between 1945 and 1960, were an unusual time for landscape architecture in Germany, since the clash between two opposing *Weltanschauungen* was reflected in professional differences in East and West Germany. During the first five of these fifteen years, there was still a considerable amount of mutual exchange between East and West; German landscape architects shared a common interest in clearing the rubble from World War II. The actual design ideas followed the naturalistic style of the late nineteenth and early twentieth centuries; the vigorous designs of the Weimar Republic period were almost forgotten. The following decade, the years between 1950 and 1960, marked recovery into prosperity, at least in West Germany. In the East, however, private landscape architecture firms and municipal park departments gradually ceased to exist. But in both East and West Germany, landscape architects avoided any reflection of National Socialism and its impact upon their profession.

A comprehensive view of the development of landscape architecture and the various aspects of design between 1940 and 1960 in Germany can come only with future research. Perhaps this essay will stimulate study for just that purpose.

NOTES

I wish to thank Marc Treib and my editors at the University of Pennsylvania Press who took so many pains to make my piece more readable to an English-language audience.

1. See Gert Gröning and Joachim Wolschke-Bulmahn, *Die Liebe zur Landschaft, Der Drang nach Osten, Zur Entwicklung der Landespflege im Nationalsozialismus und während des Zweiten Weltkrieges in den "eingegliederten Ostgebieten,"* *Arbeiten zur sozialwissenschaftlich orientierten Freiraumplanung*, 9 (Munich: Minerva Publikation, 1987), especially chapter 3.1, "Die Eroberung Polens als Meilenstein in der Entwicklung der Landespflege."

2. See Gröning and Wolschke-Bulmahn, *Die Liebe zur Landschaft, Der Drang nach Osten*.

3. Heinrich Friedrich Wiepking-Jürgensmann, "Aufgaben und Ziele deutscher Landschaftspolitik," *Gartenkunst*, 53, no. 6, 1940, p. 92 (my translation). See also Heinrich Friedrich Wiepking-Jürgensmann, *Die Landschaftsfibel* (Berlin: Deutsche Landbuchhandlung, 1942), p. 32.

4. Wiepking-Jürgensmann, "Aufgaben," p. 93 (my translation).

5. Wiepking-Jürgensmann, *Landschaftsfibel*, p. 32.

6. See Gröning and Wolschke-Bulmahn, *Die Liebe zur Landschaft, Der Drang nach Osten*.

7. Himmler was also the National Socialist Reichsführer SS; for a comprehensive account of the meaning of the SS, see Eugen Kogon, *Der SS-Staat* (Munich: Wilhelm Heine Verlag, 1945; reprint, 1977).

8. My translation; motto of the journal *Deutsche Arbeit* for nos. 6–7, June–July 1942, reprinted in Gröning and Wolschke-Bulmahn, *Die Liebe zur Landschaft, Der Drang nach Osten*, p. 62.

9. These rules have been reprinted in Gert Gröning, "Die 'Allgemeine Anordnung Nr. 20/VI/42'—Über die Gestaltung der Landschaft in den eingegliederten Ostgebieten," Mechthild Rössler, Sabine Schleiermacher, unter Mitarbeit von Cordula Tollmien (eds.), *Der "Generalplan Ost": Schriften der Hamburger Stiftung für die Sozialgeschichte des 20. Jahrhunderts* (Berlin: Akademie Verlag, 1993), pp. 131–47.

10. Erhard Mäding, *Regeln für die Gestaltung der Landschaft* (Berlin: Deutsche Landbuch-handlung, 1943), p. 51 (my translation).

11. See Louis Kniese, *Die Pflanzensoziologie in der Landschafts- und Gartengestaltung, Leistungssteigerung im Gartenbau*, no. 7 (Wiesbaden: Rud. Bechtold, 1942).

12. Erwin Aichinger, "Pflanzen- und Menschengesellschaft, ein biologischer Vergleich," *Biologia Generalis*, 17, 1943, pp. 56–79 (my translation).

13. Reinhold Tüxen, "Pflanzengesellschaften als Gestaltungsstoff," *Gartenkunst*, 52, 1939, p. 209. "Fremdkörper" has an ambiguous meaning in German; it may mean body as well as substance.

14. In 1939 Tüxen established the Central Office for Mapping the Vegetation of the Reich, in Hanover. Tüxen had become interested in plant sociology during his studies at the University of Heidelberg (1919–25); he considered Josias Braun-Blanquet, who had published his book *Pflanzensoziologie* in Berlin in 1928, as his mentor. Also in 1928 Tüxen founded the Floristisch-soziologische Arbeitsgemeinschaft in Niedersachsen and consequently edited its newsletter. In 1931 Tüxen qualified for the academic field of *Pflanzensoziologie* (sociology of plants) at the College for Veterinary Medicine in Hanover.

15. See Wiepking-Jürgensmann, "Aufgaben und Ziele," caption to figure 23, p. 88 (my translation). For a more detailed discussion of these events see Gröning and Wolschke-Bulmahn, *Die Liebe zur Landschaft, Der Drang nach Osten*.

16. Wiepking-Jürgensmann, *Landschaftsfibel*, p. 24.

17. Ibid., p. 23.

18. Midgard was a landscape of fields and gardens which in old times had to be gained from "Utgard," the virgin forest, "in a tedious fight against animals and forces of nature," ibid., p. 25 (my translation).

19. Ibid.

20. Ibid., p. 15.

21. In 1948, Georg Pniower, who was forbidden to work as a landscape architect during National Socialism, criticized this policy: "Imagine that only 7 percent of the tree and shrub species in Germany are of native origin, this is reason enough to apply the term 'rooted-to-the-soil flora' with caution and to greet the striving for the reconstruction of native plant associations with reservations. Swaggering 'over-gardeners' of the Nazi time did their best to degrade plant sociology in landscape design to a set of pat solutions. One of these 'stormers' (alien to the profession, however), to the mockery of the experts, went so far as to ban certain trees and shrubs as 'non-Aryan.'" Georg Pniower, *Bodenreform und Gartenbau* (Berlin-Charlottenburg: Siebeneicher Verlag, 1948), p. 136 (my translation).

22. In a misleading way a pathless garden by the Danish landscape architect Gudmund Nyeland Brandt (1878–1945) had been presented to the professional public in Germany as exemplifying the "coming garden" in two 1930 articles. See Gudmund Nyeland Brandt, "Der kommende Garten," *Wasmuths Monatshefte für Baukunst*, 14, no. 4, 1930, pp. 161–76, and Franz Hallbaum, "Der kommende Garten," *Gartenkunst*, 43, no. 7, 1930, p. 103.

23. Reichsminister of Science, Education, and Education of the People to the Reichsminister of Finance, both in Berlin, 17 July 1941, "Betrifft: Neuordnung der gartenbaulichen Berufs- und Fachschulen," Bundesarchiv Koblenz R2/12848.

24. Reichsminister of Science, Education, and Education of the People, 15 January 1942, memo, "Aktenvermerk," Referat I/8, Bundesarchiv Koblenz R2/12848.

25. See Erklärung in Anbetracht der Niederlage Deutschlands und der Übernahme der obersten Regierungsgewalt hinsichtlich Deutschlands durch die Regierungen des Vereinigten Königreiches, der Vereinigten Staaten von Amerika und der Union der sozialistischen Sowjet-Republiken und durch die Provisorische Regierung der Französischen Republik, Berlin, 5.6.1945, *Amtsblatt des Kontrollrats in Deutschland*, 1945, Ergänzungsblatt no. 1, pp. 7–9.

26. There were signs of unification, however. For economic reasons, the zones in West Germany administered by the United States and the United Kingdom were combined into an entity known as the Bi-Zone in 1946: see Karl Busemann, "Der Industrieplan im Zweizonenbereich," *Die Neue Stadt*, 1, no. 1, 1947, pp. 37–38. The Bi-Zone turned into a Tri-Zone in 1947, when the zone administered by France was added. On 25 February 1946 the Allied Council issued as Act 46, a law that dissolved the Prussian state; see *Amtsblatt des Kontrollrats . . .*, no. 14, 31 March 1947, p. 262. On 8 May 1949 the Parliamentary Council in the Tri-Zone accepted the constitution, the Grundgesetz der Bundesrepublik Deutschland, and thus

established the Federal Republic of Germany with the help of the Western Allies. The East Zone was administered by the Soviet Union and on 7 October 1949 turned into the German Democratic Republic.

27. See Karl Busemann, "Die deutsche Völkerwanderung," *Die Neue Stadt*, 2, no. 1, 1948, pp. 36–37.

28. See, e.g., Kurt Blaum, "Die drei Stufen," *Die Neue Stadt*, 1, no. 1, 1947, pp. 7–10; and Peter Paul Nahm, "Die Eingliederung der Vertriebenen in Hessen," *Die Neue Stadt*, 1, no. 1, 1947, pp. 22–23.

29. See Johannes Rautenstrauch, "Stadtpark Hamburg—40 Jahre alt," *Gartenwelt*, 51, no. 1, 1951, pp. 8–9. The Quonset huts disappeared only shortly before the first International Horticultural Show Hamburg in 1953.

30. Carl Alwin Schenck, *Forestry in Germany —Present and Prospective* (New York, 1948), p. 28.

31. See Johannes Reinhold, "25 Jahre akademisches Studium des Gartenbaues in Deutschland," *Archiv für Gartenbau*, 2, nos. 5–6, 1954, p. 346. In January 1950 Reinhold was appointed professor of vegetable cultivation at Humboldt University in East Berlin; see G. Friedrich and F.-P. Zahn, "Prof. Dr. Johannes Reinhold 60 Jahre alt," *Der Deutsche Gartenbau*, 4, no. 5, 1957, p. 166.

32. Hans Karl Möhring, "Zukunftsfragen des Gartenbaues," *Gartenwelt*, 49, no. 1, 1948, p. 1.

33. See, e.g., "Frankfurter Trümmerverwertungsgesellschaft G.m.b.H.," *Die Neue Stadt*, 1, no. 2, 1947, p. 89. See also the first issue of the journal *Das Gartenamt*, which appeared in December 1952. It carried several articles that referred to the greening of "rubble mountains." See Eberhard Fink, "Versuchspflanzung auf dem grössten Trümmerberg Berlins," *Garten und Landschaft*, 65, no. 8, 1955, pp. 7–9.

34. See "Betrachtungen über einen künstlichen Berg," *Das Gartenamt*, 7, no. 2, 1958, pp. 33–34; this article talks about a student housing project, which had been partially developed there between 1936 and 1939. It avoids any reference to National Socialism. This was a characteristic position in those days when National Socialist activities were played down in Germany.

35. Since it was located next to Teufelssee, it was appropriately named Teufelsberg, the "Devil's Mountain." Walter Rossow, "Trümmerberg am Teufelssee," *Garten und Landschaft*, 62, no. 9, 1952, p. 7.

36. See G. Hoffmann, "Erfahrungen aus der Begrünung Gross-Berlins," *Der Landschaftsgärtner*, 5, no. 41, 1953, pp. 37–38. And former National Socialist landscape officer Alwin Seifert now suggested that instead of planting thousands of kilometers of highways in Poland and the Soviet Union, five million cubic meters of rubble from houses in the center part of Cologne could be distributed within the open spaces of the greenbelt of the city. See Alwin Seifert, "Gutachten über die Unterbringung von 5 Mill. cbm. Altstadtschutt im inneren Grüngürtel der Stadt Köln," *Garten und Landschaft*, 60, no. 1, 1950, pp. 2–4. The city planned to create rubble hills between twenty and forty meters high in the open spaces of the "Innere Grüngürtel," but Seifert supported a height of up to twenty-five meters "designed according to the internal logic" of the inner greenbelt. The design would be a "wide-swinging hilly landscape" (p. 2).

37. See Erich Borchert, "Wir fangen wieder klein an!" *Gartenwelt*, 51, no. 8, 1951, p. 118.

38. See Werner Starke, "Baum und Strauch auf dem Schulhof," *Gartenwelt*, 49, no. 24, 1949, p. 356.

39. See Norbert Schindler, "Die Berliner Grünplanung von 1945 bis 1970," *Das Gartenamt*, 19, no. 6, 1970, pp. 288–304.

40. Karl Girt and Hirsch, "Dresden wird wieder Gartenstadt," *Der Landschaftsgärtner*, 4, no. 26, 1952, p. 10.

41. See Karl Diebolder, "Die öffentlichen Gartenanlagen der Stadt Heidelberg," *Gartenwelt*, 49, no. 12, 1949, pp. 184–185.

42. See SO 1, "Trümmerverwertung, Was geschieht mit den Bunkern?" *Die Neue Stadt*, 2, no. 2, 1948, p. 81; see W. Delenk, "Der Berliner Friedrichshain und seine Aufgaben als zentrale Parkanlage in der Hauptstadt der DDR Berlin," *Deutsche Gartenarchitektur*, 9, 1968, pp. 29–31; see also Gert Gröning and Joachim Wolschke-Bulmahn, "Volkspark und Volksgemeinschaft," Bezirksamt Wedding von Berlin, Abteilung Bau- und Wohnungswesen —Gartenbauamt (ed.), *". . . wo eine freye und gesunde Luft athmet . . .": Zur Entstehung und Bedeutung der Volksparke im Wedding* (Berlin: Kulturbuch Verlag, 1988), pp. 104–9.

43. Designed by the sculptor Jewgeni V. Vutchetetich and the architect Jakow B. Belopolski the memorial was built in the park between 1947 and 1949. See Jürgen Riese, "Eine Führung durch den Treptower Park," *Entwicklung der Volksparke* (Berlin: Druckhaus Weimar, 1979), pp. 67–69. See also Jürgen Riese, "Treptower Park," Gottfried Funeck, Waltraud Schönholz, and Fritz Steinwasser (eds.), *Park- und Grünanlagen in Berlin* (Berlin–DDR, 1987), pp. 60–78. The park and the playground were designed in the 1870s by landscape architect Gustav Meyer (1816–77) who was the first head of the newly established municipal parks department in Berlin from 1870 until his death. Before that Meyer had closely collaborated with the royal landscape architect Peter Josef Lenné (1789–1866), who is considered the forefather of professional landscape architects in Germany.

44. See Günter Winkler, "Parks in Pankow," Gottfried Funeck, Waltraud Schönholz, and Fritz Steinwasser (eds.), *Park- und Grünanlagen in Berlin* (Berlin-DDR, 1987), pp. 82 and 89.

45. Such principles were explicitly stated for architecture and city planning: see Otto Bartning et al., "Grundsätze des Wiederaufbaues," *Die Neue Stadt*, 1, no. 1, 1947, p. 41.

46. See Josef Victor, "Die Geroanlage in M.-Gladbach, Auf Trümmern entstandene Grünfläche im Zentrum einer Grossstadt," *Das Gartenamt*, 5, no. 7, 1956, pp. 125–27.

47. Camillo Schneider, "Begrünung von Flächen in ausgebombten Städten," *Gartenwelt*, 49, no. 4, 1948, pp. 59–60.

48. Ibid., p. 59.

49. See Aloys Bernatzky, "Die Tagung der Landschafter in Hannover," *Die Neue Stadt*, 2, no. 7, 1948, p. 314.

50. See Georg Pniower, "Garten- und Landeskultur," Henry Gocht et al. (eds.), *Berliner Forschung und Lehre in den Landwirtschaftswissenschaften* (Berlin: Landwirtschaftlich-Gärtnerische Fakultät, Humboldt-Universität), 1956, pp. 155–63. And see Gert Gröning and Joachim Wolschke-Bulmahn, "Zum 90. Geburtstag des Gartenarchitekten Georg Bela Pniower," *Das Gartenamt*, 35, no. 12, 1986, pp. 735–43. Pniower held this chair from 1 June 1946 until his death on 14 March 1960.

51. See map, figure 1, plan of Berlin, buildings respectively territories of the agricultural college, in Ludwig Wittmack et al. (eds.),

Königliche Landwirtschaftliche Hochschule in Berlin (Berlin, 1906), p. 27. See map "Lage der Stadtinstitute der Landwirtschaftlich-Gärtnerischen Fakultät" attached to Gocht et al. (eds.), *Berliner Forschung und Lehre in den Landwirtschaftswissenschaften*.

52. See Pniower, *Bodenreform*, pp. 123, 136, and 139; see Pniower, "Garten- und Landeskultur," p. 158.

53. Georg Pniower, "Gartenbau und Landschaftsgestaltung," *Mitteilungsblatt der Genossenschaft zur Förderung des Gartenbaues*, 1, no. 9 (offprint s.p., 4 pp.), p. 4.

54. Ibid.

55. Ibid.

56. See Georg Bela Pniower, "Un giardino esotico nella 'Gourmenia Haus' a Berlino," *Casabella*, 29, no. 2, 1930, pp. 34–38. Pniower was one of the few German landscape architects who had their design ideas published in Italian professional journals before National Socialism: see Georg Bela Pniower, "Un giardino d'abitazione, trasformato," *Casabella*, 29, no. 5, 1930, pp. 43–46; and Georg Bela Pniower, "Una casa d'artista nei pressi di Berlino," *Casabella*, 32, no. 8, 1930, pp. 27–31. Pniower's design is also cited in a post–World War II Italian publication: see Luigi Figini, *L'Elemento "Verde" e L'Abitazione*, Quaderni di Domus, 7 (Milan: Editore Domus, 1950). I thank Sonja Dümpelmann for providing me with the bibliographical data for these publications.

57. See Georg Pniower, "Rund um den Kleistpark," *Garten und Landschaft*, 60, no. 5, 1950, pp. 5–12.

58. See Pniower, "Garten- und Landeskultur." And see, for a history of the botanical garden that also mentions Pniower's design for Kleistpark, Folkwin Wendland, *Berlins Gärten und Parke* (Berlin: Propyläen Verlag, 1979), pp. 186–96.

59. In 1744 it became the garden of the newly established Royal Academy of Sciences with Johann Gottlieb Gleditsch (1714–86) as professor of botany. In 1773 Gleditsch published a list of foreign and native trees, shrubs, and perennials for the use and enjoyment of gardeners and amateurs; see Johann Gottlieb Gleditsch, *Pflanzenverzeichnis zum Nutzen und Vergnügen der Lust- und Baumgärtner und aller Liebhaber, von fremden und einheimischen Bäumen, Sträuchern und Staudengewächsen* (Berlin, 1773). In 1823 the first school for higher education for garden-

ers was established there with the help of royal landscape architect Peter Josef Lenné. From 1899 on the botanical garden moved in a southwesterly direction toward a location in Berlin-Dahlem, where it is still located.

60. Not until 1985 were the sentences of this cruelly unjust court of justice declared entirely invalid. It needed a public protest from filmmakers around Michael Verhoeven to make this happen. Verhoeven had made a film, *Die weisse Rose*, about a group of students who tried to resist National Socialism. The students were caught and decapitated in 1943.

61. Georg Bela Pniower, "Ein Vorschlag zum Berliner Tiergarten," *Die Neue Stadt*, 2, no. 7, 1948, p. 270.

62. For Hoffmann's biography, see Harald Kegler, "Das Bauhaus, eine Annäherung," Stiftung Bauhaus, Verein Industrielles Gartenreich e.V. (eds.), *Vom Bauhaus nach Bitterfeld* (Berlin: Stattbuch Verlag, 1998), pp. 18–19.

63. See Hubert Hoffmann, "Das grüne Herz Berlins," *Die Neue Stadt*, 2, no. 7, 1948, p. 274.

64. The plan is reproduced in *Die Neue Stadt*, 3, 1949, p. 104.

65. See Willy Alverdes, "Der Große Tiergarten," *Garten und Landschaft*, 62, no. 9, 1952, p. 9.

66. See a contemporary review by R.O. in *Die Neue Stadt*, 2, no. 4, 1948, pp. 188–89.

67. See especially the chapter "City Landscape or Garden-City?" in Pniower, *Bodenreform und Gartenbau*. The book also contains short chapters about the state of the agrarian reform in the American, British, French, and Russian Occupied Zones. The chapter about the Russian Occupied Zone is longer than the others because "while in the West zones the agrarian reform is still in the stage of discussions it is implemented fact in the East of Germany. By a revolutionary act large landed property has been abolished here in one stroke" (p. 42).

68. Pniower, *Gartenbau und Bodenreform*, p. 125.

69. Ibid., pp. 119, 136, 137. Pniower's plans may have been stimulated by the achievements of the Tennessee Valley Authority and the gigantic Russian plan to create a steppe agriculture. See Pniower, "Gartenbau und Landschaftsgestaltung."

70. See "Eine Beispiellandschaft entsteht," *Der Landschaftsgärtner*, 5, no. 41, 1953, p. 37.

71. Gustav Heinrichsdorff, *Erkenntnisse und Erfahrungen aus den Forschungs- und Entwicklungsarbeiten im Huy-Hakel-Gebiet*, Rat des Bezirkes Magdeburg, Abteilung Land- und Forstwirtschaft, Agrarpropaganda (ed.), *Naturschutz und Landschaftsgestaltung im Bezirk Magdeburg*, 3. Folge, Sonderdruck (Magdeburg, 1959), p. 6 (my translation).

72. See Gert Gröning, "The Idea of Land Embellishment as Exemplified in the *Monatsblatt für Verbesserung des Landbauwesens und für zweckmäßige Verschönerung des baierischen Landes* (Monthly for the Improvement of Rural Architecture and Appropriate Embellishment of the State of Bavaria)," *Journal of Garden History*, 12, no. 3, 1992, pp. 164–82.

73. Georg Pniower, "Wirtschaft und Naturschutz," *Märkische Heimat*, 3, 1956, p. 46.

74. See Reinhold, "25 Jahre akademisches Studium," p. 346.

75. See Hans-Helmuth Wundsch, "Die Landwirtschaftlich-Gärtnerische Fakultät der Humboldt-Universität zu Berlin," Henry Gocht et al. (eds.), *Berliner Forschung und Lehre in den Landwirtschaftswissenschaften* (Berlin: Landwirtschaftlich-Gärtnerische Fakultät, Humboldt-Universität, 1956), pp. 11–15.

76. See Pniower, "Garten- und Landeskultur." See also Reinhold, "25 Jahre akademisches Studium."

77. See Pniower, "Garten- und Landeskultur," p. 159.

78. Ibid., pp. 161, 162 (Forstliche Kippenkultivierung in der Niederlausitz); see also Klaus-Dietrich Gandert, "Georg Bela Pniower—Sein Leben und Wirken für die Garten- und Landeskultur," Institut für Umweltgeschichte und Regionalentwicklung (ed.), *Landschaft und Planung in den neuen Bundesländern—Rückblicke* (Berlin: Verlag für Wissenschaft und Forschung, 1999), pp. 221–35.

79. See Gröning and Wolschke-Bulmahn, "Zum 90. Geburtstag."

80. See Reinhold, "25 Jahre akademisches Studium."

81. See Klaus Dietrich Gandert, "Das Hochschulstudium in der Fachrichtung Garten- und Landschaftsgestaltung," *Der Deutsche Gartenbau*, 3, no. 4, 1956, p. 108. Regarding developments in East Germany, on 1 February 1952 the Institute for Landscape Design was established at Karl Marx University in Leipzig. It was headed by Gerhard Darmer, who left for Hanover University in West Germany in 1958. Albrecht Krummsdorf, Darmer's assistant, succeeded him. In 1955 a chair for garden art, landscape design, and engineering-biology was established at the East German Dresden University of Technology. It was given to Werner Bauch (1902–83), who held it until 1961. See "Zum Professor ernannt," *Der Landschaftsgärtner*, 4, no. 26, 1952, p. 9.

82. Ibid.

83. See Ulrich Wolf, "Die Ausbildung des Garten- und Landschaftsarchitekten," *Garten und Landschaft*, 60, no. 10, 1950, p. 5.

84. Jürgen Barth, "Aufgaben und Möglichkeiten eines Hochschulinstitutes für Grünflächenplanung und Landschaftspflege," *Das Gartenamt*, 8, no. 4, 1959, pp. 71–72.

85. Gröning and Wolschke-Bulmahn, *1887–1987, DGGL, Deutsche Gesellschaft für Gartenkunst und Landschaftspflege*, p. 66.

86. This was the West Berlin branch of the once central administration for Berlin. On 29 January 1946 the chairs of the School of Agriculture of Friedrich Wilhelm University had been approved by the German Central Administration for the Education of the People, which was located in the Russian occupation zone in what later became East Berlin. See Wundsch, "Die Landwirtschaftlich-Gärtnerische Fakultät," p. 14.

87. The SS established and administered the concentration camps where millions of Jews and other people were systematically killed during World War II. See Kogon, *Der SS-Staat*.

88. See Reinhard Berkelmann, "Der Sachsenhain bei Verden an der Aller," *Gartenkunst*, 50, no. 5, 1937, pp. 125–28; see also Wilhelm Hübotter, "Steine—auch eine Art Landschaftsgestaltung," *Garten und Landschaft*, 66, 1956, pp. 110–13. The site still exists. Basically, a flood plain is surrounded by the Saxon walk, a kind of pedestrian loop. Both sides of the walk are framed by 4,500 sizable boulders which commemorate the decapitation there of 4,500 Saxons by Charlemagne. Whether or not that took place is hard to ascertain. From a small and a

large Führerkanzel, terraces projecting into the flood plain, the Führer, Adolf Hitler, would address the assembled thousands of SS men.

89. See Joachim Wolschke-Bulmahn, "1945–1995: Zur landschaftsarchitektonischen Gestaltung der Gedenkstätte Bergen-Belsen," *Die Gartenkunst*, 7, no. 2, 1995, pp. 325–40; see also Gert Gröning and Uwe Schneider, *Die Heide in Park und Garten, Grüne Reihe—Quellen und Forschungen zur Gartenkunst*, 19 (Worms: Wernersche Verlagsgesellschaft, 1999). Two years later, in 1948, Hübotter and the fervent National Socialist Wiepking-Jürgensmann were instrumental in establishing the School of Horticulture and Culture of the Land in Hanover in the British zone. In 1954 the school became incorporated in the University of Technology, Hanover, as the Fakultät für Gartenbau und Landeskultur.

90. Schindler, "Die Berliner Grünplanung," p. 32, offprint; see also Ursula Poblotzki, "Conservative versus progressive strategies of Federal German Park Administrations in the 1950s and 1960s," *Journal of Garden History*, 12, no. 3, 1992, pp. 235–46. For a fairly comprehensive study of how landscape architects in West Germany saw people between 1945 and 1970, see Ursula Poblotzki, *Menschenbilder in der Landespflege, 1945–1970, Arbeiten zur sozialwissenschaftlich orientierten Freiraumplanung*, 13 (Munich: Minerva Publikation, 1992).

91. Fritz Schumacher, "Erkenntnisse für den Wiederaufbau zerstörter Städte," *Die Neue Stadt*, 2, nos. 5–6, 1948, p. 201 (my translation).

92. See N., "Die Akademie für Raumforschung und Landesplanung," *Die Neue Stadt*, 1, no. 1, 1947, p. 33.

93. See Bernhard Düttmann, "Ein Planungsvorschlag für Düsseldorf," *Die Neue Stadt*, 2, nos. 5–6, 1948, pp. 222–33; the section "Grünflächengestaltung" in this article included a "Grünflächenplan 1947" for Düsseldorf. See also the section "Grüngestaltung" in Hans Bernhard Reichow, "Organischer Aufbau der Stadt Kiel," *Die Neue Stadt*, 2, nos. 8–9, 1948, pp. 329–41; Aloys Bernatzky, "Begrünung Kiels," *Die Neue Stadt*, 2, nos. 8–9, 1948, pp. 376–77; and Hans Högg, "Die Durchgrünung unserer zerstörten Städte," *Baurundschau*, nos. 7–8, 1948.

94. See Theodor Joseph Bürgers, "Die Hygiene bei der Städteplanung," *Die Neue Stadt*, 1, no. 2, 1947, p. 53; see also Wilhelm Freckmann, "Die Bewässerung der Gärten," *Die Neue Stadt*, 2, no. 1, 1947, pp. 15–17.

95. Georg Heyer, "Kritik des Wohnungsreformers," *Die Neue Stadt*, 2, no. 2, 1948, pp. 72–74; Heyer responded to and supported Bürgers, see n. 94, above.

96. See Deutsche Olympische Gesellschaft, *Der Goldene Plan in den Gemeinden, Ein Handbuch* (Frankfurt am Main: Wilhelm-Limpert-Verlag, 1960, 2nd ed. 1962).

97. The group of employees of the magistrate of Berlin were Hans Scharoun, Wils Ebert, Reinhold Lingner, Luise Seitz, Peter Friedrich, Ludmilla Herzenstein (1906–94), Selman Selmanagic (1905–86), and Herbert Weinberger.

98. See Schindler, "Die Berliner Grünplanung," p. 33.

99. Göderitz published a small book *Braunschweig, Zerstörung und Aufbau, Kommunalpolitische Schriften der Stadt Braunschweig*, Heft 4 (Braunschweig, 1949).

100. See Hubert Hoffmann, "Schwerpunktsiedlung Finkenheerd," *Die Neue Stadt*, 4, no. 10, 1950, pp. 401–2.

101. Johannes Göderitz, Roland Rainer, and Hubert Hoffmann, *Die gegliederte und aufgelockerte Stadt, Archiv für Städtebau und Landesplanung*, 4 (Tübingen: Verlag Ernst Wasmuth, 1957).

102. Karl Bonatz, "Der Plan Berlin 1948," *Die Neue Stadt*, 3, no. 3, 1949, pp. 98–109.

103. Schindler, "Die Berliner Grünplanung," p. 35, offprint.

104. In the National Socialist era Wiepking had written: "A fruit landscape is a culture landscape in high culture—in contrast to a park, to a negligently used landscape, or to a nature protection area." Wiepking, *Landschaftsfibel*, p. 43. It was clear to Wiepking that "explicitly for war reasons we have to reconnect our cities as closely as possible to the fruit landscape not only in a manner of thinking that would work several 'wonders' but in a real reality," p. 44.

105. See Aloys Bernatzky, "Landschaft und Städtebau," *Die Neue Stadt*, 2, no. 1, 1948, pp. 5–9.

106. Hans Schwenkel, *Der Führer hält seine schützende Hand über unsere Hecken* (Stuttgart, n.d. [1936?]), p. 7.

107. A new West German association of landscape architects was established as the Association of German Garden Architects on 19 June 1948. See Wolschke-Bulmahn and Gröning, *1913–1988, 75 Jahre BDLA*. Their first conference was held a few months later with Josef Breloer (1898–?), a garden architect from Hildesheim, as its first president. The new statutes of the federal association and the new fee schedule for the honorarium the landscape architects wanted to collect for their services were the main points of this conference. See "Bund deutscher Gartenarchitekten," *Gartenwelt*, 49, no. 7, 1948, p. 118. The heads of the West German municipal parks departments did not organize until 1954; a number of garden and cemetery departments had formed within the association of cities that same year in Hesse. See Friedrich Heyer, "Bericht über die Arbeitstagung der Arbeitsgemeinschaft Hessischer Garten- und Friedhofsämter . . . ," *Das Gartenamt*, 5, no. 5, 1956, p. 100. Late in 1956 Konrad Glocker (1900–77), landscape architect and head of the parks department in Dortmund, Northrhine-Westphalia, from 1938 to 1965, was elected president of the newly established Association of Heads of Park Departments in Frankfurt am Main. See "'Verband der Gartenamtsleiter' gegründet," *Das Gartenamt*, 5, no. 11, 1956, p. 227.

The German Cities Diet Standing Conference of Park Department Directors in West Germany was formed in 1958 with landscape architect Johannes Joachim Sallmann (1912–96), head of the parks department in Frankfurt am Main from 1957 to 1977, as its first chairman from 1958 to 1964. See Johannes Sallmann, "25 Jahre 'Konferenz der Gartenbauamtsleiter beim DST,'" *Das Gartenamt*, 32, no. 8, 1983, pp. 481–83. For an overview of the professional status and salaries of landscape architects in the late 1950s, see Norbert Schindler, "Gartenbau-beamte im Spiegel der Beamten- und Besoldungsgesetze," *Das Gartenamt*, 8, no. 11, 1959, pp. 248–51.

108. Reinhold Lingner, "Die Verschönerung der Städte als Aufgabe des Nationalen Aufbauwerkes im Jahr der grossen Initiative," *Der Deutsche Gartenbau*, 1, no. 5, 1954, p. 129.

109. On 8 September 1949 the Action Committee of Leading Landscape Architects in Authorities and of Freelance Garden and Landscape Architects and Green Space Planners of the East Zone met, and on 9 September 1949 the Working Conference of the Garden and Landscape Architects and the Green Space Planners of the East Zone took place on the occasion of the East German Horticultural Exhibition in Markkleeberg, near Leipzig, from 7 to 18 September 1949. See "Fachtagung und Planschau der Gartenarchitekten und Grünraumplaner in Leipzig/Markkleeberg," *Die Neue Stadt*, 3, no. 4, 1949, p. 231. More time passed and hopes were dashed. In a short note from a similar event in 1950 in Erfurt, the action committee is not mentioned. See Wu. (Wulle), "Tagung der Gartenarchitekten und Grünraumplaner in Erfurt," *Die Neue Stadt*, 4, no. 7, 1950, pp. 289–90. In 1952 the heads of the East German municipal parks departments met in Halle, and again somewhat later in East Berlin, in order to form an organization; "nothing came from it, however" (Hartmut Olejnik, "Jeder arbeitet nach eigenen Richtlinien," *Der Landschaftsgärtner*, 6, no. 16, 1954, p. 55).

On 16 February 1954 the Central Professional Group for Garden Architecture and Landscape Design was founded as a subdivision of the East German Association of German Architects, which had been incorporated on 31 October 1952. On 3 February 1955 East German landscape architects met again in East Berlin to establish a Garden Architects Section within the East German Union of Architects. See "Bildung einer Sektion Gartenarchitekten im BDA," *Der Landschaftsgärtner*, 7, no. 3, 1955, p. 76. It never worked as an independent professional organization, however.

110. See Gustav Allinger, *Das Hohelied von Gartenkunst und Gartenbau* (Berlin: Verlag Paul Parey, 1963), chapter titled "1933–1944 Episode des 'Reichsnährstands.'"

111. Hans Leistikow, "Vor zwanzig Jahren," *Die Neue Stadt*, 1, no. 2, 1947, p. 50.

112. Otto Bartning et al., "Grundsätze des Wiederaufbaus," *Die Neue Stadt*, 1, no. 1, 1947, p. 41. Founded in 1907 by Fritz Schumacher and others, the Werkbund was and still is a guild of artists, architects, city planners, painters, and others which included the plant breeder Karl Foerster. The first Werkbund conference after World War II was held in Schloss Rheydt in 1948. On 3 December 1949 the Berlin group of the Werkbund reestablished itself and elected architect Heinrich Tessenow (1876–1950) as president. At the third conference in Schloss Alfter, near Cologne, the reestablishment of the Werkbund for the Federal Republic of Germany including Berlin was resolved: see Heinrich Köning, "Deutscher Werkbund auf Bundesebene," *Die Neue Stadt*, 4, no. 9, 1950, pp. 377–78; and Effenberger, "Neubegründung der Gruppe Berlin des Deutschen Werkbundes," *Die Neue Stadt*, 4, no. 1, 1950, pp. 34–35.

113. For the overall design of the Feuerbacher Heide between the Doggenburg and the Rosensteinpark in Stuttgart, H. H. (Hubert Hoffmann), "Stuttgart plant ein Wohn-, Park- und Zoogelände," *Moderne Bauformen*, 35, 1936, p. 240.

114. See Max Müller, "Wie es zur SÜWEGA kam!" *Garten und Landschaft*, 59, nos. 5–6, 1949, p. 23; see also Alfred Reich, "SÜWEGA," *Garten und Landschaft*, 59, nos. 7–8, 1949, pp. 22–24. The Leipzig exhibition was designed by landscape architect Helmut Lichey, the one in Landau by landscape architect Walter Rieger (1909–84). Compared to prewar shows the program had become enlarged to up to sixty areas, including fruit, vegetables, annuals, children's playgrounds, allotment gardens, graves, and cemeteries and many others.

115. For a critical comment, see Josef Hempelmann, "Stuttgart-Hannover," *Gartenwelt*, 50, no. 24, 1950, p. 390.

116. Since 15 October 1949 Mattern had taught "Landschaftskultur" at the Staatliche Werkakademie Kassel: see "Staatliche Werkakademie Kassel," *Die Neue Stadt*, 3, no. 4, 1949, p. 283. In 1949 Mattern designed the park area around the Bundeshaus in Bonn: see Karl Wimmenauer, "Bundeshaus in Bonn, Ausbau der Pädagogischen Akademie in Bonn als Parlamentsgebäude der Bundesrepublik Deutschland," *Die Neue Stadt*, 3, October, 1949, pp. 297–301.

117. For Funcke's work see Susanne Karn, "Freiflächen und Landschaftsplanung unter den gesellschaftlichen Bedingungen der DDR, dargestellt am Beispiel von Werken des Landschaftsarchitekten Walter Funcke (1907–87)," doctoral dissertation, Faculty of Design, Architecture, University of the Arts, Berlin, 2001.

118. Wilhelm Hübotter, "Die Gartenbauausstellung in Erfurt," *Garten und Landschaft*, 60, no. 8, 1950, pp. 12–13; see also F. W. Hübner, "Erfurter Gartenschau 1950," *Gartenwelt*, 50, no. 16, 1950, p. 258; and Alexander Steffen, "Rückblick auf die Erfurter Gartenschau," *Gartenwelt*, 50, no. 22, 1950, pp. 357–58.

119. Wilhelm Hübotter, "Zum Jadega-Wettbewerb," *Garten und Landschaft*, 59, nos. 11–12, 1949, pp. 6–7.

120. It should be noted that during National Socialism Hanover had hosted the First Reichs Horticulture Fair on the same grounds from 24 June to 10 October 1933. The design competition for it had been won by Wilhelm Hübotter and Kurt Vogler. Also Oskar Langerhans, who had won the second prize with the architects Springer and Haack, took part. See Herbert Jensen, "Jahresschau deutscher Gartenkultur in Hannover," *Zentralblatt der Bauverwaltung*, 53, no. 37, 1933, pp. 437–42.

121. Gerda Gollwitzer, "Berlin wird immer grüner," *Garten und Landschaft*, 65, no. 8, 1955, pp. 1–6.

122. See, e.g., Johannes Rautenstrauch, "75 Jahre Ohlsdorfer Friedhof," *Gartenwelt*, 51, no. 23, 1951, pp. 392–93; this brief seventy-five-year history of the Ohlsdorf Cemetery in Hamburg mentioned that "in recent years almost all war damage has been repaired" (p. 393).

123. Kurt Irmscher, "Vorgartenbegrünung," *Der Landschaftsgärtner*, 5, no. 48, 1953, pp. 41–42.

124. Andreas Seidel, "Eisenhüttenstadt, Das Freiflächensystem der Wohnkomplexe I—IV—Zielsetzungen und Gestaltungsauffassungen der frühen fünfziger Jahre," *Brandenburgische Denkmalpflege*, 5, no. 2, 1996, p. 84.

125. Gerhard Kosel et al., "Der sozialistische Wohnkomplex, Deutsche Bau-Enzyklopädie," Richtlinien, Freiflächen, 4. Blatt, rear, 1959.

126. See the reports in the various journals about the National Garden Show in Cologne, West Germany, and the Horticultural Exhibition of the German Democratic Republic in Markkleeberg, near Leipzig. Both exhibitions were held in 1957: see, e.g., *Der Deutsche Gartenbau*, 4, nos. 11 and 12, 1957.

127. Gunter A. Schoch, "Gartengestaltung in Moskau (UdSSR)," *Das Gartenamt*, 6, no. 5, 1957, pp. 108–9.

128. See Helmut Kruse, "Entwurf und Baudurch- führung des Volksparkes am Weinbergsweg," *Der Deutsche Gartenbau*, 2, no. 7, 1955, pp. 183–86.

129. Reinhold, "25 Jahre akademisches Studium," pp. 352–54; see also the short report of a visit by students from Hanover University to Humboldt University in Berlin in *Der Deutsche Gartenbau*, 3, no. 7, 1956, p. 198.

130. In 1946–47 there were 133 students; in 1954–55, 773; see "Die Frequenz der Landw.-Gärtn. Fakultät," *Berliner Forschung und Lehre in den Landwirtschafts-wissenschaften* (Berlin: Landwirtschaftlich-Gärtnerische Fakultät, Humboldt-Universität), 1956, p. 278.

131. See "Bildung einer Sektion Gartenarchitekten im BDA," *Der Landschaftsgärtner*, 7, no. 3, 1955, p. 76.

132. Hermann Schüttauf and Helmut Eue, "Ein Jahr 'Der Deutsche Gartenbau,'" *Der Deutsche Gartenbau*, 2, no. 1, 1955, p. 1.

133. Friedrich Bergann, "'Arboretum Deutschland,' Gedanken zu einer Wiederbelebung der deutschen Dendrologie," *Der Deutsche Gartenbau*, 1, no. 1, 1954, pp. 29–31.

134. See Konrad Glocker, "Zentrale für Gehölzsichtung," *Gartenwelt*, 53, no. 3, 1953, pp. 35–36.

135. See Konrad Glocker, "Zentralstelle für Gehölzsichtung beim städtischen Gartenamt in Dortmund," *Garten und Landschaft*, 62, no. 7, 1952, pp. 14–15; and Klemens Heinze, "Dendrologie und öffentliches Grünwesen (Diskussionsbeitrag)," *Der Deutsche Gartenbau*, 1, no. 9, 1954, pp. 274–75; see also the response to this article by Friedrich Bergann, "Bemerkungen zum Beitrag des Kollegen Heinze," *Der Deutsche Gartenbau*, 1, no. 9, 1954, pp. 275–76.

136. See Görlach, "Die Bedeutung der Schau- und Sichtungsgärten," *Der Landschaftsgärtner*, 7, no. 6, 1955, p. 77.

137. Walter Funcke, "Die kulturelle und volkswirtschaftliche Bedeutung der Schau- und Sichtungsgärten für Freiland-Schmuckstauden," *Der Deutsche Gartenbau*, 2, no. 4, 1955, p. 95.

138. Klemens Heinze, "Dendrologie und öffentliches Grünwesen," p. 275.

139. The West German firms that formerly bought perennials from the East German Foerster firm at a much lower price than they had to pay anywhere in West Germany no longer bought these plants after the unification. In 1990, the new privately owned firm, which established itself after the unification as a successor to the state-owned firm, had to sell the plants under market economy conditions and consequently had extreme difficulty in establishing itself economically; personal communication from Kurt Näser, head of the state-owned VEG Stauden-kulturen "Karl Foerster" from 1971 to 1989.

140. Winkler, "Kommuniqué der Sektion Gartenbau," *Der Deutsche Gartenbau*, 1, no. 4, 1954, pp. 124–25.

141. I thank Kurt Näser, who confirmed this information.

142. Simone Hain, "Reise nach Moskau: Erste Betrachtungen zur politischen Struktur des städtebaulichen Leitbildwandels des Jahres 1950 in der DDR," manuscript (Berlin, 1992), p. 7.

143. Simone Hain, "Zur historischen Bedeutung und planungstheoretischen Bewertung der 'Reise nach Moskau,'" *Regio doc, Dokumentenreihe des Instituts für Regionalentwicklung und Strukturplanung* (Berlin) no. 1, 1995, pp. 5–11.

144. See Pisternik, "Übersicht über den Verlauf der Reise nach der Sowjetunion vom 12.4. bis 25.5.1950," *Regio doc, Dokumentenreihe des Instituts für Regionalentwicklung und Strukturplanung* (Berlin) no. 1, 1995, p. 38.

145. See "Grundsätze für den Städtebau in der Ostzone," *Die Neue Stadt*, 4, no. 8, 1950, pp. 329–30.

146. See "Bekanntmachung der Grundsätze des Städtebaus vom 15. September 1950," *Ministerialblatt der Deutschen Demokratischen Republik*, 16, no. 25, September 1950, pp. 153–54.

147. "Grundsätze für den Städtebau in der Ostzone," p. 329 (my translation).

148. Ibid., p. 330 (my translation).

149. Quoted in Wulle, "Tagung der Gartenarchitekten und Grünraumplaner in Erfurt," *Die Neue Stadt*, 4, no. 7, 1950, pp. 289–90.

150. Lothar Bolz, "Erläuterungen zu den Grundsätzen des Städtebaus," *Der Städtebau der Deutschen Demokratischen Republik, Ein Beitrag zum deutschen Aufbau* (Berlin, 1950), p. 31.

151. A new communal parks department for East Berlin was established in 1960 with landscape architect Helmut Lichey as director until 1975, see Gottfried Funeck, "Die Entwicklung des Berliner Stadtgartenamtes und seine Auswirkungen auf die städtebauliche Planung," Zentrales Parkarchiv, Zentraler Fachausschuß Dendrologie und Gartenarchitektur, Kulturbund der Deutschen Demokratischen Republik (ed.), *Entwicklung*

der Volksparke (Berlin: Druckhaus Weimar, 1979), pp. 21–32. See also "Ein neuer Betrieb für die Hauptstadt Berlin" *Landschaftsarchitektur*, 3, no. 2, 1972, pp. 61–62, which says that a parks department for the city of East Berlin and parks departments for the eight districts of the city were established in 1961. For the developments in West Berlin, see Norbert Schindler, "Die Berliner Grünplanung von 1945 bis 1970," *Das Gartenamt*, 19, no. 6, 1970, pp. 257–87, 288–304.

152. See Hans Joachim Winkelmann, "Bericht zum 10. Jahrestag der DDR, Abteilung Kommunale Wirtschaft—Städtische Parkanlagen und Friedhöfe," manuscript, 15 July 1959, Berlin, n.p. As if the process of making the parks department disappear from public perception needed to be more definitive, the name of this branch of local government was changed again in East Berlin in 1952 to Department of Reconstruction—Main Subdepartment of Building Affairs—Subdepartment of Green Areas, and again in 1954 to Department of Community Economy—Municipal Parks and Cemeteries.

153. Hans-Jürgen Schwarz, "Parks and Garden Departments in the Former GDR: The Example of Leipzig," *Journal of Garden History*, 12, no. 3, 1992, p. 234.

154. See Staatliches Entwurfsbüro für Stadt- und Dorfplanung Dresden—Brigade Grünplanung, "Stufenbau für Gartentreppen," *Der Landschaftsgärtner,* 5, no. 41, 1953, pp. 38–39.

155. Schwarz, "Parks and Garden Departments," p. 230. The first meeting of the VEBs took place in Leipzig on 4 July 1948. See Volksbetriebe im Wirtschaftsplan, Der Auftakt in Leipzig, Bericht von der ersten Zonentagung der volkseigenen Betriebe am 4. Juli 1948 (Berlin, 1948); see also *Volksbetriebe im Aufbau* (Berlin, 1948).

156. Olejnik, "Jeder arbeitet nach eigenen Richtlinien."

157. A. Wunschik, "Zur Methode der Perspektivplanung in der Landschaftsgestaltung," *Der Deutsche Gartenbau*, 4, no. 12, 1957, p. 330 (my translation).

158. Wilhelm Hübotter, "Ost-West-Begegnung," *Garten und Landschaft*, 66, no. 11, 1956, pp. 332–33.

159. See Frank Erich Carl, *Kleinarchitekturen in der deutschen Gartenkunst, Schriften des Forschungsinstitutes für Städtebau und Siedlungswesen* (Berlin: Henschelverlag, 1956).

160. Schwarz, "Parks and Garden Departments," p. 230.

161. Personal communication from Kurt Näser.

162. See, e.g., Friedemann Dressler, "5 Jahre Grünflächenamt Görlitz," *Das Gartenamt*, 46, no. 1, 1997, pp. 25–26.

163. See Wolschke-Bulmahn and Gröning, *1913–1988, 75 Jahre BDLA*.

164. Dieter Hennebo, "Die letzte Chance," *Das Gartenamt*, 5, no. 6, 1956, p. 106; Hennebo agreed with an article "Vom Neuaufbau der deutschen Städte," which the city planner and architect Ernst May had published in the journal *Der Monat*, 8, 1956, pp. 31–42, and which Hennebo found "shocking and stimulating" (p. 106).

165. Johannes Babenzien, "Erhaltung oder Zerstörung der Landschaft?" *Garten und Landschaft*, 66, no. 2, 1956, p. 50.

166. See, e.g., Ludwig Römer, "Verkehrsfragen quer durch den Englischen Garten," *Garten und Landschaft*, 66, no. 2, 1956, pp. 47–49; see also Hermann Landgrebe, "Strassenbepflanzung, eine Gemeinschaftsaufgabe der Landschaftsarchitekten und Bauingenieure," *Garten und Landschaft*, 69, no. 7, 1959, pp. 200–202.

167. See Günther Grzimek, "Grünplanung in Ulm, Probleme einer wachsenden Stadt," *Garten und Landschaft*, 64, no. 6, 1954, pp. 1–21.

168. In 1996 this office was moved to Berlin.

169. They succeeded in 1970 when they were included in the National Chamber of Architects, which was established in that year—but that was already a decade beyond 1960, the limit of my research. See Bund Deutscher Garten- und Landschaftsarchitekten, "Entwurf zur Ordnung des Architektenberufes (Architektengesetz)," *Das Gartenamt*, 3, no. 7, 1954, pp. 133–34. In this proposal for an act that would upgrade the status of architects, the BDGA had suggested a few additions that referred to the profession of landscape architects: see paragraphs 3, 7, 8, 10; see also the publication of selected paragraphs of the Bavarian act concerning architects, which included garden and landscape architects, in *Garten und Landschaft*, 64, no. 2, 1964, p. 19.

170. Willibald Gutsche, "Die Geschichte des Kulturparkes Cyriaksburg," *Der Kulturpark Cyriaksburg in Erfurt und seine Geschichte,* verbesserter und erweiterter Sonderdruck der Seiten 51 bis 76 des I. Bandes der Schriftenreihe "Aus der Vergangenheit der Stadt Erfurt," 3. Auflage (Erfurt), 1956, p. 12.

On 1 May 1953 the name of the earlier flower show area was changed cultural park. See Hans Bien, "Eine gärtnerisch-dendrologische Betrachtung der Cyriaksburg," *Der Kulturpark Cyriaksburg in Erfurt und seine Geschichte*, p. 16.

171. See Gutsche, "Die Geschichte des Kulturparkes," p. 11; and Hermann Braband and Alfred Wiese, "Die Gartenanlagen der Stadt Erfurt," *Behörden-Gartenbau*, 1, no. 6, 1924, p. 21.

The Volkspark am Veteranenberg, a centrally located park in Berlin, might have qualified as a Kulturpark but instead was labeled Volkspark, or people's park, in 1954. "Ein grosser Volkspark entsteht im Zentrum Berlins," *Der Landschaftsgärtner*, 6, no. 16, 1954, p. 56. In 1955 the Klara Zetkin Park in Leipzig, which encompassed the former Johannapark, was redesigned as what then was called a contemporary Kulturpark. "Die Messestadt Leipzig erhält einen modernen Kulturpark," *Der Landschaftsgärtner*, 7, no. 3, 1955, p. 73. In the early 1950s landscape architect Walter Funcke designed what he called a people's park in the southern part of Babelsberger Park, in Potsdam. When Funcke finished his plan in 1955, he called it a Kulturpark. See Susanne Karn, "Der Kulturpark—ein sozialistischer Park oder eine Sonderform des Volksparks?" *Projekt sozialistische Stadt* (Berlin: Dietrich Reimer Verlag, 1998), pp. 193–202.

172. Helmut Lichey, "Thema und Gestaltung der Landwirtschaftlichen Unionsausstellung in Moskau 1954," *Der Deutsche Gartenbau*, 2, no. 1, 1955, p. 7.

173. Helmut Lichey, "Maitage in Moskau," *Der Deutsche Gartenbau*, 3, no. 9, 1956, p. 250. In 1957 Lichey again mentioned the Zentrale Kulturpark Maxim Gorki; see Helmut Lichey, "Frühjahrsblumenschau des Gartenbaus der DDR in Moskau," *Der Deutsche Gartenbau*, 4, no. 5, 1957, pp. 117–18.

174. Reflecting on an exchange with the park designers there, he found "that it would be necessary to stay in continuing connection via lectures with the Soviet professional colleagues." Helmut Lichey, "Aufgabe und Ausführung der Moskauer Frühjahrsblumenschau," *Der Deutsche Gartenbau*, 4, no. 6, 1957, p. 183.

175. Several years earlier, in 1951–52, there had been a competition—won by landscape architect Werner Bauch—for a redesign of the Grosser Garten zu Dresden, a park dating from the late seventeenth and early eighteenth centuries. Its new label was "Kulturpark Grosser Garten zu Dresden;" the word "Kulturpark" did not, however, appear in the title for the Dresden meeting a few years later. See "Zum Professor ernannt," p. 9.

176. Harald Linke, "Planschau Pillnitz 1956," *Der Deutsche Gartenbau*, 4, no. 4, 1957, pp. 110–11.

177. See Klarstellung des Begriffs (Eine Antwort an Dr. h.c. Steffen), *Gärtner-Post*, 6, no. 17, 1954, p. 4; "Neue Kulturparks in Berlin," *Gärtner–Post*, 6, no. 22, 1954, p. 1; "Richtlinien für die Anlage von Kulturparks," *Der Landschaftsgärtner*, 6, no. 18, 1954, p. 57.

178. See Wilhelm Hübotter, "Ost-West-Begegnung," *Garten und Landschaft*, 66, no. 11, 1956, p. 332.

179. See Gert Gröning, "School Garden and Kleingaerten: For Education and Enhancing Life Quality," Eisuke Matsuo and Diane Relf (eds.), *Horticulture in Human Life, Culture, and Environment*, Acta Horticulturae, 391, 1995, pp. 53–64.

180. See P. Gerhard Wilhelm, "Welchen Anteil nehmen die Gartenämter am Schulgartenwesen," *Das Gartenamt*, 3, no. 9, 1954, pp. 171–73.

181. See Gerda Gollwitzer, "Warum Schulen im Grün?" Schulen im Grün, *Schriftenreihe der Deutschen Gesellschaft für Gartenkunst und Landschaftspflege*, Heft 1 (Munich: Callwey Verlag, 1956), pp. 7–8. See also Ulrich Wolf, "Freiluftschulen," *Garten und Landschaft*, 60, no. 1, 1950, pp. 4–6.

182. See Ivan Wladimirowitsch Mitschurin, Ausgewählte Werke (Moskau: Verlag Kultur und Fortschritt, 1949); see also P. Roeszler, "Ivan Vladimirovic Mitschurin: 1855–1935," *Garten und Landschaft*, 60, no. 6, 1950, pp. 8–10.

183. For an overview see Gröning, "School Garden and Kleingaerten."

184. See Gert Gröning and Uwe Schneider, Anmerkungen zur "Friedhofsreform-bewegung," *Die Gartenkunst*, 12, no. 2, 2000, pp. 326–45.

A PERSONAL PROLOGUE

The notion that, having lived through the close of the twentieth century, we are at a sufficient remove in time to reflect profitably upon the history of landscape architecture in the period just after World War II seemed to me at first rather an unsettling proposition. Added to the realization that a half-century familiar through adult experience had now become "historic" was my awareness that I tended to dismiss the 1950s — without question the span of years that turned out to be the most critically important of my own life — as not having been a particularly momentous time in the cultural life of this nation. Many Americans of my generation feel nostalgia for the fifties as "the good years," characterized by the burgeoning prosperity of a middle class committed to those "family values," the loss of which is now lamented. Others view the same period with contempt, believing that an insufferably staid and bourgeois culture succeeded in enforcing a degree of conformity that reached fascistic extremes in McCarthyism. From either perspective, the decade of the fifties inevitably lies in the shadow cast by the more dramatic social and political upheavals of the (literally and metaphorically) sexier sixties.

6.   CATHERINE HOWETT

After the "Other" War: Landscapes of Home, North and South

The temptation to engage the history of those years by recalling my own experience of them — precisely because memories are so often informed, given shape and meaning, by images of a series of domestic landscapes — seems quite irresistible. So I have elected to compare residential landscape design in the years after World War II in two regions of the United States, the Northeast and the South, through the lens of a personal history. My hope is that a firsthand description and interpretation of particular lives, times, and landscapes may compensate for whatever is sacrificed in the range and comprehensiveness of this analysis. Perhaps, too, these personal recollections of my encounter with a complex configuration of traditional values and practices that found expression in house and garden design even during the postwar period of dramatic growth and change may help to balance the weight of scholarly attention focused on the reception of modernist ideas in regions of the country other than the South.

I grew up in a house on Delafield Avenue in Riverdale, a community within what is now Bronx County, for which the city of New York had in 1876 commissioned Frederick Law

Olmsted to do a planning study.[1] Olmsted argued that the topography on the heights overlooking the Hudson River was too rugged to be well suited to urban commercial, industrial, or ordinary residential uses and would be better conceived as a "specially picturesque and convenient suburb" for commuters "able to indulge in the luxury of a villa or suburban cottage residence."[2] I am confident that my parents never thought of the four-square, hip-roofed, stuccoed house they built about the middle of the 1920s as either a villa or a cottage. For me it was and has remained the Ur-house, central pivot of a serene childhood, surrounded by a genial yard—probably slightly less than an acre in size—on a graveled, deadend road that climbed a steep hill edged and crowned with those outcroppings of fissured granite and gneiss admired by Olmsted. The driveway leading to our garage divided the front yard into two areas of lawn at different elevations.

In a photograph probably taken late in the spring of 1937 or 1938 [Figure 6–1], my mother and I sit posed on the retaining wall along the drive, with the privet hedges that bordered the lawns, a flowering hydrangea, and our one great tree, an oak, visible behind. The privet and hydrangea, as well as a large specimen forsythia on the opposite lawn, were among the most popular shrubs in residential landscapes up and down the street; perhaps only the absence of a " bridal wreath" spirea saved our yard from being perfectly typical.

The onset of World War II brought about a curious destruction of these serene suburban landscapes, since a surprising number of New York City homeowners like my parents answered the national call to replace ornamental gardens with productive "Victory Gardens." Another family photo [Figure 6–2] shows my father and youngest brother (shortly before his being drafted into the army) in the very act of demolition, preparing the lower half of what had been our front lawn for eggplant, corn, and tomatoes. My father, a businessman born and raised in the city, discovered extraordinary pleasure in converting almost his entire house lot to a working farm for at least three years during the war, taking up arms against beetles and blight while his sons fought in real battles half a world away. My mother felt less enthusiasm for growing vegetables but did her part, preserving and pickling produce until she wearied of the whole enterprise and demanded that her lawns and shrubs be restored.

155

Figure 6–1.
The author with her mother.
[Family photo, c. 1937-38]

An equally convulsive if more benign transformation of this domestic landscape occurred in the years immediately after the war, when my brothers became part of the massive social reconstruction initiated by the G.I. Bill of Rights. In the brief period during which all three lived at home again before they finished school, married, bought houses with Veterans' Administration mortgages, and began raising families of their own in second- or third-generation suburban communities, they pitched in to build a flagstone terrace in our back yard, for which my parents purchased redwood lawn furniture with splashy-patterned canvas cushions. When an automatic clothes dryer joined the newly installed Bendix washer in the basement, clotheslines could be removed from the opposite side of the yard, where my father then set to work as brick mason, building an elaborate fireplace grill. "Modern outdoor living" had traveled east from California, although at the time I thought only that these dramatic changes in our lives — like my mother's renovated modern kitchen, with its refrigerator-freezer, metal cabinets, Formica counters, and chrome-and-vinyl tubular furniture — were an extended celebration of the end of the war, which seemed to have ushered in new ways of living for many families in our neighborhood.

I came to know a very different kind of residential landscape while attending a high school for girls that moved in 1951 to a sixteen-acre property that had been part of the Westchester County estate of millionaire industrialist William Boyce Thompson. Little in my education until then had encouraged me to think about architecture or gardens, but in looking back, I remember the intense pleasure, physical and psychological, with which I experienced a place that drew for its atmosphere upon remnants of the ancient world as well as the great Renaissance and baroque villas of Europe. What a more sophisticated eye might have recognized as a classic example, pretentious and formulaic, of the acquisitive and self-aggrandizing obsessions of the very rich in the era of the American Country Place, I relished as a theater of keen adolescent imagination [Figure 6–3]. To me, these dramatic gardens filled with antique statuary and architectural fragments — carved Roman sarcophagi had been converted to use as planters — radiated a palpable aura of a past that seemed inconceivably remote, mysterious, and beautiful. This was how I came to be lastingly imprinted, I suppose, as were many Americans of my generation, with the same highly resonant imagery of western European landscape models that the generations of our parents and grandparents had found so seductive.

Figure 6–2. [*facing page*]
Preparing the front yard for a "Victory
Garden."
[Family photo, summer of 1942]

Figure 6–3.
A rehearsal of *Antigone* at Elizabeth Seton
School, Yonkers, New York, spring 1952.
The author stands at left in the central group.
[*Caritas*, 1952]

Looking back from the vantage point of about 1950 at the evolution of a suburban way of life in this country, Russell Lynes — in his now-classic social critique *The Tastemakers* — noted that the wave of middle-class homeowners building, as my parents had, in the twenties and thirties, wanted the style of their suburban homes, however reduced in scale or in quality of construction, to affirm a connection with the eclectic traditions represented by country estates like Boyce Thompson's: "The models suggested [to them] by the *Ladies Home Journal* and *House Beautiful* were modest versions of the houses that sat at the ends of long driveways behind high hedges."[3] The practice of emulating upper-class taste in architectural and landscape styles and interior design was hardly new, of course. In the preceding century, books and magazine articles by such popular authors as Andrew Jackson Downing had educated earlier generations of suburban homeowners to the expressive potential of the "home scene," a harmonious composition of house and landscape that offered sure proof of an owner's refined good taste and civility. Those associative values persisted after the turn of the century, when the expansion of commuter transportation networks and exponential increases in automobile ownership accelerated the development of suburbs around major cities.

The generation of Americans buying homes during the housing crisis that followed the war in mass-produced and mass-marketed suburban communities such as Levittown outside New York City, Lakewood outside Los Angeles, and Park Forest outside Chicago also dreamed of living in genteel suburban neighborhoods, although fewer options were available to them in the models that developers offered potential buyers. The basic box could be reconfigured and decorated in a limited number of ways, among which variations of the Cape Cod cottage [Figure 6–4] or the California ranch were most popular.[4] The "Western-style" ranch obviously represented a new house type preference among easterners, and a choice with the potential

Figure 6–4.
House in Levittown, New York, 1948.
[Bernard Hoffman, *Life* magazine, copyright © *Time*, Inc.]

to be read in either (or both) of two ways: as a gesture of modernity or as a romantic evocation of the simpler lives, closer to nature, of America's pioneering forebears homesteading on the prairies and in the frontier West. Shelter magazines helped to foster the tremendous growth in popularity of the ranch (and its variant form, the "split-level") among average homebuyers in these postwar years by celebrating the emergence of a presumedly more humane, individualistic, and hence authentically American modernism, inspired by such earlier models as Frank Lloyd Wright's Usonian houses and deliberately contrasted with the "mechanistic" and "communal" aesthetic of the European school. In looking back at this changing tide of taste, William Jordy observed that "such popularization never centers in the philosophical reach of a style, but in its consumable features": "Thus the open plan, outdoor living, the interior court, the emphasis on convenience and informality — in short, the 'modern look' entered the consumer magazines; especially publicized were the cozier variants. . . . Redwood, the barbecue patio, the 'family room,' 'picture window,' the kitchen 'pass-through,' 'carport,' the 'deck,' the 'storage wall' . . . and so on: these eventually became the bywords (rather, the buy-words) of the housebuilder."[5]

Although I married a veteran of the war in 1957, we did not become homeowners until 1963, when we purchased a three-bedroom ranch [Figure 6–5] on about a quarter-acre lot in the McKinley Terrace subdivision in South Bend, Indiana, that had been built right after the war. We purchased the property quite casually one Sunday afternoon by giving its most recent owner $350 in cash and assuming the $12,500 balance on his VA mortgage. The house seemed almost deluxe to us because it had a garage rather than just a carport, and a small concrete terrace in back. By the mid-fifties, Weber grills or cheaper substitutes — right down to hibachis — had taken the place of built-in fireplace grills for young families like ours, and brightly painted metal swing-sets and redwood picnic tables were equally affordable and universal.

The landscaping consisted of a foundation planting of Pfitzer junipers along the front and one side of the house, a narrow border of hybrid tea roses along the house wall on the drive-way side, and a scraggly privet hedge along the rear lot line separating our yard from the neighbor's. I was not aware at the time that the junipers, like the house itself, repre-sented the diffusion of California style eastward to other parts of the country, since junipers were apparently among

Figure 6–5.
The Howett residence on Corby Boulevard,
South Bend, Indiana.
[Family photo, 1963]

the most popular of the many species of Asian evergreens hybridized and propagated by California nurseries after the war, then marketed nationally as "adaptable to virtually every North American climate."[6] The most exceptional feature of our yard was that a large tree had unaccountably been spared by the developer, an oak that reminded me of the one in front of the house on Delafield Avenue; its presence, and the fact that our house sat on the edge of the sub-division adjacent to an unfenced woodland, redeemed an otherwise undistinguished but therefore very typical tract-house landscape.

Russell Lynes also made the now-familiar observation that these postwar suburbs all looked alike, no matter what part of the country they were in: "If you were put down blind-folded in the new suburbs of any large American city it would be difficult to tell whether you were in the East or the West, the North or the South." He blamed this marked erosion of regional differences in architectural taste — and, by implication, landscape tastes as well — primarily on the mobility of postwar suburbanites, who absorbed influences from regional cultures to which they moved, while at the same time contributing to the transformation of their new communities. This was a process of homogenization obviously accelerated by the particular success of the California ranch style, and by the rate at which mass media, especially television, were reaching out to a national audience.[7]

MOVING SOUTH

Lynes may have been mostly right in this generalization, but I believe it would have been much less true of cities in the South in the 1950s, first because the rate of suburban growth had historically lagged significantly behind that of the North, and did still—except, perhaps, around resort and retirement cities in Florida. When we moved to Atlanta in 1966, the city was almost entirely suburban in character, even in residential neighborhoods close to downtown such

Figure 6–6.
The Howett residence on Emory Circle, northeast Atlanta.
[Family photo, 1966]

as Ansley Park in midtown, subdivided in the second decade of this century. With three thousand dollars in hand this time, we assumed the mortgage on an older, circa 1927 house [Figure 6–6] in a modest suburban neighborhood near Emory University, a pre–World War II subdivision of that earlier sort described by Lynes, graced with greater architectural distinction and with tree-lined streets and parks or at least more leftover green spaces.

Even those Atlanta subdivisions developed —still close in — in the late forties and fifties were smaller and more stylistically varied than northern examples; none of them reflected those adaptations of wartime building techniques —organizing construction teams for rapid production, using new materials and standardized components purchased in bulk from manufacturers—that northern developers like Levitt had used to create "instant communities."[8] That kind of tract development did not begin in earnest in Atlanta until the seventies, bringing with it an explosive growth of population in what had been rural counties on the city's perimeter; since that time, several of these metropolitan counties have often ranked among the fastest growing in the whole country.[9] But even in the university neighborhood to which we had come, there was little awareness, late in the sixties, of the "Sunbelt boom" already under way, except perhaps for the auspicious opening downtown of John Portman's Hyatt Regency, the first of the "atrium" hotels with exposed glass elevators scaling the lobby walls (a building whose revolving rooftop restaurant now seems quaintly dwarfed by surrounding development). There was also, of course, the conspicuously increasing presence in Atlanta of Yankees like us, learning about life in the South.

I had not thought in terms of "learning about life in the Midwest" during the twelve years we lived in Chicago and South Bend, but the South is the most self-consciously regional culture of any in the nation; the identification of who one is with where one is from is equaled only by New York City and California, neither of which is a region (except perhaps in the minds of those who live there). It has always seemed to me rather sad that the pride southerners take in being native born, and the strong ties to place so many feel from earliest childhood, are sometimes curdled by defensiveness or resentment of outsiders. The roots of this rancor lie in knowing just how much the overwhelmingly tragic economic and social consequences of the Civil War, including all the hard-fought battles of the civil rights movement, persisted throughout most of the twentieth century.

Unless one has grown up in the South, it is hard to appreciate the degree to which a catastrophe that occurred more than a century ago can be seen to have compromised the quality of life and sense of well-being that men and women of today experience. But that is, after all, the entirely appropriate perception of most African Americans, and, I suspect, a great many white southerners as well.

One must bear in mind, too, that throughout the fifties the South was still more rural than suburban, and a considerable part of that rural countryside was poor and culturally deprived; early in the sixties, John Kennedy's "War on Poverty" shocked the nation by exposing the hunger and hookworms of children in Appalachia and coastal counties in the Carolinas. At that point no city in the South had achieved a level of wealth, commerce, and urban culture equivalent to that of major cities in other parts of the country, although several, including Atlanta, were poised to do so.

Our family was welcomed graciously by our southern neighbors with such old-fashioned gestures as gifts of garden flowers left on our porch steps. Such expressions of neighborliness were particularly comforting to my husband and me, because our departure from South Bend had been sadly shadowed by the sudden rupture of a close friendship with the older couple who were our next-door neighbors —a rupture occasioned by our having sold our home to a "colored" family. Dear Gert was given the ghastly task of coming to the door to tell me that she would not be able to speak to us or to our children again, while her husband set to work promptly and dramatically digging a trench between our two houses for the line of tall evergreens meant to produce a wall between himself and his new neighbors.

Once in Atlanta, it was the place, not its people, that seemed to me unfamiliar, even exotic, in the early years of coming to know and feel at home within a southern landscape. Beneath the superficial resemblance to familiar landscapes of my childhood and young womanhood, I sensed another history, another tradition of placemaking at work, which in certain of its manifestations swept me away with admiration and delight and made me want to understand its sources and intentions.

Figure 6–7.
Magnolia grandiflora. Mark Catesby, *The Natural History of Carolina, Florida, and the Bahama Islands* (London, 1731–48).
[Collections of Emory University Libraries]

A POETICS OF PLACE

Three elements, I have come to believe, may inform a regional poetics of place, even in quite modest southern gardens and landscapes—and here I must speak of "garden" (a term many of my older southern neighbors substituted for "yard," even when they meant to describe an entire residential landscape), because the understanding of what a garden should be distills and concentrates conceptions about the larger landscape.

The first of these character-defining elements is what I think of as its Edenic quotient, and I can date the time when I first recognized its reality. My only experience of the South before coming to live there (except for visits to the nation's capital, a border town tellingly described by John F. Kennedy as having "all the charm of a northern city and all the efficiency of a southern one") had been a trip by overnight passenger train to New Orleans in late winter of 1955. What had most impressed me then—apart from the shock of "whites only" rest rooms and drinking fountains—was the palpable sensuosity of warm, moisture-laden air, heavy with the scent of earth, flowers, and roasting coffee, that greeted my early-morning arrival. The memory of that epiphanic moment stirred to life when I moved south and began to garden. Not every southern garden is sensuous—indeed, some are so strait-laced that the effort to suppress any pleasure but the security of neatness and order seems deliberate—but temperate to semitropical climates simply do nourish a greener, lusher landscape and marvelously multiply the possibilities for range and richness of color, texture, form, and fragrance—and by extension, bird song and bee hum. In the eighteenth century, images such as naturalist-explorer Mark Catesby's *Magnolia grandiflora* [Figure 6–7] seemed to confirm for Europeans the legitimacy of comparisons between the southern coast and the biblical paradise.

Moreover, because warm, moist climates and luxuriant vegetation create conditions that more swiftly and easily spill over into disorder and decay, mature gardens, even in summers of the upper South, occasionally take on an atmosphere of mystery or melancholy, as if haunted by reminders of mortality and death. The landscape that Weeks Hall created on the vestigial two acres of the property he self-consciously renamed Shadows-on-the-Teche, with its antebellum mansion fronting the main street of New Iberia, Louisiana, represented a deliberate effort on Hall's part to create just such an intensely atmospheric and theatrical—even Gothic—

Figure 6–8.
Shadows-on-the-Teche, New Iberia,
Louisiana. I. A. Martin, c. 1920s–1930s.
[Collection of Shadows-on-the-Teche, a
property of the National Trust for Historic
Preservation]

version of a romantic "Old South" landscape [Figure 6–8]. The expatriate novelist Henry Miller, after visiting Shadows, wrote in his 1945 memoir *The Air-Conditioned Nightmare* that the house and its gardens represented "one of the most distinctive pieces of art that America can boast of."[10] Hall, who had returned to his ancestral home after years spent as an emigré painter in Paris, had restructured the nineteenth-century site plan in order to change the way a visitor entered and then moved through the spaces of this garden, seductively immersed within highly original and painterly compositions of shrubs and flowering plants massed beneath a brooding canopy of live oaks draped with Spanish moss [Figure 6–9].

The second of the elements potentially informing regional landscape design is linked to this Edenic richness of the South's physical geography, and that is what I will call the culture of rural life, by which I mean something different from actual rural culture, which of course is fast disappearing in many parts of the South. Rather, I mean to suggest by this term a self-conscious cultivation and expression of values associated with a historic but romanticized agricultural and pastoral society. In 1930, when several decades of their most significant contributions to American letters still lay ahead of them, the group of writers who came to be known as the Vanderbilt Agrarians — among them the Fugitive poets John Crowe Ransom, Allen Tate, Robert Penn Warren, and Donald Davidson — published the manifesto *I'll Take My Stand*, in which they warned their fellow southerners that the latest wave of "New South" rhetoric threatened to substitute material prosperity based on the example of northern industrialization and urbanism for more spiritual values rooted in the folkways of the South's agrarian traditions.

Perhaps second in importance only to religious piety among these shared traditional values is the ceremonious

Figure 6–9.
Plantings in the formal garden, Shadows-on-the-Teche, designed by Weeks Hall. Undated photo.
[Collection of Shadows-on-the-Teche, a property of the National Trust for Historic Preservation]

nurturance of an attitude and an atmosphere of civilized leisure; its indulgence defined southerners of every class by comparison with fast-talking, commerce-consumed Yankee scalawags and southern Snopses, then and now. The description in *I'll Take My Stand* of this ideal of communal life is quite explicit and bears comparison with the classical concept of *otium*,[11] which had been seminal to the thinking of artists, philosophers, and villa-builders during the Renaissance as well: "The amenities of life . . . suffer under the curse of a strictly business or industrial civilization. They consist in such practices as manners, conversation, hospitality, sympathy, family life, romantic love — in the social exchanges which reveal and develop sensibility in human affairs. If religion and the arts are founded on the right relations of man-to-nature, these are founded on the right relations of man-to-man."[12]

Climate and culture in the South had, for the three centuries before air conditioning became commonplace in the 1950s, ratified the appropriateness of activities that took time away from the workaday world of business, especially for informal socializing with family and friends. Southerners living in towns and cities still looked upon the seasonal rituals of hunting and fishing for men (in the 1950s, native southerners in sedate suburban Atlanta neighborhoods might still keep kennels of hounds in the back yard) and gardening — even more important, garden clubbing, a hobby of both women and men — as fitting expressions of this virtuous rural sensibility. In books and in newspaper columns beginning late in the 1950s, the elegantly literate and prolific garden writer Elizabeth Lawrence—pictured in an evocative photo of her "Edenic" Raleigh, North Carolina, garden [Figure 6–10]—continually celebrated the accumulated wisdom and civility of rural people throughout the South with whom she corresponded and traded plants through the market bulletins published by departments of agriculture across the region. Perhaps the Warm Springs, Georgia, "Little White House" beloved by Franklin D. Roosevelt, the country home in which his life ended in the spring of 1945 [Figure 6–11], best epitomizes those quintessentially southern qualities of place, meant to express a particular style of unpretentious living based on an older rural culture, which attracted so many northern visitors to the South.

The third element associated with southern gardens and landscapes is not unrelated to the deliberate design strategies—or offhand gestures or omissions—that invoke memories of the culture of rural life, but is more a matter of

Figure 6–10.
Elizabeth Lawrence in her Raleigh garden.
[Elizabeth Lawrence, *A Southern Garden*. Copyright ©1967 by the University of North Carolina Press. Courtesy of the publisher]

replicable formal conventions based on historic garden styles. This fidelity to the formal vocabulary of Renaissance, baroque, and American neoclassical traditions — let us call it conservatism of southern landscape design — is undoubtedly the characteristic that comes first to mind when most people imagine a southern garden, and there is no want of evidence to suggest that they are right. Southerners, for all of their travails and the shame attached to so much of their social history, would find appalling Henry Thoreau's remark that "he is blessed over all mortals who loses no moment of the passing life in remembering the past."[13] Southern residential landscapes at every scale, at least through the period of the 1950s, mined memory — personal and communal — in the way that they were laid out and planted. However inventive the design devices by which Weeks Hall had contrived, in the thirties and forties, to invoke a distinctive southern identity through the look and feel of the landscape of Shadows-on-the-Teche, his intention was clearly to color and to frame a particular version of the shared cultural experience of the region.

But ordinary, even fairly banal residential landscapes of the period after World War II may be shown to draw in similar ways upon a sign system of landscape conventions meant to affirm connections to the historic past. Typical residential design, in actual landscapes and in the design literature, is rich in evidence of this scenography of "historic" southern landscape conventions. The 1951 publication *Garden Time in the South*, by Mattie Abney Hartzog,[14] for example, is full of such stereotypical images as the brick-walled garden room with boxwood-bordered plantings of azaleas and a "Pool with Classic Lines" [Figure 6–12]; or the photo of the South Carolina garden of Mrs. Mary Simms Oliphant, in which the central feature is an Italianate fountain "brought from the plantation of Mrs. Oliphant's grandfather, the novelist and historian William Gilmore Simms" [Figure 6–13]. Subtler but no less telling is the figural meaning to be read in the landscape of a modest suburban ranch outside Athens, Georgia, where white columns gracing not just the pedimented entrance portico but the facades of the freestanding garage and nearby storage shed suggest the dependencies associated with nineteenth-century plantation landscapes [Figure 6–14].

Is it any wonder, given this predilection for historic design traditions, that the South was the most fertile of all seedbeds for the historic preservation activities that coalesced as a national movement supported by federal legislation in the 1960s? In the mid-nineteenth century, the preservation

Figure 6–11.
The Little White House, Warm Springs, Georgia, home of Franklin Delano Roosevelt.
[Medora Field Perkinson, *White Columns in Georgia*, 1952]

Figure 6–12.
Representative southern garden.
[Mattie Abney Hartzog, *Garden Time in the South*, 1951]

Figure 6–13.
The garden of Mrs. Mary Simms Oliphant,
Greenville, South Carolina.
[Mattie Abney Hartzog, *Garden Time in the South*, 1951]

of George Washington's plantation home had been accomplished through the agency of Ann Pamela Cunningham and the Mount Vernon Ladies' Association; in the 1930s, the Ladies' Association undertook a complete restoration of the mansion and grounds. And while the "restoration" of Colonial Williamsburg was conceived and subvented by the Yankee dollars of John D. Rockefeller—beginning in 1928, interrupted by the war, and then resuming in 1948— Virginia's colonial capital was a southern town. Moreover, its architecture, interiors, and gardens are still being praised or blamed for having inspired the fervid popularity of Colonial Revival styles in this country. Yet these models— illustrated here by a formal garden in Delaware, designed in the 1930s by Marian Coffin [Figure 6–15]—seem not to have been recognized as examples of the influence of specifically southern design traditions on the styles of other regions.

THE IMPACT OF MODERNISM

The strength of this conservative tradition in the South undoubtedly explains, too, why the challenge to historic styles represented by modernism produced relatively few significant southern examples of architecture or interior design. As for residential landscape design, the modern styles illustrated in shelter magazines of the postwar period appear at first glance not to have been the sort of thing polite southerners did out-of-doors. Even a cursory survey of publications from that period, however, makes clear the perception on the part of many writers, editors, and practicing professionals that Americans generally—not just southerners—had profound reservations about modernism. A book published just before the end of the war in 1945 with the prescient title *Tomorrow's House: How to Plan Your Post-War Home Now* set the tone for the hard sell that would be needed to attract a wide audience of American homebuilders and buyers to the new style:

> If you have already glanced at the pictures in this book, you will have noticed that there are no examples of the Colonial Dream House. Interiors, exteriors, furnishings, and equipment are all modern. In other words, they were built by people who haven't been afraid to change. To date, such people have put up enough modern houses to fill several books of this size. In the next five years or so, dozens of times as many are going to be built. The Colonial Dream is approaching its end. . . . The swing to modern has definitely begun. All of our tremendous apparatus for influencing public opinion is tuning up for a new barrage in favor of these new houses. A new fashion in homes will be created, and the public will follow.[15]

It is probably telling that the appended list of architects and

Figure 6–14.
Ranch house on a dairy farm, Highway 78 outside Athens, Georgia.
[Catherine Howett, 1983]

Figure 6–15.
Boxwood Scroll Garden, Winterthur,
estate of Henry Francis Du Pont, outside
Wilmington, Delaware, 1930. Marian
Cruger Coffin, landscape architect.
[Marian Cruger Coffin, *Trees and Shrubs for Landscape Effects*, 1940]

designers whose work appeared in this book—arranged by states—included just four from the South: one each from Florida and Texas, two from North Carolina. New York, by contrast, is represented by no less than forty-one contributors, California by twenty-four.[16]

Since Atlanta had been the birthplace of the "New South" agenda late in the nineteenth century,[17] perhaps it is not surprising that at least some within the city apparently felt the same conviction about the style of house most appropriate for residential development after World War II as that articulated by the authors of Tomorrow's House. Virtually at the same historic moment, Rich's department store—since its founding an Atlanta institution that set the standard for good taste in fashion and interior design—sponsored a national architectural competition "for the design of a realistic house for a family in Georgia" in cooperation with Progressive Architecture magazine, which published the program for the competition in its October 1945 issue. Atlanta architect Henry J. Toombs and Kenneth Reid, editor of the magazine, served as advisers for the competition, and a jury of six architects—four of them Fellows of the American Institute of Architects—were drawn from various regions of the country.

While emphasizing the importance of such down-to-earth values as responsiveness to Georgia's climate (without anticipating that air conditioning would become a more common feature of southern houses)[18] and accommodation of changing living patterns within the family over time, the design criteria for the competition unabashedly implied that a "realistic" small house for a Georgia family of four with an income of three thousand dollars a year ought to be modern in style:

> The clients for whom you are to design the house are average people who have been looking forward for a long time to having their own home. They have been studying the pages of current magazines and are sympathetically aware of the contemporary trend in design, especially with regard to its greater promise of comfort, convenience, and freedom from a good deal of household drudgery. They definitely do not wish conformity with any traditional "style." At the same time they are desirous that the house they build shall take its place gracefully among its older neighbors. They have an idea that a good architect can give them something that is thoroughly modern and thoroughly appropriate to the region, not at all stodgy and imitative, yet so well proportioned and pleasant of aspect that it will excite general admiration rather than amazement.[19]

The Cambridge, Massachusetts, firm of Hugh Stubbins, Jr., won the three-thousand-dollar first prize [Figure 6–16] for a design praised by the jury for having a "charming" appearance that "would fit into any Georgia scene," although it is hard not to wonder if the rather high enclosing hedges, front gate, and fencing pictured in the perspective drawing were not as important for screening out views of the house from the street as affording a courtyardlike entrance garden for the family.

The third- and fourth-prize plans presented themselves to the street in ways much less likely to "excite amazement" in a typical southern neighborhood. [Figure 6–17]. In that respect, they probably reflected an approach to modernism that many voices within the architectural press soon embraced as a necessary accommodation to the timidity of the average client in other parts of the country as well. A 1949 article in Architectural Record, for example, ventured the optimistic view that inescapable changes in lifestyle would eventually force otherwise conservative Americans to consider functional changes in the interior plan of the house, even if the exterior retained a traditional appearance: "In . . . recent times, the powerful influence of home life on house architecture is nicely illustrated in the metamorphosis of the plan in so-called 'traditional' houses. The client was ready, perhaps eager, to preserve the externalisms of the old buildings—even to copy the furniture—but he required the architect to reorganize the plan to conform to his modern living needs, literally a marriage of convenience."[20] Such reticence to commit wholeheartedly to the new aesthetic was widely acknowledged, however, to be more common among southerners than Americans living in any other region of the country. The whole point of the title "I'm Guilty! I Built a Modern House," a 1950 Saturday Evening Post article by Joseph Alsop, was that the well-known journalist had dared to build such a house in Georgetown—"a part of Washington, but . . . also a state of mind." His choice of a modern style was considered by his neighbors "a heinous outrage against 'Georgetown charm'": "Since we Georgetownians are proud of our relics of the architectural past, most of us believe that new buildings ought to be 'in the period,' with a great quantity of Georgian fakery masking their raw novelty. Being a dissenter . . . I have been made to feel as though I were living with my own ax murder."[21]

In a similar vein, a 1953 article in American Home focused

Figure 6–16.
Prizewinning entry in the "Realistic House
for Georgia" design competition sponsored
by Rich's department store in Atlanta.
Hugh Stubbins, Jr., architect, 1945.
[University of Georgia Libraries]

Figure 6–17.
Third-prize winner, Rich's competition.
[University of Georgia Libraries]

on the fact that the client's wife was "Natchez bred" and therefore initially hostile to her husband's desire that their Dallas home be appropriately modern in style. The tone of the writing actually seems to ridicule the woman' provincial taste:

> The people down Natchez, Mississippi, way are about as house-conscious as they come, but their idea of a fine home is usually the stately ante-bellum mansion, surrounded by formal gardens and reflecting a way of life that has long since passed from the scene. Barbara Blum . . . had dreamed of owning just such a house before her husband, an electrical engineer, found that he couldn't fit his ideas on architecture and home engineering into a house that was traditional in any way, shape, or form.

> It didn't take Mrs. Blum long to admit that while her Natchez tradition is a pretty one, nothing can compare with good modern, if you want to enjoy living in your home.

> . . . For-indoors-outdoors effect, [she] . . . carried modern logic throughout the furnishings—there's no evidence anywhere of nostalgia for her deep-south background, no doting mementos mar the perfectionism of this strictly functional, but undeniably attractive, home.[22]

Although the article does not tell us what part of the country Mr. Blum came from, I am willing to argue that the odds favor his not being a southerner. I am similarly convinced that perusal of the architectural literature of the postwar years supports the observation that when modern houses built in the southern states were included at all, they were more often than not houses built either for the architects themselves or for academic clients. The 1951 publication *The American House Today* is typical in this respect. Among the very few southern houses included in its survey of modern design, two represent the architects' own homes —and one of these was dean of the School of Architecture at North Carolina State University. An entire chapter addressing the influence of regional building types and materials on specific architects in different areas of the country omits any consideration of the South at all.

The two southern examples of architects' homes in *The American House Today* do serve, however, to illustrate one aspect of the modernist aesthetic in residential design that gradually became more common in suburban southern neighborhoods, perhaps because it tapped into certain of those expressive values associated with the southern landscape traditions described earlier. Both the Raleigh, North Carolina, residence of Dean Henry Kamphoefner (designed with his associate George Matsumoto, a dedicated mod-

ernist who also taught in the architecture program at North Carolina State University in this period) and the Atlanta home of J. R. Wilkinson, partner in the local firm Stevens & Wilkinson [Figures 6–19, 6–20], are houses set within densely wooded landscapes. The houses appear to be immersed within—and to some extent dominated by —a "natural" landscape. Yet although both of these houses are grouped within a chapter addressing "Environmental Influence" on modern residential architecture, the text introducing the illustrations limits its discussion to physical aspects of the site and climatic factors, to which the corresponding design responses are exclusively technological, rather than psychological or affective.

Elsewhere in this volume, of course, conventional acknowledgment is made of the new importance the modern movement attached to the integration of interior and outdoor living spaces. Bruno Zevi had been among the first to point out, however, in his seminal study, *Towards an Organic Architecture* (1950), that the vein of American modernism influenced by the powerful example of Frank Lloyd Wright diverged from European practice in the nature—literally and symbolically—of this integration. Zevi is able to show that the Europeans themselves recognized an essential difference between their own architectural intentions and the new "naturalism" fostered by Wright's organicism, a distinctively American "conception of the relation of man to nature, or his environment."[23] Zevi even links this preoccupation in Wright to a romanticism that occasionally subverted the quality of the master' s work: "Some of Wright's houses have an exaggeratedly barbaric appearance . . . suggest[ing] that Mother Earth herself has risen up to take a hand in the building. This relic of nineteenth century romanticism, the love of wild and uncultivated nature, is often to be observed in Wright . . . but the young architects have substituted for the cult of wild nature an intelligent study of the art of garden landscape."[24]

I suspect that Zevi may not have been aware of the peculiar historical transformation of English "picturesque" theory in the late phase of what was called the "natural" or "naturalistic" style of landscape design in this country. Americans building homes in rustic or scenic locations during the heyday of the country place often favored the look of "wild" nature, since it so effectively dramatized their escape from urban environments to a life in nature radically divorced from an earlier generation's imperatives of productive use of field and forest. But the attraction was not simply escape;

Figure 6–19.
Kamphoefner residence, Raleigh,
North Carolina. Henry Kamphoefner and
George Matsumoto.
[Katherine Morrow Ford and Thomas H.
Creighton, *The American House Today*,
1951]

the peculiarly American strain of nineteenth-century romanticism, strongly infused with Transcendentalist faith in nature as the home of the indwelling Divine, continued in the present century to hold out the possibility at least of self-discovery, if not of mystical communion. Even for those of modest means, vacation cottages at the lake or cabins in the woods were associated not just with a simpler way of living but with one that was more spiritually rewarding.

I think that the very simplicity, the "stripped-down-ness" of the modern house and its furnishings may have prompted imaginative associations with these architectural prototypes. Furthermore, working to reinforce this conflation of types and meanings may have been the availability, in the postwar years, of building sites in older neighborhoods that had been considered too steep or otherwise unsuitable for building in the first wave of development. In the South as elsewhere, these were the lots on which the first modern houses were introduced. And since the new style anticipated that pleasing views of the natural world would be revealed through all those glass doors and windows, it was common practice to preserve as much as possible of the existing landscape, as any photographic survey of modern houses of the period reveals.

Modern houses of this sort, screened by groves of trees or nestled within lush vegetation, were probably less offensive to southern sensibilities than those in which the architectural forms dominated the surrounding landscape. It is important to understand that the preference of southerners for "classical" garden design traditions had not precluded acceptance of those conventions of "irregular" design made popular by the English landscape gardening school of the eighteenth century and adapted in nineteenth-century American practice. In the nineteenth-century South, a grove of irregularly composed trees and expanses of lawn frequently graced fine houses in rural settings, just as they did in the North; in early to mid-twentieth-century rural and suburban landscapes, the convention of any formal areas close to the house being enframed within an asymmetrical arrangement of lawn, grove, and drive was also common—more common, in fact, than the use of formal and axial composition throughout, which was less well suited to the conventions of romantic and picturesque suburban planning.

This popular woodland glade iconology—as characteristic of elite suburban neighborhoods of the prewar period in

Figure 6–20.
Architect's own home. J. R. Wilkinson.
[Katherine Morrow Ford and Thomas H. Creighton, *The American House Today*, 1951].

northwest Atlanta as it was in their counterparts in West-chester County, New York, or Chestnut Hill, Pennsylvania — persisted even on a much reduced scale in more modest suburban Atlanta neighborhoods of the 1950s and 1960s. It was especially favored, not surprisingly, in association with the California ranch-style house, which effected a new kind of functional integration with outdoor living spaces. In these new residential landscapes, the historic high-style tradition of grove and lawn seems to have accommodated the new imagery of a cabinlike house nestled within a natural wood-land — in other words, more trees, closer to the house, had become an acceptable stylistic variation.

The environmental awareness that grew to a national movement in the decade of the sixties lent still more authority to this naturalistic style, although it was even then much less common, particu-larly in the South, than site design on residential proper-ties that was continuous in its form and materials with pre-war patterns of practice. The Howetts, however — pre-dictable academic types — moved on to a modern house built in the mid-1960s [Figure 6–21], the design for which had begun with a stock plan for a brick ranch but gained a second story and a fine southern porch through the necessity of having to be inserted into one of those steeply sloping "unbuildable" lots that had survived in an older subdivi-sion. The house was very "sixties" in preserving not just existing trees but existing substory as well; and very southern, in looking and feeling for all the world like a mountain cabin while still within a fifteen-minute drive of the state capitol.

Figure 6–21.
Howett residence on Hertford Circle, Atlanta.
[Catherine Howett, 1970]

A SUMMING UP

I think it is probably significant that no landscape architect practicing in the South seems to have enjoyed a national reputation for the quality of his or her residential design during the postwar period. At the same time, I recognized very special qualities that seemed to me distinctly southern in gardens and grounds dating from that earlier period that I visited after moving South in 1966. Two of these qualities, as I have tried to suggest, were rather intangible — the Edenic sensuosity and lushness of some gardens; and the presence within them of expressive links to country things and rural pleasures. The latter is perhaps more easily defined in terms of what it is not; it is design that deliberately avoids the impression of high-styled sophistication in favor of a seemingly artless and insouciant rurality. The third quality I have tried to associate with a southern poetics of place still operative through the 1950s is the conservatism that looks to historic regional traditions of form-giving for the design conventions by means of which garden, yard, or grounds are structured, and prefers plants that have a long history of use in southern gardens.

In an essay written just after World War I, the architectural historian Fiske Kimball analyzed the emerging typology of the American country house, including an impressive number of southern examples illustrated with both interiors and site plans. Kimball made it clear, however, that to his mind there was no substantial difference between the architectural choices made by northern and southern clients and their architects — that in fact it was possible to speak of an American style, particularly with respect to the layout of the grounds, which he described as "less intensively developed and less formal" than their counterparts in England would be. Among the several causes he suggested for this distinction, Kimball particularly pointed to " the strength and saneness of American traditions of informal landscape design, based not on artificial picturesqueness but on preservation and expression of the native and local character."[25]

This was a telling observation because it recognized that the difference between residential landscapes North and South was not so much in their site planning as in the choice of materials, particularly trees and shrubs, that were not necessarily indigenous but historically characteristic of the region or the specific place within the region; coastal southern landscapes, for example, use a plant palette that is very different from that suitable to locations in the Piedmont. When the California ranch became such a popular national style after World War II—representing, at least in its massing and open floor plan, the modest triumph of those "progressive" but marginal ideas that Kimball had recognized in the work of Frank Lloyd Wright — it was typical-

ly surrounded by a landscape that differed in no essential respect from that American informal style that Kimball had praised in 1919. Kimball was correct, in my view, in recognizing that Americans in the Northeast and South drew upon the same landscape typology because they shared the same inherited high-style traditions — even if, in the South, these were occasionally, and to great effect, inflected by evocative traces or suggestions of rural vernacular folkways.

Unfortunately, these subtle, atmospheric, personally idiosyncratic yet still distinctively southern qualities in residential gardens and landscapes became much less common after 1966, when the publication *Progressive Farmer* changed its name and its audience, becoming the highly successful shelter magazine *Southern Living*. Quoting an editor's remark that "in 1968, nobody was saying anything nice about the South," geographer Peirce Lewis has perceptively analyzed the reasons for that success:

> Most of the magazine's subscribers were native southerners, who had been raised on farms or in small towns within the region. . . . These new southerners were migrants, to be sure, but they were social migrants, moving upward from one social stratum to another. . . . The South was not new and unfamiliar country, although, paradoxically, those subscribers (and people like them) would play a central role in converting the South into a new and far more urban kind of place than it had been before.[26]

The earlier southern landscape aesthetic that I have tried to analyze represented the perpetuation, until well past the middle of the twentieth century, of a traditional sensibility and habits of garden and landscape making that may perhaps be compared to the vibrant regional tradition of story telling that contributed so much to the literature of the twentieth-century South. The expressive values of this domestic landscape tradition, which drew upon the historic experience and resilient spirit of past generations of southerners, seem, however, to have been more easily either erased — or worse, commodified and trivialized — in the glossy pictures of the magazine that sets the standard in residential design for a new generation of homeowners in the South.

NOTES

1. Frederick Law Olmsted and J. James R. Croes, *Report of the Landscape Architect and the Civil and Topographical Engineer, Accompanying a Plan for Laying Out That Part of the Twenty-fourth Ward Lying West of the Riverdale Road*, reprinted in *Landscape into Cityscape: Frederick Law Olmsted's Plans for a Greater New York City*, ed. Albert Fein (New York: Van Nostrand Reinhold, 1981), pp. 358–773.

2 Ibid., p. 362.

3. Russell Lynes, *The Tastemakers* (New York: Harper & Brothers, 1955), p. 237.

4. Ibid., pp. 251–53.

5. William H. Jordy, *American Buildings and Their Architects: The Impact of European Modernism in the Mid-Twentieth Century* (1972; reprint edition, New York: Anchor Books, 1976), pp. 174–75.

6. Alexander Wilson, *The Culture of Nature: North American Landscape from Disney to the Exxon Valdez* (Cambridge, Mass.: Blackwell, 1992), p. 105.

7. Lynes, *The Tastemakers*, p. 254.

8. Barbara M. Kelley, *Expanding the American Dream: Building and Rebuilding Levittown* (Albany: State University of New York Press, 1993), pp. 24–26.

9. Atlanta's remarkable rate of suburban growth continues to the present. From 1990 through 1997, Atlanta led the country in new home construction. New construction in 1997 represented 41 percent of total home sales, also the highest figure in the nation. "The Housing Boom," *Atlanta Journal-Constitution*, 8 February 1988, p. H–1.

10. Henry Miller, *The Air-Conditioned Nightmare*, vol. 1 (New York: New Directions, 1945), p. 114.

11. This notion of an ennobled and productive leisure (*otium*) postulated that liberation from preoccupation with the affairs of everyday life—the getting and spending summed up by the word *negotium*—was a necessary condition not only for a richly creative and satisfying personal life but, when appreciated and pursued by the larger society, for the highest achievements of civilization.

12. Twelve Southerners, *I'll Take My Stand: The South and the Agrarian Tradition* (Harper and Brothers, 1930; Baton Rouge: Louisiana State University Press, 1983), p. xliii.

13. Henry David Thoreau, *Excursions* (1863; Cambridge, Mass.: Riverside Press, 1914), pp. 119–20.

14. Mattie Abney Hartzog, *Garden Time in the South* (Harrisburg, Pa.: J. Horace McFarland Company, Mount Pleasant Press, 1951).

15. George Nelson and Henry Wright, *Tomorrow's House: How to Plan Your Post-War Home Now* (New York: Simon and Schuster, 1945), p. 6.

16. Ibid., pp. 211–13.

17. The term "New South" was coined by *Atlanta Constitution* editor Henry Grady to describe a progressive agenda aimed at replacing the South's pre–Civil War dependence on plantation agriculture with a mix of industry, commerce, and more diversified farming.

18. Air conditioning was so much a luxury in 1947 that the owners of a modern house built in Atlanta in 1947 spent $18,000 on its construction "exclusive of the air conditioning which the Rosenthals bought instead of a new car." William M. Branham, "Sensible Modern in Atlanta," *American Home*, February 1951, p. 42.

19. "Rich's-Atlanta Presents 'Georgia Builds' Architectural Competition," *Progressive Architecture—Pencil Points*, October 1945, n.p.

20. Arthur McK. Stires, "Home Life and House Architecture," *Architectural Record*, April 1949, p. 103.

21. Joseph Alsop, "I'm Guilty! I Built a Modern House," *Saturday Evening Post*, 20 May 1950, p. 175.

22. Dorothy Monroe, "Home Without Compromises," *American Home*, January 1953, p. 33.

23. W. F. Deknatel, cited in Bruno Zevi, *Towards an Organic Architecture* (London: Faber & Faber, 1950), p. 126.

24. Zevi, *Towards an Organic Architecture*, pp. 124–25.

25. Fiske Kimball, "The American Country House," *Architectural Record*, October 1919, p. 388.

26. Peirce Lewis, "The Making of Vernacular Taste: The Case of Sunset and Southern Living," in *The Vernacular Garden*, ed. John Dixon Hunt and Joachim Wolschke-Bulmahn (Washington, D.C.: Dumbarton Oaks Research Library and Collection, 1993), p. 132.

In 1969, the American landscape architect Thomas Church published *Your Private World*, a book intended to help suburban homeowners create intimate residential gardens. But the themes, and even some of the book's text, had been appearing for decades prior in the pages of the popular magazine *House Beautiful*. One of the first mass-circulation magazines devoted strictly to residential design and among the earliest of the tastemaking journals to promote modernism, *House Beautiful* celebrated its hundredth anniversary in November 1996.[1] This essay examines a twenty-year period of the magazine's publication, between 1945 and 1965 —the era that coincides with the tenure of the crusading editor-in-chief Elizabeth Gordon. Under her guidance, the journal promoted a specific modernism for both house and garden, one that emphasized the creation of a private residential world separated from community, neighbors, and public life. As a feature article proclaimed, the three big ideas for house design in 1950 were climate control, privacy, and what Gordon and her staff called "the American Style" [Figure 7–1]. But the same three ideas had already served as *House Beautiful*'s guide to good design since at least 1945, and they continued as its sacred trinity for the next twenty years. Of the three concepts, privacy and the "American Style" received the most attention, appearing repeatedly in the magazine's pages, linked to nationalistic and social ideals. They also implied a specific design response that was linked to the emerging modern landscape aesthetic.

7.   DIANNE HARRIS

Making Your Private World: Modern Landscape Architecture and *House Beautiful*, 1945–1965

Unlike its competitors, *House Beautiful* had a distinctive approach and market, publishing sermonlike editorials to persuade a nationwide audience of a specific modernism that excluded the International Style on the basis of nationalistic arguments.[2] No similar journal approached the consistently zealous tone of *House Beautiful*. After all, the magazine's founder was a minister, William C. Gannet, whose 1885 book *The House Beautiful* "crusaded for homes dedicated to the needs of human beings instead of to show-off ostentation." The magazine became the medium for spreading the minister's gospel, which railed against "entrenched, materialistic social patterns."[3] Gannet's Veblenite attitudes and disdain for conspicuous consumption set a tone for the magazine, whose slogan was "Taste goes farther than money," and the editors emphasized this with articles published in 1904 and 1905 titled "The Poor Taste of the Rich."

Perhaps the most passionate and notorious of the magazine's editors, Elizabeth Gordon, served as editor-in-chief from 1941 to 1964, her influence spanning 276 issues. She was equal parts crusader and editor—her mission was to convert her readers to high-middlebrow taste and to extol the virtues of an American modernism rooted in specific values and political beliefs. For Gordon, there was good and bad taste; good and bad modernism; a right way and a wrong way to build. All were associated with good and bad living, a moral imperative connected with design that was not atypical for the times, but was perhaps the last time we were to see that explicit connection made in the twentieth century.

Not one to avoid controversy, Gordon challenged a number of powerful culture critics in her editorials, assuring her readers that their "taste was better than its reputation," even if it nonetheless required her guidance as an arbiter. She railed against Le Corbusier, Mies van der Rohe, the Museum of Modern Art curators who sought to elevate International Style modernism, and a variety of authors such as John Kenneth Galbraith, whose book *The Affluent Society* struck her as pessimistic and insulting to her readers.[4] Although its warnings against out-of-control consumerism were in keeping with the philosophies of *House Beautiful*'s founder, Galbraith's book likely struck a nerve with an editor of a magazine supported by advertisers who relied on exactly such enthusiasm for consumption. Postwar readers were assured that "The *House Beautiful* Look Knows that Too Much Is Just Right"—the modernist less-is-more mantra had no place at Gordon's journal.[5]

Gordon authored the most controversial editorial ever published by the magazine—a 1953 piece titled "The Threat to the Next America," which was an emotional attack on International Style modernism. She viewed the International Style as subversive, foreign, autocratic, communist, and even fascistic. Above all, its main practitioners were not American, and her comments are redolent with postwar xenophobia. Naturally, the piece provoked much reader response, both supportive and critical. In a June 1953 speech delivered to the Press Club Luncheon of the American Furniture Mart, Gordon defended her editorial, which had already gained considerable notoriety in the intervening months since its publication. In an attempt to clarify her position she stated:

> We don't believe the International Style is simply a matter of taste; any more than we believe that Nazism or Communism are matters of taste, matters of opinion. . . . We say: vote either the Nazi or Communist party into office and it

Figure 7–1.
House Beautiful's three "big ideas" for residential design in June 1950: climate control, privacy, and the American Style.

is your last election for a long time. Similarly, choose a way of life whose architecture is the International Style and whose philosophy of living is the Bauhaus and you subject yourself to something far beyond a casual change in home fashions. Why do we speak so strongly? Because in all honesty we feel that a profound choice faces us today. Either we choose the architecture that will encourage the development of individualism or we choose the architecture and design of collectivism and totalitarian control. We believe the International Style is the latter, that, whether some of the people who practice it know it or not, want it or not, it is the Procrustean bed of collectivism, conditioning people for total control. . . . The International Style is an ideal form of architecture for would-be dictators. It offers the physical structure for total control. It masses families together in one giant building so that relatively few, strategically placed, block leaders could check on all movements and conduct classes of ideological indoctrination. . . . Whether they know it or not, or want it or not, the International Style school of design, if successful, will end in imposing a design for living that we associate with totalitarianism.[6]

If Gordon believed International Style architecture was a procrustean bed of totalitarianism, she advocated Frank Lloyd Wright's work as "the democratic dream."[7] Wright recognized her editorial as an explicit promotion of his work and used it as an opportunity to forge a lasting friendship with the editor [Figure 7-2]. For Gordon, Wright's architecture epitomized American modernism and as the editor herself noted, "The architecture department [of *House Beautiful*] was an extension of Taliesin."[8] Gordon devoted three entire issues of *House Beautiful* to Wright; they appeared in 1955, 1959, and 1963 and featured his work for the duration of his career.

In 1948, Gordon initiated the annual series of Pace-Setter houses, selecting built examples from each year that epitomized her acceptable brand of modernism. All the Pace-Setter houses were American, and each exemplified a wide variety of ideals, including postwar expansionism, patriotism, and capitalist enterprise. For Gordon, Pace-Setting modernism was that practiced by Wright and a group of architects that included William Wurster and his firm Wurster Bernardi and Emmons, Harwell Hamilton Harris, John Yeon, Gardner Dailey, Cliff May, Joseph Esherick, Robert Cerny, Hugh Stubbins, John Funk, and Quincy Jones [Figures 7–3 to 7–8]. The roster of names should recall what Marc Treib has termed "an everyday modernism"—a soft brand of residential modernism that retained comforting signs of the

182

traditional such as hipped roofs, as well as familiar materials like wood and stone.[9]

Because *House Beautiful*'s brand of modernism emphasized the importance of indoor/outdoor connections, garden design received equal attention; the magazine featured the work of Marie and Arthur Berger, Jacques Hahn, Lawrence Halprin, Garrett Eckbo, Robert Royston, and their combined firms, Edward Huntsman-Trout, Douglas Baylis, and Janet Dar- ling [Figures 7–9 to 7–13]. But no landscape architect received more attention than Thomas Church, whose work covered the magazine's pages for the duration of Gordon's tenure. If Wright was her architect of choice, Church epito- mized all that she deemed appropriate for the modern residential landscape [Figure 7–14].

Although many of the showcased houses belonged to the relatively wealthy and included maid's quarters and parking for multiple family cars, the overriding concern of the post- war articles was accommodating design to small lots — the suburban-sized lots, 60 by 125 feet and sometimes smaller — that most of their readers could afford and were buying in tract developments all over the country. The magazine's readers were primarily middle-class suburban women, and Gordon herself referred to *House Beautiful* as "a woman's magazine."[10] Russell Lynes caricatured Gordon's audience in his 1954 book *The Tastemakers*, which he opened and closed with the example of a lawyer's wife, so befuddled by domestic decorating and taste choices that she flees on a vacation.[11]

Gordon and her staff clearly recognized that many of their readers were befuddled by modernism, and if they were going to sell it effectively, they would first have to demystify it. To assuage consumer anxiety about the style, they used a number of tactics that included humorous short stories such as Marguerite Nixon's "I'm Scared of Postwar Houses," from 1946, a tale of an average housewife's struggle to appear progressive by accepting modern architecture no matter how much it goes against the grain of what appears sensible and comfortable [Figure 7–15].[12] A similar short story written by designer and decorator T. H. Robsjohn- Gibbings in the same year titled "Dilemma . . . The Perils of Making a Cult of Modern" told the story of a woman named Harriet who makes an excursion to a Museum of Modern Art exhibition opening only to encounter art she cannot fathom and people who are more pretentious and rarified than the works of art.[13] The message of the story was intended to comfort insecure readers and to assure them

183

Figure 7–5.
Shainwald residence. Wurster Bernardi
and Emmons, architects; Thomas Church,
landscape architect.
This house epitomized the "American Style"
for the magazine's editors.
[Reprinted by permission from *House
Beautiful*, © November 1950. The Hearst
Corporation. All Rights Reserved]

Figure 7–6.
Haven house and garden, Berkeley,
California, 1941. Harwell Hamilton Harris,
architect.
[Marc Treib]

185

Figure 7–9.
A pierced concrete grill provided this house with "a truly private and unostentatious entrance" and grounds with ample parking. Marie and Arthur Berger, landscape architects.
[Reprinted by permission from *House Beautiful*, © November 1963. The Hearst Corporation. All Rights Reserved]

Figure 7–10.
Philip Pierpont residence. Jacques Hahn, landscape architect.
This landscape design provided "distinction for the modest house."
[Reprinted by permission from *House Beautiful*, © February 1957. The Hearst Corporation. All Rights Reserved]

Figure 7–11.
Patrick H. Peabody residence, 1959.
Lawrence Halprin, landscape architect.
An example of the enlarged terrace.
[Reprinted by permission from *House Beautiful*, © July 1959. The Hearst Corporation. All Rights Reserved]

Figure 7–12. Community Club Center, Foothill Farms subdivision, Sacramento, California, 1950s(?). Douglas Baylis, landscape architect.
[Douglas Baylis, courtesy Marc Treib]

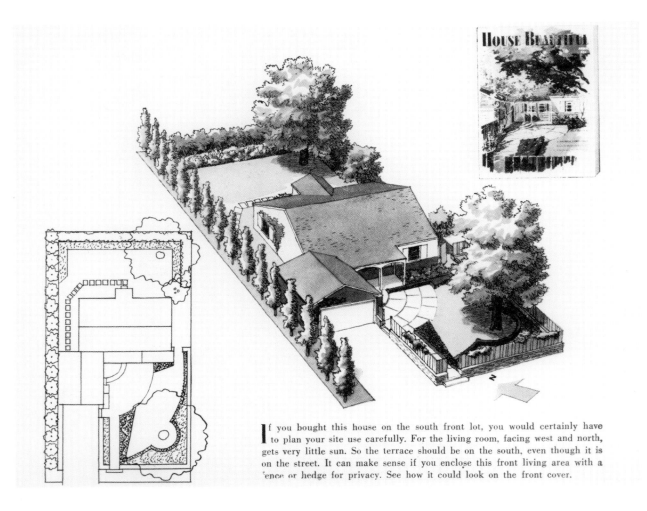

If you bought this house on the south front lot, you would certainly have to plan your site use carefully. For the living room, facing west and north, gets very little sun. So the terrace should be on the south, even though it is on the street. It can make sense if you enclose this front living area with a fence or hedge for privacy. See how it could look on the front cover.

Figure 7–13.
This garden design indicated the ways custom landscaping could individualize a mass-produced house. Janet Darling, landscape architect.

By Thomas Church
Landscape Architect

People of taste everywhere are trying to find ways to avoid reducing their standard of living because of the squeeze of the higher living costs. The trend to smaller houses is producing a parallel trend to make more use of the garden. For a house seems bigger if its outdoor spaces are contrived to carry the eye far out to the edge of the property. And a house actually *is* bigger if it provides terraces, screened porches, sunpockets for fall and winter living out of doors, and play areas for children, rain or shine.

As a result of this trend, better landscape designers in all parts of the country are trying to make a garden something more than a place of trees and flowers. The trend is to make the garden work like an extra room— or several rooms.

First necessity of such a trend is to make the garden private, so it can function truly as a room. For no one wants to carry on one's personal life—entertaining, eating, napping, and reading—under the eyes of neighbors and casual passers-by. *(Continued on page 326)*

243

PHOTOGRAPHS BY PHILIP FEIN

The recreation room (above and on opposite page) was placed between two large California white oaks. Adjoining are the dressing rooms with baths, which may conveniently be turned into comfortable guest rooms.

189

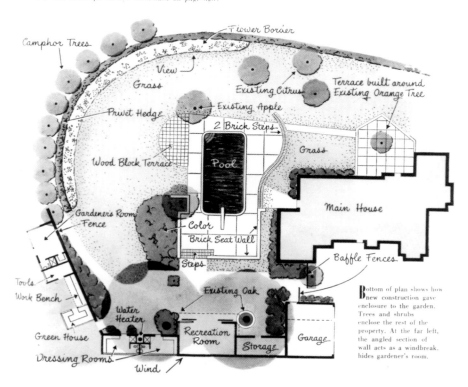

Bottom of plan shows how new construction gave enclosure to the garden. Trees and shrubs enclose the rest of the property. At the far left, the angled section of wall acts as a windbreak, hides gardener's room.

that they need not feel pressured by high-art tastemakers who, according to the story, were out of touch with reality.

But the magazine also sought to assure its readers that modernism had something important to offer them, that indeed there was an acceptable modernism, which all readers should embrace in order to live the truly American good life. Letters from subscribers such as Martha Bell's "My Love Affair with Modern" assured readers that modern design had much to offer those with even the most traditional lifestyles and tastes.[14] To further the cause, *House Beautiful* published lists of books that would help educate their readers on modernism and articles like "Do You Know the Difference Between Modern and Modernistic?" which explained that "Modernistic is bad design, very bad design," examples of which caused the author, Robsjohn-Gibbings, "unspeakable torture."[15]

By including the ever popular magazine quiz, the staff let readers test themselves on how well their taste and lifestyle measured up. Modernism might be intimidating, but after all, nobody wants to be considered old-fashioned. Quizzes like "Are You Really Living in Your Own Times?" included categories on gardening, asking readers, have you "brought the outdoors in via larger windows, bays, French doors, or sliding walls?" and included a series of seven questions under the heading "Better-Flowers-with-Less-Effort Division," which asked readers the extent to which they gardened with fungicides, fertilizers, pesticides, hormone sprays, and weed killers. Each "yes" scored the reader 5 points, and a total below 120 meant "you are still living in the horseless carriage era."[16] To assure their readers that the publication itself remained up-to-date, in 1946 the magazine guaranteed its readers that "the *House Beautiful* on its fiftieth birthday is as up-to-date as the atomic bomb, an achievement of which you may well be proud."[17]

In the pages of *House Beautiful*, taste was closely linked to personal distinction and class, and the writers seemed to recognize that their suburban readers had a particular need to mark social and economic distinction in subtle but recognizable ways through house and garden design. In *The Organization Man* (1956), William Whyte described the uniformity of suburban life with its "great forest of television aerials, the hardtop convertibles, and . . . the pink lampshade in the picture window."[18] Amidst this great sameness, it could be difficult for outsiders to distinguish the subtle differentiations of class that existed despite the relative homo-

190

I'm SCARED
of postwar houses

JOHN L. FER

Figure 7–15.
The illustration for Marguerite Nixon's short story.

geneity.[19] Although suburbia of the 1950s and early 1960s was superficially a one-class society, the insider could mark a number of distinctions. True, everyone wanted their houses to look the same, up to a point. But because the architecture of the early suburbs was so uniform, many middle-class inhabitants feared the look of the lower-class "projects" or "developments" they had lived in on their way up the economic ladder.[20] Modern home furnishings and modern gardens, then, became indispensable markers of class distinction.

A number of sociological studies from the period recorded a growing concern about the effects of mass suburban conformity, and they likewise found an antidote in the garden. David Reisman's *Lonely Crowd*, first published in 1950, is one such example. Reisman's was a study of national character formation, and he focused on a perceived trend toward postwar overconformity. He encouraged Americans to "break free of their conformist peer-group aspirations," and he sought possibilities for development of an autonomous society. Such studies undoubtedly arose from anxieties related to images from World War II and to the recognized horrors of fascism, which certainly disallowed individuality and diversity. But they also must have been linked to concerns about the growing homogeneity of suburban life. In the closing pages of his book, titled "Autonomy and Utopia," Reisman extolled the virtues of city planners whom he called "the guardians of our liberal and progressive political tradition," and advocated a view of the city "as a setting for leisure and amenity as well as work."[21] The author considered recreation and leisure vital components in the fight against the mass conformity fostered by the workplace and the suburban tract.

If individuality was to be attained, one had to have privacy as well, since privacy fostered self-expression and inward contemplation, both of which facilitated free thinking. But such free thinking was ultimately linked to democracy, to the American way of life. As Reisman wrote: "people may, in what is left of their private lives, be nurturing newly critical and creative standards. If these people are not strait-jacketed before they get started . . . people may some day learn to buy not only packages of groceries or books but the larger package of a neighborhood, a society and a way of life."[22] Back yards, then, became a key to individualization, a means to autonomy and ultimately, it was hoped, to the strengthening of democracy. The key was to increase the

amount of time suburbanites spent in leisure and to help Americans achieve a degree of distinction, without appearing eccentric or radically different. The balance was crucial: one's garden should reflect one's outlook and personality but should conform to a level of embellishment in keeping with that established in the neighborhood and following the guidelines set out in taste-making journals such as *House Beautiful*.[23] Articles like the one titled "A Garden Can Banish Subdivision Monotony" showed the importance of a professionally designed garden in distinguishing a "run-of-the-mill house from its neighbors" [Figure 7–16].[24]

Sociologists like Reisman may have seen the city planner as the savior of American freedom and individuality, but they were likely unaware of Elizabeth Gordon's efforts on her country's behalf. Like the sociologists, Gordon was deeply concerned about societal overconformity, and she used the magazine as a forum to advocate free thinking and individuality expressed through design of the home. The 1952 Pace-Setter home exemplified the American Style she repeatedly advocated. According to Gordon, the house constituted "a relaxed, democratic architecture — a modern house that belongs, yet has an individuality essential to personal culture. Just as it is the essence of Americanism for each of us to develop our differences, so the Pace-Setter, while honoring the general character of the community, arrived at distinction and originality because it freely solved the problems of a unique site and a particular owner."[25] The house struck the perfect and requisite balance for suburban dwellers, and Gordon had a keen eye for her preferred design model. But it was not enough for houses to appear merely democratic — American Style houses had to appear truly "American."

A feature from 1950, written by garden editor Joseph Howland, attempted to define the style for readers. As Howland tried to explain, "The American Style in gardens . . . is thoroughly American, a product of the melting pot that is America," and its distinguishing characteristic was freedom from "rigid imported restrictions."[26] By 1951, Gordon and Howland had become more precise. In articles titled "Why Is This an American Style House?" and "When Is a Garden American Style?" they listed features that recurred with remarkable consistency in *House Beautiful*'s pages for the twenty years of Elizabeth Gordon's editorial leadership: (1) The integration of house and garden into a single, unified composition; (2) the idea that the garden should be rationally planned and that it should be useful; (3) that it should be low in maintenance; (4) climate controlled to maximize

A garden can banish subdivision monotony

See what landscaping did for a run-of-the-mill house. Now it has a distinguished look, privacy, hidden service, safe play space

192

Nothing conventional about this "foundation" planting. Row of dwarf trees (five in all) extends across front of house, shades bedroom from afternoon sun. Owners widened drive to make enough walk space to let you pass wet car without brushing your clothes against it.

SALE PRICE	$8,500
Lot value	$750
Lot size	55 x 125 ft.
Landscaping	none
(owners spent $1,750)	
House cost	$7,750
House size	1,219 square feet
Cost per sq. ft.	$6.35
No. of rooms	5
Appliances	none

PHOTOGRAPHS BY MAYNARD PARKER

Garden designed by Thomas Church
Landscape Architect

use; (5) an aesthetic based on space, form, and texture rather than color; (6) the implementation of modern technology and materials; (7) accommodation of the automobile; (8) creation of space for children's recreation; (9) design for comfort rather than display; and (10) above all else, an insistence on privacy.[27] Taken together, these ten components defined not just modern residential landscape architecture but a so-called American Style modernism linked to Gordon's belief in the importance of autonomy to development of democratic national character.

In order to achieve an American Style garden, privacy was absolutely essential.[28] For Gordon, the right to privacy was at the core of American independence and freedom. Without privacy, there could be no autonomy, no democracy—and these were closely linked to the idea of individuality. As she stated in her 1953 speech:

> The challenge of our time is individualism versus totalitarianism—democracy or dictatorship—and this struggle is on many fronts. Our front, yours and mine, happens to be on the home front. . . . It is a time of profound spiritual crisis. . . . The individual is under assault from many sides. . . . We judge all design for the home in terms of what it offers for the encouragement of individuality, for the development of individual differences, for the provision of privacy and personal creativity, in short, for what it contributes to the humanistic values of a democratic age. . . . The modern American house—the good modern house . . . provides privacy for the family from the community, and privacy for individuals of the family from each other. It inspires democratic living by encouraging a personal life.[29]

Because Gordon equated privacy with the development of individuality and democracy, she devoted more pages to articles related to privacy than to any other aspect of modern design. The emphasis on privacy is somewhat ironic considering that the houses she used to illustrate her point were exposed to millions of readers through a vehicle of mass communication. Showcased houses included the owner's names along with the house location so that every good example of privacy achieved through design was immediately exposed to the throngs of prying eyes Gordon so vehemently tried to exclude.

In January 1950, Joseph Howland wrote a piece titled "Good Living Is NOT Public Living," which connected privacy to the American dream of individual home ownership, writing, "We Americans give much lip service to the idea of privacy.

We consider it one of the cherished American rights, one of the privileges we fought a war to preserve. Freedom to live our own lives, the way we want to live them without being spied on or snooped around, is as American as pancakes and molasses. . . . The very raison d'etre of the separate house is to get away from the living habits and cooking smells and inquisitive eyes of other people. . . .If your neighbors can observe what you are serving on your terrace, your home is not really your castle. If you can't walk out in a negligee, to pick a flower before breakfast without being seen from the street or by the neighbors, you have not fully developed the possibilities of good living"[30] [Figures 7–17 to 7–19].

Fences, then, or at the very least a dense and well-clipped hedge, were essential aspects of the modern residential garden, and the magazine featured numerous articles devoted to design of attractive fences that provided privacy without offending one's neighbors [Figure 7–20].[31] By 1960, Elizabeth Gordon found the subject compelling enough to devote an entire issue to "Landscaping and Privacy," asking her readers, "Is Privacy Your Right or a Stolen Pleasure?"[32] Linking politics and domestic design once again, Gordon urged her readers to consider their political commitment to individuality and the right to privacy. She wrote, "Does Your Front Lawn Belong to You — Or the Whole Neighborhood? The United States is split into two factions over this question — an ideological split just as real as the Republican-Democratic divide. Where do you stand? . . . The issue really boils down to whether or not others have the right to look at or onto your land." The editor encouraged her readers to stop watching each other and, borrowing a phrase used by the sociologists, asked them "to turn inward." Because fencing was the key to achieving privacy, she advised her readers to organize their communities to eliminate deed restrictions and covenants that restricted or prohibited fence construction. Although she noted that such restrictions frequently extended to "the kind of people to whom you can sell your house," she did not elaborate on the problems of racial discrimination in the residential real estate market of the early 1960s. But she did advise her readers to take the law into their own hands if conventional organizational efforts failed, writing, "If you can't get around fencing ordinances legally, there are a few ways to avoid them without breaking the letter of the law," and she recommended hedges, trellises, and climbing vines as suitable alternatives to fence construction [Figure 7–21].

by Dr. Joseph E. Howland
House Beautiful's Garden Editor

Good living
is NOT public living

We Americans give much lip service to the idea of privacy. We consider it one of the cherished American rights, one of the privileges we fought a war to preserve. Freedom to live our own lives, the way we want to live them without being spied on or snooped around, is as American as pancakes and molasses. Yet, few Americans avail themselves fully of this right.

People who must live in apartment houses or row houses automatically must accept less privacy by their choice of abode. In such close quarters the sights and sounds and smells of neighbors cannot be screened out. It's the price people in such dwellings must pay in return for not having to cope with other problems. For them we have nothing but sympathy—and no suggestions except to seal their windows and buy air-conditioning units.

People who live in single-family, detached houses are sacrificing one of the advantages inherent in that type of dwelling if they do not achieve, at least, visual privacy from their neighbors and from the street. The very *raison d'être* of the separate house is to get away from the living habits and cooking smells and inquisitive eyes of other people. The nuisance of snow shoveling and of being your own janitor can be more than offset if you achieve the advantages of privacy. But if your neighbors can observe what you are serving on your terrace, your home is not really your castle. If you can't walk out in negligee, to pick a flower before breakfast without being seen from the street or by the neighbors, you have not fully developed the possibilities of good living. On the next 32 pages you will see how other people have gained privacy in ways you may want to use.

Better your home
Better your living

PHOTOGRAPHS BY

Your whole property—garden as well as house—should permit you to relax comfortably without being constantly on view and dress parade. You cannot completely relax if the world looks over your shoulder. Securing this kind of freedom is usually very simple, sometimes as simple as putting up a good-looking fence like this.

Garden designed by James Rose
Landscape Architect

PHOTOGRAPHS BY MAYNARD PARKER

Do the neighbors
know your business?

You may love your neighbors, but you deserve a chance to live your life without constant observation. Here's how you can remodel a back yard and get privacy on a narrow city lot

Compare the big increase in usable living space gained by this family when they remodeled their 65' x 125' back yard—despite the fact the garage had to stay in its space-wasting place (¼ of lot is driveway).

You can do as much for your own yard. The elements are simple: board fence, brick wall, seat wall to accommodate many guests, paving for dry feet as well as interesting year-round ground pattern, vertical surfaces against which to feature plants. You may need a designer to sketch out the best solution for you, but building fences and walls or laying paving isn't beyond a determined handyman's ability or equipment. Study your own lot and gain virtually another living room.

Figure 7–17.
House Beautiful authors, including Joseph Howland, wrote numerous articles that, like this one, emphasized the importance of privacy in the residential garden. James Rose, landscape architect.
[Reprinted by permission from *House Beautiful*, © November 1948. The Hearst Corporation. All Rights Reserved]

Figure 7–18.
Numerous *House Beautiful* articles featured fencing and fence design as key to attaining privacy.
[Reprinted by permission from *House Beautiful*, © January 1950. The Hearst Corporation. All Rights Reserved]

Figure 7–19.
A San Francisco house that demonstrated "how to have your private bit of outdoors off a city street." Wurster Bernardi and Emmons, architects; Thomas Church, landscape architect.

Figure 7–20.
An example of a corrugated plastic panel used as a rolling privacy screen. Design by Thomas Church.

Part of the frenzy for privacy was linked to the increased use of large areas of glazing in the home. Sliding glass doors and picture windows allowed the requisite merging of indoors and outdoors, but they also caused privacy problems. In a December 1946 article titled "The Enlarging Window. . . . Straw-in-the-Wind That Shows You the Direction in Which American House Design Is Heading," a contributing author wrote, "Unfortunately, in our best residential areas, obsolete restrictions created in times before the Glass Age prevent our putting fences, hedges or walls close to our own property lines and keep us from creating privacy, both indoors and outdoors. As a result, many people who responded to the urge for more sun and light are living behind drawn venetian blinds and thin curtains to escape living like fish in a bowl."[33] Large areas of glass also caused climate control problems in the house, but the look of modernity they allowed was desirable enough that the magazine launched a Climate Control Research Program in 1949 to look for ways to make glazed expanses feasible.

In addition to the desire for autonomy and individual freedom, the obsession with privacy was linked to increased crime rates and the desire for security. A featured house from 1947 included a noteworthy attraction: "a peephole concealed in the west wall of the kitchen so that visitors ringing the front doorbell [could] be surveyed before they are admitted."[34] Within ten years' time, security concerns were such that articles featured radio-operated garage doors like the one that "enables Mrs. Lindsley to stay in her automobile until she is safely within the confines of her home" and the "built in intercom system that permits Mrs. Lindsley to answer the door from the main house."[35]

But overall, the concern with privacy was connected to the desire for a private world, secluded from the conforming masses. Home and garden were best designed when they allowed one to turn one's back on the world. As early as 1946, author Marion Gough profiled a "Honeymoon Home," which she found notable because its site was "aloof from prying neighbors . . . utterly secluded . . . turning its back on the road and all possible intruders." For the author, the house epitomized "good secluded living without ostentation or side" and a look at "what a real private world can be."[36]

But turning one's back on society meant that the garden had to play a new role. Not only should it provide much-needed additional living space for small suburban homes, but it also had to accommodate a range of activities that

Here is a typical suburban lot, 100 feet wide, in Modesto, California. On the far left, above, you can see the house of one neighbor, while at the far right appears the driveway to the garage of another. Instead of following the usual formula of placing the house in the middle of the lot and exposing it on all sides, a far better solution was found in the case. Here the owners have almost 100 per cent of land for private use.

The family consists of parents and a small daug[ht]er wanted a small, compact home which offered pr[ivacy] for the house and for the garden. Their architect [solved the] problem by placing the house at the rear of the lot [to assure] desirable garden area with southern exposure. He th[en put] a fence almost entirely around the garden to assu[re privacy.] This is the way more people should approach buildi[ng.]

A little PRIVATE KINGDOM
on a 100-foot lot

Figure 7–21.
Residence in Modesto, California.
John Funk, architect.
Designed on a 100-foot-wide suburban lot, a fence surrounds the entire property to assure privacy.

formerly took place away from the home. As one author wrote, "Today all the facilities that used to be scattered around the community we now want to exist on our own little piece of land."[37] The garden became a place for "vitamin-conscious moderns" to relax, a new place for housewives to cook on the outdoor grill, a playground for the children, a recreation center for teens complete with stereo system and swimming pool, and an extension of the living room for adult entertaining. As long as the garden was properly furnished with equipment, furniture, sound system, lighting, and climate control devices, the family need never leave their property to fulfill their recreational needs.[38] In 1948, Thomas Church informed readers that "You Don't Have to Join a Country Club," and he urged readers to "have fun and entertain right at home" by having a well-designed garden.[39] Even the controlled setting of the country club was less desirable than the insularity of one's own suburban back yard. The idea was echoed ten years later in a 1958 piece that explained how families could easily turn their ordinary back yard into "Country-Club Living" [Figure 7–22].[40] Likewise, an article on the importance of the paved terrace for the modern home noted, "A terrace helps make the home more of a play center for children. It is an ideal place for bonfires, marshmallow roasts, and wading pools. It makes home more exciting than anywhere else, canceling the need for seeking family pleasures in private clubs or public beaches."[41]

Terraces and lanais, then, were essential garden elements for several reasons. First, they facilitated the indoor-outdoor connections deemed essential for unification of house and garden. A July 1951 article titled "What Is Leading Us to Merge Indoors and Outdoors?" stated, "This business of merging indoors and outdoors is neither a fad nor architectural whimsy. Rather, it is the logical answer to the social and economic pressures of our times." The author referred, as did numerous *House Beautiful* articles from the period, to the smaller lots and houses that required homeowners to use the outdoors as an additional room.[42] The magazine urged its readers "to make the garden work like an extra room — or several rooms," thus adding usable space to small homes.[43] By 1952, the paved terrace had become the essential "Mark of a MODERN House,"[44] and by 1953, the magazine was telling its readers that to achieve "Fine Living" they should have "6 places for outdoor living for 6 kinds of weather conditions, direct access to terraces from 6 rooms, and rooms that look and live bigger, thanks to glass walls and terraces" [Figure 7–23].[45]

BEFORE

Face-lifting the existing house, done with only a few structural changes to keep it in step with the new "outdoor wing," actually helped improve the looks of the whole house.

AFTER

From ordinary back yard to country-club living

By JEAN BURDEN

You don't have to go to some mythical Pacific island or a cabin in the north woods to keep your family outings unspoiled by traffic snarls, the nerve-shattering blare of portable radios, crowded beaches, or poor restaurant food, indifferently served.

You can have your outings at home—your swimming, sun-bathing, picnics, cook-outs, dancing, cocktail parties, shore dinners at poolside, or just plain loafing—with none of the handicaps of traveling or having precious time taken from their actual enjoyment.

Shown on these pages are the facilities for such outdoor pleasures that one family installed in their own back yard. See from the photographs how skillfully Architects Robert Kliegman and

Matthew Robert Leizer used every inch of back-yard space to provide father, mother, and teen-age daughter with their favorite outdoor interests.

The old back yard had a windfall of space in a 10-foot driveway approach to an unused third garage. The garage itself was converted into a cabana with two luxurious dressing rooms and a shower room between. Beside it, cheek by jowl, a sun-catching swimming pool, shaped to make the most of its allotted space, was built. The cabana was related to the house by a stylized pergola repeated as a cover over the terrace adjoining the house.

For cook-outs, a favorite family hobby, an old fireplace was junked for an outdoor (*Please turn to page* 103)

BEFORE

AFTER

Sound planning to serve the needs of the entire family guided the architects as they fitted these many facilities into the limited space of an average-size back yard.

Figure 7–22.

The back yard as country club.

Mark of a MODERN house –
the paved terrace:

— *a great stage of glamour, day and night, winter and summer*

– *a private box from which to watch the drama of the seasons*

— *a three-season living room*

— *a private beach*

— *an outdoor play room*

— *a private dance floor, when tile-paved*

— *a low-maintenance garden*

— *a fourth dimension in modern living, because it adds*

    two to three months of outdoor living to every year

Anybody who ever added a terrace to an old house has wished he had made it three or four times larger. For it becomes a second living room, catching the overflow from indoors. On a paved terrace, you can put furniture anywhere. Trees and plants are decorative art objects. Low walls can seat dozens of people at big parties, and don't have to be taken in out of the dew at night, as would most outdoor furniture. Terrace was as carefully color-schemed as the indoor rooms.

Figure 7–23.
The terrace of a postwar garden.
[Reprinted by permission from *House Beautiful,* © November 1952. The Hearst Corporation. All Rights Reserved]

Second, paved areas provided the additional square footage required for accommodation of the new activities. Once the terrace had been created, Elizabeth Gordon urged her readers to buy things for it, to make it into what she called "a poem of loveliness . . . equip it with music, night lighting, beautiful accessories and furniture that do not try to compete for attention with the beauty of nature."[46] The lanai and terrace became crucial components in the quest for the modern garden, and the magazine promoted them as "stages for our parties, box-seats for the dramatic changes of the seasons, open-air kitchens for the new mobile kitchen units, private bathing beaches and outdoor play rooms, auditoriums for today's amplified music systems, and so on."[47] Properly furnished and concealed from neighbors, the new terrace could fulfill all the family's recreational needs so that they need venture out as little as possible [Figure 7–24].

Increased paving in the garden meant decreased maintenance, and low-maintenance gardens facilitated the increased leisure time required for the development of autonomy. As the magazine stated repeatedly, good help had become hard to find, and even if the search was successful, few people could afford to pay a gardener nor could they justify the expense, given the smaller size of suburban gardens. The problem, then, was how to maximize leisure time by minimizing garden maintenance. A 1958 piece obligingly provided easy tips for readers: "Avoid troublesome or tender plants. Also avoid the quick growing tree or shrub. It outgrows its place too fast. Dwarf types 'stay put' longer and preserve the status quo longer." The author also recommended paving as much of the garden as possible, using groundcover instead of lawn, planting shrubbery instead of annuals, and using power tools whenever possible.[48]

Essentially, the garden was to be designed for stasis. If it didn't change, its owner needn't spend time on maintenance. In a 1958 article titled "Do You Know These 26 Time-Tested Work Savers," point 16 pronounced, "Use ground cover that doesn't grow" and encouraged readers to use gravel and other inorganic materials in the garden.[49] An article titled "If You Pave It, You Don't Have to Mow It" stated, "Paving needs no mowing, no weeding, no pruning or clipping."[50] The postwar garden, then, became an increasingly paved or decked garden, which perhaps explains the decreasing emphasis on plants and planting design in schools of landscape architecture during the period. Even Thomas Church as early as 1948 recommended that "if you

199

*The Garden
of the Next America
is an*
Outdoor Room

It's furnished with plants, of course, plus stone, wood, concrete, water, texture, and the

By Dr. Joseph E. Howland
House Beautiful's Garden Editor

are a lazy gardener . . . then convert most of your property to paving, setting aside just enough ground to grow a few plants that don't need too much coddling."[51]

Part of the rationale for increased paving on suburban lots was the intrusion of the automobile, seen both as an asset and as a new burden of modern life. Parking and maneuvering cars required a great deal of space, and many of the Pace-Setter plans included an extraordinary amount of paved area devoted to parking for homeowners and guests, sometimes with space for as many as fifteen to twenty cars.[52] The 1948 Pace-Setter house focused on accommodating the car, and editor Gordon justified her choice by stating that the house "presents a new way of life that recognizes the deep changes brought about by the motor age, which has turned our streets into nuisances and robbed our home sites of their privacy . . . it [is a Pace-Setter] because it provides off-street parking by a motor court, a definite new trend in property planning."[53] The car, of course, was an asset, a status symbol, and a convenience, but it was also seen as an infringement on the quality of life, and the garden became the safe refuge from what Church called "a network of roads and freeways. . . . [We are] dodging more automobiles and people than we would have thought possible a generation ago. Our problems run like this: How to get to and from our gardens without being scalped on the highways."[54] Although Church acted as landscape architect for the General Motors corporate headquarters, he seems to have been somewhat ambivalent about the infringement of that company's product on daily life.

If cars were not uniformly embraced, the magazine considered other forms of technology essential in order make a more useful garden that required little maintenance and met the new demands of functioning as an outdoor room and a private world. For example, the magazine advocated implementation of modern outdoor lighting systems and outdoor wiring for high-fidelity sound systems, which would increase the number of hours families spent in their gardens by increasing comfort and recreational activities. By 1959, Elizabeth Gordon recommended that readers "hook up an outdoor speaker to your hi-fi system and start experimenting with which kind of music goes best with which kind of weather. Try Wagner at his most tempestuous during a raging thunderstorm. Try Segovia on some foggy autumn evening when the wet, fallen leaves are so fragrant."[55] New gas ignition systems for barbecues made it that much easier to start outdoor cooking fires and, therefore, were more desirable.

Radiant heating coils laid inside terrace paving allowed extended use of outdoor space during cool weather and, as *House Beautiful* informed its readers, helped melt snow quickly and so reduced the need to shovel.[56] The expense for installation, maintenance, and operation of such a system was seldom addressed, but it was an important innovation because it facilitated individualized climate control.[57] A 1952 article reminded readers to "Remodel Your Own PRIVATE CLIMATE," saying, "You don't have to put up with the general climate of your neighborhood;" the author provided tips on site planning and design that promised to change the temperature by as much as forty degrees in marginal weather and made it ten degrees cooler in hot weather.[58] One's house might not look much different from the neighbor's, but at least one's thermal comfort could be individualized.

Thermopane double glazing of windows helped with climate control in the house and allowed the wider expanses of glass needed to achieve the proper aesthetic integration of indoors and out; it also made steel and aluminum frame sliding windows feasible in colder climates. But the larger expanses of glass led to increased concerns for privacy, and a variety of new materials appeared that made inexpensive and attractive screens. Translucent corrugated plastic; frosted Plexiglas; Cel-O-Glass, which is a plastic-coated wire mesh; Transite fencing; and translucent Alsynite, which looks like corrugated plastic and was used as an overhead filter, all appeared in the magazine's pages.[59] Likewise, new synthetic fabrics appeared for use on outdoor furniture. These new materials, such as "Restfoam," which were cushions covered with vinyl-coated Fiberglas and guaranteed to resist fade and mildew; or Nylon frieze, the material used in the ubiquitous nylon strapped aluminum chair; or "Koolshade," a screening material that reduced sun heat and contained horizontal wires as tiny flat louvers — all these materials were considered sturdy, water repellent, and therefore perfect for outdoor use. To assure readers of their quality, the magazine noted that the materials had been tested in industrial and military installations and endorsed by professionals like Thomas Church.

A 1957 article highlighted the significance of new technology to the modern garden and pointed to wartime agricultural research as its source.[60] New propagating techniques made plants more affordable, and innovations such as preemergent weed killers and conveniently packaged pesticides with their own applicators made it easier to keep plants

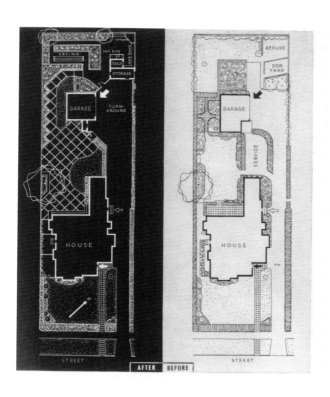

33

Brick wall now screens service area from living, something the ground-wasting twin hedges didn't do before. Gate width allows cart to enter.

PHOTOGRAPHS BY MAYNARD PARKER

Garden designed by Thomas Church
Landscape Architect

Have you a narrow border that could be used as effectively to grow your favorite cut flowers? Warmth from paving and wind protection supplied by fence foster fast growth and prolific blooming.

PHOTOGRAPHS BY MAYNARD PARKER

Hedge supplies the moving line needed to pull the eye past bulky garage which stands in the middle of things. These are original hedge plants (plan above), but now they are working part of garden design.

201

alive, as did "plant foods for every purpose" and "easy to use, highly effective garden chemicals."[61] Pesticides eliminated annoying insects from the terrace; Elizabeth Gordon endorsed "private and community insecticide systems" that help facilitate outdoor living and urged her readers to "rely on the new easy-to-apply, all purpose dusts or sprays as preventatives rather than wait for diseases or insects to attack your garden."[62] Likewise, automatic sprinkler systems with timers and remote control systems assured that plants would not die from neglect and had the added benefit of increasing leisure time by reducing maintenance.

But power tools were perhaps the most attractive of the new technological developments, since they radically reduced time spent on maintenance. With their introduction on the mass market, the home gardener, for the first time, became an important target for manufacturers, and they catered to his needs with aggressive solicitude. I use the male pronoun intentionally here — barbecues and power tools were, and still are, explicitly associated with men. *House Beautiful* articles advised homeowners to "own the specialized tools for what has to be done, and if the job recurs again and again see that the tool is motorized or electrified." In order to maximize efficiency, the authors advised that designers eliminate "sharp corners that power equipment cannot negotiate."[63] Thus, as one author pointed out, low-maintenance gardening required "plenty of weatherproof outdoor electrical outlets conveniently spaced" lest owners find themselves ill equipped to "work with those dandy electric tools like clippers, cultivators, mowers, and edgers."[64] Still, the editors wanted to assure their readers in the 1960s that "mechanization has not taken command, but is kept in a proper supporting role," and the Pace-Setter house of that year was deemed "a fusion of technological advantages with emotional values." It was modern, yet traditional and comforting.[65]

The modern aesthetic for the private garden world is familiar to us by now. Derived from the proposition that beauty follows from space, form, and texture, rather than from color or plant diversity, the new aesthetic emphasized the "pleasing pattern of permanent design, with fluid lines and informal beds" and what one author called "foliage gardening . . . the getting of exciting and permanent textural effects through the juxtaposition of different kinds of leaves as they are seen against other natural landscape materials."[66] The garden was to have its own spatial dynamic derived from architectural form, while remaining in all other ways as static as possible. A 1948 piece by Thomas Church titled "Archi-

tectural Pattern Can Take the Place of Flowers" emphasized the importance of pattern and texture in the garden. He described the importance of creating patterns in view, in paving, of line against the sky, of shadow patterns, and so on. His trademark chevron, zigzag, and checkerboard patterns played against the broad, sweeping curve of the lawn panel illustrated his points, and he emphasized the fact that such design formulas worked well to visually enlarge small suburban lots [Figure 7–25]. The Church formula was as follows: "1. No recognizable form is completed within the space, with the result that the eye has a tendency to complete them. The lawn panel has a corner which is outside the wall. . . . 2. No material completes any part of the design. This means no area is encompassed or defined and does not become static."[67] *House Beautiful* even provided careful instruction to its readers on how to achieve Mr. Church's trademark curves, advising gardeners to "be sure the curve is a sensible one: it must curve for some reason. Have it go all the way to the edge of the lawn area; never leave it stranded between two pieces of lawn. And please, no wiggles or reverse curves."[68]

It is difficult to say how many readers embraced the formula for garden design provided by *House Beautiful*.[69] Certainly fourteen hundred Church clients did. Although Elizabeth Gordon acknowledged that the examples published in *House Beautiful* did not represent the houses of typical Americans, she consistently strove to make them so; the *House Beautiful* look, as defined under her guidance, was less a style than a lifestyle.[70] Above all, it was an American style, sold to readers who were anxious to create their own self-contained universe, independent of the outside world. With food stored in the new deep freeze, a Bendix washing machine and clothes dryer, home entertainment like high-fidelity sound systems and television, and a garden that met the requirements of a country club, there was no need to venture outside the safe and controlled environment of "your private world." For, as the magazine warned its readers, "you must give your personal expression, your taste, free play—or you will emerge like an end-product on an assembly line of canned culture."[71]

NOTES

I would like to thank my research assistant at the University of Illinois, Jennifer Langworthy, whose help made this project possible. Funding for research on this project was provided by a University of Illinois Research Board Grant. I would also like to thank Robert Riley, and especially Marc Treib, who suggested this topic and has always so generously shared ideas and his enthusiasm for landscape history with me.

1. The first issue of *House Beautiful* was published in December 1896. Both Christine Pittel and Martin Filler have noted that the magazine was among the earliest of its kind. See Christine Pittel, "What Style Reveals," *House Beautiful*, November 1996, p. 29, and Martin Filler, ibid., p. 120.

2. *Ladies Home Journal* reached a similar audience but included International Style modernism among an array of design options. *Sunset* and *Southern Living* were directed at regional markets and were, as Pierce Lewis has written, entirely apolitical. Pierce Lewis, "The Making of Vernacular Taste: The Case of Sunset and Southern Living," *The Vernacular Garden*, John Dixon Hunt and Joachim Wolschke-Bulmahn, eds. (Washington, D.C.: Dumbarton Oaks, 1993), p. 118. *House Beautiful* continued to publish a wide range of domestic styles and embraced eclecticism; and *Arts and Architecture*, under the direction of John Entenza, promoted and embraced International Style modernism and reached a smaller and more specialized audience.

3. "What Inspired *House Beautiful*," *House Beautiful*, December 1946, p. 151.

4. Elizabeth Gordon, "A New Thing in the History of Man: Palatial Living for High or Low Incomes," *House Beautiful*, November 1958, p. 193.

5. Elizabeth Gordon, "What Is the *House Beautiful* Look?" *House Beautiful*, January 1958, p. 43.

6. Elizabeth Gordon, "The Responsibility of an Editor," manuscript for speech delivered to the Press Club Luncheon of the American Furniture Mart, Chicago, 22 June 1953, pp. 14, 15, 21. Thomas Church Collection, Environmental Design Archives, University of California, Berkeley. My thanks to Marc Treib for bringing this document to my attention.

7. Gordon, "The Responsibility of an Editor," p. 16.

8. Jane Margolies, "Meeting Mr. Wright," *House Beautiful*, November 1996, p. 136.

9. Marc Treib, ed., *An Everyday Modernism: The Houses of William Wurster* (Berkeley: University of California Press, 1995).

10. Margolies, "Meeting Mr. Wright," p. 136.

11. Russell Lynes, *The Tastemakers* (New York: Grosset & Dunlap, 1954). The writings of Lynes, David Reisman, and William Whyte (cited below) appear in this essay as historical documents. As Winnie Breines has noted, sociological texts of the 1950s, which were written by white male professionals, represent a limited perspective. Lynes's chauvinistic portrayal of the befuddled housewife must be seen within this context. See Winnie Breines, *Young, White, and Miserable: Growing Up Female in the Fifties* (Boston: Beacon Press, 1992), p. 26.

12. Marguerite Nixon, "I'm SCARED of Postwar Houses," *House Beautiful*, June 1946, pp. 134, 137.

13. T. H. Robsjohn-Gibbings, "Dilemma . . . The Perils of Making a Cult of Modern," *House Beautiful*, December 1946, pp. 216–17, 292–96.

14. Martha Bell, "My Love Affair with Modern," *House Beautiful*, March 1946, pp. 73, 131.

15. "Required Reading if You Don't Understand Modern," *House Beautiful*, September 1945, p. 105; "The Library of a Connoisseur of Good Living," *House Beautiful*, November 1951, pp. 242–43, 307–12; T. H. Robsjohn-Gibbings, "Do You Know the Difference Between Modern and Modern-istic?" *House Beautiful*, October 1946, p. 135.

16. "Are You Really Living in Your Own Time?" *House Beautiful*, January 1947, pp. 46–47.

17. "How We Did It in the Old Days," *House Beautiful*, December 1946, p. 250.

18. William H. Whyte, *The Organization Man* (New York: Doubleday, 1956), pp. 337–41.

19. Ibid., p. 330. Recent studies of suburban life increasingly point to the variety of social experience for children and other residents of postwar suburbs. Both the richness and the despair of suburban residential life register in numerous works of fiction and in memoirs and biographies. See, for example,

Doris Kearns Goodwin, *Wait Till Next Year: A Memoir* (New York: Touchstone Books, 1998), and D. J. Waldie, *Holy Land: A Suburban Memoir* (New York: W. W. Norton, 1996). For a fictional narrative rich in the portrayal of 1950s suburban despair, see Alice McDermott, *That Night* (New York: HarperCollins, 1987).

20. Whyte, *Organization Man*, p. 337. For a sociological analysis of postwar anxieties that focused on past living situations, see Alan Ehrenhalt, *The Lost City: The Forgotten Virtues of Community in America* (New York: Basic Books/HarperCollins, 1995), p. 197.

21. David Reisman, *The Lonely Crowd* (New Haven: Yale University Press, 1950), p. 306. For an analysis that compares the writings of Whyte and Reisman, see Breines, *Young, White, and Miserable*, p. 27. Breines called Reisman's book "extraordinarily successful" in its time (p. 30). For other sociological studies that focused on concerns about conformity and the decline of autonomy, see John Seeley, *Crestwood Heights: A Study of the Culture of Suburban Life* (New York: Basic Books, 1956), and John Keats, *The Crack in the Picture Window* (Boston: Houghton Mifflin, 1956).

22. Reisman, *The Lonely Crowd*, p. 307.

23. Russell Lynes noted the deep need to mark individual distinctions in suburban housing developments: "A home of one's own meant a house different from one's neighbors. . . . [A house that had] a semblance of individuality without a trace of eccentricity. . . . Taste was a quality to be carefully strained, and the court of appeal on all such matters was first a peek into your neighbor's window and then a careful study of the women's magazines." See Lynes, *Tastemakers*, p. 246.

24. "A Garden Can Banish Subdivision Monotony," *House Beautiful*, March 1950, p. 78.

25. Elizabeth Gordon, "The Key to Pace-Setting Living," *House Beautiful*, November 1952, p. 212.

26. Joseph Howland, "The American Style in Gardens," *House Beautiful*, May 1950, p. 278.

27. Joseph Howland, "Why Is This an American Style House?" *House Beautiful*, February 1951, p. 80; Elizabeth Gordon, "When Is a Garden American Style?" *House Beautiful*, February 1951, pp. 55-56.

28. The call for a private residential world appears pervasively in the literature on

203

domestic design in the postwar period. For a sociological analysis of the phenomenon see Elaine Tyler May, *Homeward Bound: American Families in the Cold War Era* (New York: Basic Books, 1988). Clifford Clark made a brief note of the desire for postwar domestic privacy in *The American Family Home, 1800-1960* (Chapel Hill: University of North Carolina Press, 1986), p. 219. The topic appears as a major theme in Keats's *Crack in the Picture Window* and in Roger Woods Kennedy's *The House and the Art of Its Design* (New York: Reinhold Publishing, 1953). As a planning or design issue, privacy occurs countless times in articles in shelter magazines from the period.

29. Gordon, "The Responsibility of an Editor," pp. 7, 9, 10.

30. Joseph Howland, "Good Living Is NOT Public Living," *House Beautiful*, January 1950, p. 30.

31. See, for example, "How to Get Privacy," *House Beautiful*, February 1952, p. 140; "Privacy Is Easier with Community Action—Is Costlier If You Have to Go It Alone," *House Beautiful*, May 1960, pp. 154-55; and June Meehan, "How to Arrange for Privacy in Spite of—But Not to Spite—Close Neighbors," *House Beautiful*, May 1960, pp. 164–65, 252–53.

32. Elizabeth Gordon, "Is Privacy Your Right or a Stolen Pleasure?" *House Beautiful*, May 1960, pp. 152, 232, 234–35.

33. Will Mulhorn, "The Enlarging Window—Straw-In-the-Wind . . .," *House Beautiful*, December 1946, p. 286.

34. Elizabeth Gordon, "The 12 Best Houses of the Last 12 Years," *House Beautiful*, September 1947, p. 89.

35. Carolyn Murray, "How an Interior Court Can 'Save' a Crowded Lot," *House Beautiful*, November 1957, p. 305. See also "Orientation Is More Than Just a Word," *House Beautiful*, May 1961, p. 109; and Madelaine Thatcher, "How Public Should the Front Entrance Be?" *House Beautiful*, November 1963, p. 225.

36. Marion Gough, "Honeymoon Home," *House Beautiful*, June 1946, pp. 62–63.

37. "How Our Cars Have Changed Our Gardens," *House Beautiful*, November 1956, p. 254.

38. As a 1949 Pace-Setter house plan caption stated: "Broad L-shape living porch shows how vitamin-conscious moderns turn toward outdoors. Because people now work indoors, outdoors is a symbol of relaxation. Re barbecue: cooking has prestige when you cook for fun." *House Beautiful*, January 1949, p. 57.

39. Thomas Church, *House Beautiful*, August 1948, p. 78.

40. Jean Burden, "From Ordinary Back Yard to Country-Club Living," *House Beautiful*, August 1958, p. 72.

41. "Mark of a MODERN House—The Paved Terrace," *House Beautiful*, November 1952, p. 220. The desire to avoid public recreational facilities and spaces in the immediate postwar period was no doubt connected to recurring polio epidemics as well.

42. Robert W. Carrick, "What Is Leading Us to Merge Indoors and Outdoors," *House Beautiful*, July 1951, p. 40.

43. "The New Trend in Gardens," *House Beautiful*, November 1948, pp. 242-43.

44. "Mark of a MODERN House—The Paved Terrace," *House Beautiful*, November 1952, p. 219.

45. "The Key to Pace-Setting Life—Plan Outdoors and Indoors as One Working Whole," *House Beautiful*, November 1952, p. 225.

46. Elizabeth Gordon, "Furnishing the Garden to be Another Living Room," *House Beautiful*, April 1959, p. 144.

47. "Key to the New American Look in the Garden—The Living Terrace," *House Beautiful*, June 1953, p. 141.

48. "Five Ground Rules for Playing the National Pastime: The Most Beautiful Garden for the Least Work," *House Beautiful*, April 1958, p. 101.

49. "Do You Know These 26 Time-Tested Work-Savers?" *House Beautiful*, April 1958, p. 230.

50. "If You Pave It, You Don't Have to Mow It," *House Beautiful*, April 1959, pp. 118-19.

51. Thomas Church, "How Lazy You Are Should Dictate Your Garden Design," *House Beautiful*, June 1948, p. 112.

52. See, for example, Elizabeth Gordon, "Increase Parking Space—Reduce Garden Work," *House Beautiful*, March 1959, p. 94; Dorothy Ducas, "Will Your Parking Be As Up-To-Date As Your Car?" *House Beautiful*, June 1945, pp. 45—47, 98–104; and "How Our Cars Have Changed Our Gardens," *House Beautiful*, November 1956, pp. 254–57, 344.

53. "Why This House Is a Pace-Setter," *House Beautiful*, February 1948, p. 71.

54. Thomas Church, "Musings About the Past and the Future of Our Gardens," *House Beautiful*, January 1957, pp. 88, 108.

55. Elizabeth Gordon, "Furnishing the Garden to Be Another Living Room," *House Beautiful*, April 1959, p. 144.

56. Thomas Church, "The New Kind of Garden Pampers Us—Not the Plants," *House Beautiful*, February 1951, p. 64.

57. An article in June 1951 featured the house Cliff May designed for himself with its radiant heated terrace achieved through installation of an electrical grid system in the concrete paving. The magazine reassured readers that the cost of heating the terrace was only about 25 cents an hour and was offset by the reduction in wear and tear on the house since more people preferred to remain outdoors. The article proclaimed that "the new heated terrace improved their living 200%." Marion Gough, "In America Nothing Is Ever Good Enough," *House Beautiful*, June 1951, p. 84.

58. "Remodel Your Own PRIVATE CLIMATE," *House Beautiful*, February 1952, pp. 82–83.

59. See, for example, Leavitt Dudley, "The New Plastic Panels Are Ideal for Saturday's Carpenter," *House Beautiful*, July 1954, pp. 79–81, 120–21.

60. Jean Lawson, "This Is Gardening's Golden Age," *House Beautiful*, February 1957, pp. 110–13, 156.

61. "Do You Know These 26 Time-Tested Work-Savers?" p. 107.

62. Elizabeth Gordon, "Designed For Comfort—Not Show," *House Beautiful*, February 1951, p. 55.

63. "Five Ground Rules," p. 101. For another interesting source on the promotion of power tools, see the film collection "Industry on Parade," produced by the National Association of Manufacturers, located in the Smithsonian Institution's National Museum of American History Archives Center, Washington, D.C. The films appeared regularly on television throughout the 1950s. See reel 31, 5/4/51, "Lawnmowing Made Easy!;" reel 68,

1/22/52, "Hobby Help"; reel 128, 3/26/53, "Goodbye Grass!"; reel 192, 6/15/54, "More Power to the Householder!"; and reel 405, 7/12/58, "Power in the Yard."

64. "Do You Know These 26 Time-Tested Work-Savers?" p. 107.

65. "The House as a Work of Art," *House Beautiful*, February 1960, p. 89.

66. John A. Grant and Carol L. Grant, "The Style Trend Is to Texture and Pattern in Your Garden," *House Beautiful*, November 1951, p. 232.

67. Thomas Church, "Worth Looking At All Year," *House Beautiful*, January 1948, pp. 40-41, 105. See also Grant and Grant, "The Style Trend Is to Texture," pp. 232–33, 318–20.

68. "The Curve Makes a Graceful Entrance," *House Beautiful*, October 1954, p. 299.

69. In 1945, *House Beautiful* records indicate 288,906 paid subscribers. By 1955, the number had more than doubled to 628,942, and by 1965 the magazine had 977,672 paid subscribers. My thanks to Steve Chiarello at *House Beautiful* for furnishing this information. Although the impact of shelter magazines on consumers is difficult to measure, it is clear that the building trades took them seriously and believed their impact on prospective home buyers to be significant. In 1955, *House & Home*, a magazine that targeted builders, developers, and architects, began a monthly series of articles surveying the latest trends in a range of consumer and shelter magazines. As the author wrote, "*House & Home* feels that the consumer magazines are such an important barometer of what the home-buying public is going to want—and going to get—that we will, henceforth, publish a monthly pictorial review of what consumers are finding on their newsstands. We hope that this feature will help builders to gauge accurately the demand for better design that is being created throughout the U.S." "Better Keep Your Eye on the Newsstands ... Because Your Customers Do," *House & Home*, May 1955, p. 175. The writer estimated that 50 million Americans read these magazines each month, noting that circulation figures represent a fraction of the actual readership: "Most magazines figure that each copy is read by five or six people" (p. 169).

70. Elizabeth Gordon, "The Typical Versus the Unique," *House Beautiful*, March 1959, p. 89.

71. Joseph Barry, "Free Taste: The American Style of the Future," *House Beautiful*, October 1952, p. 178.

ROSSANA VACCARINO

The Inclusion of Modernism:
Brasilidade and the Garden

Brazil's physical and cultural development has run parallel to that of the Spanish American countries only in the broadest sense. Brazil, in many ways, cannot be discussed within a generalized Latin American cultural framework, since it is a country all its own, with a distinct language, racial composition, natural environment, culture, and history. Moreover, Brazil is an extremely complex nation, where a diversified and stratified society produces and reflects multiple and contradictory cultural influences. These contradictions have several sources, the first being the biological and cultural collage of people — indigenous, European, African, Asian — which binds in apparent harmony a society that has long lacked legally defined racial barriers. Contradictions are also produced by the original promises of freedom and socioeconomic opportunity and their continuous negation by the realities of marginalization and violence.[1] Urbanization in Brazil occurred later and has been slower than in many other Latin American countries. Cities still coexist today with a large and populous countryside. The huge Brazilian territory, larger than the continental United States, still falls into three broad zones of development: an urbanized seacoast on which industry, technology and population are concentrated; an upland and "back country" behind it, with farming, plantations, and agribusiness; and, to the northeast and the northwest respectively, the desert and the Amazon region with its forests and surviving aboriginal cultures. This division is maintained by great distances and lack of adequate infrastructure, and has been perpetuated since colonial times by the establishment of an integrated social hierarchy, which allows the elite to dominate society with little fear of challenge.

The period from the 1930s to the mid-1960s witnessed the physical manifestation of Brazilian modernism in literature, the arts, and architecture. This was a period of dramatic change in the spirit and aspirations of the country, which was then undergoing a substantial transformation due to industrialization and immigration by a large section of the rural population to the two main urban centers, São Paulo and Rio de Janeiro. Similar to other Latin American nations, Brazil's industrial sector underwent large-scale expansion in the 1930s and 1940s. In fact, both the Great Depression and World War II reduced the available supply of manufactured goods from abroad while increasing Brazilian export of basic products.[2] The war cut off trade with Europe and increased political, economic, and cultural ties with the United States. The U.S. presence became increasingly noticeable, not only through *Reader's Digest* (which became the country's most popular magazine) and Hollywood movies, but also in the technical missions sent officially to Brazil to recommend programs for the country's economic development.[3]

Economic growth continued during the two decades thereafter, when Brazil invested in heavy industries such as steel and automobile production. This economic renaissance was coupled with political optimism. After Getúlio Vargas's twenty-five-year regime, both the new federal republic and the constitution of 1946 raised major hopes in Brazil for democratization and social mobility. A spur in urban growth and a real estate boom marked the presidencies of Enrico Gaspar Dutra (1945–50) and Juscelino Kubitschek (1955–60).[4] The tendency to foster large, prestigious projects, which became symbolic achievements of a particular presidency, operated at all levels in Brazilian politics, from the parochial to the national.[5] The rapid proliferation of modernist architecture, which achieved its fame abroad through many international publications, is one of the iconic expressions of this period.[6] In Brazil, no *reconstruction* was necessary after the war. There was no sense of loss: instead, Brazil was under *construction*. The new buildings came to symbolize cultural ambition, the construction of a vision — a new nation and a better future.[7]

The Brazilian phenomenon, as it has been called, was spurred by cultural and political ferment dating back to 1922, which is considered the symbolic year marking the beginning of an active repudiation of the past. That year, the Copacabana revolt in Rio, coupled with the pronouncements culminating in the Modern Art Week at the municipal theater of São Paulo, announced that a new generation — primarily composed of the urban middle class — had challenged the nation's corrupt political, economic, and social institutions and was ready to propel Brazil into the future.[8] The Brazilian modernist movement was a broad-based intellectual phenomenon that brought about a considerable re-orientation of Brazilian culture in the first years after World War I. It affected and correlated many areas of cultural production, such as literature, music, the visual arts, and architecture.[9] Another important political event in the formation of the new movement was the Revolution of 1930 in Rio de Janeiro, which formed a part of the larger upheaval that arose out of the crisis sweeping through the capitalist world after 1929. The revolution reinforced Getúlio Vargas's right-wing regime at all levels of administrative, social, and economic life in Brazil. Many artists and intellectuals, like the painter and muralist Candido Portinari and the architect Oscar Niemeyer, were leftist or belonged to the Communist Party without hiding their views. This was possible because Vargas's Estado Novo did not attempt to create its own aesthetic ideas, and the modernists were able to produce work commissioned by the government without being identified with the regime.[10]

Roberto Burle Marx (1909–94), Latin America's most influential landscape architect and internationally renowned figure in the modern arts, played an important role in this period of cultural evolution. A multitalented artist, he witnessed and contributed to an unusually broad cultural formation at a time when professional specialization was becoming internationally pervasive. Trained as a painter and musician, he practiced simultaneously in diverse media, including drawing, painting, etching, sculpture, tile mosaics, tapestry, printmaking and fabric design, stage-set design, and jewelry design. Amateur botanist and expert horticulturist, he was among the first advocates of protecting the Brazilian forests, and he discovered many new botanical species, forty of which now bear his name. During his sixty-two-year career, he designed thousands of gardens, parks, and urban public spaces, for which he received popular appreciation and international acclaim.

When, in the fall of 1929, Burle Marx returned to Rio from an eighteen-month sojourn in Berlin — where he had studied music and painting and was directly exposed to cubism, expressionism, De Stijl, Bauhaus, and other vanguard movements in theater, opera, and music — he found that Le Corbusier had left his mark on Rio's and São Paulo's intellectual circles. Rio's cultural institutions were to become the center of the "spiritual revolt," as had happened in the early 1920s in São Paulo. Burle Marx's enrollment in the National School of Fine Arts would place him directly in the intellectual tumult led by the young architect Lúcio Costa, who, as a result of the revolution led by Vargas's forces, assumed the direction of the school in 1930 with a mission to revise and modernize its architectural program.[11] Burle Marx's training at the National School of Fine Arts under Leo Putz (a painter from Munich, one of Costa's appointments) and Candido Portinari were very important in his artistic formation. He identified with the school's philosophy of rejecting academism, valorizing local culture, and respecting functionalism, as well as the multiple cultural movements and debates stirring its students.

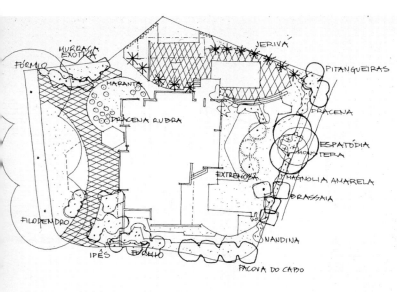

Figure 8–1.
Ilda Zarzur Garden, Jardim América, São Paulo, 1962–63. Roberto Coelho Cardozo. Garden plan.
[Drawing by Omar de Almeida Cardoso, after sources from FAUUSP Archives]

Figure 8–2. [facing page, top]
Abraão Huck Garden, Jardim Paulista, São Paulo, 1956. Waldemar Cordeiro.
View of front garden.
[Courtesy of Ana Livia Cordeiro]

Figure 8–3. [facing page, bottom]
Ubirajara Keutenedjan Garden, Jardim Europa, São Paulo, 1955. Waldemar Cordeiro.
View of side garden.
[Courtesy of Ana Livia Cordeiro]

Burle Marx's direct engagement in, and unique contribution to, the modernist movement, together with his incredible versatility in many media, made his art resonate beyond the boundaries of landscape architecture. Thus he overshadowed the work of other design contemporaries, such as Carlos Perry, Mina Kablin Warchavchik, Waldemar Cordeiro, and Roberto Coelho Cardozo. In fact, it is possible to identify two different tendencies, or schools, in landscape design in the 1950s and 1960s in Brazil: one occurring in Rio de Janeiro, under the leadership of Burle Marx, and another in São Paulo, under the leadership of Roberto Coelho Cardozo and Waldemar Cordeiro.

Roberto Coelho Cardozo and his wife, Susan Osborn, studied landscape architecture at the University of California at Berkeley and are both responsible for having introduced the North American modernist garden design tradition in Brazil. Their work can be seen as a transposition of the California modern garden, and especially the ideas of Garrett Eckbo, into the Brazilian tropical context.[12] Indeed, Cardozo and Osborn worked in Eckbo's office after graduation before moving to Brazil in 1950s. After a brief association with Burle Marx in Rio de Janeiro, they established themselves in São Paulo, where they opened an office. With the exception of Praça Roosevelt (1970) and a few streetscapes, their work concentrated on small private urban gardens, built mostly in the mid-1950s and throughout the 1960s.[13] In rapidly growing São Paulo, single-family houses for an affluent population were built in "garden city" neighborhoods with perfectly landscaped plots, side by side with more dense neighborhoods with multistory apartment and office buildings.[14] Thus the transposition of Eckbo's design principles became possible. The articulation of the garden space in different functional zones was the driving concept for the composition: a service area, a driveway and garage, a paved area, and a planted zone with grass and decorative trees. Water features were rare and the vegetation (native or exotic tropical species) was mostly used for space articulation or screening [Figure 8–1]. Cardozo published his ideas in a few issues of Acrópole and taught landscape architecture courses in the Department of Architecture and Urbanism of the University of São Paulo for many years.[15] The formation of a whole generation of architects as paisagistas—who in turn taught the following generation — is perhaps his most important contribution. Cardozo's students—who included Rosa Kliass, Luciano Fiachi, Miranda Magnoli, Francisco Segnini, Ayako Nishikawa, and Jamil Kfouri —incorporated in their work the influence of both North American modernism and Burle Marx.[16]

Waldemar Cordeiro, the other Paulista exponent, contributed design projects in São Paolo during this same period. Cordeiro, born in Rome, studied at the Beaux Arts Academy there before his arrival in São Paulo in 1946, when he was twenty-one years old. Like Roberto Cardozo and Susan Osborn, his formative years were spent in a country outside of Brazil. A caricaturist, art critic and sculptor, he is mostly known as a painter, moving gradually from expressionism to cubism to concretism, and eventually to computer art. Since Cordeiro sold only a few of his two hundred and fifty artworks, he took advantage of his knowledge of botany (his father was an agronomist) and supported himself as a landscape designer.[17] He designed about two hundred gardens in the years between 1950 and 1973.[18] Besides a few *fazenda* (farm) gardens, these were generally in small urban residential lots, condominium shared spaces, and office frontages or atrium gardens under *pilotis*. In later years he also designed a number of urban plazas and larger landscapes, including subdivisions and planning projects. The transposition of the painter's concretist sensibility into landscape work is discernible in all of Cordeiro's productions, but in different ways during his career. In the first phase, he used the ground as a graphic canvas, applying a rigorous geometry of lines and forms, as if he were creating a painting or a collage [Figures 8–2, 8–3]. Shrubs and groundcover plants alternated or intersected with paving materials (that included textured concrete and wood) to create color and textural contrasts or to set off furniture or sculptural elements, also designed by Cordeiro.[19] Asymmetrical and diagonal lines were used, as they were in Cardozo's designs, to increase the apparent dimension of space. Later, with the change of scale and scope of his projects, volumes and spatial composition acquired more importance, and vegetation was used to counterpoint the orthogonal lines of modernist architecture.[20]

Burle Marx's school or tradition had a stronger and much greater resonance in the architectural and landscape architecture fields in Brazil (São Paulo included) and abroad and, therefore, will be the focus of the remainder of this essay.[21] Acclaimed by the American Institute of Architects as "the real creator of the modern garden," Burle Marx was unquestionably a major force in the theory and practice of modern landscape architecture.[22] In fact, he came forth with bold, fresh solutions just at the time when the traditional constructs and manifestations of the garden were becoming precarious due to modernization and the establishment of a more democratic urban society, especially in Europe.[23] In

effect, the location, conceptual inspiration, symbolism, construction, use, and maintenance of the garden, as it was envisioned in the eighteenth- and nineteenth-century Western tradition, had become incompatible with the standardization of modes of production, internationalization of culture, speeding up of time, needs for public space and recreation, and different modes of life in modern capitalist society. Burle Marx used to his advantage the favorable political, social, and cultural circumstances of his country in the post–World War II decades and proposed a new synthesis that brought garden design to the same level of artistic ambition as the modernist movement in the arts and architecture. He was also able, even if not to the extent that he might have wished, to create a new sociocultural vision in the design of the modernist city, advocating and exemplifying with his work the importance of gardens, parks, and recreational space in improving the quality of urban life.

Burle Marx made his ideas known nationally and internationally through his interviews and lectures, but especially through innumerable exhibitions, where paintings, tapestries, sculptures, and garden plans were shown side by side. He collaborated with and influenced greatly almost all of the modernist Brazilian architects then on the national and international scene, including Oscar Niemeyer, Lúcio Costa, Rino Levi, Jorge Machado Moreira, Affonso Eduardo Reidy, Gregori Warchavchik, and Marcelo and Milton Roberto. Burle Marx also partnered with Richard Neutra in Los Angeles and Havana, and with Marcel Breuer, Pier Nervi, and Karl Mang, and befriended Le Corbusier and Walter Gropius. From these interactions, a passion for pure volume and inventive concrete structures developed. Moreover, Brazil, and South America in general, offered him the resources of a tropical flora particularly well suited to the plastic forms, textural contrasts, and pure color schemes called for by the modernist vanguard. Indeed, the lack of a gardening tradition in Brazil has been a problem in the maintenance and survival of his work. Yet, the availability of inexpensive craftsmanship and the support of a number of key people in the political and cultural arena have created the social conditions for his garden art to flourish.[24]

TRADITION, EMANCIPATION, AND THE QUESTION OF IDENTITY

In the second half of the nineteenth century, neoclassicism and art nouveau from Europe were the fashionable styles in

Figure 8–4.
Praça Paris, Rio de Janeiro, 1929.
Alfred Agache. Photograph c. 1940.
View of formal gardens.
[Courtesy Arquivo Geral da Cidade do Rio de Janeiro]

architecture, urban design, and the plastic and decorative arts. In the twentieth century, both São Paulo and Rio de Janeiro initiated many public works, among which was the carving of great avenues in Rio similar to the undertaking of Haussmann under Napoleon III in France, the country that had most influenced the Brazilian elite at the time. The straightening and widening of streets had the objectives of functional planning, sanitation, beautification and regulation of traffic and included extensive demolition of densely occupied areas.[25] President Vargas Avenue, originally recommended by French urbanist Alfred Agache, necessitated the razing of 525 buildings between 1941 and 1944, including four churches, four banks, and a marketplace. These urban renewal projects transformed Rio, the seat of the national government, into an efficient symbol of modernity and progress, aiding the propaganda of the new regime.

Until the first decades of the twentieth century, like architecture and urban design, Brazilian park design followed European models. Agache's Praça Paris (built in 1929) stems from this period. It was, in Claude Vincent's words, an "arid and senseless expanse" with its "clipped *ficus-bush* animals and birds and its lack of shade-giving trees" [Figure 8–4].[26] Praia da Botafago and Quinta da Boavista are examples from the late nineteenth century, when French hydraulic engineer and amateur botanist Auguste François-Marie Glaziou came to Rio to do work commissioned by Emperor D. Pedro II on the renovation of several squares and parks [Figure 8–5]. Glaziou made an original synthesis of two traditions fashionable in France at that time: the picturesque of the English landscape garden tradition and the formalism of the French garden tradition. In the Passeio Publico park, Glaziou dramatically changed the original formal design by the introduction of log fences, grottoes with stalactites, pyramids, boulders, and chalets, all built in concrete, similar to those found in the park of Buttes-Chaumont in Paris [Figure 8–6].[27] Although in Brazil there are more than fifty thousand autochthonous species, there was a common prejudice at the time that exotic species brought from distant lands would be preferable. Pioneering a different perception, Glaziou mixed baobab, traveler's palm, and many kinds of nonnative fig trees (*Ficus* spp.) with plants that he collected himself in the course of numerous expeditions into the hinterland of Brazil, thus setting a precedent for the design approach and the botanical expeditions of Burle Marx.[28]

The first signs of Brazilian nationalism can be traced back

Figure 8–5.
Gardens of the Praia de Botafogo, end of nineteenth century. Paul Villon, a disciple of François-Marie Glaziou. Site plan.
[Courtesy of Museu da Cidade do Rio de Janeiro]

Figure 8–6.
Passeio Publico, Rio de Janeiro, end of nineteenth century. François-Marie Glaziou. View of stone obelisks.
[Courtesy of Museu da Imagem e do Som]

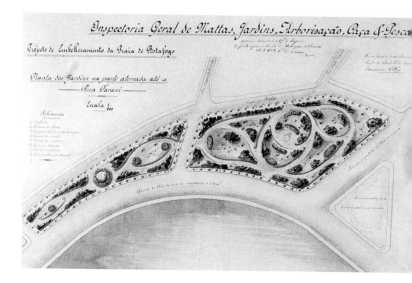

to the political and economic transformations of the last decades of the nineteenth century. Just when European fashions and styles seemed to have spread across the private and public spaces of the Brazilian elite, Brazil began to see itself with new eyes. A new romantic-realist depiction of everyday life infused by indigenous tones arose in painting, literature, and music.[29] In particular, the political emancipation of Brazil from Portugal with the proclamation of the republic in 1889 (one year after the Abolition of Slavery) was the beginning of a romantic sensibility that brought, in the early twentieth century, the "cult of the Indian" and "myth of the jungle" in literature and the plastic and decorative arts. Decorative artists, such as Theodoro Braga and Manuel Pastana, started using nativist elements in creating objects that still had a strong Belle Epoque accent or Art Deco influence, and thus they signaled a premodernist moment. From the 1920s to the 1940s, the Marajoara style became fashionable in Brazil in the applied arts and was widely adopted in ceramics, rugs, cushions, furniture, architectural ornamentation, and carnival costumes. This style was a syncretism of Art Deco references with basic patterns from pre-Columbian tribes of the Amazon, which produced the most complex ceramic artifacts of the entire Brazilian territory.[30]

The perception of the "self" as a hybrid culture, the awareness of the conditions and consequences of colonization, and the contradictions of a cultural and economic dependence on Europe were the very characteristics that the Brazilian avant-garde embraced in the twenties. Indeed, the various Brazilian modernist manifestoes in the arts and architecture of the time called for emancipation from the passive assimilation of foreign models and advocated for *brasilidade* (Brazilianness)—that is, a true Brazilian national identity or essence.[31] The paradox within brasilidade was that the struggle of a search for a national identity that would resist foreign influences was coupled with the opposite desire to be what Brazil could not be—that is, the wish to be French or English or, best of all, American.[32] This pervasive ambiguity found expression in Oswaldo de Andrade's influential *Manifesto Antropofago* (Anthropophagous, or Cannibal Manifesto) of 1928, which became one of the intellectual vehicles advocating a return to primitive sources: it demanded that the artist "devour the enemy," or whatever had been imported from the outside (largely European cultural traditions), in order to *repropose* art in a way that was typically Brazilian. Thus anthropophagism was a form of syncretism used to metaphorically combine and reconcile

Figure 8–7.
O Lago, 1928. Tarsilia do Amaral. Oil on canvas.
[Courtesy of Sérgio Estanislau Amaral]

the best efforts of the European literary and artistic vanguard with Brazilian values, traditions, and history. Lúcio Costa has described this paradox, explaining that in Brazil, it was exactly those who struggled in favor of an opening toward the modern world who also plunged into the history of the country to search for its roots, its tradition.[33] Therefore, similar to other Latin American avant-garde movements, the Brazilian modernist break with the past was rarely expressed as brutally as in Futurism or Dada. Even if emotional commitment lay with Brazil, a total rejection of European influence was probably never possible, nor even desired. In fact, the penetration of modernism into Brazil and its implementation as a cultural paradigm remained within the agenda of the liberal bourgeoisie and postcolonial social elite, formed by wealthy proprietors and those artists and intellectuals educated or well traveled in Europe or North America.[34]

Directed by writer Màrio de Andrade to go "back to her roots," Tarsilia do Amaral — who would become one of the leading artists of the anthropophagic movement — left Paris in the middle of 1922, just a few months after the now-famous Week, and returned to Brazil. Here, through both forest excursions and painting, she rediscovered the colors and exuberance of her country's wild interior. Hers was a first, albeit rudimentary, ecological relation to wild nature, one that recaptured a lost sense of naive happiness as a way to reconfigure the atavistic hostility and suspicion of the forest — the forest's richness reduced to *mato*, the invader, the "green hell."[35] Tarsilia do Amaral's anthropophagic assimilation is quite clear because, as stated by Olívio Tavares de Araújo, "one cannot ignore Léger's influence on [her] *pau-brasil* phase, although it is not considered an influence, as such, but rather a desired presence, a way to show how the Brazilian reality could also be learned through the international language of the time" [Figures 8–7, 8–8].[36]

Flávio de Carvalho (1899–1973) was another important exponent of the vanguard movement. A civil engineer from England, he was also a painter, stage-set designer, playwright, writer, and caricaturist. Carvalho had multiple intellectual interests that covered all artistic endeavors; he mixed rationality and experimentation with iconoclasm, mysticism and anarchic rebellion. His design for the Governor's Palace in 1927 was actually a manifesto, the first modern proposal for a Brazilian architecture. In Carvalho's proposal for the Columbus Memorial Lighthouse, bold modernist forms coalesce with a commitment to tradition. His design for the ceramic flooring elaborates on Marajoara Indian motifs

Figure 8–8.
Antropofagia (Cannibalism), 1929. Tarsilia do Amaral. Oil on canvas.
[Courtesy of Paulina Nemirowsky]

seen from a distance of 160m. from a height
of 2m. above the black disc level, and making
an angle of 57° with the front face of the monument

1:20

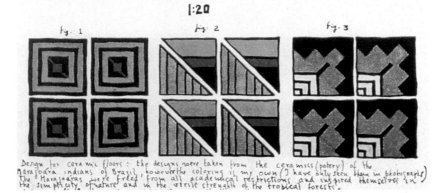

Design for ceramic floors: the designs were taken from the ceramics (potery) of the
Marajoara indians of Brazil, however the coloring is my own (I have only seen them in photographs)
The Marajoaras were freed from all academical restrictions and inspired themselves in
the simplicity of nature and in the virile strength of the tropical forests.

Figure 8–9.
Columbus Memorial Lighthouse design;
and design of ceramic flooring with
Marajoara motifs, 1928. Flávio de
Carvalho. Gouache from an album pub-
lished by competition organized in 1931.
[*Journal of Decorative Arts*, no. 21,
Brazil Theme Issue, 1995, p. 198, The
Wolfson Foundation of Decorative and
Propaganda Arts]

Figure 8–10.
Painting XIV, 1965. Ruben Valentim.
Gouache on canvas.

[Figure 8–9]. In his handwriting below the drawing we read: "The Marajoara were freed from all academic restrictions and inspired themselves in the simplicity of nature and in the virile strength of the tropical forest."[37] This tradition resurfaces over and over again in Brazilian art: one can compare, for instance, Carvalho's drawing with *Painting XIV*, by Ruben Valentim (1965) [Figure 8–10].[38]

The return to the forest and to its indigenous cultures needs to be seen in the context of those social changes brought by the republic and the Abolition of Slavery, which created the preconditions of modernity. These included the migration of free labor to the city, the end of nobility's privileges, and the introduction of new cultural habits that promoted industrialization and determined the apparent democratization and mixture of classes.

It is important to mention that modernization in Brazil has not run throughout the whole country. It was a phenomenon occurring within major urban centers, such as São Paulo, Rio de Janeiro, and, after the 1960s, Brasilia. Modernity and modernism are in many ways an imported concept, one belonging to the elite culture, one that is, as Eduardo Mendes de Vasconcellos states, "sometimes frightening and unreal, sometimes anxiously desired and almost within reach," and thus modernity in Brazil "should be realized through metaphors, through magic and dreams."[39] Indeed, popular values such as emotion, sensuousness, gesture, remembrance, and sacredness were always surfacing and partly responsible for the peculiarly Brazilian cultural forms and aesthetics. As seen in Rio at this time, ancient stone clashed with concrete, mysticism with functionality, passion with rationality. Thus, the skyscrapers that were towering in the 1950s in the photos of Jean Manzon seem to have been built with a sort of imagination projected into the future. Like architecture on paper, they seemed to be fantastic constructions from a century to come and, in a poetic sense, to look at the same time both strikingly beautiful and absurd.[40]

Brasilia is another, poignant example of the paradox between multiple historical times in the Brazilian modernist city. The inauguration of the nation's capital in the middle of the state of Goias in 1960 affirmed the significance of the vast interior, which was so well known to the Brazilian imagination through the book *Os Sertoes* (Rebellion in the Backlands), by Euclides da Cunha. The roads radiating from Brasila brought in pioneers, tying the West and the still much unexplored interior or "backlands" to the rest of the country. The people that Euclides da Cunha called "back-woodsmen," or "the very core" of Brazilian nationality, "the bedrock" of the nation's race, could now find their home in the most strikingly modernist environment.

ANTHROPOPHAGISM AND THE MODERNIST GARDEN OF BURLE MARX

One example of how Roberto Burle Marx transformed the expressive values from the past into his forward vision is in his use of the traditional Portuguese mosaic sidewalk, or black-and-white *pedra portuguesa*, which was adopted in Brazilian coastal cities such as Rio de Janeiro, Recife, and Salvador. For instance, in the plaza facing the Amazon Theater in Manaus, built in 1856, the metaphorical subject of the pavement had been the confluence of the black currents of the Rio Negro with the clay-colored waters of the Rio Solimo, which together form the Amazon River. This mosaic was transposed by Burle Marx to the design of Terrero de Jesus (1952) and Praça Tres de Maio (1954), both in Salvador, Bahia, and in Largo do Machado (1954) in Rio [Figure 8–11]. In these examples, Brazilian modern space, like colonial space, was being constructed with leitmotifs drawn from both the jungle and Europe, stretching across two different natural and cultural territories. The paving pattern was a pretext to rediscover the old within the new. Burle Marx's gigantic graphics were not prefabricated geometries made with prefabricated materials, as in many European modernist examples of open space. They were made by hand, following an ancient and patient craft by inlaying small bits of minute mosaic stones, compressing them bit by bit with a wooden pole. The pedra portuguesa was used later in many other projects, including the famous Copacabana Beach sidewalks (1969–70) and the Largo da Carioca (1981), both in Rio de Janeiro, and the courtyard for the headquarters of Bank Safra (1988) in São Paulo.

A remarkable permutation of the tradition of patterned walking surfaces is what can be called Burle Marx's "grass terrace." This was usually a relatively large, perfectly flat rectangular area of the garden, usually in proximity to a building or to a pool, with which it shares continuity in the overall orthogonal framework. It was an area meant to be walked upon, although it had a dual function as a grass "parterre," since it was graphically articulated into a pattern of alternating light and dark green lawn. The design motif could be a fluid one, such as the waves literally transposed from the Portuguese pedra portuguesa patterns into the

Figure 8–11.
Terreiro de Jesus, Salvador, Bahia, 1952.
Roberto Burle Marx.
[Courtesy Burle Marx & Cia Ltda.]

216

grass terrace of the Museum of Modern Art in Rio (1954). Alternatively, it could be made of generous checkerboard squares, such as for the Edmundo Cavanellas garden, in Pedro do Rio, Petrópolis (1954) [Figure 8–12] and the Francisco Pignatari garden, in São Paulo (1956). The grass was sometimes patterned in alternating stripes, as seen in the garden design for the campus of the University of Rio de Janeiro (1953).[41] Upon this formal platform, sculptures would often be placed, like "oversized chess-men." The attempt to transform something alive into a permanent pattern of "grass paving" was a difficult endeavor, perhaps less in terms of construction than of maintenance. In fact, the lighter colored grass (*Stenotaphrum secundatum* "Variecatum"), being a recessive mutation of the deep green variety, easily became hybridized if not maintained properly and changed into the darker color.

Another example of Burle Marx's anthropophagic transformations can be found in his murals of *azulejos*, or walls covered with glazed ceramic, again a reinterpretation of a Portuguese tradition with Arabic origins. The azulejo tiles were suitable to figurative design but not to realism, and in Brazil they became a perfect material for the expressionist style of artists and muralists such as Candido Portinari, Firminio Saldanha, Emiliano di Cavalcanti, and Paulo Verneck, among others. Burle Marx learned the azulejo technique from Portinari, and, along with his master, produced the greatest number of azulejo murals in modern Brazil.[42] His approach in azulejo design was unique in that he displaced the ceramic tiles from their conventional place (exterior and interior building walls) and used them in the garden as the medium of two-dimensional art (freestanding walls). Once in the garden, the panel could be associated with a reflecting pool, which would provide a foreground of depth. Moreover, selected colors and textural variations of aquatic plants or nearby vegetation could be exploited to create unusual contrasts with the smooth and glaring, blue, lilac, and white azulejo tiles. Early remarkable examples of these compositions can be seen in Arnaldo Aizim garden (1948) and Walter Moreira Salles garden (1951), both in Rio [Figure 8–13].[43] Here the panel designs show the expressionist and cubist influences (especially Picasso's) so clear in the early azulejo designs of Portinari as well. The flowing bands and abstract, organic forms and figures intersecting with areas of small figures of fishes or shells multiplying across would be replaced in the mid- to late1950s by more abstract geometric patterns, with interlocking areas of contrasting colors that recall the concrete art production in

Figure 8–12.
Edmundo Cavanellas garden. Pedro do Rio, Petrópolis, 1954. Roberto Burle Marx.
[Marcel Gautherot, courtesy of Olivier Gautherot]

vogue at the time. Pushing further the possibilities of the azulejo mural, Burle Marx was able to establish a "cubist interaction" with the landscape, in the fragmentation and refraction of forms established by shifting and echoing variations of their pattern into the ground plane.[44] This was due to his ability to work out the plan of the garden simultaneously with the design of the panel's elevation, and transposing the ideas from one to the other.[45] It would not be far-fetched to say that the azulejo mural is one dimension that helps situate the garden within the modernist arena, just as modernist architecture had incorporated ceramic tile panels as a way to broaden its relationship with both art and tradition.

In the desire to articulate space or to give a more permanent frame to the ephemeral and transitory structure of the garden, Burle Marx used many other kinds of panels and freestanding walls whose inspiration appears to come from other places and times. Made of composite construction or of highly patterned reliefs, they would often be associated with falling water and still water surfaces, to refract or multiply the effect of their texture and composition. In general, these are artistic explorations that began in the mid-1950s. Among the best examples is the vertical structure that separates the water garden from the driveway in his home, the Sítio Santo Antonio da Bica (built in the early 1970s), which was an abstract assemblage of large blocks of granite reclaimed from colonial mansions [Figure 8–14]. More than an aesthetic object, this wall was an act of recycling facades that were demolished in Rio de Janeiro to make space for large avenues and modernist buildings. It could also be seen as an act that calls forth the image of a Mayan or Aztec ruin devoid of pastiche or melancholy.[46] Specific extrusions and edges were planted with bromeliads to appear as if colonized through time by wind or dispersion of seeds by birds. The collage quality of the Sítio mural had a precedent in the granite mural of the Candido Guinle de Paula garden (1966), for which the assemblage of the block was done, as in the Sítio, on site and without prior design. Other concrete mural designs derive their graphism and relief pattern from carving or sculpting a flat surface rather than from the assemblage of parts. Thus their conceptual origin can be found not in the ceramic muralist or the assemblage technique but in the sculptor and artist who is familiar with carving techniques with different surfaces, at a different scale — necklace jewelry plates, bas-reliefs, woodcuts, etching plates. The panels framing the already mentioned Francesco Pignatari garden, and the many murals

Figure 8–13.
Walter Moreira Salles Garden,
Rio de Janeiro, 1951. Roberto Burle Marx.
Azulejo mural.
[Rossana Vaccarino]

Figure 8–14. [facing page]
Sítio Santo Antonio da Bica,
granite mural and water garden, c. 1970.
Roberto Burle Marx.
[Rossana Vaccarino]

designed for the walled gardens proposed for the International Exposition of Caracas (which in 1956–58 would become the Parque del Este) are examples of this category of works.[47]

A number of "vertical gardens" that explore the possibility of using roughcast concrete planters of different sizes also belong to this typology of structures. The planters protrude at different levels from a wall that seems somehow "historic" and impossible to date, despite its pseudo-cubist articulation of volumes, reliefs, polished areas, and openings.[48] As seen in the vertical gardens at Hospital Souza Aguiar (1955) and at the Edificio Manchete (1969), Burle Marx took the opportunity to display on these walls epiphytes or creeping plants from the *Araceae* family, bromeliads, *Clusia* spp., and other rock-loving species [Figure 8–15]. He then syncretized and crossbred this idea in the design of many roof gardens and cantilevered plazas. The concrete planters, in fact, were multiplied on the ground and clustered at different levels to achieve volumetric complexity (which otherwise would not be possible on a roof structure), while plant material was rhythmically alternated with areas filled with river stone or mosaic paving. Textural contrasts were further increased by the projection of linear shadow patterns cast from a concrete lattice above, as in the interior garden of the Ministry of Exterior Relations (1965) in Brasilia. It is important to stress these not as examples of the development of a style — something that could be repeated over time as a trademark—even if that became an inevitable consequence. The repetition of forms and patterns in many permutations or at different scales was, rather, the result of a process — the working process of an artist unable to end the creative possibilities of an idea, always inventing new solutions from one single and promising inspiration.

The *xaxim* columns represent still another inventive cultural synthesis. These are vertical sculptures that Burle Marx made with bromeliads or philodendron plants embedded into a structure of metal and tree fern bark (a species of *Cyathea*) or cork. These living columns reinterpreted both popular traditions and plant physiology, since these plants grow naturally high up in the tree trunks and branches of primary Brazilian forests [Figure 8–16]. Epiphytic plants — such as bromeliads, orchids, ferns, and philodendrons—are insignificant in number in secondary forests and, in the tertiary forests, disappear completely. Thus, one might argue that the xaxim columns used by Burle Marx in many urban spaces are like totem poles from a primitive past, erected

Figure 8–15.
Hospital Souza Aguiar, vertical garden, Rio de Janeiro, 1966. Roberto Burle Marx.
[Marcel Gautherot, in Flávio Motta, *Roberto Burle Marx e a nova visão da Paisagem*]

Figure 8–16. [*facing page*]
Sítio Santo Antonio da Bica, xaxim sculptures, 1994. Roberto Burle Marx.
[Rossana Vaccarino]

to exorcise or challenge modernization and its practices of environmental destruction. Yet, eventually, the xaxim "object" transmutes into "space" itself, that is, into an aerial environment structured by many horizontal and vertical integrated parts. Indeed, in the modern city, where green areas are constantly replaced by paved surfaces, there is less and less room for trees and green areas. In this condition, Burle Marx's creative vertical gardens — as mentioned before — are also joined by xaxims projected into fantastic vertical heights from within the core of skyscrapers. Like rainforest plants fighting against the tall canopies above in search of light, so these aerial structures colonize the air space, escaping the shadow cast from the concrete forest of buildings of the modern city.[49]

The vertical floral arrangements prepared for banquets and parties are another variation of the archaic-looking xaxim totems. These assemblages of dried and fresh flowers, fruit pods and seeds, Spanish moss or feathers, were meant to display the seasonal treasures of his own tropical garden at the Sítio Santo Antonio da Bica.[50] They would also transform any simple interior and exterior space into a royal, magnificent environment. As Flávio Motta has stated, "they suggest altar pieces, triumphal arches, awaiting a new Madonna or a new fertility Goddess."[51] The flower/composite arrangements were always used at Burle Marx's parties to accompany the visual delight and profusion of dishes (always a celebration of culinary variety from different regions of Brazil), dishes that, in turn, were always placed as sculptural objects, by Burle Marx himself, in specific areas of his famous hand-painted tablecloths. From the ceiling, floral and seed arrangements would hang majestically, like the candelabra in a baroque church.

THE DISCOVERY OF NATIVE PLANTS IN THE GARDEN

The story of how Burle Marx discovered the beauty of the Brazilian flora is well known. During his short stay in Germany in 1928, he recognized the "disquieting beauty of cacti" and other Brazilian plants organized in ecological groups by the botanist Henrich Engler in the Dahlem Botanical Gardens of Berlin. Yet, when he came back to Rio, just when Agache was building the fin-de-siècle Praça Paris, somebody had already made the discovery of native plants in the modern garden: Mina Kablin Warchavchik.[52] Mina Kablin was married to the Russian architect Gregori Warchavchik, who had studied under Marcelo Piacentini in Rome before emi-

grating to São Paulo in 1923. Kablin's pioneer work is limited to the gardens of Gregori's early houses [Figure 8–17]. In Warchavchik's residence, she used a limited palette of tropical plants mostly consisting of palm trees, cactuses, agave, and dracenas. The gardens did not have a precise plan, and the plants were specified during construction. Planting was organized in small groups, often in planters around the foundations or steps, to contrast or frame the orthogonal lines of the building or to add texture by the windowless walls. The Casa Modernista of 1927, in rua Itapolis, is considered the first modernist house and garden in São Paulo [Figure 8–18].[53] By reviewing the archival drawings and photographs of these gardens, it is possible to speculate that Kablin's work could not afford a strong formal design of its own — being mostly a complement to her husband's striking architecture—nor would she intentionally state a philosophical position vis-à-vis the relationship of the garden to the Brazilian natural environment: that task was left to Burle Marx.[54]

Burle Marx's first garden was built in 1932 for the residence of Alfredo Schwartz, designed by Lúcio Costa and Gregori Warchavchik in Copacabana.[55] This garden drew attention and led to the appointment of Burle Marx, then only twenty-five years old, as Director of Parks and Gardens for the city of Recife, in Pernambuco, in 1934. During the following three years Burle Marx remodeled Recife's old squares and dilapidated nineteenth-century public spaces, but experienced difficulty in finding both native plants in the quantity needed and reliable, skilled plantsmen.[56] The Praça Euclides da Cunha and the Jardin da Casa Forte date from this period. There, Burle Marx was able to display the unlimited richness of the plants from the *caatinga*, the so-called *silva horrida* of Recife's northeastern scrubby, stunted landscape. Among other native cactus plants, he used the *mandacarus*, with its phallic and slightly pot-bellied form, the same cactus studied by Tarsilia do Amaral beginning 1923 and presented then as a symbol of national modernity.[57]

The park for the spa town Araxá, in the state of Minas Gerais (1943), marks an outstanding moment in Burle Marx's design approach with native plants [Figure 8–19]. He collaborated in this project with the self-taught botanist Henrique Lahmayer de Mello Barreto, who would become his mentor in the following years. Mello Barreto was not a traditional botanist — he had little interest in herbaria but loved living plants in their environment. He basically introduced Burle Marx to a surrogate ecology, taking him on excursions in

the various *Serras* and *Lagoas* landscapes surrounding Belo Horizonte. There they observed unique formations of sandstone, limestone, iron conglomerate, quartzite, and granite-gneiss, each one associated with its own autochthonous flora. Burle Marx learned at this time the importance of studying plants in situ before using them in a design, valuing the unique relationships that develop in nature among rocks, soil, climate, altitude, vegetation, and animals. Of all the ecological factors, the correlation among rock formation, soil, and plant association was the easiest to study and emulate in the garden, and the most promising in terms of creative reinterpretation. This seems obvious today but was new at the time, and is precisely what Burle Marx focused on for the rest of his career.

In the Araxá Park, plant masses were organized according to different phytogeographical regions — such as caatinga, sandstone and quartzite formations, desert, and others.[58] Local stones and vegetation were collected with the intention of reconfiguring the park using the characteristic structures of different regional landscapes. In one of the park sections, for instance, eight hundred square meters of ironstone rocks were "transplanted" from surrounding sites so that the rock plants would have "the soil they love."[59]

Yet, as the Araxá project shows, the intent was not to literally reproduce a natural landscape but to "distill the essence of it into a few concentrated images."[60] A more direct and abbreviated relationship with nature was established, one that exemplified the elementary play of natural forces in a given environment — it would be easier for the people to understand and, therefore, value. Nature then was a pretext, a point of departure for Burle Marx's brasilidade in the garden. Plants found elsewhere under comparable climatic and pedological conditions would soon find a place with their fellow natives in the creation of strikingly new, contrasting associations.

Araxá paved the way for a number of projects, several only designed and never implemented. These included the botanical sector of the Zoological Garden of Rio de Janeiro (1946) and the campus design for the Federal University of Rio de Janeiro (1953). The latter project included a proposed garden so the School of Architecture could teach classes in landscape architecture outdoors. This was a complex proposal that had nothing "naturalistic" in its forms despite its didactic intentions. It was concentrated in a small space and within an abstract geometrical layout; it contained a number of dif-

Figure 8–17. [*facing page, top*]
Vila Mariana, rua Santa Cruz, São Paulo, 1927–28. Gregori Warchavchik, architect; Mina Kablin, garden design.
The first modernist house in São Paulo.
[Courtesy Carlos Eduardo Warchavchik]

Figure 8–18. [*facing page, bottom*]
Casa Modernista, rua Itapolis, São Paulo. 1930. Mina Kablin, garden design.
[Courtesy Carlos Eduardo Warchavchik]

Figure 8–19.
Araxá Park, Minas Gerais, 1943. Roberto Burle Marx. Aerial view, 1945.
[Courtesy Laura Mourao]

Figure 8–20. [*facing page*]
Zoo-Botanical Garden of Brasilia, Brasilia,
1961. Roberto Burle Marx. Flora of the
granite-gneiss formation. Perspective by
Roberto Burle Marx.
[Courtesy Burle Marx & Cia Ltda.]

Figure 8–21.
Zoo-Botanical Garden of Brasilia, 1961.
Roberto Burle Marx. Flora of calcareous
formations. Perspective by Roberto
Burle Marx.
[Courtesy Burle Marx & Cia Ltda.]

ferent regional plant communities associated with their rock formations, together with an area for aquatic plants and one for shade-loving vegetation. Later projects that attempted to transplant native vegetation in a public space with a pedagogical program include the Zoo-Botanical Garden in Brasilia (1961) [Figures 8–20, 8–21]; the Botanical Garden of São Paulo (1961); the Park of the Americas, in Santiago, Chile (1962); the Botanical Garden for the Federal University of Minas Gerais, in Belo Horizonte (1970); and the Botanical Garden of Maracaibo, in Maracaibo, Venezuela (1981).[61]

The botanical research in situ in the Brazilian forests or remote landscapes was never an ascetic or mystical experience in wild nature. Burle Marx's excursions, in fact, were not the enactment of the romantic spirit, of the pioneer going into the primeval forest or into the inhospitable brushwood *sertão* in the far interior of Brazil. The mines he discovered were not filled with gold, emeralds, and diamonds, but with treasures of indigenous species never seen before.[62] The act of collection, identification, propagation, and recomposition of the native flora turned the wilderness of the *Mata*, Brazil's biological endowment, into an intimate garden experience to appreciate and value. As Pietro Bardi has stated, Burle Marx was aware that "to remove a plant from the forest and take it to a garden or collection is to remove it from the anonymity of the Mata, it is to introduce it to the people and give it an urban dimension."[63]

The Parque del Este in Caracas, Venezuela (1957–63) [Figure 8–22], and Parque Flamengo, in Rio (1959–63) [Figure 8–23], are examples of Burle Marx's ability to confer this idea of "urban dimension" in Brazilian nature. These two parks remain among the major urban green areas realized in Latin America in the twentieth century but will not be described here in any detail. There are, however, at least five peculiar aspects of their design that should be mentioned in this discussion, since they represent a synthesis of Burle Marx's conception of the garden in its relationship to nature, and these aspects can be seen as important paradigms in his unique design process.

First, Burle Marx created complex plant compositions — what he called "artificial ecological associations" — where exotic plants from different tropical countries found expression in many possible permutations among the Brazilian natives, regardless of their original genotype or taxonomy. If their morphology or physical characteristics (phenotype) could be integrated visually and artistically to his advantage,

the overall ecological distortion would not be, so to speak, a sin.[64] Thus, if in the Parque del Este he used an existing forest to shelter the growth of a whole new community of native and nonnative species, in Flamengo he adopted an empty landfill exposed to seasonal salty winds to test the pioneering and adaptive capacities of a wide range of trees and palms growing in nature under the most adverse conditions. Both parks remain today successful ecological experiments and incredible "botanical gardens," but of a unique kind. Here, unusual species are recognizable not from a label on the ground but from their distinction in terms of relative placement and massing.

Second, Burle Marx rarely undertook an important project in a new region or country without first directly exploring the key natural habitats. These excursions became a fundamental component of his design process. They were, as Haruyoshi Ono has stated, an "idea always in the air."[65] They were not only a direct source of autochthonous species: they also allowed Marx to observe in loco and to receive inspiration from the structure and visual richness of a variety of tropical regions, their dominant morphology, and their ecological associations. These were well-organized scientific expeditions, funded through the design fee of a project (as in both the Parque Flamengo and the Parque del Este) or by various sponsoring activities. They lasted one to two weeks according to the itinerary and benefited from the participation of a multidisciplinary team — usually a congregation of naturalists, botanists, gardeners, architects, and other staff from his office. The learning opportunity was reciprocal. On the one hand, the partnership with botanists or plant lovers frequently extended to commissions or collaborations in garden projects. On the other, Burle Marx would transmit his aesthetic appreciation and design talents to his travel companions, and nearly all the architects, botanists, and naturalists who shared these experiences with him started designing gardens of their own.[66]

Third, Burle Marx felt the necessity to create a *viveiro*, or nursery area, within the park, both during construction and after its completion, to ensure the continuous supply of otherwise difficult-to-find plants. This was a place where the *coletas*, or live material, collected from the excursions would be acclimatized and kept under observation for several months, before transplanting on site. If only seeds or one or two specimens were obtained from the wild, and if a number were called for in the design, the waiting time was often years. That is the reason why the Parque Flamengo was still

Figure 8–22.
Parque del Este, Caracas, Venezuela,
1957–63. Roberto Burle Marx.
Aerial photograph of park after construction,
date unknown.
[Courtesy INPARQUE]

being planted fifteen years after its inauguration. And it is also the reason why the Parque del Este gradually lost a huge number of plants from its original collections as the viveiro closed and was abandoned. The viveiro was to be a place under direct supervision of the botanist collaborating in the project, and was to become a laboratory for training workers and maintenance staff.[67] Unfortunately, in Brazil and Venezuela political changes directly affect policy. In the case of the viveiro, this resulted in discontinuity of planning and management of park personnel.

Fourth, Burle Marx had the capacity to wait and imagine his landscapes changing in time. He preferred to plant small tree specimens a few feet tall rather than large ones, because they would establish themselves more successfully in the long run.[68] Also, because they were small, he could move plants easily around in the park during construction, and could adjust the design to perfection. It was not unusual for him to dig up the trees and replant them elsewhere. The interruptions during the process of planting — waiting for new plants, waiting for them to grow in the nursery — were moments for reflection, gestation, and incorporation of new ideas. This would have not been possible by following the planting plan literally and all at once. In this process, by incorporating temporality and change, he generated projects with the character of a living organism.[69] The delayed construction and the possibility of watching progressive growth provided, in fact, the time for both Burle Marx and the park users to establish a deep relationship with the landscape, in a way very similar to the relationships that humans develop among themselves.[70]

Fifth, Burle Marx believed that the role of the designer should not be restricted, as he said, to "executing projects." An equally important responsibility was that of a proactive participation in the preservation and conservation of the environment. The choice of native plants in the specifications of a project would thus be part of this larger endeavor: beyond a pedagogical intention or personal aesthetic, it would save many plants from extinction. In his travel to study and collect plants, Burle Marx directly experienced the sheer magnitude of deforestation and unsustainable development taking place in many environmentally sensitive areas of his country. This compelled him to become, beginning in the late 1960s, one of the most dedicated and incisive fighters against the destruction of Brazil's ecological endowment. He soon became engaged in a passionate dialogue, which would be a lifelong project, between two intercon-

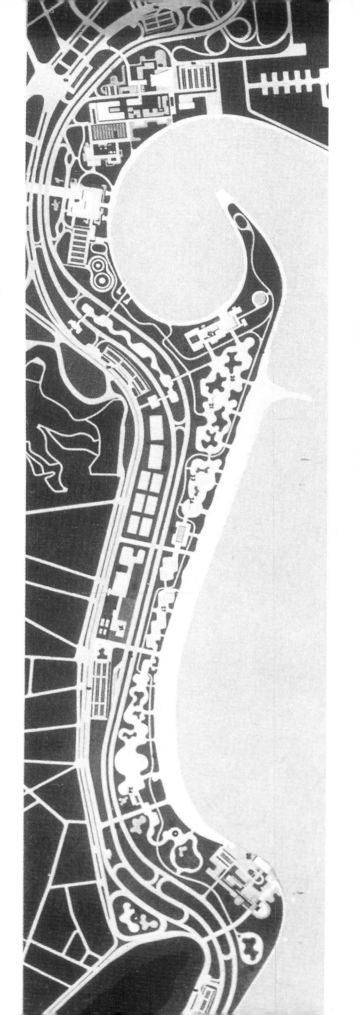

nected typologies and conceptual realms—the garden and the natural environment. Burle Marx described the garden as the place to display, conserve, and perpetuate the existence of native species otherwise threatened in the wild.[71] The natural environment, in turn, would be a larger reference, readable and meaningful to people through direct experience of the details of the designed garden.

BRASILIDADE, CULTURAL DIVERSITY, AND THE PRACTICE OF INCLUSION

As discussed above, the use of autochthonous flora and indigenous crafts and materials, together with plants and construction technologies assimilated from other countries and now naturalized in a new context, became fundamental tenets of Burle Marx's modernism. Yet there is another important aspect of his anthropophagic notion of brasilidade, notably the incorporation of aesthetic sensibilities from cubism, expressionism, and surrealist avant-garde movements into the design of the garden. The influence of Pablo Picasso, Henri Matisse, Alexander Calder, Joan Miró, and especially Jean Arp has been widely discussed elsewhere. It can be seen not only in the abstract curvilinear layout and inter-locking biomorphic forms of several gardens—especially those produced by Burle Marx between 1940 and 1950—but also in the painterly renditions he produced for them, which are mistakenly considered "garden plans."[72] In the abstract compositions of the vanguard European painters, Burle Marx probably recognized the bold contrasts among the pure primary colors of his Brazilian environment—from the bright yellow-red and yellow-green contrasts of flowers and leaf buds in the forest, to the color of tropical birds, amphibians, and butterflies, to the stark hues of the "body paints" (*arte do corpo* and *arte plumaria*) of the indigenous Brazilians. Thus, when Burle Marx used the juxtaposition of reds, blues, yellows, and oranges in his paintings and his gardens, he syncretized a modernist aesthetic with natural and cultural phenomena specifically Brazilian.

The notion of brasilidade, as discussed in this essay, should not be seen necessarily as the expression of the desire for a fixed cultural "essence." In fact, rather than the result of a cohesive or reconciliatory practice of assimilation, Brazil-ianness can be the outcome of an ambivalent and polymor-phic condition of identity. Expressing cultural difference from an established hegemonic or monologist form of nationalism, this condition reflects the transposition, inter-section, and overlay of multiple and often contradictory

Figure 8–23.
Parque Flamengo, Rio de Janeiro, 1959–63.
Roberto Burle Marx. Gouache on paper.
Site plan of 1961.
[Courtesy Burle Marx & Cia Ltda.]

cultural modes and practices. The construction of cultural identity through the inclusion of diversity and difference is one of the most important themes of Latin American cultural discourse in postcolonial societies.[73] In Brazil, it is the expression of the process of democratization and the resistance to a number of doctrines of scientific racism from Europe and North America, which were embraced by many among the Brazilian elite. The practice of intercultural mixing in Brazil traces back to colonialism and its patriarchal society, in which the disparate elements of European, Native South American, and African cultures were juxtaposed, and to a certain extent fused, by a gradual miscegenation.[74] After World War I, the Brazilian population was further diversified by the arrival of millions of immigrants from non-Portuguese Europe, Asia (especially Japan), and the Middle East. All the different ethnic groups and cultural customs have continued to mix relatively freely in a fluid continuum, never resulting in a static, single act of incorporation between two original "extremes."[75] The Brazilian modernist garden, as a cultural artifact, may be discussed within this multivalent social perspective. As in Brazilian society, it would not reflect a bipolar system of relations—for instance, building its identity through exclusive dialectics such as native/exotic, past/present, or tradition/modernity. Instead, the garden would exemplify its composition as a spectrum, that is, articulating many temporal and historic intersections, and with a certain ambiguity in expressing its physical and conceptual characteristics. This is specifically how in Brazil the aristocratic or elitist heritage of garden art may find a place in a modern, democratic society.[76]

The precondition for a vanguardist departure from established canons almost always requires a position of radical exposure and a capacity for being at the edge, rather than within, the paradigm of an established system. The precondition of a reformist activity, in contrast, implies the capacity to speak the local language and reinvent the future from within, using the means available. Burle Marx was comfortable with and skilled in both these approaches. He was able to speak the many languages necessary to communicate with outsiders and insiders, treating on an equal footing the politician, the associate, the consultant, and the gardener.[77] Practicing in the everyday the existential condition of exposure and inclusion, he was able to invent a field for landscape architecture that is not autonomous or self-referential: in fact, to call it just landscape architecture would be simplistic, because it embodies so many other things.[78]

In practicing brasilidade as discussed in this essay, Burle Marx brought landscape architecture to the level of art, on the same footing as other important artistic expressions of the time. Even in a literal sense, the garden was able to enter the gallery space and the architectural space as art. In fact, having trained as an artist, Burle Marx felt the need to be featured in gallery exhibitions as a way to connect with and gain recognition from the public. Thus, as projects would be conceived and built, he would transform garden plans and construction drawings in painterly renditions or models to be exhibited nationally and internationally as art, among his paintings, sculptures, tapestries, and dyed fabrics.[79] One wonders whether Burle Marx would have invested so much time and money in this kind of marketing strategy had he been trained just as a landscape architect. Moreover, from their inception, Burle Marx's gardens entered the space of architecture as a fundamental part of modernist space in Brazil. Whereas Burle Marx was able to expose garden design to the Bauhaus and CIAM, and thus reinvent both with a fresh eye, so architecture opened up its windows and walls to what was previously considered a hostile nature, and included the tropical garden of Burle Marx on its roof gardens and within its pilotis. The garden did not "naturalize" modernist architecture: it made it more humane, more inhabitable. Further, the tropical luxuriance of Burle Marx's landscape corresponded so well to the exuberance of Brazilian architecture that in some cases it is difficult to imagine how they could be separated from each other. Thus, landscape and architecture began to share space and fame in the most important international architectural magazines of the time.[80] The garden of Burle Marx became another artistic inflection, another construction specification of architecture, just as a tile mural of Candido Portinari or a sculpture from Bruno Giorgi would become an integral part of a holistic cultural expression in building design.[81]

The feedback between architecture and landscape architecture in Brazil was also related to a shared need for climate control. Thus, on the one hand, we see the transformation of the modernist flat wall in response to the tropical climate and the articulation of exterior building surfaces with the greatest variety of sun-screen devices—from permanent brise-soleils in concrete, to movable louvers or jalousies in asbestos or wood, to openwork screens of tile and perforated concrete blocks with vines growing on them. On the other, we find Burle Marx's designs progressively including architecture's vocabulary, besides the above-mentioned tile murals and lawn "terraces." For instance, pavilions and pergolas made of horizontal concrete latticework and perforated brick walls were used to solve the need for immediate and more permanent sun control in the garden while vegetation was still undeveloped.

The reciprocal influence between landscape and architecture extended beyond function and included shared forms. A most remarkable example is found when comparing the work of Burle Marx and Oscar Niemeyer. One may even speculate that the volumes, flowing curves, plastic freedom, and lightness that begin to characterize Niemeyer's work from the design of the Pampulha complex in Belo Horizonte in 1942–43 have a partial origin in the Matisse- and Arp-inspired biomorphic forms proposed first by Burle Marx in his famous roof garden for the Ministry of Education and Health Building in Rio (1938).[82] From the 1950s, while Niemeyer's architecture became more gestural and organic, an interest in more linear, orthogonal forms on the ground plane prevailed in Burle Marx's work, along with the recurrent interjection of fragments of the circle and other geometric forms.[83]

EPILOGUE

The period from 1940 to 1960 was critical in the artistic evolution of a whole generation of architects and artists in Brazil. It was also the period when Burle Marx refined his approach to landscape design, and the period that holds the most original exemplification of his work. The projects designed and built at that time influenced not only a whole generation of landscape architects in Brazil and Venezuela — including Fernando Tabora, John Stoddard, Haruyoshi Ono, Fernando Chacel, Rosa Kliass, Koiti and Klara Mori — but also led to a worldwide school of ardent followers, which embraced Burle Marx's ethical and philosophical attitudes, his conceptual artistic and ecological principles, and even some of his formal solutions, especially in similar tropical regions.

From 1964 to 1985 Brazil was governed by a succession of authoritarian regimes, each headed by a four-star general. The return of military rule and the dissolution of Burle Marx's association with the architects Monte, Pessolani, Tabora, and Stoddard in those years mark a decline in his creative activity that would begin again only with the formation of a new office in Rio in association with Haruyoshi Ono. With the Brazilian economy's return to a growth path after 1967 (which duplicated the record of the 1950s), the

office was busy again designing from twenty-five to forty gardens per year, reflecting in its activity the "miracle" of the Brazilian economy.[84] But if we look carefully at the built projects, there are no more parks of the stature and social importance of the Parque Flamengo or the Parque del Este. As previously stated, in Brazil and elsewhere in Latin America, public authorities turned to architecture and public art as iconic expressions of their cultural ambitions. Government and local officials had an open-minded attitude toward modern art and architecture, and in Brazil they played an important role in sponsoring the artistic activities that included the establishment of modern landscape architecture as well. Yet, after 1964, the favorable association of intellectuals and visionary politicians, typical of the postwar decades, seems to have been lost: we do not find leaders with the audacity of a Gustavo Capanema, we do not find another Carlota Macedo Soares, a Carlos Lacerda, or a Juscelino Kubitschek. These people were responsible for the promotion of major public buildings and open spaces, and they supported large-scale urban projects in Rio de Janeiro and Brasilia that are an exception in the otherwise general lack of urban planning in Brazil. The 1940s–60s marked, therefore, a unique cultural circumstance of osmosis between nationalist and populist agendas, of visionary politicians, and of powerful imagery generated by artists who disregarded professional boundaries. The question remains whether the current and future work produced in Brazil in the field of landscape architecture will ever be able to situate itself in comparable social, political, and cultural conditions so it can carry on the legacy of Burle Marx with equal coherence and depth.

NOTES

Among the many people I wish to acknowledge, my gratitude goes in particularly to Haruyoshi Ono, Burle Marx's associate in the office in Rio since 1965 and now principal of Burle Marx & Cia, Ltd., for sharing his archives and information on many occasions; to John Stoddart and Fernando Tábora, Burle Marx's associates in the office in Caracas, for their invaluable contribution to my neverending questions; Dr. Leandro Aristeguieta and Prof. Luiz Emygdio de Mello Filho, for their vivid recollections of the botanical expeditions and the importance of native plants in Burle Marx's designs.

1. As Aracy Amaral has stated, "Following the end of the Second Empire in 1889, Brazil emerged as a contradictory reality, with disproportionate wealth and poverty and flagrant regional differences in terms of development and quality of life, particularly between the South and the Northeast. Not until the Vargas era (1930–45) did Brazil begin to perceive itself as a unified whole." "Stages in the Formation of Brazil's Cultural Profile," *Journal of Decorative and Propaganda Arts*, no. 21, 1995, p. 9. According to Thomas Skidmore, the ultimate contradiction in Brazil is between the justifiable reputation for personal generosity ("cordiality") of the Brazilian people and the fact of having to (still) live in one of the world's most unequal societies. See his *Brazil: Five Centuries of Change* (New York: Oxford University Press, 1999), p. xiii.

2. In São Paulo, the center of industrial growth, 15 percent of Brazil's population was producing about 50 percent of the country's manufactured goods by the 1940s. Between 1947 and 1961 manufacturing output increased at an annual rate of 9.6 percent, compared to 4.6 percent for the agricultural sector. By 1960 industrial production amounted to more than 25 percent of the gross domestic product, and by 1975 it was up to nearly 30 percent. This diversification helped Brazil reduce its economic dependence on the outside world and lent credibility to its claims that the country would someday join the ranks of the superpowers. See Thomas Skidmore and Peter Smith, *Modern Latin America* (New York: Oxford University Press, 1989), p. 153.

3. Likewise, in the United States, Brazil became a fashionable cultural topic. Movies like *Flying Down to Rio*, with Fred Astaire and Ginger Rogers, presented the first popular images of Brazil to an American audience. Others followed with stories set in Brazil—such as Alfred Hitchcock's *Notorious*—although filmed on Hollywood's backlots.

Heitor Villa-Lobos's compositions as well were starting to be included in the repertory of American orchestras.

4. During certain periods, some of the largest cities increased in population at the rate of 10 percent a year. In 1920, approximately 25 percent of the population lived in urban areas; by 1940 the proportion reached 31 percent, it climbed to 36 percent in 1950, 45 percent in 1960, and 50 percent in the 1970s. The growth is concentrated in the two metropolitan giants, Rio and especially São Paulo: Rio went from 1,157,000 inhabitants (1920) to 1,781,000 (1940) to 3,372,000 (1960); São Paulo went from 579,000 (1920) to 1,308,000 (1940) to 3,825,000 (1960). It is important to mention that Rio and São Paulo accounted for only 10 percent of the nation's population in this period and that most of the 2,763 cities had populations of fewer than 5,000 inhabitants. Brazil thus had no urban concentrations comparable to those of other Latin American countries. See Bradford Burns, *A History of Brazil* (New York: Columbia University Press, 1970), p. 467.

5. Examples are the President Vargas Steelworks, the Dutra Highway, the Branco Dam, and Kubitschek's Brasilia.

6. In 1942 the Museum of Modern Art held its exhibition Brazil Builds, accompanied by a publication by Philip L. Goodwin with photographs by G. E. Kidder Smith, which made Brazilian achievements known to the world at large. The event was an obvious reflection of the effort in the United States to establish political ties with Brazil. The vitality of that production spread through South America, led by the Brazilian reviews *Habitat* and *Modulo*, and through *L'architecture d'aujour-d'hui* in France, *Architectural Review* in England, *Domus* in Italy, and *Architectural Forum* in the United States. A second survey was done by the Museum of Modern Art in 1955, covering the work done after 1945 not only in Brazil but throughout Latin America, and published in Henry-Russell Hitchcock, *Latin American Architecture Since 1945*. This was followed a year later by Henrique E. Mindlin's book *Modern Architecture in Brazil*.

7. The eyes of Europe and the United States were on Brazil, quizzing how the country could change so quickly. (Brazil was still importing all its basic furbishing materials from Europe and the United States, and its construction techniques were based on artisan processes, employing mainly traditional craftsmanship.) The *Architectural Forum* spe-

cial issue on Brazil in 1947 saw it this way (p. 66): "Ever since the Ministry of Education Building in Rio was first photographed, it has been apparent that a spectacular architectural development has occurred below the Equator. To North Americans, smug in their technical wealth, this phenomenon is especially intriguing. How does it happen that a 'backward' country can suddenly produce so vibrant and up-to-date an architecture? Brazilian architects have a simple answer: Their work is an expression of cultural maturity, not technological wealth. They seem both surprised and unimpressed by the sensation which their recent work has created in this country and Europe. Seen in the flesh, they are a modest, assertive and surprisingly youthful set of men. They are quick to point out that not all Brazil is built in image and that—as yet—only a small portion of their countrymen have access to such buildings."

8. The Roman Catholic Church and the Communist Party (whose founding was also in 1922) joined to voice a radical program of change.

9. The Semana de Arte Moderna (Modern Art Week) of 1922 in São Paolo was the official public manifestation of the Brazilian modernists and promoted avant-garde artistic expression in all areas of creative work. It included exhibitions (featuring the sculptures of Vitor Brecheret and the paintings of Di Cavalcanti, Anita Malfatti, and Vincente do Rêgo Monteiro, among others), readings in poetry, philosophy, and modern criticism, and dance and music recitals (showcasing Villa-Lobos, in particular, with his original incorporations of folkloric melodies, rhythms, and popular musical instruments into his symphonic and chamber work). Attacking old preconceptions and the prevailing eclecticism, the event burst like a bombshell of spiritual revolt in the Parnassian and academic atmosphere of São Paulo. The Semana was financed by the highest bourgeoisie of the time—the so-called coffee barons—and was a deliberate rupture, a gesture of self-revision on the part of a group of people who wanted to put their country's art in tune with that of their European contemporaries. As Olívio Tavares de Araújo has stated, "It was only for this intellectual elite (and the financial elite that supported it) that the Semana did not explode like a bomb; for the rest of the audience (in the literal and figurative senses), it did. There was more booing than applause." See his *Brazilian Twentieth-Century Paintings: Significant Trends* (Rio de Janeiro: Estaçoes Ltda, 1998), pp. 8–10.

10. In the desire to mark a new era, and in the attempt to control the wave of democratic opinions building up during and after the war, Vargas's strategy, particularly under the Estado Novo (1937–45), aimed at a nationalist pattern of economic development and diversification and included a number of populist measures. Among these were a greater emphasis on Brazilian history in school and the decree that all instruction be given in Portuguese. Vargas guaranteed a minimum wage, a social security system, state schools, libraries, medical assistance, and maternity leave. The coup deposed the landed oligarchy (the old coffee barons) of São Paulo and Minas Gerais states, centralized power in Rio de Janeiro and allowed the rise of reformist sectors of the lower middle class. For details, see Burns, *A History of Brazil*, pp. 385–439; Michael L. Conniff, *Urban Politics in Brazil: The Rise of Populism*, 1925–1945 (Pittsburgh: University of Pittsburgh Press, 1981), pp. 160–73; Skidmore and Smith, *Modern Latin America*, 155–66; and Skidmore, *Brazil*, pp. 93–125.

11. In the 1930s, the National School of Fine Arts was the only school of fine arts in Brazil and was the most important center of architectural study. Music was taught by composer Heitor Villa-Lobos, literature by writer Mário de Andrade, and painting by Candido Portinari, among others. Lúcio Costa's brief tenure as director (December 1930–September 1931) was sufficient to induce immediate organization of an active group of architects ready to risk new paths of action and to make their mark at the first opportunity. See Eduardo Mendes de Vasconcellos, "Modernism in Brazil: A Cultural Project–Architecture and Urban Planning, 1930–1960" (University of London, 1994), pp. 103–10; see also Henrique E. Mindlin, *Modern Architecture in Brazil* (Rio de Janeiro: Colibris Editora, 1956), pp. 4–5.

12. Omar de Almeida Cardoso, "Roberto Coelho Cardoso—A Vanguardia da Arquitetura Paisagística Moderna Paulistana," in *Paisagem e Ambiente, Ensaio IV* (São Paulo: Faculdade de Arquitetura e Urbanismo, Universidade de São Paulo, 1992), p. 173.

13. For a list of projects, reconstruction of garden plans, and sources, see dissertation by Omar de Almeida Cardoso, "Arquitectura Paisagistica e a Cidade: Do Eclectismo ao Moderno" (Universidade de São Paulo, Faculdade de Arquitetura e Urbanismo, 1990), pp. 171–85.

14. As Aracy Amaral has written, "São Paulo's sudden growth during this century's first two decades led to a revised concept of residential urbanism introduced by the English Companhia City, which planned residential areas for an affluent population. Their 'City Gardens' distinguished the emerging metropolis: Jardim América, Jardim Europa, Alto da Lapa, Paecambu, and Alto de Pinheiros are made up of winding tree-lined streets and homes, from neocolonial to ultramodern, set in the midst of perfectly landscaped plots." See "Stages in the Formation of Brazil's Cultural Profile," p. 20.

15. Cardoso became involved in academia because he was interested in officially establishing the field and profession of landscape architecture in Brazil, but he never actually started a degree program.

16. Conversations with Roberto Cardozo, Miranda Magnoli, and Silvio Soares Macedo, February 1997.

17. Interview with Helena Cordeiro, widow of the artist, in Almeida Cardoso, "Arquitectura Paisagistica e a Cidade," p. 168. A list of Cordeiro's projects and illustrations is included here.

18. In addition to garden design, Cordeiro continued his activities as painter and art critic, being the primary organizer of the "Ruptura" manifesto of 1952, which gathered signatures of abstract and concretist artists. He also promoted and participated in a number of exhibitions, such as the First National Exposition of Concrete Art. See Marco Castilha, "O Moderno na Arquitetura da Paisagem e a Obra de Waldemar Cordeiro," in *Paisagem e Ambiente, Ensaio IV* (São Paulo: Faculdade de Arquitetura e Urbanismo, Universidade de São Paulo, 1992), p. 159.

19. Waldemar Cordeiro, "Para uma justa proporção entre volumes edificados e espaços livres," *Acrople*, 223, 1957, pp. 244–46.

20. Marco Castilha, "O Moderno na Arquitetura da Paisagem e a Obra de Waldemar Cordeiro," p. 163.

21. Burle Marx was not involved in formal academic teaching, although he gave occasional lectures and in 1954 taught a course on landscape architecture in the department of architecture of the University of Rio de Janeiro. His "school" was in his atelier-office, where he instructed a great number of designers during his lifetime. Many disciples who had been educated as botanists or architects worked as landscape architects after that experience.

22. This quote is included on a 1965 AIA award displayed, among so many others, at the Sítio Burle Marx.

23. Jean-Pierre Le Dantec, "L'éclipse moderne du jardin" in *Dans Les Jardins de Burle Marx*, Jacques Leenhardt, ed. (Crestet Centre D'Art/Actes Sud, 1994), pp. 111–17.

24. As opposed to the situation in North America, building materials were expensive and labor cheap in Latin America. Therefore it would not cost much more to cover a wall with an artistic stone mosaic than it would to cover it with mechanically produced material. The same applied to constructing walls and paving surfaces in the garden, though it was much more difficult to find skilled labor to plant and take care of plant material, and Burle Marx had to teach his workers and constantly supervise the implementation of his planting schemes.

25. See Rachel Sisson, "Rio de Janeiro, 1875–1945: The Shaping of a New Urban Order," *Journal of Decorative and Propaganda Arts*, no. 21, 1995, pp. 139–54. The demolition of substandard residences in densely occupied low-income areas created a serious housing crisis. Yet there was now room for new spatial landmarks and public buildings, such as the Biblioteca National and the Teatro Municipal in Rio (modeled on the Paris Opera). The Rio elite described this rebuilding program as "Rio civilizing itself," but the rebuilding touched only the traditional downtown, doing nothing for those *favelas* (shantytowns) already covering the hills of the city. See Skidmore, *Brazil*, p. 77.

26. Claude Vincent, "The Modern Garden in Brazil," *Architectural Review*, 101, no. 605, May 1947, p. 165.

27. The fifty-acre area was originally designed by Valentim da Fonseca e Silva, or "Master" Valentim, who in 1779–83 completed the construction of what was to be the first public garden in Rio. Though Master Valentim privileged fruit-bearing and exotic species, he used Brazilian fauna and flora motifs in his sculpture and architecture. Thus he may be considered among the creators of nationalism in the Brazilian arts. See Cecilia Beatrix da Vega Soares, *A Mais Belas Arvores Da Mui Formosa Cidade de São Sebastião do Rio de Janeiro* (Rio de Janeiro: Nova Fronteira, 1994), pp. 19–27. See also P. M. Bardi, *The Tropical Gardens of Roberto Burle Marx* (New York: Reinhold, 1964), pp. 13–14.

28. Among the native plants that Glaziou introduced into the urban landscape were the Oiti, Painera, Pau-Ferro, Pau-Brasil, Embauba, and Babacu.

29 For details, see Amaral, "Stages in the Formation of Brazil's Cultural Profile," pp. 13–14.

30. Paulo Herkenhoff, "The Jungle in Brazilian Modern Design," *Journal of Decorative and Propaganda Arts*, no. 21, 1995, p. 258.

31. The manifestoes for the avant-garde in the arts include "Statement of Intent" by the Editorial Board of Klaxon, Monthly Review of Modern Art, in *Revista Klaxon*, no. 1, São Paulo, May 1922; Oswald de Andrade, "Pau Brasil Poetry Manifesto," *Correio da Manha*, Rio de Janeiro, 18 March 1924; and Oswald de Andrade, "Anthropophagous Manifesto," *Revista de Antropofagia*, no. 1, São Paulo, May 1928.

32. Vasconcellos, "Modernism in Brazil," p. 12.

33. Lúcio Costa, *Lúcio Costa: Compilaçao de Sentido Autobiografico, Fundaçao Cultural Banco do Brasil* (Rio de Janeiro, 1993). Quoted in Vasconcellos, "Modernism in Brazil," p. 19. Costa also said: "Modern architecture should be understood as an inclusive proposition capable of becoming either a classical crystal or an organic flower, but also capable of subsuming the classical crystal within the organic flower and vice versa." (Quoted by Carlos Eduardo Dias Comas, in "Niemeyer's Oasis: A Brazilian Villa of the Fifties," paper presented at "The New Inside the New: Latin American Architecture and Urbanism and the Crisis of the International Style, 1937–1954," a conference at the Harvard Graduate School of Design, 19–20 April 1996. This proposition poetically articulates the metaphor of anthropophagism. In a way, it suggests a form of assimilation and reinterpretation of modernist canons not dissimilar to what has been proposed so eloquently by Kenneth Frampton with the notion of "critical regionalism." Anthropophagism is in fact close to what Frampton calls "locally inflected manifestations of 'world culture,'" and is also an aspiration to "some forms of cultural, economic and political independence." See Kenneth Frampton, "Critical Regionalism: Modern Architecture and Cultural Identity," in *Modern Architecture: A Critical History*, 3rd ed. (New York: Thames and Hudson, 1992), pp. 314–27.

34. Vasconcellos, *Modernism in Brazil*, 110. According to the author, "things go slowly in

Brazil," and, in general, "the modern movement was seen with a disguised suspicion." For many exponents of the social elite, "to be modern was merely a fashionable thing to be," and if on the whole "there was a small pressure group that argued and claimed modernity's benefits, there was also the almost insurmountable tropical laziness and conservatism, expressing an unmentionable and veiled wish to resist the impulse of change."

35. *Mata Atlantica* is the botanical appellation of the forest formation in coastal southeast Brazil. *Mato* or *Mata* is a popular appellation that, similar to the word weed, lumps together native plants with no aesthetic or functional use for people. Burle Marx often referred to the atavistic fear of the forest, which shelters the enemy's poisoned arrow, the serpent, the wildcat, the ant, and the spider.

36. See Araújo, *Brazilian Twentieth Century Paintings*, p. 54. When Tarsilia went back to Paris in 1923, she took some classes with André Lhote and Fernand Léger. If, as she said, she discovered modernism in Brazil, then she also discovered Brazil in Europe.

37. Rui Moreira Leite, "Flávio de Carvalho: Modernism and the Avant-Garde in São Paulo, 1927–1939," *Journal of Decorative and Propaganda Arts*, no. 21, 1995, p. 198. See also Luiz Carlos Daher, *Flavio de Carvalho: Arquitetura e Expressionism* (São Paulo: Projecto, 1982).

38. For works of Ruben Valentim, see Roberto Pontual's *5 Mestres Brasileiros* (Rio de Janeiro: Livraria Kosmos Editora, 1977).

39. Vasconcellos, "Modernism in Brazil," p. 255.

40. Jean Manzon, *Féerie Brésilienne* (Neuchâtel: La Baconnière, 1956), p. 6. "Brazil has no iron," Sigfried Giedeon has stated, "Brazil has a few industries for concrete, and yet one sees the skyscrapers rising everywhere. There is something of the irrational in the growth of Brazilian architecture . . . the new Brazilian architecture grows all at once as would do a tropical plant." In "Le Brésil et l'architecture contemporaine," *L'Architecture d'Aujourd'hui*, 23, nos. 42–43, August 1952, p. 3.

41. Even in the gardens he built in Caracas, Venezuela, Burle Marx continued to design such patterned lawns, as for instance in the Inocente Palacios Garden (1957), which has a checkerboard design; the garden for Diego Cisneiros (1957), with patterned stripes; and

the third walled garden in the Parque del Este, which had circles of dark *Stenotaphrum* grass on a field of the lighter variety and also included areas with circles of *Coleus hybridum* cultivars in yellow and purple for additional contrast.

42. Rejected at first by modern Brazilian architects as a relic of colonial architecture, azulejos were revived in the Ministry of Education and Health Building, at Le Corbusier's suggestion. Since then, azulejos have again become a typical feature of Brazilian architecture, introducing a lively note of regionalism. See Paul Damaz, *Art in Latin American Architecture* (New York: Reinhold, 1963), p. 88. The tiled exterior walls or hallways under pilotis of modernist architecture constitute a link between painters' and architects' expression. Burle Marx created a number of azulejo designs for the exterior walls of buildings. For building interiors, he would generally be commissioned for large tapestries, paintings, or bas-relief sculptures.

43. For images of these two gardens, see Flávio Motta, *Roberto Burle Marx e a Nova Visão da Paisagem* (São Paulo: Nobel, 1984), pp. 74–75, 82–83.

44. A "cubist interaction" of this sort between the ground plane composition and the vertical dimension of the garden was explored in Fazenda Marambaia, near Petrópolis (1948–52), where contrasting hues and intensities of color fragment perspective and increase the complexity of space. The flowering trees from the garden edge begin a dialogue with the groundcover in the open, illuminated areas of the garden. This occurs especially as light shifts or weather changes, as changing value or brightness of plant masses against a simultaneous changing background accentuate the phenomenon known in color theory as "afterimage." See Rossana Vaccarino, "The Correspondence of Time and Instability: Two Gardens," in *Roberto Burle Marx: Landscapes Reflected*, Rossana Vaccarino, ed. (New York: Princeton Architectural Press/Harvard School of Design, 2000), p. 48.

45. Examples of this resonance between the mural design and the ground plane design can be found in the above-mentioned Diego Cisneiros garden, where a dialogue between the striped lawn and the horizontal pattern of the ceramic tiles of the mural was established; and again in Caracas, a similar relationship was established in the third walled garden of the Parque del Este, where the contrasting circles of the lawn and groundcover

were to be echoed by a ceramic mural that would be patterned with circles of different color at a different scale and composition (the mural was not built).

46. A later example of such recycled structures is the Sítio atelier, the painter's studio constructed in the late 1980s. A bold treatment of natural light and modernist design of the interior space are folded into an archaic facade, a shell of granite from an old coffee warehouse demolished in Praça Mauá in Rio de Janeiro. The granite facade was rescued more than forty years before and was erected in the late 1970s around what would eventually become the foundations of the new building. For some ten years it looked like an archaic ruin under restoration rather than the first phase of a new building.

47. The concrete mural geometry and relief pattern were, once again, transmuted and incorporated in the design of other projects. We see for example a series of playground designs from the early 1960s (such as the Pampulha late Club in Belo Horizonte) based on a similar "carving" strategy of a two-dimensional plane. In other words, the play areas, water pools, or sinuous concrete walls seem to be a three-dimensional blow-up of one of Burle Marx's murals or jewelry pieces, lying now huge on the ground.

48. The weathering effects of water, changes in temperature, and bright sunlight, and the process of colonization by vegetation—planted or brought in by wind or birdseed dispersion—have transformed the concrete into a kind of organic system that seems to age and evolve in time.

49. Examples of xaxim columns may be found in the winter gardens of the Ministry of Foreign Affairs (1965) and of the National Theater (1976) in Brasilia; in the BNDES (1974) atrium space in Rio, and in the forecourt garden for the Banco Safra (1982) in São Paulo. An impressing aerial garden as described in the text is observable at the Xerox do Brasil (1980–82) in Rio.

50. For examples of his flower arrangements, see Sima Eliovson, The Gardens of Roberto Burle Marx (New York, Abrams, 1991), pp. 33–34; and Marta Iris Montero, Burle Marx: paisaje lírico (Buenos Aires: IRIS, 1997), pp. 33, 38, 44, 183. The flower arrangements were a normal feature at his Sítio home and gardens. As these became famous, friends and clients soon commissioned them for private and public events.

51. Motta, Roberto Burle Marx e a Nova Visão

da Paisagem, p. 238.

52. As previously said, Glaziou is the first to have "discovered" the beauty of native plants and their potential for use in urban parks. Yet his park settings and designs were still traditional, and the use of native plants is not sufficient to make him a real precursor of the modern garden in the sense that is meant in this essay.

53. The Casa Modernista inspired other gardeners and the plastic and decorative artists of the time. Mina and Gregori were in fact very close to the avant-garde artists, whose meetings usually occurred in their house. Warchavchik's early houses closely followed the "scandal" provoked by Flávio de Carvalho and prepared the ground for the visit of Le Corbusier to Brazil in 1929. For images of Kablin's gardens see Geraldo Ferraz, Warchavchik e a Introduçao da Nova Arquitectura no Bresil: 1920 a 1940 (São Paulo: Museo de Arte de Sao Paulo, 1965), and Catalogo de desegnos de arquitetura da Biblioteca da FAUUSP (Universidade de Sao Paulo, 1988), pp. 143–59.

54. It should not be forgotten, however, that Mina Kablin, as a member of a rich industrial family of São Paulo, was continuously in contact with all intellectual circles of the local elite. It was actually through her that her husband was able to develop strong ties with the proponents of the modernist movement. Kablin was aware of the "myth of the jungle" and the nativism advocated by Tarsilia do Amaral and other artists of the time. It is possible that, had she the opportunity to design larger gardens or gardens for buildings other than Warchavchik's, she could have developed more complex schemes.

55. It is possible that Burle Marx became acquainted with Kablin's work on that occasion, even though he had already been experimenting with strikingly colored leafy plants and native plants in his own garden.

56. In Pernambuco, the state where his mother was born, Burle Marx came in contact with cultural diversity and local folklore, as well as the torrid landscape, which was completely ignored by the people. In Recife, he became friends with a group of intellectuals, including sociologist Gilberto Freyre, painter Cícero Diaz, art critic Clarival do Prado Valladares, and poet-engineer Joaquín Cardoso.

57. As Guilherme Mazza Dourado has written, "Burle Marx knew these [Tarsilia's] surrealist works, he knew the Abaporu, from 1928,

evoking a seated human figure alongside the mandacaru and his vision was no doubt influenced by this experience." In his "Green Modernity: The Transcendence of the Work of Burle Marx," DOCOMOMO Conference Proceedings (Bratislava: DOCOMOMO International, 1997), p. 151.

58. This is an early conceptualization of ecology and ecological design, one that came to the profession of landscape architecture from the field of biogeography dating back to the nineteenth century and the work of Ernst Haeckel. For this, see Donald Worster's Nature's Economy: A History of Ecological Ideas (Cambridge: Cambridge University Press, 1977), p. 194.

59. Vincent, "The Modern Garden in Brazil," p. 169. The site was divided into twenty-five sections, of which only fifteen were completed, due to a later lack of governmental support. As Laurence Fleming has written, Burle Marx "had learned in Recife how little municipal workers understood about the treatment of plants and he now planned, as far as such a thing was possible, a park full of plants that could look after themselves." See Laurence Fleming, Roberto Burle Marx: A Portrait (Rio de Janeiro: Editora Index, 1996), p. 51. The transportation of rocks from the surrounding natural landscape into the garden has been repeated in many projects: Burle Marx maintained a love for rock gardens—in addition to water gardens—and would continually attempt to create new ones with different regional influences.

60. Anthony Walmsley, "South America: Appraisal of a Master Artist," Landscape Architecture, July 1963, p. 264.

61. The excursions became a regular routine after Burle Marx's acquisition of the Sítio Santo Antonio da Bica in 1949. This was a farm property of 800,000 square meters, about twenty-eight miles from Rio de Janeiro, where Burle Marx established his home and studio, several greenhouses, and a nursery, which became world famous. The Sítio nurseries became an important source of plants for his design projects, at a time where native plants were still not appreciated nor cultivated in commercial nurseries.

62. Besides collecting native plants, Burle Marx collected other kinds of partially known "nativism," including pre-Columbian pottery, clay figurines from the Jequitinhonha Valley (traditional to the region of Minas Gerais), ex-votos and sacred paintings, altarpieces, and gargoyle figureheads from Brazilian ship prows. As per Tarsilia do

Amaral back in 1924, Burle Marx surely "rediscovered" the same "pure blues, violet pink, bright yellow, or singing green" in Minas Gerais's interior decoration of churches, images of saints, furniture, and carnival costumes. The objects of his collections would be displayed in his house side by side with his own paintings and sculptures, botanical watercolors by Margaret Mee, glass objects from Scandinavia, ethnic embroideries and fabrics, and Brazilian furniture from the eighteenth and nineteenth centuries alongside Bauhaus chairs. Burle Marx did not surround himself with art and craft objects to reveal his refined taste, like a number of architects and artists of his time. His collection of cultural artifacts would be for him a source of inspiration and would also reflect his appreciation of the creative manifestations of the so-called popular cultures, with their unexpected formal inventions. He demonstrated his respect for works of craft and cult objects at the same level as high art by placing both on the same aesthetic footing. Yet he said that it was not enough to appropriate folk elements as a means of producing art of national expression: the artist was required to go beyond a superficial "appearance" to the foundations of popular culture in order to re-create a new synthesis, a new language.

236

63. Bardi, *The Tropical Gardens of Burle Marx*, p. 221. The cultural relevance of such a project was the ability to show and perpetuate the botanic structure of different Brazilian landscapes, since a garden could trigger people's emotional appreciation, understanding, and therefore attachment, not so differently from what had happened to him in experiencing the botanical garden in Dahlem, Germany. His gardens, in Burle Marx's mind, would become a similar discovery for the people of Brazil: something they had never seen before. Thus the significance of Burle Marx's work transcends the innovative act of merging art, tradition, and botany. His work creates something truly new in that it is an act of interpretation, via aesthetics, of an undefined value: he does so by transforming the texture and colors of the forest into comprehensible, human-scale experiences that elicit an emotional response from the viewer. See Vaccarino, "The Correspondence of Time and Instability," p. 52.

64. As a Portuguese saying goes, "Beneath the equator there is no sin." This aspect, I would argue, interestingly correlates the daring, bold associations of Burle Marx with the erotic images and descriptions of Brazil since the time of its discovery. Burle Marx's deep knowledge of plants and their needs in rela-

tion to physical conditions allowed him to play intensely with very unusual combinations of species, with surprisingly harmonic or daring results.

65. "If one person would speak to Roberto about a certain plant seen in a certain region, he would start thinking of a trip right away," Ono continued. "While we would start a whole mechanism for its organization—Which is the region? Which is the best season to collect this plant?—several experts would be consulted to establish the itinerary. Often people from abroad would join in the trip, together with friends, architects, and botanists—all with the same interest in common. Us in the office, we were completely involved with this." "Entrevista com Haruyoshi Ono," *Folha—Sociedade dos Amigos de Roberto Burle Marx*, no. 13, August 1999, p. 12.

66. Throughout his life Burle Marx sought to duplicate with other botanists the working relationship established with Mello Barreto. They included Luiz Emygdio de Mello Filho (who collaborated on many projects in Rio, especially on the Parque Flamengo), Grazilea Barroso, Aparicio Duarte, Luiz Mathis, Hermes Moreira de Souza, and Adolpho Ducke, among the Brazilians; and Leandro Aristeguieta (crucial for the Parque del Este in Caracas), Abalo, Wirdack, and many others, among the foreigners.

67. Interviews with Luiz Emygdio de Mello Filho, the botanist collaborator on the Parque Flamengo (December 1999), and with Leandro Aristeguieta, the botanist collaborator on the Parque del Este (January 2000).

68. It is important to mention that for lack of both nurseries and a demand by landscape architects, large specimens such as we are used to seeing today in gardens and parks were unthinkable in Brazil in the 1940s and 1950s. Large plants (such as coconut palms) were available for the Parque Flamengo only if reclaimed in Rio during the conversion of garden properties into apartment buildings. But I am sure that given a price, and having a choice, Burle Marx would have preferred to buy ten small trees rather than one large one, since he needed several plants from the same species for his grouping design.

69. The early phase of his designs would derive its power from the interesting contrast of color, texture, and forms of the groundcover and shorter plants massed in "special gardens" featured within the park (for instance, the walled gardens and the

north lake with a profusion of aquatic plants in the Parque del Este, and the gardens by the Museum of Modern Art in the Parque Flamengo). Indeed, in many projects the small trees and palms would often serve in the first years as part of or complement to this groundcover composition, and quite effectively so. Compare, for instance, the difference between the historical photographs of Fazenda Marambaia (1950s) and the situation today.

70. In many ways, in this process, people who had never cared about trees and parks in Brazil or Venezuela became attached, as if personally related to "their" trees and parks. We could say, then, that Burle Marx succeeded in his mission to teach people to respect their flora. Paradoxically, this very success has also fortified a strong conservation movement to the extent that today in both parks it is nearly impossible to eliminate trees that have accidentally grown owing to seed dispersion, thus compromising the original design and altering Burle Marx's spatial and compositional intentions.

71. Roberto Burle Marx, "Jardim e Ecologia," in *Arte e Paisagem: Conferência Escolhidas* (São Paulo: Nobel, 1987), pp. 37–44.

72. See Vaccarino, "The Correspondence of Time and Instability," pp. 42–43.

73. See Jeffrey Lesser, *Negotiating National Identity: Immigrants, Minorities, and the Struggle for Ethnicity in Brazil* (Durham, N.C.: Duke University Press, 1999); Amaryll Chanady, ed., *Latin American Identity and the Construction of Difference* (Minneapolis: University of Minnesota Press, 1994); and Bill Ashcroft, Gareth Griffiths, and Helen Tiffin, eds., *The Post Colonial Studies Reader* (London: Routledge, 1995).

74. Miscegenation, or interracial crossing, comes from the Latin *miscere*, mix, and *genus*, race. This process created the emergence of mixed bloods, producing *caboclos* from the union between the white Portuguese and the indigenous, mulattoes or *mestiço* from the union between Portuguese and Africans, and *mamelucos* between indigenous and African. The Portuguese themselves included racial and cultural elements of Celtic, Nordic, and Mediterranean origin, and especially in the south of Lisbon there was a large mixture of Moorish blood and of Moorish and Semitic culture traits. This diversity was counteracted and controlled politically in Brazil by many members of Brazil's upper classes, which supported eugenics-influenced policies that promoted the entry of those immigrants

able to "whiten" or "bleach" Brazilian society, such as Italians, Germans, Poles, Jews, Spaniards, Russians, Syrians, Lebanese, and Japanese. The cultural elite felt that Brazil's inferior status among nations was due to the racial inferiority of the native Africans and Native Americans, and, to a lesser extent, the mixed offspring of these darker races and the Europeans. Even the darker Mediterranean Europeans from whom the Portuguese descended were considered inferior to the lighter Nordic northern Europeans. Yet miscegenation did not create a uniform Brazilian "race" but a constellation of different identities, a multiplicity of hyphenated Brazilians. See Lesser, *Negotiating National Identity*, p. 5.

75. Brazil houses the largest population of African descent outside Africa and has one of the most richly varied indigenous populations. When Cabral landed in Brazil in April 1500, the native populations numbered more than one hundred separate language groups, almost all unintelligible to one another. See Skidmore, *Brazil*, pp. 14–15.

76. In the Parque Flamengo and the Parque del Este, for instance, the educational program and the artistic intention of specific gardens within the park are only one agenda, one aspect of the programmatic spectrum. Side by side there are other kinds of social spaces, all overlapping in proximity with one another or claiming the same territory at different times of the day. For example, jogging and tai chi are practiced by middle- and upper-class groups only in the early morning or late afternoon; people-watching, soccer playing, picnicking, and sunbathing are practiced during the day by the masses coming from less affluent areas of the city. Both parks negate the assertion that geography or birthplace, in terms of specific metropolitan areas of origin, can be the basis of class hierarchy or racism. There is no Europeanlike national identity constructed in the park design or use that would suppress the mixed-blood populations with its superiority. Different people identify themselves with the park at different levels and in different ways. In both parks, the merging of different users coming from the most disparate neighborhoods of Rio de Janeiro or Caracas needs to be understood as a joining (rather than mixing) of different identities.

77. Burle Marx has been described many times as a generous and humble being, making every guest or worker feel at ease; he also had an extroverted, "solar" personality, capable of shining in the middle of any conversation. He attracted many people to him—intellectuals, politicians, the affluent—

and his wonderful parties and banquets were nationally and internationally renowned.

78. Even today in Brazil, in the early 2000s, there is not an academic landscape architecture program that prescribes a specified curriculum for attaining professional competence. Classes on landscape architecture are usually offered within architectural curricula, and landscape professionals contribute background and experience from other fields.

79. Two out of his four partners from the 1950 and 1960s, Mauricio Monte and Julio Pessolani, were nearly always involved in the office in helping him prepare large gouaches or mixed media presentation artwork with the sole purpose of being used in exhibitions.

80. See, for instance, the importance of gardens with architecture in Lina Bo Bardi, "Lettera dal Brasile," *L'architettura, Cronache e Storia*, anno II, no. 9, July 1956, pp. 182–87; and Vincent, "The Modern Garden in Brazil," pp. 165–70.

81. Architects and artists were trained in the same schools across Latin America in the postwar decades. Cultural milieux were rather small: architects, artists, writers, and other intellectuals would maintain close social contacts, would organize cultural events, and were often close friends. Architecture in Brazil, as in other Latin American countries, was considered an art among the others. Architects were expected to provide more than purely "functional" solutions, and ambiguous professional boundaries were not uncommon: for instance, a muralist could have been trained as an architect or an architect could receive, and succeed in executing, an art commission. See Damaz, *Art in Latin American Architecture*, pp. 68–69, 84–85. The most significant indication of the close relationship of the arts may be seen in professional publications.

Architectural magazines (*Modulo* is an example in Brazil) devoted much space to articles on painters or sculptors, reviews of exhibitions nationally and abroad, and important theatrical or musical events. *Modulo*—which was published in both Portuguese and English and had French and Spanish translations to address the four official languages of the country—also covered folkloristic Brazilian traditions side by side with important visits of architects from abroad. Burle Marx's travels and exhibitions were usually featured in *Modulo*'s *noticiario*.

82. For example, the Niemeyer house in Canoas, built in 1953—for which Burle Marx designed the garden—is considered the purest example of free-form modernism in domestic architecture. The building derives its expressive power from the biomorphic stylization of the architectural elements, the fluidity of its spaces, and the attention given to the natural elements of the site—stone, water, and vegetation. The roof is a flowing curve, a topographical plane rising metaphorically from the land. The inside becomes an exuberant landscape of plants and stones without architectonic boundaries.

83. This evolution can be attributed to many factors, among which are the continuous collaboration of Burle Marx with architects and the direct influence of Fernando Tabora and John Stoddart, the two architects associated with Burle Marx from 1956 to 1964 who helped design and construct many projects carried out during those years.

84. As Skidmore and Smith have stated, "From 1968 to 1974 the growth rate averaged 10 percent, and exports more than quadrupled. . . . [M]anufactured goods replaced coffee as the country's leading export product. Outside observers soon talked of the 'Brazilian miracle,' [which was actually] achieved by low wages and easy credit to purchasers of consumer durable goods" (*Modern Latin America*, p. 178). The "miracle" ended in the early 1980s, when the world recession depressed the value of Brazilian exports, and inflation and the international deficit skyrocketed.

Australia grew up quickly in the twenty years after 1940. A world war on its doorstep and bombs falling on its shores were a shocking introduction to the project of modernity, a jolt that wakened the nation from the peaceful cultural distance from Europe and the Americas that Australia had enjoyed in the 1930s. Being part of the team that developed the atomic bomb, hosting an Olympic Games, winning an RIBA Gold Medal in Architecture, a Nobel Prize in Physiology and Medicine, launching a new Australian operatic diva, and announcing the winning design for the Sydney Opera House in 1957 were high points of the two decades in which Australia, a vast country the size of the United States and with a fraction of its population, became wealthy and earned the title of "the Lucky Country."[1] Growing up and becoming rich meant clearing the land, mining the ground, and damming the rivers—all part of modernity and progress. Landscape was largely not designed but engineered or, in some few cases, it was simply left alone. If the period from 1940 to 1960 was Australia's pimply adolescence, the experience left its scars. Its culture persisted then, and in many ways still persists today, in believing itself to be youthful and yet to come of age. It talked, and still talks, of a new land and a new language.

9. PHILIP GOAD

New Land, New Language: Shifting Grounds in Australian Attitudes to Landscape, Architecture, and Modernism

Between 1940 and 1960, relationships between architecture and landscape in Australia shifted their philosophical and aesthetic allegiances. Critical was the interruption of World War II when for the first time Australia found itself as "A Nation of trees, drab green and desolate grey; / In the field uniform of modern wars."[2] Critical was the subsequent acceptance of international modernism as a generalized vocabulary for postwar architecture. In the dissemination of this vocabulary, landscape and landscape design played a complicit and central role. This essay examines the ways in which these new allegiances were made manifest: how the Australian bush came to be regarded as an appropriate backdrop for a new language of architecture; how, by contrast, influences from the United States, Latin America, and Asia gave primacy to compositional and pictorial values in the designed landscape; and how the projects of postwar Australian modernity demanded large-scale and often sweeping responses to the landscape.[3] Landscape was coupled with the rise of the postwar skyscraper, new emphases on recreation and national tourism, and dramatic changes in the design of the Australian house. The factory, the highway, the mining town, and the damming of Australian rivers also gave the landscape and its design a significant role in their ambitious development.

Landscape design in postwar Australia unconsciously followed, as it did in other Western countries, then-unwritten axioms for a modern landscape, which have since been formulated by Marc Treib.[4] Specifically local themes also appeared: an unspoken nationalism and circumstantial pragmatism that encouraged expedient ecological design and a culture of artless naturalism; a hybrid design ethos (also linked to identity) that tentatively blended East and West; and a parallel and largely uncritical pursuit of the engineered landscape. Yet by 1960, formalized traditions in both postwar Australian architecture and landscape architecture had not emerged. The experiments of the 1950s had produced tension and revelation about a phenomenon still tantalizingly unresolved: the nature of design in a postcolonial landscape.

The scope of this essay is thus intentionally broad. With the exception of a very few sources, there is inadequate documentation of Australian landscape design in the 1940s and 1950s and its relationship to architecture.[5] My aim is therefore to demonstrate the subject's breadth in an attempt to initiate a more complete discourse, exposing the masked view given by the garden designer monograph and answering Australian academic David Yencken's call for research for a better "view from within" and hence a better "view from without."[6]

PRELUDE TO A WAR

In the 1930s, the Melbourne-based landscape designer Edna Walling (1896–1973) was the dominant figure in Australian garden design, her work representing prevailing loyalties to English landscape traditions. Walling's gardens were an assured and inventive blend of both her idols: the architectural structuring of Gertrude Jekyll and William Robinson's conception of the wild garden.[7] In the city, Walling's gardens were commissioned by a wealthy urban elite. Her garden for Ringland Anderson, Esq., in Toorak (1934) was intended to complement a new house designed by society architect Marcus Martin [Figure 9–1]. It combined both formal and natural styles.[8] Walling inserted a swimming pool and flanking Ionic columned pergolas between two tennis courts to create a dominant axis, while to one side of the house, above this urbane terrace, a relaxed planting scheme based on large existing trees created intimate outdoor rooms and carefully controlled distant views. Propriety in garden style

Figure 9–1.
Garden for Ringland Anderson, Esq.,
Toorak, Victoria, Australia, 1934.
Edna Walling.
[Edna Walling, *Gardens in Australia* (1943)]

matched the subdued, tasteful, modern Georgian of Martin's house design.

Edna Walling also designed for the so-called squattocracy of rural Australia. A similar sense of propriety toward location and character determined her 1937 pergola at Boortkoi for Andrew Manifold's large country station at Hexham, in the Western District of Victoria [Figure 9–2]. Walling's fondness for the pergolas of Amalfi was realized as a series of roughly plastered white rubble columns covered by a framework of saplings supporting wisteria.[9] The Long Walk at Boortkoi was romantic and rustic and indicated a not uncommon idea in terms of architecture as well as landscape architecture, that an appropriate idiom for Australia was one that was modeled on something from somewhere else.[10]

Gardens such as these, and others like them of the 1930s, represented a belated golden summer for Australia as colony in both the city and the country. Conceived by a small number of society garden designers such as Walling, Paul Sorensen, and Jocelyn Brown, or by gifted amateurs, these gardens invariably complemented existing and period-style homes designed by society architects. The common aim was, as Helen Proudfoot suggests, the search for grace via "restfulness and the Rule of Taste."[11] The presence of the Australian landscape was understandably and often conspicuously absent from these gardens, which were created as Arcadias of exotic descent. Owing to the harsh climate and difficult soil conditions across much of Australia, English and European conditions could be replicated only in urbanized areas, on prosperous country grazing properties, or in wet temperate mountain areas such as the Blue Mountains in New South Wales, the Dandenong Ranges, and "the Simla of the South," the Macedon Ranges in Victoria.[12] An added restriction was that propagation techniques for Australian native trees and plants were at that time largely undeveloped by local nurseries.[13] The notion of a bush palette applied to garden design was thus in its infancy. For the most part, therefore, the Australian landscape, its flora and its peculiar colors and patterns, instead of availing itself as a new design repertoire, was largely consigned to the status of "other."

The Australian landscape was, however, not unwelcome in the nation's depiction of itself. With the success of the romantic Heidelberg School paintings of the 1890s, the landscape became a virtual national obsession.[14] By the 1930s and 1940s, the acceptance of this "other" landscape

Figure 9–2.
The Long Walk at Boortkoi, Hexham, Victoria, Australia, 1937. Edna Walling.
[Peter Watts, *Edna Walling and Her Gardens* (1991)]

Figure 9–3.
Spirit of Endurance, 1937. Harold
Cazneaux, photographer.
[Historic Houses Trust of New South Wales,
Harold Cazneaux Photographs (1994)]

Figure 9–4.
Rocks, French's Forest, New South Wales,
Australia, c. 1955.
[Max Dupain, *Max Dupain's Australian
Landscapes* (1988)]

was also being explored by photographers such as Harold Cazneaux, who was able to match the romanticism of the 1890s with his evocative images of the Adelaide Hills (c. 1938).[15] At the same time he was also exploring other evocations. Cazneaux's *Spirit of Endurance* (1937) depicted the eucalyptus as timeless icon withstanding the ravages of time and erosion introduced by the colonizers [Figure 9–3].[16] This was sublime survival. Similarly, Max Dupain's *Newport Landscape* (1939) depicts a group of gums reading virtually as a series of classical ruins more grandiose than the humble timber structures nearby.[17] Dupain's later black-and-white photographs of a creek and wattles (1946) and rocks (c. 1955) at French's Forest, near Sydney, however, revealed new compositional details, textures, and reflections of light available with the bush [Figure 9–4].[18] But these were all depictions of Australian landscape as opposed to its actual design and manipulation.

Exceptions to the apparent habit of omission of Australian plants in garden design had existed for many years; bunya-bunya pines and Moreton Bay fig trees in gardenesque idiom had graced the parks of the nineteenth century. In the early twentieth century, Edna Walling herself had no negative predisposition toward Australian trees and had planted the now-renowned avenue of lemon-scented gums at Cruden Farm, Langwarrin (1929) [Figure 9–5]. But these were techniques that drew Australian flora into, on the one hand, the nineteenth-century gaze of the specimen and, on the other, conventional architectural adaptations of landscape flora. While often visually striking, these gestures did not challenge the dialogue of architecture and landscape in new terms, in the terms of the modern.

Three projects of the 1930s, however, foreshadowed critical themes of the modern in landscape design, which would recur in the two decades after 1940. The first project was the insertion of a swimming pool within a garden at Olinda, in the Dandenong Ranges in Victoria [Figure 9–6]. The pool, its amoebic shape and giant rock as diving board and planting intended to eventually screen and conceal a carefully engineered scum gutter, was made to appear utterly natural against a backdrop of mixed exotic and native trees. Design was recessive, humble, and a seamless fit within the existing landscape. The pool was designed in 1939 by Edna Walling for Miss E. Hughes-Jones.[19] Assisting Walling in the pool's construction was Ellis Stones, whose expertise in the placement of rocks would become legendary in the following three decades.[20] This apparently natural swimming hole was not like Thomas Church's famous pool in the Dewey Donnell Garden, Sonoma, California (1948), of nearly ten years later with its clear overlay of architectural modernism, nor was it like the curiosity of a reconstructed bush setting within a grand nineteenth-century garden.[21] The intention was a coexistence with the landscape, an acceptance of modified wilderness above romantic association and also above avant-garde compositional dexterity. It was an example of the artless naturalism that would pervade the ideas of a nascent bush movement in the 1950s and find its greatest popularity in the Australian bush gardens of the late 1960s and 1970s.[22]

The second harbinger of new themes in Australian landscape design was another insertion within an existing garden. In 1937 at Everglades, in Leura in the Blue Mountains of New South Wales, Danish emigré landscape architect Paul Sorensen introduced a linear terrace opening off the undercroft of an elevated studio of cubist design.[23] Containing a swimming pool, Sorensen's studio terrace was a simple flat plane with the Australian landscape as backdrop and timeless foil to the severe lines of brick edging to either side and a framing pergola at the terrace's distant end [Figure 9–7]. The retention of an ancient eucalyptus took on the appearance of a piece of modern art. It was an abstract sculpture placed on its own podium — the Australian tree as surrealist *objet d'art*. A dialogue of rich spatial, textural, and formal contrast between the designed landscape elements and the natural landscape was introduced. This was a feature of Sorensen's designs, which otherwise included eclectic pieces of architectural fragments as counterpoints and his favored dry-stone walls with their drumlike ends. The freedom of the Australian landscape, lacking reference and contextual value, was intended to complement and accentuate the severe modern forms of the architecture, a habit taken up by architects in the next two decades, partly by circumstance and partly by a similar aesthetic intent, to make landscape complicit in the promotion of the architecture.

The third emergent theme was an attempt, more often than not on the part of architects, to place landscape and architecture into dialogue not as accentuation by contrast but more by an informing of the architecture by the landscape itself, as a part of justification for the apparent naturalness of the architecture. The colors and qualities of the Australian landscape were to merge with the forms of a new architecture. For example, this was how the Dudok-inspired forms of Wildfell, the Critchley Parker House,

Figure 9–7.
Studio terrace, Everglades, Leura,
New South Wales, Australia, 1937.
Paul Sorensen.
[Richard Ratcliffe, *Australia's Master
Gardener: Paul Sorensen and His Garden*]

Upper Beaconsfield (1933), were described in 1934: "The main walls are silver white to provide a glistening background for the everchanging shadows of the trees. The rust-red window frames and fascia reflect the peeling bark of honey eucalypts. Shade and a gayer note is sung by the striped awnings which fold away to oblivion when winter's sun is searching hopefully to live within the rooms. This is La Mabeillion—Modern by circumstance."[24] The red brick plinth, quarry-tiled terraces, silver-painted bricks coupled with the allusion to the play of light among the ochers, silvers, and reds of native trees, the stripes of the blinds interacting with the shadows of trees, were part of the rhetoric for the acceptance of the new forms and the sprawling plan of the house.[25] Its architect, Roy Grounds, also often employed a dusky pink-gray stucco for his understated modern houses and blocks of flats, another reference to the subtle pink trunks of lemon-scented gums. Similarly, in a house built for Betty Ramsay (which was later to become his own), amid the coastal ti-trees of the Mornington Peninsula in 1938, Grounds employed white-painted window joinery, oiled weatherboards, and a roof of timber shingles left to weather to a natural gray [Figure 9–8].[26] Grounds created a subtle dialogue with the ti-trees' tiny gray-green leaves, their tight white floral balls, and the peeling gray bark of their spindly gnarled trunks. Modern architecture was represented as natural and importantly at one with an Australian rather than an introduced landscape.

The three themes of artless naturalism, dramatic contrast as backdrop for modernism, and a natural and hence native modernism interacting with the landscape, were indicative of not only experiments with new forms of architecture but also, in each case, the crucial complicity of the Australian landscape in achieving a convincing aesthetic resolution of each project.

LANDSCAPE AND DISCOURSE: THE GROUND SHIFTS

In 1942, the evolutionary development of a respectful and subtle inclusion of modernism in architecture and landscape halted. Australia entered World War II, and a new culture of pragmatism, scientific rationalism, economy, and repressed dreams was instated. Housing starts diminished almost to nothing, and all energy went toward planning for the war effort and, as the war progressed, hopes for a new future. Australian men and women joined the landscape as camouflage, many experiencing outback Australia for the first time

Figure 9–8.
Ramsay House, Mount Eliza, Victoria, Australia, 1938. Roy Grounds, architect.
[Robin Boyd, *Victorian Modern*]

Figure 9–9.
Chancellor House, Mount Eliza, Victoria, Australia, 1952. David Chancellor, architect.
[Kenneth McDonald, *The New Australian Home*]

in training or awaiting departure for the theaters of war in Southeast Asia. The less lucky found themselves tramping the jungles of New Guinea, or in Singapore or Burma. For some it was battles once again halfway round the world in the deserts of Egypt or in the air over Europe.

In Australia, as in the United States, the focus of postwar dreams centered squarely on the single-family house. There were numerous books written about the ideal postwar house, as well as competitions like the 1945 *Sun* postwar home competition,[27] which was typical of many such morale-boosting exercises. Gone were the 1930s romantic water-colors; house and landscape were delineated in dense black ink with rapid and efficient strokes of the pen [Figure 9–9]. Less studied, artless, and spontaneous, this was the message of postwar production. The circumstantial adoption of modern architecture — it was cheap and simple — brought a discursive shift in the framing of architecture and landscape. In subsequent depictions of the garden, the landscape was radically functionalized. This idea was, of course, not radically new — nor was it particular to Australia — but its appearance at a time of postwar austerity carried a special sense of immediacy. Two suburban plot designs of the early 1940s demonstrate this shift. Jocelyn Brown's 1942 garden design for the "upmarket women's magazine," *The Home, The Australian Journal of Quality*, comprised axial vistas, compartmentalized planting rooms, and a formal arrangement of exotic plants.[28] A detailed plan of the house was omitted from her drawing [Figure 9–10]. By contrast, Karl Langer's 1944 design was published in a scientific pamphlet.[29] House and garden were inseparable elements of a greater whole as external and internal spaces all interrelated [Figure 9–11]. Plant types were not discussed. The garden became a diagram of rendering techniques indicating function rather than a predestined botanical choice shaping a future garden.

Critical differences among 1950s Australian landscape designers soon became apparent. There were those with a horticultural background and those with an architectural training. A strong cohort of garden designers, mostly women, trained in horticulture at the first school of its kind in Australia, Burnley Horticultural College, established in Melbourne in 1891. They included designers such as Edna Walling, Emily Gibson, Olive Mellor, Mervyn Davis, John Stevens, Grace Fraser, and Phyllis Simons.[30] The other group, who were architects, went on to develop a strong and then professional interest in landscape architecture. Among this group there was John Oldham, Beryl Mann (who also

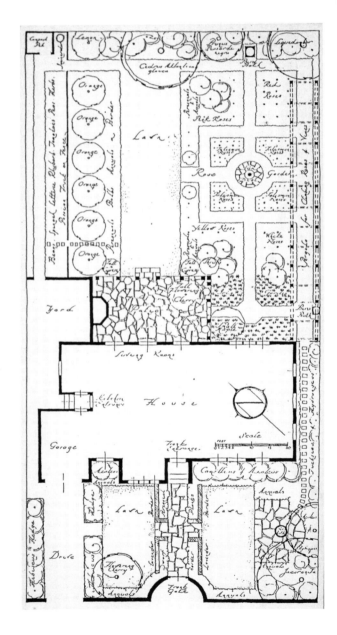

Figure 9–10.
Garden design for *The Home*, 1942.
Jocelyn Brown.
[Helen Proudfoot, *Gardens in Bloom*]

Figure 9–11. [*facing page*]
Garden and house design, 1944.
Karl Langer, architect.
[Karl Langer, *Sub-Tropical Housing*]

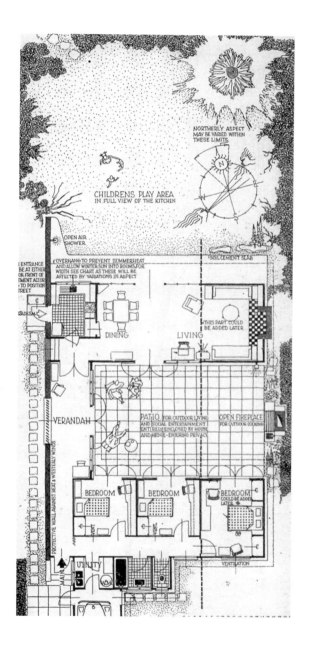

completed the course at Burnley), Ron Rayment, Bryce Mortlock, Peter Spooner, Trevor Westmore, Richard Ratcliffe, and Malcolm Munroe. A third group comprised designers such as Ellis Stones, Eric Hammond, and Gordon Ford; they were self-taught, either by association with a prominent figure such as Walling or from a lifetime of contracting. A very few such as Paul Sorensen, Richard Clough, and Allan Correy were qualified landscape architects but they had been trained elsewhere. No dedicated course in landscape design existed in Australia until 1965 (and that was a postgraduate course), and it was only from 1974 that Australian students were able to study landscape architecture at the undergraduate level.[31] Nineteen fifties landscape architecture therefore lacked a common forum in which to draw together these coexistent strands of training and outlook.

Despite an apparent vacuum of discourse, garden design was well popularized during the 1940s through books, newspapers, and homes journals.[32] Edna Walling's public profile was at its highest. Both her *Gardens of Australia* (1943) and *Cottage and Garden in Australia* (1947) went into successive reprints over the next two decades. When Walling discussed architecture, however, reference was made to her own Arts and Crafts–inspired house designs at Bickleigh Vale, Mooroolbark, or she quoted the reassuring homilies of East Coast American architect Royal Barry Wills. She assiduously avoided the modern. But in other 1940s texts, architecture was making a different appearance. In Elynne Mitchell's *Australian Treescapes* (1950), in a few pages at the end of her series of impressive illustrations of Australian trees, the native bush surrounded a Wurster-inspired house design by Ellice Nosworthy and an unassuming modern flat-roofed house by Arthur Baldwinson.[33] In *Victorian Modern* (1947), Robin Boyd, a young Melbourne architect, soon to become Australia's most vocal proponent of modern architecture, described a brief history of architecture in Victoria. But in many of his figure captions, reference was made to the backdrop of Australian gums that graced houses such as Harold Desbrowe Annear's Broceliande (1918) and J. F. Spears's own house at Beaumaris (1947).[34] Boyd was constructing his own local picture of modernism, and it was as if the backdrop of Australian trees gave the buildings credibility as logical precursor and contemporary outcome. The landscape setting released the building from any reference to time or context. There was no discussion, however, of any self-conscious designing of the landscape.

Importantly, Boyd brought back into discussion, at least among architects, a figure whose architecture and whose ideas on landscape were largely undiscussed during the 1930s: Walter Burley Griffin (1876–1937). As James Weirick has noted, Griffin was Australia's first and perhaps most important landscape architect.[35] But in Boyd's attempt to construct a history of modern architecture for Australia, Griffin is nominated solely as a prophet of modernist architecture. His contributions and those of his wife, Marion Mahony (1871–1961), to landscape architecture, in particular their designs for Canberra and their understanding of its landscape, are largely unacknowledged by Boyd. Despite this omission, Boyd's rediscovery of Griffin in 1947 is timely. The presence of Griffin buildings in Castlecrag, Sydney, and Mount Eliza, just outside Melbourne, and their forms and siting, which appear to gain inspiration from their immediate locale, cannot be overlooked. In the late 1940s and early 1950s these would be the same locations for some of the most advanced examples of postwar modernist domestic architecture.

Boyd was not alone in his use of the landscape to promote modern architecture. Sydney Ancher's 1940s and 1950s houses were often published as perspective drawings of white planar forms collaged onto a black-and-white photograph of a site [Figure 9–12].[36] Set within an apparently virgin landscape, between trees and around giant boulders, heroic new forms were pitted against heroic wilderness. But the most persuasive image was Marcell Seidler's photograph of the Rose Seidler House, Turramurra (1947–50), a freestanding house of pure East Coast Bauhaus International style [Figure 9–13]. Paul Rudolph was to describe it as the Harvard house incarnate.[37] The only thing that contextualized Harry Seidler's design was the eucalypts in the background. No one observed that the site had been scraped clean to create a tabula rasa for a sculptural terracing in readiness for the placement of the house as isolated art object. For many architects in Australia, this image represented the most convincing postwar argument for modern architecture. Historian J. M. Freeland described its effect on Australian architecture as "tremendous. . . . Imitations and virtual copies in whole or in part sprang up all around Australia immediately and for five years afterward."[38]

It could be argued that these depictions of the Australian landscape as backdrop to the high points of Australian postwar modernism were conscious decisions to promote modern architecture. But, at a time when money for external landscape design in Australia was virtually nonexistent, to retain existing old and sometimes visually dramatic native trees and boulders made economic as well as aesthetic sense, enhancing the minimalism of the architecture. Architects

Figure 9–12.
P. B. Hart House, Wahroonga, New South Wales, Australia, 1953. Sydney Ancher, architect.
[*Architecture and Arts*, January 1954]

Figure 9–13. [*facing page*]
Rose Seidler House, Turramurra, New South Wales, Australia, 1947–50.
Harry Seidler, architect. Marcell Seidler, photographer.
[Harry Seidler, *Houses, Interiors, and Projects*]

also had to deal with difficult sites that had steep slopes or creek gullies or were often undeveloped, in distant suburbs and hence in bush, or on the beach amid coastal scrub. Landscape design thus followed artless naturalism by default —it was an expedient complicity between new building and existing landscape.

LANDSCAPE AND THE POSTWAR HOUSE

For the majority of urban Australians in the postwar years, a new house was placed on a typical suburban block, 50 by 150 feet deep, the ubiquitous quarter-acre site that had been ruthlessly cleared. The habit was also to fence these blocks, both sides, front and back in an English tradition of coveted privacy and territoriality. The austere postwar bungalow almost always had its dearly loved manicured front garden and a rear back yard (rather than back garden), often ignored, and the repository of a rotary clothes-drying rack, the ubiquitous lemon tree, and a lawn to occupy the husband with mowing on the weekend. Architects and garden designers contended with a resistant mentality to changing not just the look of the postwar suburban house but also the look of its garden, and what Robin Boyd described in *The Australian Ugliness* (1960) as "arboraphobia," a peculiarly Australian hatred of trees and obsessive preoccupation with clearing any land of existing planting.[39]

The enforcement of building sizes and materials restrictions after World War II meant that new architect-designed houses were modest in scale and finish. Landscaping was thus intrinsic to efforts in making these very small houses seem very large.[40] Concerted attempts were made at better interaction between house and landscape. Robin Boyd's and later Neil Clerehan's weekly articles from 1947 until 1961 in *The Age* newspaper for the RVIA Small Homes Service encouraged use of the entire block and a subtle infusion of a more progressive image for the small home. A competition held in 1953 by the service demonstrated the attention that architects were expending on the landscape.[41] Pergolas and decks delineated outdoor rooms, barbecues were set into external walls creating external kitchens within carports, isolated single trees gave areas of shade and sculptural interest, and as a garden signature, a collection of visually interesting rocks, a geometric flowerbed, and perhaps an existing tree could become a feature or eye-catcher from the street. The signs of postwar recreation also appeared in these drawings: chairs and chaises of steel rods and woven string; butterfly chairs; the open sportscar; and if one had it

all, the yacht parked in readiness in the drive. The houses themselves were tiny. Designed landscape and the entourage of the good life, outdoor furniture, were used to sell a lean architecture.

Australia in the 1950s was enchanted with things American. It had been ever since the impetus for victory in World War II seemed to emanate from the other side of the Pacific rather than from Great Britain. Architects and garden designers were thus not the only ones looking to the United States for inspiration. Much of the exposure to 1940s and 1950s American architecture came not just from the plethora of books and architectural journals emanating from the United States but also via the English journal, *The Architectural Review*. When little was being built in England, work in Scandinavia, or by Californian architects such as Richard Neutra, John Ekin Dinwiddie, Harwell Hamilton Harris, and others, was regularly published. The frequent publication of regionalized versions of modernism at a time when Australian architects were eager to find out more about this new architecture meant an exposure to the textural and carpenterlike simplicity of Sweden and California. This confirmed the local need to make do and to respond simply to the question of the postwar house. The Melbourne magazine *Architecture and Arts*, which began in July 1952, in name and style was a direct switch of the well-thumbed California-based journal *Arts and Architecture*. While Christopher Tunnard's *Gardens in the Modern Landscape* (1938) was well known in Australia, the articles and books of Californian landscape architects Thomas Church and Garrett Eckbo were equally well assimilated into local design culture. In 1948, Robin Boyd went so far as even to say that California and Australia were architectural twins.[42] When it came to designing, however, architects in Australia did not replicate American models. They could not do so because of dramatically inferior budgets and a limited availability of sophisticated building materials and technology. The results in almost every case were tempered with Australian expediency in construction technique, size, and lean gestures in terms of a designed landscape. For the most part architects generally designed the landscape and, if money was available, a consultant was brought in to advise on plant selection and little more. The case of an entire domestic garden design being commissioned was rare.

Hundreds of 1950s architect-designed houses in Australia indicate parity with the postwar architecture and landscape design of California. Ron Rayment's Mervyn Harry House,

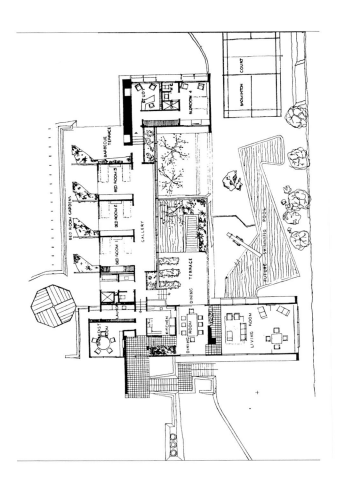

Figure 9–14.
Mervyn Harry House, Mount Coot-tha, Queensland, Australia, 1954–55. Ron Rayment, architect (for Lund Hutton Newell). Plan.
[*Architecture*, January–March 1955]

Mount Coot-tha, Brisbane (1954–55), was a typical example.[43] Its plan comprised zoned wings with similarly zoned barbecue terrace, dining terrace, and a free-form-shaped swimming pool [Figure 9–14]. The construction of the rubble rock wall and terrace at the heart of the C-plan was based on Frank Lloyd Wright's techniques for rock wall building at Taliesin West.[44] Garden and house were designed as coexisting platforms, or "shelves," terraced onto a steeply sloping site with a bedrock of shale not far beneath the surface. In addition to preserving much of the natural bush, several bold species of succulents, which grow to profusion in Brisbane, were planned for the garden. Trained as an architect and familiar with Garrett Eckbo's *Landscape for Living* (1950), Rayment was one of an emerging group of architects who were to later become prominent designers and leaders of an eventual Australian landscape architecture profession.[45]

Direct American influence could be seen in Douglas Snelling's Sydney houses. Snelling, who had been chief designer for Los Angeles architect Douglas Honnold before coming to Australia during the war to set up the U.S. Navy Clubs, imported the glamorous modern architectural vocabulary and landscaping style of Richard Neutra and the *Arts and Architecture* Case Study Houses.[46] Employing accomplished rendering techniques that effortlessly included a completed landscape with each house, these designs included a landscaping of biomorphic-shaped pools, lawns and rockeries of succulents, features intrinsic to the house conceived as elegant machine in the garden [Figure 9–15].[47] While Snelling brought direct American experience and expertise to Australia, the influence of the *Arts and Architecture* Case Study House program was pervasive and felt in all Australian states in the 1950s and well into the 1960s.[48]

The notion of landscape's directly informing the architecture under the mantle of Frank Lloyd Wright's concept of the "Natural House" also appeared. In 1953, Peter Muller, the first Australian architect to receive a Fulbright Traveling Scholarship (1949), returned home after graduating with a master of architecture degree from the University of Pennsylvania in 1950. One of his first houses was the Audette House (1953) built on the Griffin-designed estate at Castlecrag in Sydney.[49] Despite his American sojourn, Muller had not visited a single Wright building; this house indicates intimate knowledge of the organic architecture of Wright and his American followers. Massed with battered brick walls and puddled joints (i.e., with the mortar left to ooze out between the joints) and with floating fascias of wide

Figure 9–15.
House, Bellevue Hill, New South Wales, Australia, 1954–55. Douglas Snelling, architect.
[*Architecture and Arts*, September 1954]

varnished Australian bluegum boards, the large multilevel house was made up of overlapping and interlocking single-room-width wings. The surrounding landscaping was totally native. Unlike the Rose Seidler house, which gained its visual impact through contrast, this house seemed totally at one with the colors and forms of the landscape. Even more integral with its local landscape was Muller's design for his own house at Whale Beach (1955).[50] While Wright's forms and ideals are invoked, the Muller House also recalls a house in Belvedere, California (1950), designed by Jack Hillmer.[51] On a beautiful and sloping site, Muller retained as many natural features as possible. Tree branches made their way inside the living room and a fireplace was built into a giant rock [Figure 9–16]. With large expanses of glass and flat oversailing roofs, the only vertical elements were isolated brick piers. The Muller House, as Jennifer Taylor has observed, appeared to dissolve distinctions between shelter and site.[52]

Other solutions of the time were more idiosyncratic and local in inspiration. Robin Boyd's series of parasol houses was an attempt to resolve the opposites of the rational versus the organic by means of an intellectual approach with which to tackle the harsh Australian climate and, if desired, to provide a sheltered contained garden.[53] In his design for Pelican, the Ken and Prue Myer House, Daveys Bay, Mt. Eliza (1956), Boyd's parasol was a giant flat roof made up of a series of plywood box beams. Beneath was a free arrangement of spaces including enclosed sleeping blocks and a vast living room with doors that slid away. Landscape, lawn, and terrace were all included beneath the overhang. It was as if Boyd's conception of the ideal way to live in Australia was under a beach umbrella. At the request of the Myers, the garden was planted completely with Australian natives and designed by landscape consultant John Stevens. Boyd's Clemson House on a steep site in Kew (1959) followed a similar principle. A parasol formed by a scissor truss had the blocks of the house floating freely beneath and painted dark green to disappear. Ellis Stones was the landscape designer employed to place giant slate steps between a rational white post frame and the green house forms. He added Australian native groundcover plants, rock terracing, and a row of lemon-scented gums to match the white sticks of the parasol. The parasol could also roof an enclosure that mixed garden and the rooms of a house as platforms. The Date House, Molesworth Street, Kew (1955), was an early attempt by Boyd to achieve this ideal with internal spaces separated by tiny garden strips. The aim was to create the sense of living in a garden under one

Figure 9–16. [facing page]
Muller House, Whale Beach, New South Wales, Australia, 1955. Peter Muller, architect.
[Architecture in Australia, January–March 1956]

Figure 9–17.
Boyd House, South Yarra, Victoria, Australia, 1957. Grounds Romberg and Boyd, architects.
[Mark Strizic]

large single pitch roof. Boyd's second house for himself in South Yarra (1957) was a series of platforms underneath a draped parasol of steel cables, the center of which was open to the sky [Figure 9–17]. His Featherston House, Ivanhoe (1969), had an internal garden running underneath floating platforms and a translucent roof. In this latter set of houses, Boyd created a self-contained living / garden environment.[54] It was an attempt to harness the landscape in a new way, controlled within and wild without, keeping separate what Boyd regarded as two incompatible design palettes.

Each of the seven Australian states had its own specifically regional influences in terms of the promotion of landscape during the 1950s. Common to each state, however, was that these influences and ideas were not institutionalized or codified. That lack was something which the adoption of modernism had exposed and was to problematize. In New South Wales, the teachings of conservationist Myles Dunphy and painter Lloyd Rees within architectural schools were influential in bringing the special qualities of the Australian bush, its landforms and its flora, to the attention of young Sydney student architects.[55] In Sydney, there was also the example of the Griffins at Castlecrag and returning young scholars like Bruce Rickard, who had completed his master's degree in landscape architecture at the University of Pennsylvania and been in Ian McHarg's first class there. Rickard, like Muller, came back an advocate of Wright's organic approach to building in the landscape.[56] There were other returning NSW Government Scholarship winners such as Ken Woolley and Tony Moore, who brought back notions about the naturalness of materials espoused in differing ways by Aalto, the Smithsons, and Team 10.[57] But Sydney was a special case also because of its own landscape. The benefits of sloping sites, enviable harbor vistas, and bushy rock outcrops contributed to the dominance of landscape in Sydney's domestic architecture. The idea of an organic architecture seemed not only natural but inevitable.

In the other states, influences were less focused. In Brisbane, Karl Langer's teachings and articles on building in the tropics did much to focus attention on using the landscape for functional ends.[58] In Perth, John Oldham's appointment as landscape architect for the Public Works Department of Western Australia in 1956 was an unusually enlightened step, and his landscaping of low-income housing estates did much to improve government attitudes toward the necessary provision of landscaping in future multihousing projects.[59]

Figure 9–18.
Freiberg House, Kew, Victoria, Australia, 1960. Chancellor and Patrick, architects; Edna Walling, garden designer.
[Trisha Dixon and Jennie Churchill, *Gardens in Time: In the Footsteps of Edna Walling*]

In Victoria, the influences were different again. On the one hand, there was the strong horticultural basis for a garden design tradition, which emanated from Burnley graduates.[60] On the other hand, there was also already a tradition of building and amateur landscaping in the bush centered around artistic circles in Eltham and Warrandyte, outlying communities on the fringe of Melbourne. Dating from the early years of the century and developing most strongly from the late 1930s, artists and intellectuals made the bush their home. In the late 1940s, with shortages of materials, building mud-brick houses took on a new sense of expediency as well as cultivating rustic simplicity. Alistair Knox designed and built numerous houses from the late 1940s with landscaping designs from Ellis Stones and his limited but strong palette of bush garden designs, or from Gordon Ford who had trained with Stones in the early 1950s.[61] Indeed, it was Ellis Stones who bridged the decades and also different client groups. He had worked on and off for Walling since the 1930s and did landscaping for architects during the 1950s as well as for other landscape consultants such as John Stevens. Then in the 1960s and up to his death in 1975, Stones helped popularize the bush garden style in Victoria.[62]

The postwar house effected the greatest change with respect to relationships with the Australian landscape and inculcated a tradition of artless naturalism and resourceful use of the existing landscape. Perhaps best of all, Edna Walling, who herself had gone native sometime around 1950, in her 1948 design for Kildrummie, a country property at Holbrook, NSW, and her 1960 garden design for the Freiberg House, Kew, demonstrated the relaxed freedom that the 1950s released into the consideration of the designed landscape in Australia [Figure 9–18]. The benefits were a new understanding of the local when, by 1950, given advancements in propagation techniques, many garden designers were specifying greater quantities of native plants and exploring new planting combinations. A negative aspect, however, was the tendency among designers to favor a morality of landscape nationalism based on exclusive use of natives. For some, the reasons for this shift were emotional rather than carefully considered. Ignorant of the aesthetics and frequent short life span of the formal structure of native plants, few people realized the demanding requirements of managing a native garden.

LANDSCAPE AND THE PROJECTS OF POSTWAR MODERNISM

In the Australian city, the new dialogue with the local was not experienced. With rare exception, there was virtually no major piece of urban design within an Australian capital city between 1940 and 1955, the exception being Czech émigré architect Ernest Milston's prizewinning design for a commemorative forecourt (1950–53) to Melbourne's Shrine of Remembrance at the end of the Swanston Street axis in the King's Domain [Figure 9–19]. More like a giant piece of symbolic urban design with its huge paved cross in plan, its placement of flags on one side and an elevated sculptural tableau on the other, this project foreshadowed notions of a new urban landscaping that was not about the City Beautiful but instead involved bold formal statements in hard and soft landscaping and almost always included semi-abstract murals or sculpture.[63]

Before 1956, most Australian capital cities were dense conurbations based on 1920s street architecture, a metropolitanism of restricted building heights where the skyline was still the prerogative of the cathedral and the pinnacles of the commercial moderne. That picturesque skyline was soon to change at the horizon and also at ground level. The completion in 1958 of the freestanding skyscraper ICI House, Melbourne, signaled the dramatic changes that would be wrought on the postwar city. Designed by architects Bates Smart and McCutcheon in 1955, ICI House broke the city's 132-foot height limit, and, in recompense, an open and public landscaped plaza was provided at ground level [Figure 9–20]. While the building's model was the recently completed United Nations headquarters in New York and Skidmore Owings and Merrill's Lever House, New York (1952), the model for the garden had its sources in Latin America, in Roberto Burle Marx's landscape design for Niemeyer and Costa's Ministry of Education and Health, Rio de Janeiro (1937–43), a building well known to Melbourne architects.[64] Lever House also had its own plaza garden and a podium roof garden, but both were rigidly formal in layout. The postwar corporate skyscraper required a landscape architecture fully and instantaneously integrated with its new high-style image. With a radically new language for the urban building, there came a radically different garden — one of succulents, cacti, water, stones, and luxuriant curves — garden as public sculpture. It was to be permanent, low maintenance, and resistant to the vagaries of wind, shade, and pollution.

Figure 9–19. [above]
World War II Forecourt, Shrine of
Remembrance, Melbourne, Victoria,
Australia, 1950–53. Ernest Milston,
architect.
[Milston Collection, University of Melbourne
Archives]

Figure 9–20. [right]
ICI House, Melbourne, Victoria, Australia,
1955–58. John Stevens, Gerald Lewers, and
Bates Smart and McCutcheon.
[Wolfgang Sievers]

Figure 9–21. [facing page]
Garden for South British Insurance
Company, Melbourne, Victoria, Australia,
1961. John Stevens, Gerald Lewers, and
Bates Smart and McCutcheon.
[Wolfgang Sievers]

In Melbourne, the design of the ICI House garden, foyer, and plaza area was a collaboration between the architects led by Osborn McCutcheon and Alan Ralton, landscape consultant John Stevens, and sculptor Gerald Lewers.[65] With the building raised on pilotis to house a small parking lot beneath, the foyer and garden were to read as a single three-dimensional sculptural field. Rocks inserted into the lift core wall spouted water and appeared within the foyer amid Arp-like curves of floor tiling. All were part of an unashamedly stylish visual foil to the efficiency and scientism of the construction and hence, by implication, the corporation above. Garden/foyer as art and curtain wall as science — the two components of the skyscraper were complicit in their statement of the modern and explicit in their separation of roles.

Between 1956 and 1964, John Stevens, an acknowledged admirer of Burle Marx, completed numerous landscaping commissions in Melbourne for Bates Smart and McCutcheon and other architects, including the landscaping for the CRA Building, Collins Street (1960), and another sign of American influence, the Chadstone Shopping Centre (1960–61).[66] Stevens's garden for the South British Insurance Company, Melbourne (1961), was a treatment of a central city corner site with a sculptural arrangement of cacti, pool, blocks of Melbourne's local bluestone, tiled planes, and a wall-hung sculpture by Gerald Lewers, a sort of three-dimensional art installation [Figure 9–21].[67] The provision of this garden at ground level also meant that real estate return could be maximized — the more garden, the higher the building.

Corporatized postwar modernism also extended to the landscaping of the postwar factory.[68] The sculptural canopies and murals of Niemeyer and Burle Marx's biomorphic beds of agave and succulents were invoked to compensate for the suppression of symbolism, ornament, and formal variation in the architecture as well as to give a complete, permanent, and low-maintenance landscape. In South Australia, the ETA Foods and the Sisalkraft Factories (1957), both in suburban Adelaide, South Australia, by architects Lawson Cheesman Doley and Partners were typical examples where the architects took control of the landscape and provided a modernist overlay to not just the building but the entire site [Figure 9–22].[69] At other factories, rockeries and the obligatory organically formed porte-cochere presented dazzling fronts to coolly banal factory buildings behind. Embellishment coupled with function. The exotic garden inspired by Burle Marx took the place of ornament, as the architecture was

Figure 9–22.
Factory, warehouse, and offices for ETA
Foods, Adelaide, South Australia,
Australia, 1957. Lawson, Cheesman, Doley
and Partners, architects.
[*Cross Section* Archive, Architecture Library,
University of Melbourne]

Figure 9–23.
Garden for Lennon's Broadbeach Hotel,
Surfer's Paradise, Queensland, Australia,
1957. Karl Langer, architect.
[*Cross Section* Archive, Architecture Library,
University of Melbourne]

drained of its art and its artifice. The removal of symbolism, ornament, and formal variation in the architecture found its outlet and opposite in the foyer, the introduced artwork or — if the budget permitted it — in the garden. In other situations, landscape consultants were brought in to solve pragmatic problems. Australian natives were used as functional screening for massive refineries on windswept and barren sites where only Australian trees would survive without the importation of topsoil.[70] For the most part, the impetus for this architecture and this landscaping were again part of the irresistible embrace of America by Australian industry and commerce during Sir Robert Menzies' conservative Liberal government.

Enthusiasm for the apparent magic of America could also be observed in postwar tourism with the rise of the motel and the opening of resorts, accessible by airplane, on islands off Queensland such as Hayman Island and Dunk Island in the early 1950s. On Queensland's Gold Coast, the mood was positively buoyant as rapid development of its dunes swiftly created an antipodean Miami. The extraordinary stretch of perfect beach at Surfer's Paradise was the focus. The symbol of this location's rapid rise in popularity during the late 1950s was Karl Langer's Lennon's Broadbeach Hotel, Surfer's Paradise (1957).[71] The hotel garden was a direct blend of Burle Marx, Morris Lapidus, and Edward Durrell Stone's resort modernism with its recreational accouterments — the swimming pool terrace, the open air dance floor and bandstand, and the covered cabana — all contained by a sinusoidal brick screen wall [Figure 9–23]. Langer also relandscaped the space between the dunes and the foothills beyond as the region's first of many canal housing estates.[72] This time the model was Florida, providing the answers in form and in name, the Miami Keys and Rio Vista estates. Inverting Clarence Stein and Henry Wright's Radburn principle of vehicle-free green spaces forming a network of parks behind superblocks of low-rise housing, the green strips were replaced by waterways. There was no question as to the validity of such gestures in terms of ecology — this was optimistic faith in the future of tourism and in the ability of the land to sustain radical restructuring. In motel design, the same emulation of American prototypes was eagerly followed, the exception being Grounds Romberg and Boyd's Black Dolphin Motor Inn, Merimbula (1958), with its Australian native landscaping by Gordon Ford.[73] Here, unusually, existing trees were carefully respected and echoed by Boyd's use of bare log columns in the colonnades and balconies of the motel complex.

A different reason lay behind the landscaping of other recreational building types in the late 1950s. With Australia's dominance in the swimming pool at the 1956 Olympic Games, the design of municipal swimming pools received enthusiastic attention as training grounds for the nation's youth and locations for family recreation. Brisbane City Architect James Birrell's Centenary Pool (1958) employed exuberant Latin American modernist forms in building and landscaping, specifically Marcel Breuer and Eduardo Catalano's Ariston Restaurant, Mar del Plata, Argentina (c. 1948).[74] In Perth, in a more restrained fashion, Howlett and Bailey's kiosk for the Beatty Park Pool (1962) was encircled by giant curving screen walls to define protected seating areas.[75] In these and other projects of postwar modernism, the exotic cocktail of the Americas was imbibed with unashamed admiration. While Boyd, typically ambivalent and a repressed Americaphile himself, described in 1960 these influences as signs of "Austerica," austere versions of America whose "religion [was] glamour," they were ultimately liberating as European and English traditions could be happily purged.[76]

LANDSCAPE AND THE PROJECTS OF MODERNIZATION

Outside Australia's urbanized centers, there was a different purging, one of conscience, as Australians developed the land in dramatic ways as never before. Postwar confidence bred a mentality of development rationalism. As Prime Minister Menzies stated in 1958, "Our prime duty is to develop the country. Let us not worry too much about other things."[77] This development can be judged harshly four decades later, but the 1950s need to be understood in terms of recovery, growth, and willing ignorance. Radical changes were wrought on the natural landscape as it was engineered for modernity. The highway, dams for water supply and hydroelectricity generation, and mines and mining towns — the projects of modernization — replaced agriculture as the most powerful colonizing force within the landscape.

The construction of freeways and highways in the 1950s and early 1960s was one of the most graphic demonstrations of Australia's modernization. As new roads connected the major cities on the eastern seaboard and plans for new freeways inevitably were chosen to follow existing creek beds, Edna Walling, now in her fifties, produced in 1952 one of her most influential texts, *The Australian Roadside*, in which she argued eloquently for an ecological approach to planting alongside these new stretches of bitumen.[78] The lack of development of much of Australia's rural infrastructure meant that her peaceful and romantic photographs and ideas were persuasive. It was a carefully argued case for a responsible and resourceful naturalism, which Ellis Stones and others would champion in the 1970s as Melbourne's creeks were being commandeered for freeways as it and other Australian cities ballooned with new suburban growth.[79] In New South Wales, in the construction of the Newcastle Expressway (1962–67) between Sydney and Newcastle, landscape architect Peter Spooner (employed by the NSW Department of Main Roads) attempted to diminish the impact of the great, scarring cuttings through Sydney sandstone with careful chemical treatments of the stone to make it age prematurely as well as, in some sections, highlighting the dramatic sculptural possibilities of such development by leaving monumental pylons of stone [Figure 9–24]. In 1964, John Oldham set an important precedent with his inclusion of a pedestrian park beneath the Narrows Interchange in Perth. For the most part, however, such sensitivity was lacking. In the rapacious drive to modernize, careful landscape design was often last on the list, or omitted altogether.

In the Australian outback and in the Australian Alps, there were also signs of modernization. The Snowy Mountains and Kiewa Valley Hydro-Electric Power schemes of the 1940s were beacons of national pride. Massive projects involving new townships and numbers of reservoirs and power stations, they were Australian equivalents of the Tennessee Valley Authority scheme. Giant concrete dam walls and huge reservoirs filled bush valleys. In new townships such as Mt. Beauty, Eildon, and Jindabyne, avenues of prunus and suburban plots planted with exotics and garden city layouts were comforting and safe, apparently "normal" environments, havens from battling the wilderness. Parks and barbecue areas adjacent to artificial lakes were planted with poplars, ash, and elms to introduce a new and picturesque counterpoint to the virgin bush. They were designed fundamentally to cater to tourist traffic, citysiders who had come to marvel at scientific modernity's triumph over the landscape. In Western Australia, John Oldham's attempts at sympathetically landscaping such vast projects were more thoughtful. In 1961, at the Serpentine Dam, built to serve as water supply to Perth, Oldham planned for an expected peak attendance of fifteen hundred cars per day. Using many West Australian trees and experimenting in transplanting dozens of large grass trees (*Xanthorrhoea australis*) and placing carefully grouped specimens of native trees labeled for

Figure 9–24.
Newcastle Expressway, New South Wales, Australia, 1962–67. Peter Spooner, landscape architect.
[New South Wales: Department of Main Roads, Annual Report]

ease of identification, Oldham's terracing, which followed the existing contours, was designed to provide walks among a miniature Australian botanical garden.[80] At the spillway, he introduced a decorative fountain with a giant boulder of local granite set within a pool in which, in a faintly corny note, there were the compass points of the meridian [Figure 9–25]. And in one of the earliest attempts in landscape with reference to indigenous culture, Oldham inserted a large formal parterre adjacent to the restaurant. This garden used rocks and small plants in the shape of a mythical totemic snake, linked by the local aboriginals with fertility, rain, and an assured water supply.[81] While Oldham's attempts may seem tokenistic, this was nevertheless one of the earliest attempts to translate indigenous culture into landscape design.

On a similar scale, out in the far reaches of Australia, the mining of vast tracts of land rich with iron ore, bauxite, and uranium meant that a new industrial landscape appeared in locations like Rum Jungle, Broken Hill, and Weipa, and on the coast where ore was refined in locations like Newcastle, Bell Bay, and Kwinana. One result of these developments was the inevitable scarring of the landscape. The other was the introduced landscaping of mining towns. Milston and Fulton's Radburn-inspired planning of Mary Kathleen (1956) brought an idealized and supernormal suburbanism to the outback.[82] In the late 1940s, at Mount Kembla, Edna Walling made much of the function of mining in her landscaping of employee housing designed by Marcus and Alison Norris, directing giant boulders to be placed around the house sites.[83] These were the better attempts to ameliorate the rate of change in the natural landscape. Designed landscape in these remote locations provided amenity and relief from blistering heat as well as, in the interests of the mining corporation, a visually apparent social equilibrium.

By the end of the 1950s, the voracious development of Australia's cities and its far-flung industrial sites, while exciting and financially rewarding, had begun to raise concerns. During the late 1950s, there had been quiet murmurings of discontent by Peter Spooner, Milo Dunphy, and Bruce Rickard concerning the state of the designed landscape.[84] In March 1960, *Architecture in Australia* devoted its entire issue to conservation; later that year, Boyd's *The Australian Ugliness* (1960) became a seminal diatribe nationwide, read by designers, schoolchildren, and politicians, and in which Boyd railed against the visual desecration of Australian cities; the national fetish for arboraphobia; and, in design terms, what he described as shallow "Featurism."[85] Boyd's book was inspired

Figure 9–25.
Serpentine Dam, Western Australia, Australia, 1961. John Oldham, landscape architect. Fountain court at spillway.
[*The Architect* (Perth), March 1962]

Figure 9–26. [*facing page, top*]
Grounds House, Toorak, Victoria, Australia, 1953. Roy Grounds, architect. Plan.
[*Architecture and Arts*, October 1954]

Figure 9–27. [*facing page, bottom*]
Grounds House, Toorak, Victoria, Australia, 1953. Roy Grounds, architect. Courtyard.
[*Architecture and Arts*, October 1954]

by Englishman Ian Nairn's plea for better roadside development and for ridding English cities of visual pollution in *Outrage* (1955), and it predated Peter Blake's very similar book of four years later, *God's Own Junkyard: The Planned Deterioration of America's Landscape*.[86] But Milo Dunphy criticized Boyd for his lack of understanding of the Australian bush, in particular his description of the Australian landscape as "the monotony, the infinite sameness of the eucalyptus bush, the awe-inspiring plainness of it all [which] encourages the thought of setting up features."[87] Even Boyd, it appeared, was typical of most Australians who should have known better.

LANDSCAPE AND THE PROBLEM OF THEORY

Part of the limitations of the two decades after 1940 was that no one attempted to codify or theorize landscape designs of the period. This was not part of any local agenda; these were decades of production, not of reflection. There was, however, one less well-articulated theme being explored during the 1950s. Australia's proximity to Asia had never been completely explored, either intellectually or aesthetically. In the 1920s, Australian architect Hardy Wilson (1888–1955) attempted to resolve the nation's mixed cultural and geographical location in an idealized blending of the best of Eastern and Western cultures. Importantly, indigenous conceptions of the landscape formed no part of these suppositions, which had at their basis notions of fundamental purities and absolutes. With a series of books, personally illustrated and authored by him, Wilson set out strong, if at times racially offensive, arguments for Australia being perfectly situated to achieve a synthesis of Eastern and Western ideas in architecture and in landscape design.[88] Between 1924 and 1925, he proposed a series of three Chinese-Australian houses and gardens at Pymble, NSW, one for himself, one for his partner, John Berry, and one for Professor E. G. Waterhouse, who was promoting the camellia in Australia and who had his first house, Eryledene (1913), designed by Wilson.[89] Wilson had designed for Eryldene's exquisite garden a number of intriguing garden structures of hybrid architectural pedigree such as a neo-Georgian pigeon coop with a golden tympanum and a Chinese temple tennis pavilion. At Pymble, Wilson's design for himself was a symmetrical Chinese-Grecian house, which he called Celestion. Its garden had perimeter beds of red China roses in front of a stone rainwater channel and in the courtyard at its very center, an erythrina, or coral tree, with its clusters of blood red flowers, was flanked by oleanders and Madonna grandifloras. The scheme for the three houses never went

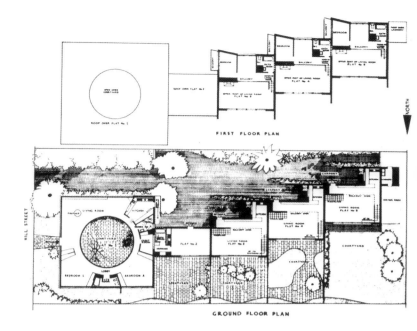

FIRST FLOOR PLAN

GROUND FLOOR PLAN

263

ahead, but Wilson's naïve idealism found its echo in the 1950s. In 1953, architect Roy Grounds designed a house for himself and his wife in Hill Street, Toorak. The plan of the house was a perfect square with a circular courtyard at its center. Built to fit four flats at the rear of the site, the house was located close to the street like an urban townhouse. By concealing the circular courtyard and providing perimeter windows only at eaves level, Grounds created a totally inward-looking composition, almost Japanese in its introspective retreat from the outside world [Figure 9–26]. The symmetry and hovering roof recall Frank Lloyd Wright's Winslow House and Palladio's ideal villas, but also Chinese courtyard houses. Grounds also designed the landscaping. From the street, an existing mature elm provided dramatic contrast to the delicacy of a Japanese maple near the front door. In the courtyard, a persimmon tree and a copse of black bamboo provided yet more Oriental ambience [Figure 9–27]. Down the side, Grounds planted coastal ti-trees as an Australian sculptural contribution and then, along the fence, a series of olive trees to form a screen.

In later buildings, Grounds continued to pursue this East/West theme, culminating in his design for the National Gallery of Victoria (1959–68), a giant, fortified, Chinese gateway to Melbourne's colonial grid plan. Inside were three perfectly square courtyards, one of which was planted with bamboos and paved in loose bluestone pebbles to complement the gallery's adjacent and prestigious Oriental collection. In the central sculpture court there was another carefully placed persimmon tree like the one in his own home. Grounds never wrote about his designs, but it appears that in his drawing together of eclectic sources for both architecture and landscape design, the spirit of Hardy Wilson's idea of a new Australian design ethos blending East and West might be possible, or at the very least explored for its formal and symbolic potential. His innocent gestures toward a hybrid landscape design idiom also hint at the possible transcendence of the artless naturalism of the bush garden.

Explorations of hybrid design by others were similarly furtive, intuitive interpretations of Japanese garden style, hybrid gardens that included the twisting trunk of a eucalyptus, river pebbles, native grasses, and perhaps a large stone perceptively placed by Ellis Stones. These tended to be picturesque vignettes at best. The artless naturalism of the Australian bush and its (albeit limited) visual affinity with

the artificial naturalism of the Japanese garden were conflated as one.

SHIFTING THE GROUNDS

By 1960 there were grounds for concern in Australian landscape design circles. For one, there was no Australian landscape architecture profession, despite the inclusion of landscape design subjects within architecture and town planning degrees; it would not be until 1966 that an institute of landscape architects was finally formed. Ironically, the location where matters would be brought to a head was the place where Australia had its best example of the bones of a nationally significant landscape architecture—in its own capital. In the 1960s Canberra became the place to start again, the richest venue for discussion of an Australian landscape design culture.[90] That in itself is another story.

The decades between 1940 and 1960 experienced extraordinary development, much of it insensitive, much of it liberating design from the precious herbaceous border and the military avenue of honor. The circumstances of war and the notion of making do in the landscape deterred a strong designed landscape ethos. There has since been realization of the scope and overwhelming presence of the indigenous landscape, but a subsequent humility on a broad scale has limited the formal and aesthetic possibilities within the designed landscape. While indigenous understandings of the landscape were not widespread, in the 1950s, a fortuitous coincidence of circumstance engendered at once a responsible ethos of ecology and one of antidesign. There were also other complicating factors. Australian trees and shrubs lack guaranteed structure and require constant maintenance, contradicting purist and nationalistic overtones to landscape design which have tended to override the need for intervention, assimilation, and difference. An ethos of leaving things alone does not work in the Australian city. The tension between the indigenous, the colonial, and the postcolonial still remains and should still be visible, not erased. The designed landscape therefore has yet to find both a coherent voice in Australia and a critical history that does not make hagiography its purpose. The decades of experiment now need a discourse that the period did not have.

The untutored stones, the rocks of Australia, seem to cross time. They are the country's great architectural and landscape monuments. But they avoid the question of design. Perhaps though it is still to rocks that one has to look, to critically analyze the work of feted designers such as Ellis Stones, the rockeries of Jocelyn Brown, the drystone walls of Walling and Sorensen, in order to find a meaningful symbology that crosses into the realm of the Aboriginal, the stones of Japan and China, the abstract realms of modernism and perhaps most important of all, the great stone piles of buildings and hill that were to be the Griffins' Canberra. Allegiances need shifting again. They also need speculation and a little self-irony. To look at the period 1940 to 1960 in Australia is to include Ellis Stones's charming and coy placement of Amanda (1938) on a simple rock for Sir Russell Grimwade at Miegunyah in Toorak and contrast it with the great manmade rock of Jørn Utzon's 1963 Sydney Opera House with its plateau-like base [Figure 9–28]. One thing is certain: they both seem to say Australia.

Figure 9–28.
Sydney Opera House, Sydney, New South Wales, Australia, 1957–73. Jørn Utzon, architect. Mid-construction, 1963.
[*L'Architecture d'aujourd'hui*, February 1993]

NOTES

1. (Sir) Mark Oliphant, nuclear physicist; Olympic Games, Melbourne, 1956; (Sir) Arthur Stephenson, RIBA Gold Medalist, 1954, the 1953 recipient had been Le Corbusier; (Sir) Macfarlane Burnet, Nobel Prize in Physiology and Medicine, 1960; (Dame) Joan Sutherland, opera singer, Covent Garden debut, 1952, by 1960 she is hailed as La Stupenda; Danish architect Jørn Utzon, architect for the Sydney Opera House, 1957. Donald Horne, *The Lucky Country: Australia in the Sixties* (Harmondsworth, Middlesex: Penguin, 1964).

2. A. D. Hope, Australia (1930), from *A. D. Hope, Collected Poems, 1930–1970* (Melbourne: Angus and Robertson, 1972).

3. Catherine Howett, "Modernism and American Landscape Architecture," in Marc Treib (ed.), *Modern Landscape Architecture: A Critical Review* (Cambridge: MIT Press, 1993), p. 32.

4. Treib, "Axioms for a Modern Landscape Architecture," in *Modern Landscape Architecture*, pp. 53–64. These axioms include denial of historical styles; concern for space rather than pattern; landscapes for people; destruction of the axis; plants as botanical entities and sculpture; integration of house and garden.

5. Important works include Anne Latreille, *The Natural Garden: Ellis Stones—His Life and Work* (Ringwood: Viking O'Neill, 1990); Peter Cuffley, *Australian Houses of the Forties and Fifties* (Knoxfield: Five Mile Press, 1993); Jane Shepherd and Simone Slee, "Pruning Back: The Australian Garden in Transition," *1956: Melbourne, Modernity and the XVI Olympiad* (Melbourne: Museum of Modern Art at Heide, 1996), pp. 80–89.

6. David Yencken, "The View from Within and the View from Without: Australian Landscape Research," *Landscape Review* 1995, no. 1, pp. 40–53.

7. Peter Watts, *Edna Walling and Her Gardens* (Balmain, NSW: Florilegium, 1991), pp. 57–74. Of architectural interest to Walling was Lewis Mumford's *The Culture of Cities* (1938) and *Sticks and Stones* (1925), and more particularly the work of American architect Royal Barry Wills. See Walling, *Cottage and Garden in Australia* (Melbourne: Oxford University Press, 1947), pp. 2–3, 33, and 54, where she quotes directly from Wills's *Better Homes for Budgeteers* (1946). It is likely that Wills's designs influenced Walling's house designs at Bickleigh Vale,

266

Mooroolbark, during the 1940s. In this book, Walling also indicates her knowledge of Edith A. Roberts and Elsa Rehmann, *American Plants for American Gardens* (New York: Macmillan, 1929).

8. Watts, *Edna Walling and Her Gardens*, pp. 85–87.

9. Edna Walling, *Gardens in Australia: Their Design and Care* (Melbourne: Oxford University Press, 1943), p. 20; and Trisha Dixon and Jennie Churchill, *Gardens in Time: In the Footsteps of Edna Walling* (North Ryde, NSW: Angus and Robertson, 1988), p. 70.

10. This tradition goes back to the adoption of various architectural styles on the basis on their suitability to Australian conditions such as Joseph Reed's use of Lombardic Romanesque in Melbourne residences and churches in the nineteenth century; Leslie Wilkinson's use of Andalusian models for houses in 1920s Sydney as part of a Mediterranean Revival; and Marshall Clifton's interpretations in Perth of Los Angeles's Spanish Colonial Revival houses.

11. Helen Proudfoot, *Gardens in Bloom: Jocelyn Brown and Her Sydney Gardens of the Thirties and Forties* (Kenthurst: Kangaroo Press, 1989), pp. 19–21. Proudfoot uses Conrad Hamann's discussion of the architectural culture of the 1920s and 1930s to form a context for the placement of Jocelyn Brown's garden designs. See Conrad Hamann, "Paths of Beauty: The Afterlife of Australian Colonial Architecture," pt. 1, *Transition*, no. 26, spring 1988, pp. 27–44.

12. Paul Fox, "The Simla of the South," *Australian Garden History* (Journal of the Australian Garden History Society), 6, no. 4, 1995, pp. 10–14.

13. Latreille, *The Natural Garden*, pp. 78–88.

14. Anne-Marie Willis, "Nation as Landscape," in *Illusions of Identity: The Art of Nation* (Sydney: Hale and Iremonger, 1993), pp. 61–92.

15. *Sunlight and Gums, Adelaide*, by Harold Cazneaux, in Elynne Mitchell, *Australian Treescapes* (Sydney: Ure Smith, 1950), pp. 42–43.

16. *Cazneaux: Photographs by Harold Cazneaux 1878–1953* (Canberra: National Library of Australia, 1978), p. 75; *Harold Cazneaux Photographs*, exhibition catalogue (Sydney: Historic Houses Trust of New South Wales and National Library of Australia, 1994), p. 7.

17. Max Dupain, *Max Dupain's Australian Landscapes* (Ringwood, Victoria: Viking, 1988), p. 103.

18. Ibid., pp. 28, 66.

19. The pool was initially published in *Australian Home Beautiful*, April 1941. Another description of the pool can be found in Walling, *Gardens of Australia*, pp. 94–97.

20. Latreille, *The Natural Garden*, pp. 53–58.

21. Thomas Church, "A Free-Form Pool Is At Home in This Natural Setting," in *Gardens are for People* (1955; New York: McGraw-Hill, 1983), pp. 227–28.

22. Edna Walling moved over to virtually an entirely Australian native repertoire around 1950. During the 1960s and 1970s, the Australian bush garden was popularized especially by garden designers Ellis Stones and Gordon Ford in Victoria, and in New South Wales by Betty Maloney and Jean Walker's books *Designing Australian Bush Gardens* (Melbourne: Horwitz, 1966), and *More About Bush Gardens* (Belrose: Mulavon, 1967).

23. Richard Ratcliffe, *Australia's Master Gardener: Paul Sorensen and His Gardens* (Kenthurst: Kangaroo Press, 1990), pp. 30, 42–43.

24. "La Mabeillion—Modern by Circumstance," *Australian Home Beautiful*, January 1934, p. 25.

25. Philip Goad, "The Modern House in Melbourne, 1945–1975" (Ph.D. diss., University of Melbourne, 1992), pp. 1/30–32.

26. Robin Boyd, *Victorian Modern* (Melbourne: Victorian Architecture Students Society, 1947), p. 40; the Ramsay House reveals Grounds's admiration for William Wurster's restrained modernism in the selection of materials and forms, and in its planning. The house has a so-called kitchen cave, a Wurster space that comprises a kitchen-living-dining room that opens up to an outdoor terrace/living space. See Philip Goad, "This Is Not a Type: Robin Boyd's 'Victorian Type' and the Expression of the Modern House c. 1933–1942," *Architecture Australia*, June 1988, pp. 56–64.

27. For example, John D. Moore, *Home Again! Domestic Architecture for the Normal Australian* (Sydney: Ure Smith, 1944); Walter Bunning, *Homes in the Sun* (Sydney: W. J.

Nesbitt, 1945); Kenneth McConnel, *Planning the Australian Homestead* (Sydney: Ure Smith, 1947); and Eve Gye (ed.), *Home Plans* (Sydney: Australian Women's Weekly, c. 1945). Entries for *The Sun*'s postwar home competition were published as a book of designs. See *The Sun Postwar Homes Competition* (Melbourne: Sun News Pictorial, 1946).

28. Proudfoot, *Gardens in Bloom*, p. 19.

29. Karl Langer, *Sub-Tropical Housing* (Brisbane: Faculty of Engineering, University of Queensland, 1944), plate 2.

30. An important article detailing the contributions of many of these women is Jane Shepherd, "Early Women Landscape Architects: Olive Mellor and Emily Gibson," *Transition*, Winter 1988, pp. 61–63.

31. Jeremy Pike, "The Development of the Landscape Architecture Profession in Australia," *Landscape Australia*, no. 2, 1979, pp. 85–87; Jeremy Pike, "Landscape Architecture Education in Australia," *Landscape Australia*, no. 3, 1980, pp. 199–206.

32. Emily Gibson wrote for *The Argus*, 1922–46, and Olive Mellor was a constant contributor to *Australian Home Beautiful* during the 1940s and 1950s. For further reading see Cuffley, *Australian Houses of the Forties and Fifties*, pp. 142–46.

33. Elynne Mitchell, *Australian Treescapes* (Sydney: Ure Smith, 1950). I am grateful to Christopher Vernon for bringing this book to my attention.

34. Boyd, *Victorian Modern*, pp. 23, 63.

35. James Weirick, "Walter Burley Griffin, Landscape Architect: The Ideas He Brought to Australia," *Landscape Australia*, no. 3, 1988, pp. 241–46, 255–56.

36. For example, the collaged image of the P. B. Hart House, Wahroonga, NSW, 1953, in *Architecture and Arts*, January 1954, p. 24, and when built, the image of the W. R. Hamill House, Killara, NSW, 1948–49, in *Architecture and Arts*, February 1954, p. 21.

37. Paul Rudolph, "Regionalism in Architecture," *Perspecta*, no. 4, 1957, p. 13.

38. J. M. Freeland, *Architecture in Australia: A History* (Melbourne: Cheshire, 1981), p. 273.

39. Robin Boyd, *The Australian Ugliness* (Melbourne: Melbourne University Press, 1960), pp. 74–100.

40. For a discussion of the large-small house of the postwar years, see Sally Woodbridge, *Bay Area Houses* (New York: Oxford University Press, 1976), pp. 155–227.

41. For example, entries by architects Parry and Paxton and by S. C. G. McConnel. See "Small Homes Competition," *Architecture and Arts*, January 1954, pp. 25–37.

42. Robin Boyd, "California and Victoria: Architectural Twins," *The Age*, 9 October 1948.

43. "A Sub-Tropical House at Mt. Coot-tha Range, Queensland," *Architecture and Arts*, May 1954, pp. 24–29; "House at Mt. Coot-tha Range, Queensland, for Mervyn Harry, Esq.," *Architecture*, January–March 1955, p. 7. Ron Rayment is listed as chief assistant within the architectural firm of Ford Hutton Newell.

44. Interview with Ron Rayment, 24 January 1997.

45. Interview with Ron Rayment, 24 January 1997. Rayment, after working for a series of architects during the 1950s and 1960s, and after studying biology under controversial conservationist John Salmon at Victoria University of Wellington, New Zealand, in 1961, turned his hand more to landscape design. While working for James Earle and Associates (later Earle Shaw and Partners), Rayment designed much of the initial landscaping along the South Eastern Freeway in Melbourne. In 1967 he became the first graduate in landscape design in Victoria, gaining the degree from the Royal Melbourne Institute of Technology. At the end of 1969, RMIT approached Rayment to run its landscape program, which he did from 1970 until 1976. In 1970, he joined briefly in partnership with Ellis Stones. Their major work was the award-winning South Lawns, University of Melbourne (1971–72). Rayment continued in private landscape design practice until 1985.

46. Biographical notes on Douglas Snelling, *Architecture and Arts*, September 1954, p. 19. Snelling, born in London in 1916, had studied architecture while working in various movie studios in their design departments, before working in a number of architects' offices in Los Angeles and later becoming chief designer within Douglas Honnold's Beverly Hills office.

47. For example, Snelling's "Four Courters House," St. Ives, NSW, c. 1954, and Bellevue Hill House, Sydney, 1954–55. See *Architecture and Arts*, September 1954, pp. 22–29.

48. Architects whose work gained sustenance from the Case Study Program included, among others in Victoria, Guilford Bell, Neil Clerehan, Hipwell Weight & Mason, Bernard Joyce, and David McGlashan; in New South Wales, W. E. Lucas, Bryce Mortlock, and in the 1960s, Glenn Murcutt; in Perth, Jeffrey Howlett and Geoffrey Summerhayes.

49. "At Castlecrag," *Architecture in Australia*, July–September 1955, pp. 76–77. The Audette House in its form and detail recalls characteristics of Wright's Taliesin West, 1938–59, and the Rose and Gertrude Pauson House, Phoenix, Arizona, 1938–41.

50. "House at Whale Beach, NSW," *Architecture in Australia*, January–March 1956, pp. 6–9; "Whale Beach House and Office," *Architecture and Arts*, December 1955, pp. 21–23.

51. "Ebony, Granite, Steel and Skill," *Architectural Forum*, April 1951, pp. 110–17.

52. Jennifer Taylor, *An Australian Identity: Houses for Sydney, 1953–63* (Sydney: Department of Architecture, University of Sydney, 1972), pp. 26–28.

53. Philip Goad, "New Eclecticism: Ethic and Aesthetic: Robin Boyd and the Design of the House, 1959–1971," *Transition*, no. 38, September 1992, pp. 160–85.

54. It was almost as if Boyd was trying to rationalize the organic fantasies of Bruce Goff's Bavinger House and to realize simply Buckminster Fuller's fantasies of an environmentally controlled paradise within a geodesic dome. Other Boyd parasol houses include the Holford House, Ivanhoe (1955–56), and McClune House, Frankston (1965).

55. Interview with Graham Brawn, 5 February 1997; Jennifer Taylor, *Australian Architecture Since 1960* (Sydney: Law Book Co., 1986), p. 35.

56. Telephone conversation with Bruce Rickard, 31 January 1997; Taylor, *Australian Architecture Since 1960*, pp. 36–37.

57. Interview with Graham Brawn, 5 February 1997; Taylor, *Australian Architecture Since 1960*, pp. 38–39.

58. Ian Sinnamon, "An Educated Eye: Karl Langer in Australia," *Landscape Australia*, no. 1, 1985, February 1985, pp. 48–56.

59. Telephone conversation with John Oldham, 27 January 1997; "Landscaping of Wandana Flats, Subiaco," *The Architect* (Perth), March 1957, pp. 29–31. John Oldham, "Early Landscape Architecture in Western Australia," *Landscape Australia*, no. 2, 1985, pp. 102–6; no. 3, 1985, pp. 219–21.

60. Edna Walling, Emily Gibson, Mervyn Davis, John Stevens, and Beryl Mann (who worked within Mockridge Stahle and Mitchell's office for twenty-eight years) were the major Melbourne practitioners who had graduated from Burnley.

61. Latreille, *The Natural Garden*, pp. 91–95, 101–3.

62. For a complete study on Ellis Stones, See Latreille, *The Natural Garden*.

63. Photographs of 1939–45 Commemorative Forecourt, Shrine of Remembrance, in Milston Collection, University of Melbourne Archives.

64. The Crown Zellerbach Building, San Francisco (designed by the San Francisco office of Skidmore Owings and Merrill in association with Hertska & Knowles) was completed in 1959 and is an exact contemporary of Melbourne's ICI House.

65. "ICI House, Melbourne," *Architecture in Australia*, September 1959, pp. 80–83.

66. John Stevens's commissions from Bates Smart & McCutcheon began with Wilson Hall, University of Melbourne (1956); and thereafter ICI House, East Melbourne (1955–59); ICIANZ Factory, Deer Park (1958); Bates Smart & McCutcheon offices, St. Kilda Road, Melbourne (1958); Monash University (1960–64); South British Insurance Building, Queen and Bourke Streets, Melbourne (1961); Prudential Building, Queen and Bourke Streets, Melbourne (1959–60); and in the early 1960s, much of the first landscaping at Monash University, Clayton. These commissions were collaborations rather than authored solely by Stevens, a Burnley graduate, or the architects. With the lack of a formalized profession of landscape architecture, this was successful collaboration between horticultural and architectural experts to produce a convincing modern landscape in an entirely new and different language for the center of old-fashioned Melbourne. Architects for the CRA Building, 95 Collins Street, Melbourne, were Bernard Evans and Partners. See "Melbourne's Newest Skyscraper," *Architecture and Arts*, April 1962, pp. 33–35. Architects for Chadstone Shopping Centre were Tompkins Shaw and Evans. See *Architecture in Australia*, December 1961, pp. 90–91.

67. "Melbourne Offices," *Architecture in Australia*, March 1962, pp. 104–7; "New Insurance Building in Melbourne," *Architecture and Arts*, February 1962, pp. 46–47.

68. A study of American responses to the corporate factory or office park can be found in Peter Rowe, *Making a Middle Landscape* (Cambridge, Mass.: MIT Press, 1991), pp. 149–81.

69. "Factory Warehouse and Offices, Adelaide, S.A. for Sisalkraft Distributors (S.A.) Pty. Ltd.," *Architecture in Australia*, April–June 1957, pp. 52–53.

70. For example, Emily Gibson's landscaping at the Vacuum Oil Factory, Altona (1953); Gibson and John Stevens's landscaping for the housing and refinery for Shell at Corio, Victoria (1955); and Stevens's landscaping for Gibson-Kelite Chemical Factory, Cheltenham (1956).

71. "Hotel at Broadbeach, Queensland," *Architecture in Australia*, December 1957, pp. 49–52; *Architecture in Australia*, January–March 1959, p. 63; *Cross Section* Archive, Architecture Library, University of Melbourne.

72. Karl Langer, "Development of Canal Estates on the Gold Coast," *Architecture in Australia*, January–March 1959, pp. 66–67.

73. "Black Dolphin Motor Inn, Merimbula, NSW," *Architecture in Australia*, December 1961, pp. 98–101.

74. Architectural Record, *Motels, Hotels, Restaurants and Bars* (New York: Dodge, 1953), pp. 135–37.

75. "Kiosk and Residence for Perth City Council," *Architecture Australia*, December 1963.

76. "Austerica," *Age*, 21 September 1957.

77. Robert Menzies in his address at the official opening of the new uranium township of Mary Kathleen in northern Queensland, "Our North's an Eye Opener," *Herald*, 28 June 1958.

78. Edna Walling, *The Australian Roadside* (Melbourne: Oxford University Press, 1952).

79. Latreille, *The Natural Garden*, pp. 245–46.

268

80. Another common name for the austral grass tree is the blackboy. Included in the landscaping at the Serpentine Dam were Mallee eucalypti, grevillea, hakea, melaleuca, and wattles.

81. "Serpentine Dam," *The Architect* (Perth), March 1962, pp. 30–34.

82. Philip Goad, "Mary Kathleen and Weipa: Two Model Mining Towns for Post-War Australia," *Transition*, nos. 49–50, 1996, pp. 42–59.

83. Watts, *Edna Walling and Her Gardens*, p. 42.

84. Milo Dunphy, "Up the Garden Path," *Architecture in Australia*, January–March 1956, pp. 6–9; Peter Spooner, "Landscape Versus Architecture," *Architecture in Australia*, January–March 1958, pp. 68–69, 97; Milo Dunphy, "From Space to Place," *Architecture in Australia*, April–June 1958, pp. 62–63, 72, in a plea for a more coordinated approach to landscape with specific reference to church architecture; Bruce Rickard, "Landscaping," *Architecture in Australia*, December 1959, pp. 69–72.

85. Robin Boyd, *The Australian Ugliness* (Melbourne: Melbourne University Press, 1960).

86. Ian Nairn, *Outrage* (London: Architectural Press, 1955). This was a reprint of the special "Outrage" issue of *Architectural Review*, June 1955. Peter Blake, *God's Own Junkyard: The Planned Deterioration of America's Landscape* (New York: Holt, Rinehart and Winston, 1964).

87. Robin Boyd quoted in Milo Dunphy, review of Robin Boyd, *The Australian Ugliness* (1960), in *Architecture in Australia*, March 1961, p. 102.

88. Hardy Wilson authored the following books: *The Dawn of a New Civilization* (Covent Garden, London: Cecil Palmer, 1929); *Yin-Yang* (Flowerdale, Tasmania: H. Wilson, 1934); *Collapse of Civilization* (Kew: H. Wilson, 1936); *Grecian and Chinese Architecture* (Melbourne: H. Wilson, 1937); *Eucalyptus* (Wandin: H. Wilson, 1941); *Solution to Jewish Problem* (Wandin: H. Wilson, 1941); *Instinct* (Melbourne: Ruskin Press, 1945); and *Atomic Civilization* (Kew: H. Wilson, 1949).

89. John Pearman, "Houses He Built," in *William Hardy Wilson: A Twentieth-Century Colonial, 1881–1955* (Sydney: National Trust of Australia [New South Wales], 1980), pp. 31–32.

90. The December 1959 issue of *Architecture in Australia* was devoted entirely to Canberra with attention given to architecture, planning, and landscape.

PARIS, 1937. As the third decade of the twentieth century inches toward its closure, a world's fair opens in the City of Light. Avoiding direct eye contact with the gathering clouds of war and shunning any confrontation with Japan's militaristic imperialism on the Asian mainland, the Western nations instead proffer the familiar themes of commerce and culture. Japan's national pavilion, designed by Junzo Sakakura (1901–69), is unabashedly modern. A regular grid of steel columns structures the free development of the plan, elevates its principal exposition spaces above the ground, and graces the building with an elegant lightness. The ramp—a hallmark of French modernism at the time—invites visitors to witness displays of artworks and industry or to taste the green tea of Japan while looking outward to the park [Figure 10–1].

An alumnus of Le Corbusier's atelier in Paris, Sakakura explores modernist themes of space and technology: little of the building's exterior, for example, distinguishes it from the pavilion of Spain, by José Luis Sert.[1] The modern myth holds sway—if ever more tenuously, if inflected by the political underpinnings of their programs—in both structures. Sakakura injects few traditional Japanese touches in the landscape development on the pavilion's perimeter.[2] The existing trees are spared and will remain; their naturalistic pattern serves as a foil for the constructed box and recalls the Parisian park as much as it recalls the traditional garden of Japan [Figure 10–2]. Only perhaps in a terrace for drinking tea, in the decorative arts on view, in the color scheme, or in the use and placement of the steppingstones can one read the endeavor as Japanese.[3] These appear essentially as signs of Asian origins, and thus the experience of a Japanese garden succumbs to a reading that relies on signals or markers. National identity as the determinant of architecture and landscape falls at the hands of modernity and international outlook; the feeling is that of a building benignly occupying its site rather than an architectural expression resolutely Japanese, despite all signs to the contrary.

NEW YORK, 1939. Two years later, in what would be the world's last optimistic view of technology and the future, the Japanese exposition committee drastically changes its tune [Figure 10–3]. Now the buildings shun any vestige of modernity and internationalism and return instead to structures derived from the Ise shrines, the *ur-arkitektur* of Japan.[4] The decorative devices on the buildings' gables—reflecting the imperial chrysanthemum—are as potent as a corporate

10.   MARC TREIB

Converging Arcs on a Sphere: Renewing Japanese Landscape Design

Figure 10–1. [*left, above*]
Japanese Pavilion, World's Fair, Paris, France, 1937. Junzo Sakakura.
[*Gendai Kentiku*]

Figure 10–2. [*left, bottom*]
Japanese Pavilion, World's Fair, Paris, France, 1937. Junzo Sakakura.
The surrounding landscape is less a garden than terrain minimally converted from existing park space.
[*Gendai Kentiku*]

Figure 10–3. [*below*]
Japanese Pavilion, World's Fair, New York, 1939. Y. Uchida, Yasuo Matsui, architects; Go Tamura, landscape architect.
The garden accompanying these buildings, based on the Ise shrines, incorporates all the features of the foreign stereotype.
[*Gendai Kentiku*]

logo or the swastika soon to be allied to its imperialistic cause. Elements of the traditional Japanese garden, designed by Go Tamura, play a larger role in suggesting the dignity and achievement of the island nation. As architecture advances, landscape recedes. A pond occupies much of the unbuilt site; rocks line the shore; there is a pavilion where visitors can sample Japanese tea and view the garden. Clearly, the Japanese exposition committee retreated from the unabashed modernity of the pavilion at the Paris fair. No new Japanese garden greets the international public here in Flushing Meadow.[5]

THE SITUATION AND ITS LANDSCAPE

By the time the United States entered the Pacific War in the aftermath of Pearl Harbor, militarism had held Japan in its grasp for almost a decade. The inequities of early treaties with the West, early successes in belligerence toward China and Russia, and the growing need for natural resources, all fueled the ideology of the Japanese military machine. In the 1930s Japan expanded under the rubric of the Greater East Asia Co-prosperity Sphere, occupying Manchuria and increasing areas of China as the decade progressed.[6] These provided the theaters for the period's major architectural projects, as Japanese business interests paired with nationalistic urges, ever-spreading across the seemingly endless miles of Chinese terrain.

Site planning became the most extensive and intensive of landscape design activities. If we lack the detailed development of landscapes for these housing estates or extensions of cities, we can nevertheless understand the striving for order and control that joined, in tandem, the military/organizational mind with the rationalism of Western modernism. A noted architect such as Kunio Maekawa (1905–86), another graduate of the Le Corbusier office in Paris, drew up expansion plans for occupied territories such as a neighborhood sector for the city of Daido, probably in Manchuria, although possibly an extension to Shanghai [Figure 10–4]. The lessons of the German planning prototype *Zeilenbau* and the *Siedlung* were not lost in far Asia, although they were adapted to the prevailing political aspirations and the particular conditions of the site. The written description accompanying the publication of this project is sparse, but one sees in the site plan houses loosely based on a traditional courtyard model; these are fed the Corbusian trinity of air, light, and greenery through a number of linear parks.[7] An elementary school, with its accompanying sports facilities,

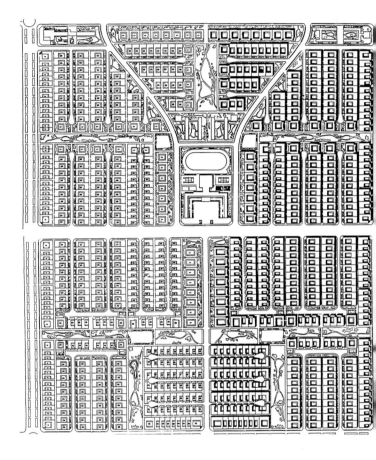

Figure 10–4.

Neighborhood sector, Expansion plan for Daido, probably Manchuria, c. 1940. Kunio Maekawa.

The plan relies on three types of housing, including a courtyard model, and centers around a school. Little suggests historical Chinese precedents.

[*Gendai Kentiku*]

272

provides the focus for this residential tract which includes three types of housing of varying density. Vegetation appears only as a signifier of planting, with neither a major presence nor a discernible form to its planning.

As a totality, there is little in this scheme that acknowledges or evokes the air of tradition, any tradition, either Chinese or Japanese. Instead, a symbiotic schism in the conception of architecture divides building from its accompanying land-scapes at this time. Architects and planners cited rationalism to bring large areas of dwellings and services into being — and under control — quickly and efficiently. Typical conditions such as orientation and circulation suggested typical solutions and arrangements — access to air, light, and movement, if not always to greenery. The drawings — which tend to be limited to site plans — treat landscape as a condition rather than as a specific design; it appears that each section of the park areas, for example, could be exchanged for one another with no harmful result. The design of individual green spaces or gardens is left on hold.

In contrast, buildings with cultural expression at their root — the monument or religious structure, for example — drew upon the specific precedents of history: one assumes under implicit, if not explicit, prompting. What seems anomalous in the diachrony of Kenzo Tange's modernist work — his winning competition entry for a Japanese cultural center in Bangkok (1943), for example — is quite explicable when viewed in the synchrony of its era.[8] Projects by Tange, Maekawa, and other architects all utilized the symmetrical planning of the Ise shrines or the formal organization of the *shinden* or *shoin* styles for projects such as these.[9] Although aspects of their typologies governed the relation of building parts, these historic prototypes allowed for restrained vari-ance or adjustment for the specific qualities of the site.

Thus, on the home islands and abroad, landscape design and architecture served equally as propaganda and as amenity. A number of proposed complexes illustrate the enfolding of ideology and physical development — the male body viewed as the mental and physical agent of the nation, that is to say, of the emperor. In 1939 a major competition for a memorial to those fallen in war — the Chureito — was held, to be set on an unspecified site in metropolitan Tokyo.[10] A prominent architectural ideologue, Sutemi Horiguchi, proposed a monumental complex on the edge of a new Yasukuni Shrine to be reconstructed on the western edge of the capital [Figure 10–5]. The existing Yasukuni Shrine had

been constructed in the waning years of the nineteenth century as part of the government's program to restate the divinity, and reinstate the temporal power, of the emperor. It had served (and continues to serve) as a topos for the soldier and war dead.[11] Thus, its selection as the site was obvious in terms of its military associations.

The entries in the idea competition fell into several groups, among them the tower, the pyramid, and the massive block. Horiguchi's design, which received one of the second-stage awards, was uncompromising in its formality and monumen-tality. A columbarium in the form of a memorial tower, intended for the ashes of citizens as well as soldiers, formed the central feature of the scheme. A rigid symmetry was common to all premiated schemes; Horiguchi explained that because Japan would serve as a central forum for many eastern countries in the future, he had drawn upon forms common to several cultures. The front and rear gardens were carefully considered in detail: the entry courtyard would feature white sand, red pines, camellia, and the sasaki bush sacred to Shinto [Figure 10–6]. In the rear, however, cedars would be prominently featured to blend with the intended greenbelt beyond the borders of the memorial.[12]

Although the architecture of the Horiguchi proposal em-ployed the rigorous symmetrical ordering of Japan's early Shinto shrines and Buddhist temples, the placement of the plantings departed from an architectonic order to create a more naturalistic effect. This in itself was a Japanese trait; rarely did the pure symmetry and geometry of the Asian continent long remain after its importation to Japan. More often one found a give-and-take between geometry and naturalism, between imposing an order and accepting what nature and the *kami* (the Shinto deities) had ordained. Even in the planning of the high shrines at Ise, allowing trees within the rectangular sites or utilizing a diagonal approach rather than one uncompromisingly axial tempered the pre-vailing symmetry. Over the past three centuries, this play of orders — formal, semi-formal, and informal — found a near codification in applications to calligraphy, flower arrangement, and garden design.[13] In this important memorial to those fallen in war, Horiguchi played the planted against the con-structed, massing vegetation around the architectural zone of the central precinct; vegetation was critical for spatial enclosure and for its role in naturalizing the monument's courtyard spaces.[14]

Although his proposal was now intended for nationalistic

Figure 10–5.
Chureito Memorial Competition Entry,
Tokyo, 1939. Sutemi Horiguchi.
Perspective.
[*Gendai Kentiku*]

Figure 10–6.
Chureito Memorial Competition Entry,
Tokyo, 1939. Sutemi Horiguchi.
Site plan.
[*Gendai Kentiku*]

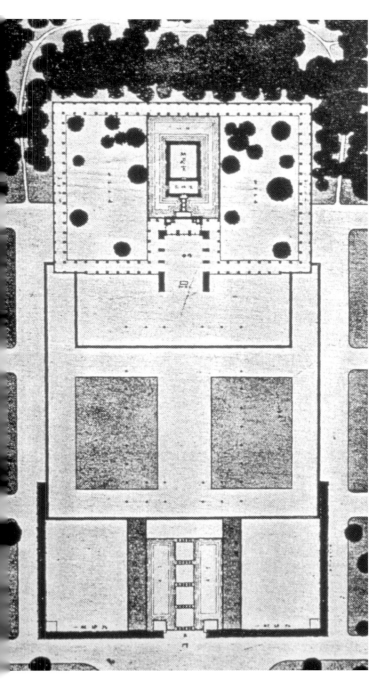

rather than purely aesthetic domestic pleasures, Horiguchi drew upon ideas he first formulated in the mid-1930s. In a key essay from 1932, "The Garden of Autumn Grass," the architect — now landscape designer and aesthete — looks to works by the seventeenth-century artists Ogata Korin and Tawaraya Sotatsu to reinvigorate the Japanese garden for today.[15] Despite the intricacy of the imagery or the lushness of the background materials, these artists reduced painting to three essentials: the frame, the ground, and the subject, whether flower or tree. The new garden for Japan can translate these ideas from painting into three dimensions, wrote Horiguchi; indeed, the sixteenth-century rock garden at Ryoan-ji had already provided such a model. At this celebrated Zen temple, its sixteenth-century maker had utilized the simplest of vocabularies — rock, gravel, and moss — deftly employed. The void equaled in power the mass of the rocks, as silence equaled in power the unformed noise of the quotidian world.

To Horiguchi, no contradiction confronted the simultaneous presence of both East and West: the white walls of modernism offered the garden a simple ground, as gold leaf had provided a background for the painting, or patinaed walls the frame for the gravel garden at Ryoan-ji. Photographic images of Horiguchi's Okada garden, taken almost sequentially, revealed the coexistence of an International Style frame, a traditional column, the smooth white planes of the enclosing walls, or a straight water channel; the bamboo deck in the foreground extended the veranda's transitional zone, engaging steppingstones characteristic of the tea garden [Figure 10–7]. The transitions among the garden's elements were virtually seamless despite the anachronistic mix of architectural and landscape elements.

While accomplished in its resolution of parts and scales, the more unusual aspect of the master plan of Horiguchi's Chureito project was its incorporation of a major sports complex of fields and gymnasiums, including a stadium for 100,000 spectators or participants in national conferences. Characteristically for the era, the superstructure of the scheme was based on the right angle and symmetrical layout. Within the areas of greenery, however, the meandering path and freely planted trees again undermined the severity of the plan, this time at the macroscale. Horiguchi's proposal, as well as other premiated schemes in the Chureito competition, demonstrated that although constrained by nationalism, the civic monument — perhaps ironically — drew as much from Western classicism as it did from Japanese history.

Figure 10–7.
Okada Garden, Tokyo, 1934.
Sutemi Horiguchi.
The garden wall frames the composed
planting; the relation between them
recalling paintings by Ogata Korin.
[Christopher Tunnard, *Gardens in the
Modern Landscape*]

But without question, the participating architects shunned the influence of contemporary ideas in the arts and some of the freedoms already common to Western modernism.

HIROSHIMA, 1945. All that was solid melted into the white heat of nuclear fission. Within days, the hostilities that had engulfed Japan for almost a decade came to a halt. The losses from the years of war were staggering.[16] Two million of its citizens were dead, a third of them civilians; 40 percent of the aggregate urban areas were devastated; industries and infrastructure were in ruins.[17] In Tokyo alone, one-third of the housing had been destroyed. And on top of all this, for the first time in its two-thousand-year history, Japan had been defeated and occupied by a foreign nation. That nation, the United States — as the principal representative of the Allied powers — sought to stabilize the political structure of the country bolstered by a new, and forcibly imposed, constitution intended to bring democracy to the modern feudal structure of interlocking monopolies and trusts.[18]

Although housing the displaced became a national priority, housing — rather than houses — did not. The apartment had never found fertile ground in Japan, where the Asian version of the American Dream was firmly rooted. In Tokyo, for example, only the intellectual, the artist, and the ambivalent would accept apartment living if they could afford any other vehicle in which to dwell. In the late 1920s and 1930s, the Dojunkai building association had launched a program to construct much-needed housing, but their cause had proved to be unpopular.[19] Even in 1945, in the wake of mass nuclear destruction, the Japanese remained distant from the economies of the apartment block.[20]

The houses that slowly increased in number among the reemerging middle class in the late 1940s and 1950s (there were virtually none built before then) featured little open space, and books such as the 1954 publication *Konichi no jutaku: 30 shuh* (Housing of Today: 30 Examples) rarely depicted any truly designed garden spaces [Figure 10–8].[21] Given the long history of gardening in Japan, this lacuna is curious. Since the literature itself provides no explanation, we can only speculate on the reasons for this omission, at least until further research confirms or contradicts these interpretations. First, due to increasing population and limited available land, the size of the house lot was shrinking, reducing building sites to minuscule proportions that could barely support the house itself. At the same time, the architect-designed single family house was more broadly available

Figure 10–8.
House, Tokyo.
[Yasukichi Watanabe and Sei-Ichi Shimizu, *Konichi no jutaku: 30 shuh* (Housing of Today: 30 Examples)]

—and fashionable—than in the prewar period, allowing better-off families minimally larger dwellings. Second, maintaining a traditional garden had become prohibitively expensive; as in the United States, few families could afford the services of the professional gardener.[22] Third, to suggest the modern, the novel, the democratic, one had to avoid ideas and symbols of the aristocratic tradition of historical Japan. Like the design of the house itself, the garden was to speak of the modern, that is to say, the foreign: normally, that was the (suburban) American.

The most common design response to these considerations was the grass lawn, which became the stock solution for most house sites [Figure 10–9]. Pushing plantings to the perimeter of the lot ensured privacy, kept the central lawn open, and maximized the sense of space. Perhaps to those fortunate enough to be upwardly mobile, the lawn also suggested the American residential landscape, itself suggesting democracy.[23] Upkeep was simplified; periodic mowing and pruning were sufficient to produce order. Certainly, none of the nearly constant care endemic to the traditional Japanese garden was required; even if one desired such a garden, few had the economic means to maintain it.

The house form answered the developments in the garden, or perhaps vice versa. Many of the more innovative architectural solutions elevated the house above the ground, creating a complete living story on the lower floor. We see this schema used, for example, in Tokyo houses by the architects Kiyonori Kikutake and Kenzo Tange dating from the early 1950s [Figure 10–10].[24] While stacking floors permitted designers to maximize the available land, leaving more space unbuilt, it also reflected the influence of Le Corbusier on postwar Japanese residential design. With this idea of a house elevated on posts, the sliding panels—the *fusuma* and *shoji*—at times gave way to Western-style doors and windows, which restricted access to outdoor spaces. In many instances, in the Tange house, for example, the building sat as a carefully positioned structure on a lawn; an earthen mound with a small stand of bamboos and some mature trees bounded the site and enclosed the lawn [Figure 10–11].

Often, a terrace extended perpendicularly from the house, joining house and garden as a diving board joins paving and pool. This new element—the ground-level terrace or deck —superseded the veranda of the historical garden. Most of the houses included in Kiyoshi Seike and Charles Terry's 1964 survey *Contemporary Houses of Japan*, for example,

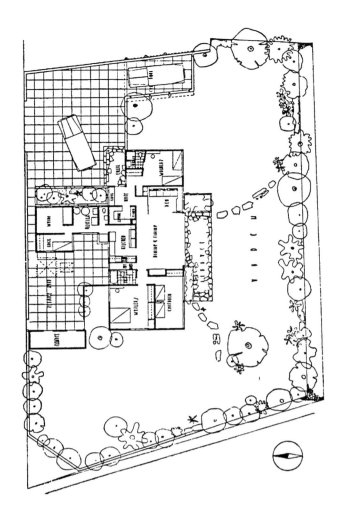

Figure 10–9.
Aurell House and Garden, Tokyo, c. 1957.
Kunio Maekawa. Plan.
[*Gendai Kentiku*]

Figure 10–10. [*facing page, top*]
Tange Residence, Tokyo, 1953.
Kenzo Tange. Site plan.
The orthogonal geometry of the building and path counters the freer handling of the earthen mound and planting.
[Courtesy Kenzo Tange Associates]

Figure 10–11. [*facing page, bottom*]
Tange Residence, Tokyo, 1953.
Kenzo Tange.
View from the lower floor.
[Courtesy Kenze Tange Associates]

employed the terrace or deck as the only bridge between architecture and landscape; the lawn remained essentially detached and mute. A house by Kiyoshi Tanaka in Hiroshima, described only as "House with a Pool," used — untypically — both a modern terrace in black tile and an open lattice in wood to replace the traditional engawa, or transition zone.[25] Thus, in the postwar landscape, modernism and the democratization of domestic space banished, if not killed completely, historical forms. Openness and potentially useful ground prevailed over intricacy and detail; space prevailed over form and vegetation.

THE PARK, PRE- AND POSTWAR

The plot of Akira Kurosawa's film *Ikiru* revolves around the transformation of an ill-drained, mosquito-breeding triangle of land in a somewhat squalid district of the capital into a children's park. "And my child got a rash from the water," says one of the women petitioning for the park; "It smells bad too. . . . There are millions of mosquitoes. . . . Why can't you do something with the land? It would make a good playground."[26] The question of its actual design never enters the discussions: it is a sufficient challenge just to negotiate the bureaucratic jungle in order to realize a simple park space for the local children: clean, well-drained, and furnished with the simplest of play equipment. The emotional climax of the film shows the protagonist, Kanji Watanabe, played by Takashi Shimura, tranquilly swinging in the playground, distracted yet fulfilled by his final gesture to realize, at all costs, the project before he dies [Figure 10–12]. "When he looked at that park," murmurs one of his fellow bureaucrats, "his face just glowed. It was . . . well it was like a man looking at his own grandchild."[27] In that pivotal scene, we see only a glimpse of the landscape itself; in its place: the figure, the swing, and the sky. These make a park.

But postwar parks were requested to communicate as well as to function. To commemorate the lives of those lost at Hiroshima and in the war—and to ensure that the horrors of that war would never be repeated—a competition for a peace memorial near the epicenter of the blast was first organized in 1946. The jury selected Kenzo Tange's submission as the winning project. The master planning of the greater site included provision for recreation, sports, and cultural activities on a parcel of land adjacent to the Peace Park and was laid out without formal order. Tange's plan for the memorial portion of the park was rigidly axial, linking at one end the burned-out dome of a bank (which stood

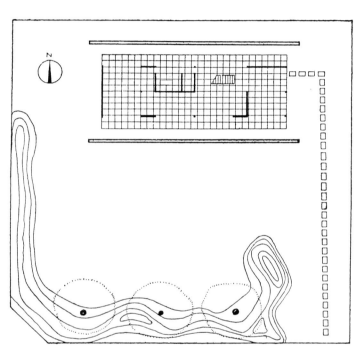

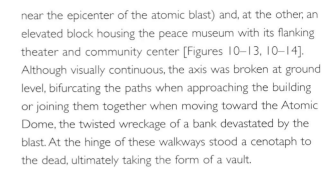

Figure 10–12.
Still from *Ikiru*, 1951. Akira Kurosawa.
Kanji Watanabe (Takashi Shimura) swings
alone in the completed park.
[Museum of Modern Art Film Stills
Department]

near the epicenter of the atomic blast) and, at the other, an elevated block housing the peace museum with its flanking theater and community center [Figures 10–13, 10–14]. Although visually continuous, the axis was broken at ground level, bifurcating the paths when approaching the building or joining them together when moving toward the Atomic Dome, the twisted wreckage of a bank devastated by the blast. At the hinge of these walkways stood a cenotaph to the dead, ultimately taking the form of a vault.

The design was established by the Japanese American sculptor Isamu Noguchi. Accepting Tange's invitation to create the cenotaph/memorial, Noguchi proposed a tubular arch form linking the underworld of the dead with the hope of tomorrow.[28] It was a form at once abstract and specific, general and universal, bearing resemblances to certain third- to fifth-century bronze bells (*dotoku*), or ceramic *haniwa*, fashioned in the shapes of houses.[29]

Noguchi had returned to Japan in 1950 on a personal odyssey, and his presence there would strongly influence Japanese landscape design in the second half of the century. The product of a Japanese father and a Scottish-American mother, he had received his high school education in the United States. After a brief apprenticeship with Constantin Brancusi in Paris, Noguchi began to attain increasing celebrity as both a sculptor and a designer of functional objects.[30] His 1945 coffee-table design demonstrated the smooth fusion of utility with the most stylish of biomorphic forms, as well as his resolution of art and design. His *Radio Nurse* (an intercom system intended as protection for infants), in contrast, suggested the mask used in *kendo*, or Japanese fencing. In coming to Japan, Noguchi sought further spiritual and aesthetic connections with his father's homeland.

The green landscape of the Hiroshima design was essentially lawn, bounded or punctuated by clumps of trees, for the most part planned without formal order — very much the Corbusian concept of greenery.[31] Although the site design of the park was simple and informal, suggesting the urban parks of the 1930s, the spatial organization of the memorial was highly effective. The museum block, raised on a field of piers, formed a gateway to the site, cropped the view, and directed the visitor's sight through the cenotaph toward the dome. We must recall that at the time of construction, no building within view rose higher than the tree line or the dome, which would be silhouetted against the sky. And as rebuilding continued amid the ruins of Hiroshima, the Peace

Figure 10–13.
Peace Park, Hiroshima, 1949-56.
Kenzo Tange. Model.
The axis commences with the elevated museum block, continues through the vaulted cenotaph, and terminates in the destroyed cupola of the bank. The remainder of the park plan is treated in a more naturalistic manner.
[*Kentiku to Shakkai*]

Figure 10–14.
Peace Park, Hiroshima, 1949-56.
Kenzo Tange.
The cenotaph, commemorating those who died in the bombing, with the Atomic Dome of the bank in the distance.
[Marc Treib]

Park at Hiroshima displayed some signs of hope, and of green tranquillity.

In truth, by proclamation, the Hiroshima memorial was a peace park rather than a peace garden, and its constituent elements were broadly sketched rather than presented in precise detail. The prevailing model for the Japanese public park was entirely Western, as there had been no prototype for public green space in Japan until the modern era and contact with the landscape traditions of Europe and the United States. In Tokyo, five imperial estates had been converted into parks during the closing years of the nineteenth century, and they were planned for activities common to their Western cousins. Tokyo's Hibiya Park, for example, linked fragments of Japan's past with a bandstand and promenade characteristic of modern life, although the sense of its overall design drew little from the historical garden tradition.[32] Thus, the park played an important role in signaling the development of a modern and cosmopolitan Japanese urban culture.

Japan's parks suffered cataclysmically in the war years, however. Rather than sites of recreation and display, their value as refuge compounded in the aftermath of the 1923 Kanto earthquake. Here the displaced and homeless withdrew as fire ravaged the capital; here they camped while the slow process of reconstruction unfolded. During the early 1940s, as food shortages became more acute, public open spaces — including some schoolyards — were given over to raising vegetables for those sufficiently unfortunate to remain within the cities [Figures 10–15, 10–16]. First used for artillery emplacements in 1936, for security reasons, Hibiya Park lost all its treetops in the direction of the palace as the war progressed. "The lawns and parterres became vegetable patches. Iron artifacts were stripped away," wrote Edward Seidensticker. "Some bronze remained, to meet the hostility of the Americans, who found certain of its applications warlike."[33] Metallic elements were converted to war materiel; during this time, the course of park design moved essentially backward. At war's end, the need for green spaces again became all too clear, despite the new openness created by continued American bombing. The Occupation forces did little to help the situation, and gardens in the historical manner suffered the indignities accompanying the pervasive phobia against all things Japanese. The park never enjoyed the priority assigned to housing, however, and even today Tokyo suffers one of the lowest per capita ratios of green space to citizen of any major world city.

282

Figure 10–15.
Schoolyard used for raising food during the war.
[Courtesy Minato Ward, Tokyo]

Figure 10–16.
Parkland converted to agricultural use during war years.

The Occupation brought an influx of social reforms and civic institutions that either differed significantly from their prewar incarnation, or had never before existed in Japan.[34] A new educational model revamped the school program, and the civic center and the town hall lucidly demonstrated the thoroughness of the reconstitution of community and citizen relations.[35] The art museum as an institution underwent a major transformation: the number of museums increased, the perspective of the national museums broadened, and new buildings dedicated to contemporary art were inaugurated. The major architectural work of this period was the Museum of Modern Art in Kamakura, designed by Junzo Sakakura and opened in 1951 [Figure 10–17]. The building, in many respects, harks back to the formal elegance of the Heian Period shinden palace with its symmetry and elevation on columns. The grounds for the museum, which usurped a portion of the Tsurugaoka Hachiman shrine, centered on a substantial pond bounded by masses of trees that buffered the building from its neighboring townscape with a soft green wall. Lifted above the water on steel columns resting on natural stones, the building was doubled in its reflection, recalling the so-called fishing pavilions of the Heian palatial style.[36] The building and its landscape still rank among the most simple yet sophisticated of the postwar period and suggest that the naturalism of the paradise garden tradition remains viable in contemporary landscape design.

Institutions dedicated to understanding among nations blossomed with the arrival of peace and reconstruction. The United Nations, and later its scientific and cultural branch UNESCO, were principal among them. In Japan, the need for international understanding and smoother trade operations instigated the formation of a host of cultural and economic organizations, both in the capital and disseminated through the country in its major cities. Among these was the International House of Japan, founded in 1951 in Roppongi, Tokyo, on the site of an old *daimyo* estate. The trio of architects for the building, which was funded by John D. Rockefeller III, had all worked for Le Corbusier in the prewar era: Kunio Maekawa, Junzo Sakakura, and Junzo Yoshimura. Their design for the building and landscape expressed its heritage, focused on a singular block with two floors of public spaces capped by two floors of guest rooms for foreign and Japanese visitors. Projecting from the principal block and into the garden were the restaurant and library wings.

The building itself, executed in reinforced concrete and wood, was a handsome essay in the Corbusian manner, a

foreign import domesticated by its proportions, its materials and finishes, and its rusticated stone base that recalled the walls of the seventeenth-century Japanese castle. Most distinctive, perhaps, was the adept fitting of the building to the sloping site and to the historical garden. Here Maekawa and company utilized modern interpretations of historical methods to "naturalize" the roofs of the projecting spaces, creating a transition between architecture and landscape [Figure 10–18]. In an almost voyeuristic manner, earth and lawn covered the roof of the restaurant, exposing the roof's gravel surface only in the far corner. On another roof surface, the central plane of gravel was bounded by low shrubs disguising the edge of the roof and blending it with the clipped vegetation of the venerable garden beyond. This merging of near and far paralleled certain historic garden-making practices, in particular the use of "borrowed scenery," which brings elements of the landscape into the garden from far beyond its borders. Thus, in the garden at the International House we find a brilliant mixing of the old and the new, with landscape architecture ideas and methods that spanned both cultures and eras.

Economic change accompanied the political and cultural transformations of the Occupation years.[37] American money also invaded Japan, following as it often does in the wake of military conquest. At the end of the 1940s, *Reader's Digest* received permission to erect the first permanent building in Tokyo after the war.[38]

The architect for the publishing house's new quarters on the edge of the Imperial Palace grounds was the Czech-born Antonin Raymond.[39] Less attached to prior architectural vocabularies than Frank Lloyd Wright, for whom he had worked on the construction of the Imperial Hotel, Raymond can be credited with some of the first truly modernist work in Japan. He also believed in the lessons of Japanese tradition, and despite his unforgiving use of concrete and other inorganic materials, he sought in his residences to integrate interior and exterior space. His own house in Reinanzaka in Tokyo (1924), while De Stijl in style, used the court and the sliding glass wall to minimize the distinction between inside and out [Figure 10–19]. It was this house that later served as one of few images used by Christopher Tunnard to represent Japan in his 1938 *Gardens in the Modern Landscape*.[40]

Why Raymond invited Noguchi to design the grounds for the Reader's Digest Building has not been ascertained.[41]

Figure 10–17.
Museum of Modern Art, Kamakura, 1951. Junzo Sakakura.
Despite the overall modernist purity of the mass, the building's structural columns rest upon stones set into the pond—recalling practices from historical architecture.
[Marc Treib]

Figure 10–18.
International House of Japan, Tokyo, 1951.
Kunio Maekawa, Junzo Sakakura,
Junzo Yoshimura.
The view over the roofs of the library and
restaurant contrast, yet blend, with the gar-
den, which dates to the eighteenth century.
[Marc Treib]

Figure 10–19.
Raymond House, Reinanzaka, Tokyo, 1924.
Antonin Raymond.
[Christopher Tunnard, *Gardens in the
Modern Landscape*]

Perhaps Raymond felt a lack of expertise in executing landscape ideas; perhaps he felt there were no native Japanese capable of creating a garden equally as modern — or American — as his structure. In a letter to Noguchi, Raymond wrote: "I know that I could never hope to make the Reader's Digest site anywhere near as interesting alone, without you, as with you."[42] Perhaps Raymond was impressed with the celebrity that had preceded Noguchi's arrival—although at that time the sculptor's spatial exercises could be found only in unexecuted monuments or in the theater.[43]

The sculptor's contribution to the Reader's Digest project can be traced in a number of existing photographs [Figures 10–20, 10–21]. In addition to at least one freestanding sculpture, Noguchi seems to have relied on mounded forms in stone or covered with grass; a meandering watercourse prefigured his garden for the UNESCO Building in Paris, some five years later. The shapes he employed in the garden drew in part upon a biomorphism characteristic of the time — in California, for example — as a signal of contemporaneity. Neither formal nor natural, the biomorphic shape could be taken only as modern and sculptural. Although it was less emphatically stated as form than most of his later garden designs, the Reader's Digest commission was of considerable importance for Noguchi. Denied the execution of the cenotaph of Hiroshima, the artist received this needed confirmation of an inhabitable sculpture executed at full scale. The Reader's Digest garden provided a new arena in which to work, simultaneously enriching the conception of the garden as essentially a sculptural enterprise.

Although Noguchi was well known in Japan, as a citizen of the Occupation country, he was suspected as well as respected. As a sculptor, there was little question of his influence, however; and although the precise nature of this influence has not been established with certainty, there is little doubt that Noguchi also nudged Japanese garden design in a new direction, or at least reinforced tendencies already under way.[44] Throughout the war years the Japanese garden tradition — what landscape architect Shiro Nakane has described as the stone lanterns, stone basins, and pine trees — held sway.[45] But over time, the sense of garden space had broadened to some degree, and the horticultural specimens that accompanied the opening of Japan to the West in the late nineteenth century had achieved greater currency. But these new influences tended to modify the pieces of the historical garden rather than displace them. Nature, however abstracted, still provided the basis for the garden's

Figure 10–20.
Reader's Digest Building, Tokyo, 1951.
Antonin Raymond, architect;
Isamu Noguchi, garden designer.
The artist's primary contribution was the
modeling of the land contour to create
linear watercourses and mounds.
[Courtesy Isamu Noguchi Foundation]

Figure 10–21.
Reader's Digest Building, Tokyo, 1951.
Antonin Raymond, architect;
Isamu Noguchi, garden designer.
Although set primarily as a foil against the
building prism, in selected locations the
garden elements engaged the architecture
directly.
[Courtesy Isamu Noguchi Foundation]

NOTES

Thanks are due Ken Oshima and Makoto Suzuki for their help with translation and securing photographs.

1. The reaction to the pavilion's design from the foreign modernists was unanimously positive, stressing the young age and the pedigree of its designer. Sigfried Giedeon, for example, wrote in *Die Weltwoche* that "the Japanese pavilion is probably the most beautiful one. . . . Though the rooms are small, we can feel the strong bond between garden and building. While the pavilion has a Western design, the Japanese spirit dominates the building." Most of them read into the structure and its grounds the Japanese sensibility and linking of indoors and out. "The Paris Exposition: Critiques of the Japanese Pavilion—Extracts from Foreign Publications," *Gendai Kentiku* (Japan), no. 6, 1939, pp. 12–34. The article also contains extensive photographic and drawn documentation.

Sakakura (1904–69) worked in the Paris office of Le Corbusier from 1931 to 1936, which positioned him strategically to receive the commission for the pavilion's design—although Kunio Maekawa's design had been selected in the initial invited competition. Sakakura maintained amicable relations with Le Corbusier and participated in the 1937 modern architectural congress (CIAM) held in the French capital. In 1940, he opened his own office in Tokyo.

2. The description of the pavilion, probably by Sakakura himself, listed four instigating characteristics of the pavilion's design: "1. The clarity of the plan; 2. The clarity of structure; 3. The respect for the natural beauty of materials; 4. The harmony between architecture and nature." He stressed that these were characteristic of past Japanese architecture as well. *Gendai Kentiku*, no. 6, 1939, p. 20.

3. The French architect Jacques Lambert stressed the elegance of the building and its grounds in his article on the foreign section of the exposition: "refined structures of steel, walls of wood set upon a traditional base of stone, light passageways" referred to "proven techniques" long in use. He seems to have missed the fact that the building had no real precedents in the land that it was representing in Paris. Jacques Lambert, "Les sections étrangères," *Illustration*, "Exposition Paris 1937," special issue, n.p.

4. A guidebook to the fair captions an image of the Japanese pavilion thus: "surrounded by a garden adorned with pools, Japanese trees and shrubs, . . . modeled after an ancient Shinto Shrine." Historical references were not lost on the writer. *New York World's Fair, Illustrated by Camera* (New York: Manhattan Post Card Publishing Co., 1939), n.p.

For the origins and architecture of Ise, see Kenzo Tange and Noboru Kawazoe, *Ise: Prototype of Japanese Architecture* (Cambridge, Mass.: MIT Press, 1965).

5. For an overview of the issues facing the design of the pavilion at the 1939 World's Fair, see Akiko Takenaka, "Orientalism and Propaganda: The Construction of a Wartime National Identity," *Thresholds* no. 17, 1998, pp. 63–68. The author argues that the building was highly successful in realizing the propagandistic program of its organizing committee. Less convincing is her argument that in so doing, the building's architects created a design that paralleled the architectural achievements of its times.

6. See Saburo Ienaga, *The Pacific War, 1931–1945* (New York: Pantheon Books, 1978), pp. 153–180; and W. G. Beasley, *The Modern History of Japan* (Tokyo: Charles E. Tuttle Company, 1963, reprint 1986), pp. 236–278.

7. In the early decades of the twentieth century, the Swiss-French architect Le Corbusier had formulated his urban program around the triad of light, air, and vegetation. It was adopted as a battle cry for a generation of architects and urban planners.

8. David Stewart is one of the few Western authors to include images of this project in their books. *The Making of a Modern Japanese Architecture, 1868 to the Present* (Tokyo: Kodansha International, 1987), pp. 157–58. More commonly, Tange's career is depicted beginning with the Peace Memorial at Hiroshima (1949–56). Kultermann states, "During the war Tange was for a time engaged in planning projects. During this period he also participated in three important competitions and on every occasion he was awarded first prize. These projects, however, were not executed." Perhaps that is why they were not illustrated. Udo Kultermann, *Kenzo Tange, 1946–1969* (New York: Praeger, 1970), p. 8.

9. The *shinden* style, dating from the Heian Period (roughly the eleventh and twelfth centuries), employed a central structure flanked by two or more pavilions connected by roofed, yet open, corridors. The later *shoin* style, developing from the fifteenth century on, was a more compact and integrated arrangement that departed more freely from the inherent, if not perfect, symmetry of the *shinden-zukuri*. To the architects working in the 1930s and the war years, these two historical modes provided viable models for a compromised modernity. They appear in several cultural center proposals by Tange and Maekawa, for example. See Stewart, *The Making of a Modern Japanese Architecture*, pp. 152–58.

10. Sutemi Horiguchi, "Chureito no hyogen to sonoichishian" (The Soldiers' Memorial, Expression and Proposals), *Gendai Kentiku*, April 1940, pp. 5–15.

11. Although a relic of the modern period, the shrine was rigidly laid out to emulate Ise and historical Shinto architecture, executed in past centuries when the imperial house held true control of the state (as opposed to its figurehead status during the years of the shoguns). In practice, it was virtually impossible to extract the purely Shinto from the amalgam of Buddhism and Shinto that had evolved intertwined from before the tenth century.

12. Horiguchi, "Soldiers' Memorial," pp. 5–15.

13. See Marc Treib, "Modes of Formality: The Distilled Complexity of Japanese Garden Design," *Landscape Journal*, spring 1993, pp. 2–16.

14. Horiguchi, "Soldiers' Memorial," pp. 5–15.

15. Sutemi Horiguchi, "Akikusa no niwa" (The Garden of Autumn Grasses), *Shiso*, 1932; reprinted in *Space Design*, "Sutemi Horiguchi," special issue, 1983, p. 155.

16. Japan's writers have left some of the most poignant testimony concerning the atomic holocaust and its aftermath. In "Summer Flower," for example, Tamiki Hara describes the slim remains of the Hiroshima vegetal and human landscape: "The bamboo grove had been mowed down, and a path made through the grove under the tramping feet of refugees. Most of the trees overhead had been torn apart in midair, and this famous old garden on the river (Asano Park) was now disfigured with pockmarks and gashes. Beside a hedge was a middle-aged woman, her ample body slumped over limply." Translated by George Saito, in *The Crazy Iris, and Other Stories of the Atomic Aftermath*, ed. Kenzaburo Oe (New York: Grove Press, 1985), p. 41. Oe's own *Hiroshima Notes* (Tokyo: YMCA Press, 1981), ed. David Swain, translated by Toshi Yonezawa, examines the existential and moral questions raised by the bomb as well as the horror of its destructive and murderous force.

17. Edwin O. Reischauer, *Japan: The Story of a Nation* (Rutland, Vt.: Charles E. Tuttle Company, 1970), p. 218.

18. The new constitution was written by the Americans and more or less forced upon the Japanese. Among its tenets were the strict adoption of a truly democratic society and government and the resolution to eternally shun the making of war. See Mark Gayn, *Tokyo Diary* (1948; reprint, Rutland, Vt.: Charles E. Tuttle Company, 1981), pp. 125–31.

19. For a detailed study of the works of the Dojunkai, the predecessor of the postwar Japan Housing Association, see Shigeru Satoh, *Shugo jutaku danchi no hensen* (Change in Urban Housing) (Tokyo: Kajima Publishing, 1989).

20. This was the case even in Hiroshima, where authorities issued makeshift dwellings in an attempt to mitigate the complete dearth of suitable housing stock for the homeless and for refugees. "When the city was reduced to rubble, not a single house was left standing. The makeshift shacks were erected on the training ground, which was still strewn with the bones of numberless soldiers who had been burned to death there.... The facilities should have been able to house everybody, since the number of survivors was not that great. But because all the older houses had been destroyed, and because repatriates from abroad and discharged soldiers were pouring into the city, the shacks were soon filled up.... That was at the end of 1946. The shack had two rooms, one designed to be floored with six tatami mats, the other with three mats. But at first the rooms were not even floored with mats because there were too many thieves and beggars around to make off with them.... None of the poorly-made tatami mats and doors fitted properly, so they had to wedge and stuff them into place as best they could." Yoko Ota, "Fireflies," trans. Koichi Nakagawa, in Oe, ed., *The Crazy Iris*, p. 89.

20. Editors of Shufunotomo, *Konichi no jutaku: 30 shuh* (Housing of Today: 30 Examples) (Tokyo: Shufunotomo Publishing, 1954).

22. American landscape literature of the 1950s addressed this issue of owner-maintained gardens in varying ways. In *Landscapes for Living* (New York: Duell, Sloan & Pearce, 1950), Garrett Eckbo argued for simplifying maintenance by reducing areas of plants and lawn and replacing them with increased expanses of paving. In *Gardens Are for People* (New York: Reinhold Publishing, 1955), Thomas Church, California's best-known

landscape architect, cited maintenance as one of the key issues in formulating a private garden. He incorporated a number of features in his designs—such as the concrete mowing strip to reduce hand clipping—that eased the work of the owner-gardener.

23. See Georges Teyssot, ed., *The American Lawn* (New York: Princeton Architectural Press, 1998).

24. Tange's house and garden no longer exist, having been replaced in succeeding decades by a large-scale apartment block. Kikutake's "Sky House" (1958) was widely published as the harbinger of a new era in Japanese residential design. Architectural critic Robin Boyd described the house as "simply one open square room with the plumbing compartments appended on two sides, the whole wrapped by a veranda and held high above the ground on four pylons." *New Directions in Japanese Architecture* (New York: George Braziller, 1968), pp. 38–39. Over time, the architect took advantage of the sloping site and open lower floor to add additional interior space to the original construction; there was no garden design to speak of.

25. Kiyoshi Seike and Charles Terry, *Contemporary Houses of Japan* (Tokyo: Kodansha International, 1964), pp. 105–18.

26. Akira Kurosawa, with Shinobu Hashimoto and Hideo Oguni, *Ikiru*, screenplay, English translation in *Contemporary Japanese Literature*, ed. Howard Hibbett (New York: Alfred A. Knopf, 1986), p. 146.

27. Ibid., p. 182.

28. Noguchi writes: "Unfortunately, neither Tange nor the mayor had consulted with the committee in charge before suggesting that I design the memorial, and my proposal was rejected. Was it because I was an American or was it a case of someone not having proper authorization to which my proposal fell victim? Tange was obliged to draw up a design himself, within a week, to meet the deadline and have something ready for the anniversary celebration. This is what is there now in Hiroshima." Isamu Noguchi, *The Isamu Noguchi Garden Museum* (New York: Harry Abrams, 1987), p. 156.

29. Of all the elements of the memorial park, the cenotaph seems to have undergone the greatest modification in the course of the project's development. Its initial form—that of the monumental arch—recalls precedents in the unrealized proposal for the

entry to the 1941 Esposizione Universale di Roma (EUR) and the Jefferson Memorial Arch in St. Louis, designed by Eero Saarinen in 1949 but constructed only in the early 1960s. Tange called upon Isamu Noguchi to design the cenotaph; the sculptor's investigations of the earthenware tomb figures of preliterate Japan provided his point of departure. In the end, it was Tange himself who designed the cenotaph, although its relation to Noguchi's earlier form is obvious.

30. See Dore Ashton, *Noguchi: East and West* (New York: Alfred A. Knopf, 1992); and Isamu Noguchi, *A Sculptor's World* (New York: Harper and Row, 1968), pp. 26–28.

31. For Le Corbusier's concept of landscape and his turn toward a landscape of undifferentiated greenery, see Dorothée Imbert, *The Modernist Garden in France* (New Haven: Yale University Press, 1993).

32. The land was used as a military parade ground, having been converted to that purpose in 1873. In time, it became a popular destination for amorous trysts. Edward Seidensticker, *Low City, High City: Tokyo from Edo to the Earthquake* (Rutland, Vt.: Charles E. Tuttle Company, 1983), pp. 122–23.

33. Edward Seidensticker, *Tokyo Rising: The City Since the Great Earthquake* (Cambridge, Mass.: Harvard University Press, 1990), p. 138.

34. For a humorous and touching short story about the postwar Japanese school and the model of American education, see Nobuo Kojima, "The American School," in Hibbett, ed., *Contemporary Japanese Literature*, pp. 119–44.

35. See Kazuo Kawai, *Japan's American Interlude* (Chicago: University of Chicago Press, 1979).

36. Common to the *shinden* type were pavilions extending outward from the main building, linked to it or to subsidiary structures by covered corridors. At times these pleasure pavilions sat upon the pond—a required element of the naturalistic garden that accompanied this Chinese-derived style. It is believed, for example, that the celebrated Golden Pavilion (originally built in the thirteenth century but rebuilt in the early 1950s after its destruction by fire) served just this purpose. The term fishing pavilion, however, should not be taken as a literal description of its use.

37. Although the new constitution had been adopted, that is to say, after it was imposed upon the Japanese by the Occupation forces,

the program for dismantling the interlocking structure of economic and political institutions was left incomplete. When hostilities began in Korea in 1950, the American government saw Communism as a greater threat than a Japan that had resurrected its historical, social, and economic structures. The Occupation ended in 1952; many of the old ways resumed. See Beasley, *The Modern History of Japan*, pp. 279–98.

38. A proscription against using metals for nonessential construction had been in force since the mid-1930s. The building's architect, Antonin Raymond, underscored the quest for all metals in the closing years of the war: "The Japanese army, during the last stages of the war, confiscated all metal that they could find in all public and private buildings: railings of bridges, statues and even street lamp posts and lanterns, boilers, radiators, everything from all the buildings." Antonin Raymond, *An Autobiography* (Rutland, Vt.: Charles E. Tuttle Company, 1973), p. 199.

39. The company had first asked Frank Lloyd Wright, who was slow to accept the commission. Ibid., p. 211. Despite Raymond's many claims for the building's innovations, it does bear certain similarities to Tange's Hiroshima project. Although the memorial park was completed in 1954, the design dates from 1946 and was thus probably familiar to Raymond.

Born in 1888, in what later became Czechoslovakia, Raymond came to the United States in 1910 and first worked with Cass Gilbert in New York. He entered the employ of Frank Lloyd Wright at Taliesin in 1916 but returned as a soldier to Europe in World War I. Thereafter, he rejoined Wright's atelier and in 1919 arrived in Japan to work on the construction of the Imperial Hotel. Unlike Wright, Raymond stayed in Japan for the remainder of his life, give or take a few years during the Pacific War. Ibid., pp. 8–65.

40. Christopher Tunnard, *Gardens in the Modern Landscape* (London: Architectural Press, 1938), p. 88. The other principal example is Sutemi Horiguchi's Okada House in Tokyo (1934).

41. Raymond tells us only this: "For the gardening, I asked Isamu Noguchi to come and help me, which he did. We built on only part of the ground instead of filling it up to the legal capacity, thereby hoping to set an example of unselfish utilization of the ground for the sake of good city design, with ample gardening around the building." Raymond, *An Autobiography*, p. 219.

42. Antonin Raymond to Isamu Noguchi, 22 November 1950. Isamu Noguchi Foundation.

43. Noguchi, *A Sculptor's World*, p. 163. See also Marc Treib, "A Sculpting of Space," *Landscape Design* (England), February 1998, pp. 21–31; and "Noguchi's Spiritual Quest," *Landscape Design*, April 1998, pp. 29–38.

44. Noted art critic Alexandra Munroe writes: "Although he was never officially accepted as a Japanese artist because of his American background and nationality, Noguchi's collaboration on several major Japanese projects with leading figures of the local art community, his profound contribution to the ongoing discourse of modernism and tradition, and his vast production of sculptures made at his studios in Japan from the early 1950s until his death in 1989, establish him nonetheless as a preeminent figure in postwar Japanese art history." "Circle: Modernism and Tradition," in *Japanese Art After 1945: Scream Against the Sky*, ed. Alexandra Munroe (New York: Harry Abrams, 1994), p. 133.

45. Shiro Nakane, "Traditional Japanese Gardens: Design and Concepts," in *In the Japanese Garden*, ed. Michael Yamashita (Washington, D.C.: Starwood Publishers, 1991), p. v.

46. Noguchi, cited in Munroe, *Scream Against the Sky*, p. 133.

47. The Funda-in (Sesshu-in) garden at Tofuku-ji in Kyoto, where Shigemori executed his series of gardens for the Abbot's Quarters, is normally attributed to Sesshu. Two temple gardens —Mampuku-ji and Iko-ji—in the small town of Masuda on the west coast, and Joei-ji near Yamaguchi appear to have a more credible claim to the painter's design. For an overview of Funda-in, see Marc Treib and Ron Herman, *A Guide to the Gardens of Kyoto* (Tokyo: Shufunotomo, 1980), p. 178; for the other gardens, see Lorraine Kuck, *The World of the Japanese Garden* (New York and Tokyo: Weatherhill, 1968), pp. 152–53.

48. This is not to say that many of the new gardens by Shigemori and others were not for religious institutions. In addition to his work at Tofuku-ji, Shigemori also completed a suite of gardens at the Matsuo-taisha (a Shinto shrine) in Kyoto (c. 1962) and other designs for Buddhist complexes. Kinsaku Nakane's practice included numerous works for temples, either as restorations, renovations, or completely new designs.

49. See Kuck, *World of the Japanese Garden*, pp. 374, 384; and Dorothy C. Miller and

William S. Lieberman, *New Japanese Painting and Sculpture* (New York: Museum of Modern Art, 1966), p. 62.

50. In a series of buildings from the mid-1950s to the mid-1960s Tange turned from his earlier efforts to modernize traditional forms, for example in his own house of 1953. This school of thought has been termed Japonica, its basis rooted in historical architecture but treated with a new spatial organization and a more terse approach to materials and detail. In the later works, such as the Kagawa Prefectural Offices and the town hall at Kurashiki (1960), it is the architecture of Le Corbusier that more obviously provided his starting point. European ideas were then tempered by selected aspects of historical Japanese architecture; for example, the translation into concrete of certain elements of timber construction.

The antithesis of this approach, perhaps, was the so-called Imperial Crown Style, which domesticated a basic box with traditional roof forms, a manner common to China-towns throughout the world. To Japanese architects such as Maekawa, Tange, and Sakakura, this architecture was an anathema, scenographic rather than essential, relying too much on the eye and not enough on the soul.

51. Shigemori aided Noguchi in selecting rocks for the UNESCO project on the island of Shikoku. The sculptor later referred to Shigemori as "a man of tea (reflective taste), of knowledge (twenty volumes on gardens) and a master garden designer." Noguchi, *A Sculptor's World*, p. 166.

52. The theme structure for the pavilion was a giant version of the steel molecule used as the fair's observation tower. For a survey of the exposition, see Marc Treib, *Space Calculated in Seconds: The Philips Pavilion, Le Corbusier and Edgard Varèse* (Princeton: Princeton University Press, 1997). Coverage of the fair can be found in special issues of almost every major architectural journal— among them *The Architectural Review*, *L'Architettura*, and *Casabella*—published between May and July of 1958.

53. An unnamed French reviewer made just this observation: "At the angle between the two buildings, the space has been developed as a Japanese garden where one finds the traditional elements: water, sand, stone, and shrubs." The resemblance to French comments about the Japanese pavilion at the 1937 fair is notable. Little seems to have changed. *L'Architecture d'aujourd'hui*, June 1958, p. 28. See also note 3, above.

299

Thorbjörn Andersson is a practicing landscape architect with FFNS Architects in Stockholm, Sweden, and former editor of *Utblick Landskap*. Among his key design projects are Daniaparken, Malmö (2001), and Holmentorget, Norr-köping (1999). He has authored and edited several books, most recently *Svensk Trädgårdskonst under fyrahundra år* (Swedish Landscape Architecture Through Four Hundred Years).

Philip Goad is Associate Professor and Reader in Arch-itecture at the University of Melbourne, Australia. A historian and critic, he is the author of *Melbourne Architecture* and *Troppo: Architecture for the Top* (both 1999). He is also a con-tributor to the *Oxford Companion to Australian Gardens* (2002).

Gert Gröning is Professor of Landscape Architecture and Open Space Development at the Institute for History and Theory of Design at the University of Arts, Berlin, Germany. He has published extensively on German landscape archi-tecture and planning policy in the twentieth century, popular gardening, and the landscape profession.

Contributors

Dianne Harris is Assistant Professor of Landscape Architec-ture and Architecture at the University of Illinois, Urbana–Champaign. Co-editor of *Villas and Gardens in Early Modern Italy and France* (2001) and the author of *Landscape and Enlightened Absolutism: Villa Culture and Representation in Eighteenth-Century Lombardy* (forthcoming), she has also published articles that focus on twentieth-century landscape architecture in the United States.

Malene Hauxner is a landscape architect, Doctor of Agronomy, and Associate Professor of Landscape Planning and Landscape Architecture at the Royal Veterinary and Agricultural University in Copenhagen. She has written extensively on modern landscape architecture, including the thesis *Fantasiens Have* (Gardens of Imagination), published in 1993. Her most recent book is *Med himlen som loft* (The Sky as Ceiling), published in 2001.

Dianne Harris is Assistant Professor of Landscape Architecture and Architecture at the University of Illinois, Urbana–Champaign. Co-editor of *Villas and Gardens in Early Modern Italy and France* (2001) and the author of *Landscape and Enlightened Absolutism: Villa Culture and Representation in Eighteenth-Century Lombardy* (forthcoming), she has also published articles that focus on twentieth-century landscape architecture in the United States.

Catherine Howett is Professor Emerita in the School of Environmental Design at the University of Georgia and has served as Senior Fellow for the Landscape Studies Program at Dumbarton Oaks. She has written extensively on the history of American landscape architecture and is currently completing a book on Reynolda House and its gardens in Winston-Salem, North Carolina.

Dorothée Imbert is Assistant Professor of Landscape Architecture at Harvard University, a practicing landscape architect, and scholar of modern landscape architecture. Her numerous publications include *The Modernist Garden in France* (1993), and *Garrett Eckbo: Modern Landscapes for Living* (1997), which she co-authored. Current research includes a projected monograph on the work of landscape architect Jean Canneel-Claes.

Alan Powers is a lecturer at the University of Greenwich and a historian specializing in twentieth-century art, design, and environment. His most recent book is *Serge Chermayeff: Designer, Architect, Teacher* (2001).

Marc Treib is Professor of Architecture at the University of California, Berkeley, and a practicing designer. He has published extensively on architecture, art, landscape architecture, and graphic design; books include: *Modern Landscape Architecture: A Critical Review* (editor, 1993); *Garrett Eckbo: Modern Landscapes for Living* (co-author, 1997); and *Space Calculated in Seconds: The Philips Pavilion, Le Corbusier, Edgard Varèse* (1997). Current projects include an edited monograph on Thomas Church and a study of modern architects and the site.

Rossana Vaccarino is Associate in Landscape Architecture at the Harvard University Graduate School of Design. She has published articles about contemporary landscape architecture and is currently completing a book on Roberto Burle Marx. Vaccarino is a landscape architect and president of Paradigm Design, Inc., a multidisciplinary design firm in

Index

The symposium "Landscape Architecture 1950: Recovery into Prosperity" was held in February 1997 at the University of California at Berkeley. Co-sponsored by the College of Environmental Design and the Berkeley Art Museum / Pacific Film Archive, the program paralleled the exhibition "Garrett Eckbo: Modern Landscape For Living," curated by Marc Treib and Dorothée Imbert, then on view at the Berkeley Art Museum. During the two days of the symposium, the eleven speakers from nine countries focused on identifying and explaining currents in landscape architecture during the 1940s and 1950s. By examining this period synchronically, sets of differences, parallels, and intersections emerged: in the formation of the profession and the education of its practitioners; in the publication of key literature; in the creation of new ideas of space, form, and the cultivation and employ of vegetation; in a rising consciousness for ecology, and perhaps above all, in the social patterns and political agenda that instigated so much of these developments in landscape architecture.

It has taken several years to realize the project for a book that expands upon the material originally presented at the symposium. Each of the speakers has now become an author, substantially developing the ideas and the factual material first presented at the symposium. Unfortunately, personal reasons have prevented Erik de Jong from contributing an essay to this book; his participation in the symposium, however, was a critical ingredient, and I wish to thank him in print. Some authors address only a portion of our twenty-year period; some start before and/or end much later (history never falls into neat decades, no matter how we may try); some regard broader tendencies; some concentrate on detailed analysis of particular projects. Some have used archives, others magazines; still others their eyes on site — or a combination of these methods. All the authors, however, have unearthed intriguing materials and ideas — much of it new, even in their home countries — which suggest that in the postwar period, geographic limits began to melt, and in their place arose a sense of world developments and an international community of values and design ideas. The result is a series of essays that offer a comprehensive glimpse into the state of landscape architecture at mid-twentieth century and which provide a solid foundation for future study.

Acknowledgments

Numerous people have helped to realize this project. For their help with the symposium, I would like to acknowledge the support and help of Dean Harrison Fraker of the College of Environmental Design; and Jacquelynn Baas, James Steward, Janine Sheldon, and Nina Zurier at the Berkeley Art Museum. For assistance with program organization, thanks are due Ari Seligman. Because the program developed so quickly, I am particularly grateful to those people and institutions who supported the symposium: landscape architect Ron Herman, San Leandro; Achva and David Stein, landscape architect and architect, respectively, now in Raleigh, North Carolina; the Center for German and European Studies, University of California at Berkeley; the Embassy of Denmark; the Embassy of Sweden; the Royal Danish Veterinary and Agricultural University; and the University of Melbourne. Without their help, there would have been no program, and ultimately no book.

The Hubbard Educational Trust, and the College of Environmental Design and Department of Architecture at the University of California at Berkeley provided critical funding for making this book a reality. Thanks are due to John Furlong, Dean Harrison Fraker, and former Chair Donlyn Lyndon, respectively, for their support. Karen Madsen gave the page proofs a careful review, for which I am most grateful.

My gratitude, also, to John Dixon Hunt, series editor, who saw the merits of the project and backed its implementation.

At the University of Pennsylvania Press, I must acknowledge the help of editor Jo Joslyn, who fostered this book into the light of day, in addition to the editorial contributions of Noreen O'Connor and Carol Ehrlich, and Carl Gross and George Lang, who saw the book through production.

Marc Treib

311